The Book of Practice Tests

Published by Private Prep
Printed by Kindle Direct Publishing, an Amazon.com company
Version 2019-2020

Contents

1   **ACT0 - A0318 - Starter Test**   5

2   **ACT1 - A0116**   59

3   **ACT2 - A0316**   113

4   **ACT3 - A0516**   165

5   **ACT4 - A0117**   217

6   **ACT5 - A0317**   271

6   **ACT6 - A0118**   325

7   **ACT7 - A0119**   379

8   **Answers and Scales**   435

ACT0 - A0318

Practice Test

ENGLISH TEST
45 Minutes—75 Questions

DIRECTIONS: In the five passages that follow, certain words and phrases are underlined and numbered. In the right-hand column, you will find alternatives for the underlined part. In most cases, you are to choose the one that best expresses the idea, makes the statement appropriate for standard written English, or is worded most consistently with the style and tone of the passage as a whole. If you think the original version is best, choose "NO CHANGE." In some cases, you will find in the right-hand column a question about the underlined part. You are to choose the best answer to the question.

You will also find questions about a section of the passage, or about the passage as a whole. These questions do not refer to an underlined portion of the passage, but rather are identified by a number or numbers in a box.

For each question, choose the alternative you consider best and fill in the corresponding oval on your answer document. Read each passage through once before you begin to answer the questions that accompany it. For many of the questions, you must read several sentences beyond the question to determine the answer. Be sure that you have read far enough ahead each time you choose an alternative.

PASSAGE I

Pride and Prejudice and Historical Accuracy

Ranging from teleplays to full-length motion pictures,
$\overline{}$
1
adaptations of *Pride and Prejudice* are as varied as they are
numerous. Countless writers have transformed Jane Austen's
1813 novel into screenplays for both film and television. [A]
While the original novel follows Elizabeth Bennet as she
slowly finds the means to live an authentic life in Regency
England, some writers opt to only utilize the skeleton of this
story in their own modern-day tellings. A select few,
consequently, find that only a textually accurate telling can
$\overline{}$
2
proper-like express the rigid laws of class and custom as
$\overline{}$
3
originally described by Austen herself.

[B] Writer and director Nina Clemens made her
intentions clear before production began. She saw herself as a
$\overline{}$
4
translator of the text rather than an artistic interpreter.

1. A. NO CHANGE
   B. They range
   C. The range extends
   D. The wide range consists of everything

2. F. NO CHANGE
   G. furthermore,
   H. on the other hand,
   J. obviously,

3. A. NO CHANGE
   B. proper
   C. most proper
   D. properly

4. Which of the following alternatives to the underlined portion is LEAST acceptable?
   F. began: She
   G. began; she
   H. began, she
   J. began: she

Of course, Clemens had given herself a more <u>emboldened</u> task
₅
than first meets the eye. Equipped with a computer and the

novel, <u>she would transcend space and time to put herself in</u>
₆

the mindset of an author <u>whom</u> lived two centuries before her.
₇

To do so, she began—of course—with the novel itself.

[C] Clemens noted every descriptor, every detail as she read

the novel over and over until <u>ones's</u> spine had worn to nothing.
₈
With a solid understanding of its tone and theme, the

screenwriter then turned to an intensive historical analysis.

By reading <u>a wide array of period-specific literature of the</u>
₉

<u>era, Clemens slowly amalgamated</u> an acute understanding of
₁₀
how the English language functioned during Austen's time.

Then, and only then, did she put pen to paper—or

fingers to keyboard, as it were. [D] Clemens painstakingly

<u>having outlined</u> the feature over and over, grappling with the
₁₁
task of parsing down the length of the work.

5. Given that all of the choices are true, which one most effectively emphasizes the seeming difficulty of Clemens' task?
   A. NO CHANGE
   B. foreseeable
   C. consistent
   D. daunting

6. F. NO CHANGE
   G. time and space would be transcended when she
   H. the screenplay would transcend space and time if she could
   J. her screenplay would transcend space and time if she could

7. A. NO CHANGE
   B. which
   C. that
   D. she

8. F. NO CHANGE
   G. their
   H. its
   J. our

9. Given that all of the choices are true, which one most specifically describes the kinds of literature Clemens used for research?
   A. NO CHANGE
   B. various pieces specific to the
   C. other novels, letters, and even advertisements from that
   D. piles of Regency writings from the

10. F. NO CHANGE
    G. this amalgamation slowly formed
    H. Clemens' amalgamation slowly formed
    J. Clemens' slow formation of an amalgamation produced

11. A. NO CHANGE
    B. outlines
    C. will outline
    D. outlined

Even if she had preferred to include every detail of the novel, the timing confinements of a feature film would not allow it. As Clemens cut entire scenes, and characters she dissected the novel to find its essential essence.

And with so many details left on the cutting-room floor, Clemens still estimates her film adaptation of *Pride and Prejudice* will last about three hours—nearly an hour longer than how long a movie usually should be. Accuracy, as it turns out, requires a longer running time.

12. F. NO CHANGE
G. cut entire, scenes and characters,
H. cut entire scenes and characters,
J. cut entire scenes and characters

13. A. NO CHANGE
B. the running length of most other movies.
C. the two hour standard associated with films.
D. the industry standard.

Questions 14 and 15 ask about the preceding passage as a whole.

14. Upon reviewing the essay and finding that a transition has been left out, the writer composes the following sentence incorporating that transition:

> A forthcoming addition to the *Pride and Prejudice* canon does just that.

If the writer were to add this sentence to the essay, it would most logically be placed at:

F. Point A in Paragraph 1.
G. Point B in Paragraph 2.
H. Point C in Paragraph 3.
J. Point D in Paragraph 4.

15. Suppose the writer's primary purpose had been to review Clemens' new adaptation. Would this essay accomplish that purpose?

A. Yes, because it boasts about the stellar quality of the film.
B. Yes, because it creates a clear comparison with other adaptations.
C. No, because it does not offer an analysis of the film's quality.
D. No, because it fails to mention its box office sales.

PASSAGE II

Sporting Abroad

My family is, always has been, and always will be, an American football family. As fifth-generation season ticket holders, we spend every Sunday watching in awe as our team of heroes battles whoever dares to challenge them. By the age of two, <u>beginning</u> to decipher when to yell in anguish by
16
following the lead of adults around me; by the age of four, I was calling out to players by name.

My love for the game deviated from that of my <u>family's</u>
17
in that I fancied myself a player. While my first five years of playing consisted of aimlessly running around the field, I eventually found my stride <u>after not really knowing what</u>
18
<u>to do for half a decade.</u> Endless practice
18

<u>which landed</u> me the starting position of running back on my
19
high school's varsity team; I beamed with pride as I ran out and squared up during our first game.

When a student exchange program brought me to Dublin, Ireland, I <u>am</u> disappointed to learn that the school I
20
would be attending for the next three months had no football team. After a brief moment of <u>panic,</u> I composed myself; I
21

would continue my workout <u>consternation</u> and catch game
22
highlights on my computer.

Any leftover fears melted in an instant, <u>therefore,</u> when I
23
arrived on campus. Students filled the quad playing something that seemed at once entirely familiar and completely foreign: rugby.

16. **F.** NO CHANGE
    G. I began
    H. having begun
    J. when I began

17. **A.** NO CHANGE
    B. familys'
    C. families
    D. families'

18. **F.** NO CHANGE
    G. following the confusion of half a decade.
    H. by conquering the confusion of the five years prior.
    J. DELETE the underlined portion and end the sentence with a period

19. **A.** NO CHANGE
    B. landing
    C. that landed
    D. landed

20. **F.** NO CHANGE
    G. was
    H. will be
    J. would have been

21. **A.** NO CHANGE
    B. panic and alarm,
    C. alarming panic,
    D. panicked alarm,

22. **F.** NO CHANGE
    G. regalia
    H. correspondence
    J. regimen

23. **A.** NO CHANGE
    B. however,
    C. accordingly,
    D. additionally,

GO ON TO THE NEXT PAGE.

Specific rules seemed reversed, and players passed backwards
exclusively. I felt the experience was something akin to a
native Spanish-speaker watching a film in Italian; I couldn't
explain the intricacies of this game, yet I recognized the
patterns without having ever studied them.

For the remainder of my exchange program, I would
race to the quad after class to lace up my cleats. I ate up every
detail, every rule, until I felt proficient. Rugby posters, gear,
and memorabilia filled my suitcase when it was time to return
home. On the flight, I used my new rugby ball, a gift—from
my host family—as a pillow. Rest would be an imperative part
of my new training schedule. After all, I was about to be quite
busy as both a starting football player and, founder of my
schools's new rugby club.

24. Given that all of the choices are true, which most
    specifically illustrates a difference between the sports?

    F. NO CHANGE
    G. The crowd wildly cheered,
    H. Drop-kicks replaced field goals,
    J. I eagerly noted the differences,

25. A. NO CHANGE
    B. of my exchange program in Dublin,
    C. of what little time I had left in my exchange pro-
        gram,
    D. of what little time I had left in my exchange pro-
        gram in Dublin,

26. Given that all of the choices are true, which one best
    emphasizes the narrator's excitement to reach his des-
    tination?

    F. NO CHANGE
    G. meander
    H. stroll
    J. saunter

27. A. NO CHANGE
    B. ball, a gift
    C. ball a gift
    D. ball—a gift

28. F. NO CHANGE
    G. player, and
    H. player and
    J. player; and

29. A. NO CHANGE
    B. school
    C. schools'
    D. school's

Question 30 asks about the preceding passage as a whole.

---

30. Suppose the writer's primary purpose had been to
    describe the historical evolution of rugby within the
    United States. Would this essay accomplish that pur-
    pose?

    F. Yes, because it gives a timeline of the sport's
        popularity.
    G. Yes, because distinguishes between rugby in Eu-
        rope and the United States.
    H. No, because it does not mention any historical
        figures.
    J. No, because it focuses primarily on the narra-
        tor's personal relationship with the sport.

PASSAGE III

Jacques E. Brandenberger: Accidental Inventor

Jacques E. Brandenberger, a Swiss textile engineer, originally worked, as most did in his field—by filling the orders of his clientele. Faced with any fabric-related request, Brandenberger designed and produced the processing, procedures, and equipping to manufacture desired textiles. A change in this methodology, however, accidentally produced his most memorable creation.

Inspiration struck Brandenberger in 1900, while dining, at an upscale restaurant, he witnessed a patron spill their glass of wine on a white tablecloth, rendering the textile useless to the restaurant. What if there were a cloth that repelled liquids rather than absorbing them? Meanwhile, restaurants and various other industries could utilize their textiles for extended periods with less damage. [A]

Brandenberger rushed to his laboratory, keen to create a cloth that repelled liquids. His first thought was, to find an adhesive that created a thin plastic sheet over the cloth. He opted to try viscose due to its waterproof nature. To his dismay, the cloth having been sprayed with viscose stiffened and were rendered useless. Still, as the experiment dried, Brandenberger noticed a clear, thin film that easily separated from the cloth. [B] This breakthrough

31. **A.** NO CHANGE
    B. processes, procedures, and equipping
    C. processes, procedures, and equipment
    D. processes, his procedures, and equipment

32. **F.** NO CHANGE
    G. 1900, while dining
    H. 1900 while dining
    J. 1900. While dining

33. **A.** NO CHANGE
    B. he will witness
    C. he witnesses
    D. he will have witnessed

34. **F.** NO CHANGE
    G. In contrast,
    H. Then,
    J. Likewise,

35. **A.** NO CHANGE
    B. first thought, was to find
    C. first thought was to find
    D. first, thought was to find,

36. **F.** NO CHANGE
    G. spraying
    H. sprays
    J. sprayed

37. **A.** NO CHANGE
    B. was
    C. have been
    D. are

11

<u>sudden</u> ended Brandenberger's experiment, changing his
38
purpose completely.

<u>Notwithstanding,</u> cellophane, Brandenberger's
39
accidental creation, is a staple of modern day wrappings. [C]

Over time, the formula has undergone some changes: the

addition of glycerin, nitrocellulose lacquer, and

<u>a lot of other composition differences.</u> |41|
40

Brandenberger almost immediately began selling the

material to a variety of vendors and merchants, including

Whitman's Candy, which used cellophane

<u>to wrap its signature candy box.</u> Although Brandenberger did
42
eventually face fierce competition,

<u>they stand</u> as an exemplar of deviating from the norm and
43

---

38. **F.** NO CHANGE
  G. abruptly
  H. forceful
  J. casual

39. **A.** NO CHANGE
  B. Thus,
  C. Above all,
  D. DELETE the underlined portion and change capitalization as needed

40. **F.** NO CHANGE
  G. other changes similar to those.
  H. more chemical alterations.
  J. the like.

41. At this point, the writer is considering adding the following information:

   These innovations have allowed for new applications of the product beyond wrapping, such as self-adhesive tapes, membranes within batteries, and dialysis tubing.

   Given that the information is accurate, should the writer make this addition here?

  A. Yes, because it explains the consequences of the preceding sentence.
  B. Yes, because it proves that everyone uses the product.
  C. No, because it contradicts a point made earlier in the passage.
  D. No, because it does not specify Brandenberger's relationship to these uses.

42. Given that all of the choices are true, which one most specifically describes how the company used the material?

  F. NO CHANGE
  G. with a myriad of products.
  H. to the joy of its customers.
  J. as an industry first.

43. **A.** NO CHANGE
  B. who stands
  C. it stands
  D. he stands

accepting seeming mistakes as gifts. [D] By following his instinct, Brandenberger eschewed his habitual process and, in turn, accidentally created a product that consumers still use today.

Questions 44 and 45 ask about the preceding passage as a whole.

44. Upon reviewing the essay and finding that some information has been left out, the writer composes the following sentence incorporating that information:

> From gift baskets to food packaging, this material with low-permeability has a myriad of uses today.

If the writer were to add this sentence to the essay, it would most logically be placed at:

F. Point A in Paragraph 2.
G. Point B in Paragraph 3.
H. Point C in Paragraph 4.
J. Point D in Paragraph 5.

45. Suppose the writer's primary purpose had been to advocate for more accidental inventions. Would this essay accomplish that purpose?

A. Yes, because it offers advice on how to create one.
B. Yes, because it uses positive language regarding Brandenburger.
C. No, because Brandenburger's invention was not accidental.
D. No, because it focuses primarily on a single incident in history.

PASSAGE IV

Skiing the Never Before Skied

Every year, countless daredevils having tested their
46
skiing or snowboarding abilities off of the beaten path in an act of pure adventure called heli-skiing. Heli-skiing is an off-trail, downhill skiing and snowboarding experience that participants can only access via helicopters. These choppers drop adventurerers in remote areas that ski lifts cannot access, allowing you to test their prowess on completely untouched
47
powder.

46. F. NO CHANGE
G. who test
H. testing
J. test

47. A. NO CHANGE
B. it
C. him or her
D. them

GO ON TO THE NEXT PAGE.

Who could be more prone to seeking thrills than the absolutely amazingly skilled skiers and snowboarders
48
participating in heli-skiing? Well, their highly skilled guides surely give them a run for their money.

Being paid to fly around in a helicopter and ski breathtaking bounties does sound like an ideal job, but only
49

the most elite skiers qualify to do so. The job, physically
50
demanding, requiring that guides be able to ski and wander the backcountry for hours—or sometimes even days—at a time. As a result, many guides were once professional or paraprofessional skiers or snowboarders.

[1] Training programs include both classroom and hands-on lessons, that test the balance between mental aptitude and physical dexterity. [2] Logistical skills are nearly as important for heli-ski guides as physical ability. [3] Guides must complete a certificate course
51
on mountainous terrain that includes skills like properly

planning for weather executing emergency medical services,
52
and intensive navigation. [4] Prospective guides must

complete a fairly lengthy list of requirements before even
53
applying to one of these programs, including having skied on many different kinds of terrain and snowpacks. [5] In fact, many students having failed their final exams and need to
54

re-take them in order to obtain certification. [55]

48. **F.** NO CHANGE
    G. highly, extremely
    H. exceedingly highly
    J. highly

49. **A.** NO CHANGE
    B. localizations
    C. locales
    D. landscaping

50. **F.** NO CHANGE
    G. job is physically
    H. job, being physically
    J. job that is physically

51. **A.** NO CHANGE
    B. how they can use their physical bodies.
    C. the agility of their athletic physiques.
    D. their abilities to use their athletic statures.

52. **F.** NO CHANGE
    G. weather executing emergency medical services
    H. weather, executing emergency medical services,
    J. weather, executing emergency, medical services

53. **A.** NO CHANGE
    B. fairly, lengthy, list
    C. fairly lengthy, list
    D. fairly, lengthy list

54. **F.** NO CHANGE
    G. failing
    H. failed
    J. fail

55. For the sake of logic and cohesion, Sentence 1 should be placed:
    A. where it is now.
    B. after Sentence 2.
    C. after Sentence 3.
    D. after Sentence 5.

GO ON TO THE NEXT PAGE.

Although a lesser obstacle, seasonal employment

which plagues heli-ski guides,
56

guides are forced to find other means of making money
57
during the off-season. That often means splitting time

between a winter and summer home, making the occupation

a difficult path to take when compared to most office jobs.
58

In fact, those individuals who are employed as heli-skiing
59
guides find great satisfaction in it. Fresh air, beautiful

mountains, and infinite opportunities for exploration—what

more could a skiing enthusiast want? 60

56. F. NO CHANGE
G. that plagues
H. plaguing
J. plagues

57. A. NO CHANGE
B. forcing them
C. they are therefore forced
D. that forces them

58. Given that all of the choices are true, which one most effectively emphasizes the difficult life changes required of heli-ski guides due to seasonal employment?

F. NO CHANGE
G. something they must be extremely passionate about.
H. more of a complete lifestyle and less of a typical job.
J. a distraction from other interests and activities.

59. A. NO CHANGE
B. Even so,
C. Correspondingly,
D. Thereafter,

60. The writer is considering deleting the preceding sentence. Should the writer make this deletion?

F. Yes, because it does not specify that the sentence is about heli-skiing.
G. Yes, because it adds unnecessary information.
H. No, because it expands upon the previous sentence and concludes the passage.
J. No, because it is the only instance of the narrator asserting their opinion.

PASSAGE V

The Retro Noise of Tim Ardel

Tim Ardel has always preferred music albums with scratchy, somewhat distant melodies underscored with reverb. [A] That style of recording harkens back to the birth of rock, when talent reigned supreme and an accidental wrong note could be seen as an asset. In the age of autotune and digital mixing, though, Ardel is considered somewhat of an
_____
61

anachronism. [62]

61. **A.** NO CHANGE
    B. mixing though,
    C. mixing though
    D. mixing, though

62. At this point, the writer is considering adding the following information:

> While most contemporary record producers chase perfection, he chases the age of grit.

Given that the information is accurate, should the writer make this addition here?

   F. Yes, because it summarizes Ardel's job.
   G. Yes, because it illustrates how Ardel differs from others in his profession.
   H. No, because it does not specify which contemporary producers.
   J. No, because it detracts from the main idea of the paragraph.

Today, most recording studios advertise as having the latest, most coveted equipment. While Ardel's Los Angeles
_____
63
studio is well-stocked with the most expensive

recording gadgets money can buy, he opts for the old analog
_____
64
tools whenever possible. Slightly out-of-tune guitars pay homage to Bob Dylan and the Rolling Stones, varied tape speeds creates key changes with different timbres, and
_____
65

it is vintage microphones that catch every sound as full bands
_____
66
play together in a single take. The end result is more akin to a live performance than a polished product. While that kind of sound may seem accidental to some—or the product of a bad recording—the process is in fact often more time consuming

63. **A.** NO CHANGE
    B. latest most coveted
    C. latest, most, coveted
    D. latest—most coveted

64. **F.** NO CHANGE
    G. lowbrow
    H. archeological
    J. stratified

65. **A.** NO CHANGE
    B. create
    C. has created
    D. does create

66. **F.** NO CHANGE
    G. catching every sound are vintage microphones
    H. vintage microphones catch every sound
    J. caught sounds by vintage microphones

than using all contemporary equipment. [B] Ardel considers this time well spent, of course, as he hopes to make listeners feel like <u>its</u> hearing a raw, uncut take meant just for them.
67

67. A. NO CHANGE
    B. there
    C. their
    D. they're

Unfortunately, the current popularity of Ardel's methods is not an indication of consistent, unwavering success. <u>His methods weren't always so popular.</u> [C] As the wave of
68
90's grunge bands dissipated, most artists opted for clean recordings that were further perfected with autotune and mixing. Ardel happily obliged—and still <u>obliges; almost all</u>
69
recording requests, but he refuses to give up his old equipment. [D] As bands began requesting vintage sounds,

Ardel's <u>studio, having</u> a constant influx of artists coming to
70
use some of the most well-kept, authentic recording devices.

As technologies change, Ardel's <u>work, which stands</u> as
71

a reminder of the beauty that <u>rested</u> in the seemingly outdated.
72
Just as an antique car show might, his recordings showcase

68. F. NO CHANGE
    G. Business has been up and down for Ardel.
    H. Ardel's methods were sometimes unpopular.
    J. DELETE the underlined portion

69. A. NO CHANGE
    B. obliges, almost
    C. obliges: almost
    D. obliges—almost

70. F. NO CHANGE
    G. studio had
    H. studio that had
    J. studio, which had

71. A. NO CHANGE
    B. work stands
    C. work that stands
    D. work, standing

72. F. NO CHANGE
    G. rests
    H. resting
    J. did rest

17

that the sturdy and sometimes impractical can transport

individuals to simpler times when <u>other sounds were</u>
₇₃

<u>preferred.</u>
₇₃

73. Given that all of the choices are true, which one most effectively illustrates the time period in question?

    A. NO CHANGE
    B. things weren't always like this.
    C. vinyl ruled supreme.
    D. music was different than it is today.

Questions 74 and 75 ask about the preceding passage as a whole.

---

74. Upon reviewing the essay and finding that some information has been left out, the writer composes the following sentence incorporating that information:

> He somehow knew that a global nostalgia would return his methods to popularity, this time prompted by the ever-growing Indie genre and a return to classic rock.

If the writer were to add this sentence to the essay, it would most logically be placed at:

    F. Point A in Paragraph 1.
    G. Point B in Paragraph 2.
    H. Point C in Paragraph 3.
    J. Point D in Paragraph 3.

75. Suppose the writer's primary purpose had been to give a general overview of Ardel's identity within the music business. Would this essay accomplish that purpose?

    A. Yes, because it discusses his personal role as a producer.
    B. Yes, because it gives an example of his typical day.
    C. No, because it does not mention any specific musicians.
    D. No, because it focuses primarily on Ardel's relationship to the past.

END OF TEST 1.
STOP! DO NOT TURN THE PAGE UNTIL TOLD TO DO SO.

THERE ARE NO TESTING MATERIALS ON THIS PAGE.

MATHEMATICS TEST
60 Minutes — 60 Questions

DIRECTIONS: Solve each problem, choose the correct answer, and then fill in the corresponding oval on your answer document.

Do not linger over problems that take too much time. Solve as many as you can; then return to the others in the time you have left for this test.

You are permitted to use a calculator on this test. You may use your calculator for any problems you choose,

but some of the problems may be best done without using a calculator.

Note: Unless otherwise stated, all of the following should be assumed:
1. Figures are NOT necessarily drawn to scale.
2. Geometric figures lie in a plane.
3. The word *line* indicates a striaght line.
4. The word *average* indicates arithmetic mean.

---

1. Betty the baker can make a cake with 3 different types of batter (white, yellow, and chocolate), 4 different types of filling (strawberry, raspberry, chocolate, and cream), and 5 different types of icing (vanilla, chocolate, butterscotch, strawberry, and mint). If each cake will be made of 1 type of batter, 1 type of filling, and 1 type of icing, how many different types of cake can Betty make?

   A. 3
   B. 12
   C. 15
   D. 36
   E. 60

2. Stephan has a coupon for 30% off the purchase of a single item at a local clothing store (in a state that does not collect sales tax). If Stephan buys a jacket that has a retail price of $85, how much money will Stephan save by applying his coupon?

   F. $19.62
   G. $25.50
   H. $30.00
   J. $55.00
   K. $59.50

3. If $\sqrt{x} > 8$ and $\sqrt{x} < 10$, which of the following numbers could be the value of x ?

   A. 3
   B. 9
   C. 64
   D. 75
   E. 100

4. In a standard deck of cards, the probability of selecting a heart is $\frac{1}{4}$ and the probability of selecting a queen is $\frac{1}{13}$. What is the probability that a randomly selected card is the queen of hearts?

F. $\dfrac{17}{52}$

G. $\dfrac{13}{17}$

H. $\dfrac{9}{52}$

J. $\dfrac{9}{13}$

K. $\dfrac{1}{52}$

5. A survey found that 4 out of 5 tutors use CREST on the Reading section. There are about 192 tutors at Private Prep. Based upon the results of the survey, approximately how many Private Prep tutors use CREST?

A. 39
B. 48
C. 145
D. 154
E. 160

6. In the figure below, $\overline{DE}$ is a part of a diagonal of parallelogram $ABCD$. If $\angle A$ measures $45°$ and $\angle CDE$ measures $75°$, what is the measure of $\angle ADE$?

F. 30°
G. 45°
H. 60°
J. 75°
K. 120°

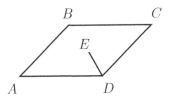

7. What is the sum of $5x^2 + 3x - 7$ and $4x^2 - 3x + 8$?

A. $9x^2 + 1$
B. $x^2 + 6x - 15$
C. $9x^2 + 6x + 15$
D. $20x^2 - 9x - 56$
E. $20x^4 - 3x^3 + 31x^2 + 45x - 56$

Use the following information to answer questions
8-11

The figure below depicts a scale drawing of a triangular park, with each line segment representing a walkway. $\overline{DE}\|\overline{AB}$. One coordinate unit represents 10 *yards*.

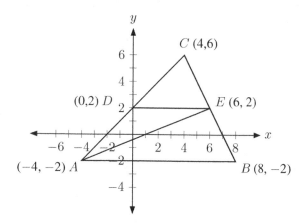

8. A water fountain will be placed halfway between points A and E when the park is constructed. If point F will represent the fountain, where should point F be placed on the graph?

    F. (1,0)
    G. $(2\frac{2}{3}, \frac{2}{3})$
    H. $(3\frac{1}{2}, 1)$
    J. (3,2)
    K. (5,2)

9. The trapezoidal region bound by points A, D, E, and B will be covered with grass. If each bag of grass seed can cover an area of 100 square yards (1 square coordinate unit), how many bags of grass seed will be needed to completely cover this region?

    (Note: the area can be found by multiplying the height of the trapezoid by the average of its bases.)

    A.   3.6
    B.   36
    C.   360
    D.   3,600
    E. 360,000

10. The two walkways that cut through $\triangle ABC$ will be constructed from slate stones that are each 1 yard long. If 60 stones are needed for walkway $\overline{DE}$, how many stones will be needed for *both* walkways?

    F.   17

    G.   60

    H. 108

    J.   168

    K. 323

11. A circular fountain, with a radius of 5 yards, will be placed in the center (centroid) of the region bound by $\triangle CDE$. Which of these could be the equation of the circle that represents the fountain?

    A. $(x + \frac{10}{3})^2 + (y + \frac{10}{3})^2 = \frac{1}{4}$

    B. $(x + \frac{10}{3})^2 + (y + \frac{10}{3})^2 = \frac{1}{2}$

    C. $(x - \frac{10}{3})^2 + (y - \frac{10}{3})^2 = \frac{1}{4}$

    D. $(x - \frac{10}{3})^2 + (y - \frac{10}{3})^2 = \frac{1}{2}$

    E. $(x - \frac{10}{3})^2 + (y + \frac{10}{3})^2 = \frac{1}{4}$

12. For which value of x would the expression $\dfrac{x + 4}{x}$ simplify to a *negative* number?

    F. -7

    G. -1

    H. 2

    J. 3

    K. 5

13. Megan and Keara are 7 years apart. Megan is 25% older than Keara and Keara is 20% younger than Megan. Which of the following are their ages?

    A. Megan is 20 and Keara is 16

    B. Megan is 21 and Keara is 14

    C. Megan is 28 and Keara is 35

    D. Megan is 30 and Keara is 23

    E. Megan is 35 and Keara is 28

14. What is the value of the expression
$|(3-8)-(12-4)|$?
F. 21
G. 13
H. 3
J. −3
K. −13

15. $\dfrac{(6x^3)^2}{4x^3}$ is equivalent to:

A. $1.5x^2$
B. $9x^2$
C. $9x^3$
D. $32x^3$
E. $24x^9$

16. In the standard (x,y) coordinate plane, what is the slope of the line $7x + 4y = 12$?
F. -7
G. $-\dfrac{7}{4}$
H. $\dfrac{7}{12}$
J. 3
K. 7

17. When Ryan decided to start exercising (Week 0), he found that he could do 15 push-ups in a row. Once a week, he did more push-ups to track his progress, and the results of how many push-ups he could do at the end of each week are shown in the table below:

Weeks (w)	0	1	2	3	4
Push-ups (p)	15	21	27	33	39

If this trend continues, which of the following equations could he use to determine how many pushups (p) he will be able to do after w weeks?
A. $p = 6w$
B. $p = 15w + 6$
C. $p = w + 15$
D. $p = 6w - 15$
E. $p = 6w + 15$

18. At Elite High School, there are 75 athletes competing on three sports teams: Football, Baseball, and Hockey. Students can compete on one, two, or all three teams. Based on the Venn diagram below, how many students play on all three sports teams?

Elite High School Athlete Distribution

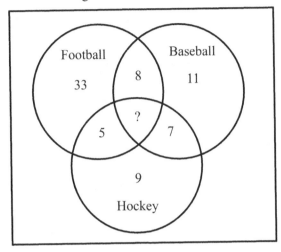

F. 0
G. 2
H. 20
J. 22
K. 53

19. The expression $\dfrac{4 + \frac{1}{7}}{2 + \frac{1}{14}}$ is equal to:

A. $1\frac{7}{29}$
B. 2
C. $2\frac{14}{29}$
D. 4
E. $4\frac{1}{7}$

20. A right triangle has legs of 5 inches and 8 inches The length of the hypotenuse, in inches, is between:

F. 4 and 5
G. 5 and 8
H. 8 and 9
J. 9 and 10
K. 10 and 13

21. Circle A, shown below, has a radius of 10 inches. What is the circle's circumference, in inches?

A. 10π
B. 20π
C. 25π
D. 100π
E. 400π

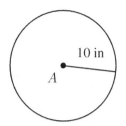

10 in

A

22. Which of the following is NOT true about $\triangle ABC$ below?

F. $\sin A = \dfrac{7}{\sqrt{65}}$

G. $\cos C = \dfrac{7}{\sqrt{65}}$

H. $\tan A = \dfrac{4}{7}$

J. $\sin C = \dfrac{4}{\sqrt{65}}$

K. $\cos A = \dfrac{4}{\sqrt{65}}$

A

$\sqrt{65}$

4

B 7 C

23. If all angles are right angles, what is the area of the figure below, in square centimeters?

A. 25
B. 40
C. 48
D. 63
E. 66

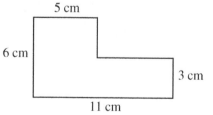

5 cm

6 cm

3 cm

11 cm

24. If $f(x) = -3x^2 + 11x - 8$, what is $f(-5)$?

    F. -138

    G. -122

    H. -28

    J. 12

    K. 122

25. Which of the following equations could be used to solve the problem: 42% of what number is 63?

    A. $\dfrac{42}{100} = \dfrac{x}{63}$

    B. $\dfrac{63}{100} = \dfrac{x}{42}$

    C. $\dfrac{100}{42} = \dfrac{63}{x}$

    D. $\dfrac{42}{100} = \dfrac{63}{x}$

    E. $\dfrac{x}{100} = \dfrac{63}{42}$

26. There are 7 members in a school's chess club. One afternoon, each member of the club played against each other member once. How many total chess matches were played that afternoon?

    F. 14

    G. 21

    H. 42

    J. 49

    K. $5,040$

27. Jordan is planning his birthday party. The party will involve games requiring teams of 2, 3, or 5 players, depending on the game. What is the minimum number of people (including Jordan) that must attend the party in order to ensure that all guests will be able to be evenly divided among teams for any of the games?

    A. 5

    B. 10

    C. 15

    D. 30

    E. 60

28. In the figure below, $\angle WVY$ measures $80°$, $\angle XVZ$ measures $85°$, and $\angle WVZ$ measures $140°$. What is the measure of $\angle XVY$?

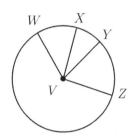

F. $5°$

G. $15°$

H. $25°$

J. $55°$

K. $60°$

29. Bennie paid $147.45 for 4 beach chairs and 7 beach towels. Mary paid $95.65 for 3 beach chairs and 4 beach towels. If each beach chair (c) cost the same amount of money and each beach towel (t) cost the same amount of money, which of the following systems of equations could be used to find the cost of 1 beach chair and 1 beach towel?

A. $4c + 7t = \$147.45$
$3c + 4t = \$95.65$

B. $4c + 7t = \$95.65$
$3c + 4t = \$147.45$

C. $4c + 7t = \$147.45$
$c + t = \$95.65$

D. $c + t = \$147.45$
$3c + 4t = \$95.65$

E. $4c - 7t = \$147.45$
$3c - 4t = \$95.65$

30. In physics, the coefficient of performance (C) is a function of work (W) and heat (Q) and can be modeled by the equation $C = \dfrac{Q + W}{Q}$. Which of the following expressions represents Q as a function of C and W?

F. $Q = \dfrac{W}{C - 1}$

G. $Q = \dfrac{W}{C + 1}$

H. $Q = \dfrac{W}{1 - C}$

J. $Q = \dfrac{C - 1}{W}$

K. $Q = \dfrac{C + 1}{W}$

Use the following information to answer questions
31-33

The figure below depicts the target for a darts game. The diameter of the board is 20 inches, each outer ring has the same width, and the radius of the innermost circle is half the radius of the circle that defines the 50 point ring. The point values for each ring are shown in the figure:

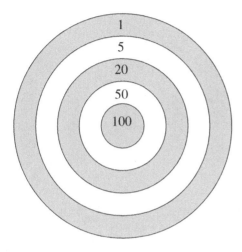

31. What is the width of the 1 point ring?

    A. 1 inch

    B. 2 inches

    C. 4 inches

    D. 10 inches

    E. 20 inches

32. What is the fewest number of darts needed to score *exactly* 99 points?

    F. 1

    G. 6

    H. 8

    J. 9

    K. 12

33. The area of the center region is what percentage of the area of the whole dartboard?

    A. 4%

    B. 8%

    C. 10%

    D. 16%

    E. 20%

34. Rectangle $ABCD \sim$ Rectangle $BCEF$ in the figure below. If $\overline{AB}$ is 10 cm and $\overline{AD}$ is 4 cm, what is the length of $\overline{CE}$ in centimeters?

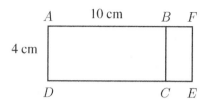

   F. 1.0 cm
   G. 1.5 cm
   H. 1.6 cm
   J. 2.0 cm
   K. 2.5 cm

35. Consider the following system of linear equations

$$2x - 5y = 43$$
$$5x - 2y = 34$$

   If (x, y) is the solution to the system, what is the value of $x - y$?
   A. -7
   B. -3
   C. 4
   D. 11
   E. 77

36. The first term of an infinite geometric sequence is 243. The common ratio for the sequence is $\frac{2}{3}$. How many terms in this sequence will be *integers*?
   F. 1
   G. 2
   H. 3
   J. 5
   K. 6

37. Which of the following is equivalent to $f(x) = x^2 - 6x - 16$?
   A. $f(x) = (x - 3)^2 - 25$
   B. $f(x) = (x + 8)(x - 2)$
   C. $f(x) = 2(x^2 - 3x - 8)$
   D. $f(x) = x(x - 22)$
   E. $f(x) = -(x^2 + 6x + 16)$

38. In the figure below, $\triangle DEF$ will be reflected over the x-axis to create $\triangle D'E'F'$. What will be the coordinates of F'?

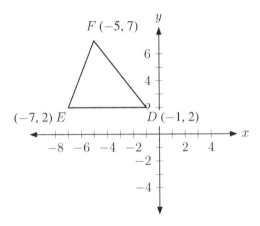

F. $(5, 7)$

G. $(7, 5)$

H. $(5, -7)$

J. $(-7, -5)$

K. $(-5, -7)$

39. A construction brick, shown below, has dimensions of 4 inches by 4 inches by 9 inches. If the entire brick is to be painted, how many square inches of surface will the paint cover?

A. 36

B. 68

C. 88

D. 144

E. 176

40. The variable z is dependent on the behaviors of independent variables w, x, and y, as well as a constant k. If z varies *inversely* with w and *directly* both with the square of x and with y, which of of the following equations could model this relationship?

F. $z = \dfrac{kx^2y^2}{w}$

G. $z = \dfrac{w}{kx^2y}$

H. $z = \dfrac{k(xy)^2}{w}$

J. $z = \dfrac{k\sqrt{x}y}{w}$

K. $z = \dfrac{x^2y}{kw}$

41. If x is an integer, which of the following could NOT be the value of y when $y = i^{3x}$? (Note: $i = \sqrt{-1}$)

  A.   0

  B.   1

  C.   −1

  D. i

  E. $-i$

42. A survey of pet owners found that $\frac{1}{2}$ preferred dogs, $\frac{1}{4}$ preferred cats, and $\frac{1}{10}$ preferred fish. If the remaining 24 participants had no opinion, how many people were included in the survey?

  F.   24

  G.   48

  H.   80

  J.   160

  K.   240

43. The graph of the function $f(x) = -3\cos(4x - \pi) + 2$ is shown on the figure below. Which of the following correctly state the period and amplitude of this function?

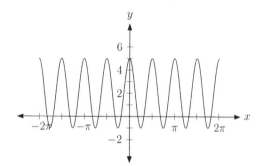

  A.   period = $\frac{\pi}{2}$, amplitude = 3

  B.   period = 3, amplitude = $\frac{\pi}{2}$

  C.   period = $\frac{\pi}{2}$, amplitude = 5

  D.   period = $\frac{\pi}{4}$, amplitude = 3

  E.   period = $\frac{1}{2}$, amplitude = 3π

44. When $(3x - 5)^2$ is expanded to the form $ax^2 + bx + c$, what is the value of $a + b + c$?

  F.   −16

  G.   −4

  H.   4

  J.   14

  K.   54

45. In the figure below, a battleship has spotted a submarine that is 250 meters away at an angle of depression of 55°. Which of the following expressions represents the depth (d) of the submarine?

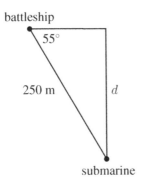

A. $250 \sin(55°)$

B. $250 \cos(55°)$

C. $250 \tan(55°)$

D. $\dfrac{\sin(55°)}{250}$

E. $\dfrac{\cos(55°)}{250}$

46. The figure below shows 3 trees — tree A, tree B, and tree C — where the distance between tree A and tree C is 16 yards and the distance between tree A and tree B is 11 yards. The angle formed at tree A is 14°. The distance between tree B and tree C, d, can be modeled by which of the following equations?

(Note: The law of cosines states that for any triangle with vertices A, B, and C and the sides opposite those vertices with lengths a, b, and c respectively, $c^2 = a^2 + b^2 - 2ab \cos C$)

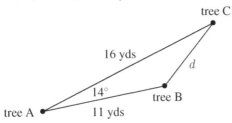

F. $d = \sqrt{16^2 + 11^2}$

G. $d = \sqrt{16^2 + 11^2 - 2(11)(16) \cos(14°)}$

H. $d = \sqrt{16^2 + 11^2 + 2(11)(16) \cos(14°)}$

J. $d = \sqrt{16^2 + 11^2 - 2(11)(16) \cos(76°)}$

K. $d = \sqrt{16^2 + 11^2 + 2(11)(16) \cos(76°)}$

GO ON TO THE NEXT PAGE.

47. An ID Badge consists of an ID Code that contains 1 digit, then 4 letters, then 1 digit. The letters O and I are excluded to avoid confusion with the digits 0 and 1. If the digits (0-9) may be repeated, but letters (taken from the remaining 24) must each be different, how many possible unique ID Codes are possible?

- **A.** 22,952,160
- **B.** 25,502,400
- **C.** 32,292,000
- **D.** 33,177,600
- **E.** 35,880,000

48. What is the value of $\log_3 \sqrt{27}$?

- **F.** $\dfrac{2}{9}$
- **G.** $\dfrac{2}{3}$
- **H.** $\dfrac{3}{2}$
- **J.** $\dfrac{9}{2}$
- **K.** 3

49. On a Wednesday, Seth realized that it was 100 days until his next birthday. On what day of the week will Seth's next birthday fall?

(Note: there are 7 days in a week)

- **A.** Friday
- **B.** Saturday
- **C.** Sunday
- **D.** Monday
- **E.** Tuesday

50. Jodie is constructing an obtuse, scalene triangle that has a perimeter of 24 inches and side lengths that are all whole numbers. Which of the following could be the side lengths of Jodie's triangle?

- **F.** 6, 8, and 10
- **G.** 7, 8, and 9
- **H.** 7, 7, and 10
- **J.** 5, 7, and 12
- **K.** 6, 7, and 11

Use the following information to answer questions
51-53

At the end of each 10 question quiz, Ms. Krabappel asks her students how many hours they spent studying for that quiz. She then compared her students average quiz score (y-axis) to the average amount of time they studied (x-axis). For example, Lisa averaged 6 hours of study time and had an average score of 8, while Bart averaged 4 hours of study time and had an average score of 5. She then determined that the line of best fit to be $y = 0.3x + 5$, shown below:

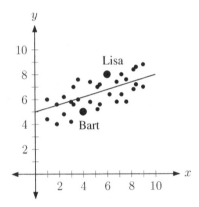

51. Based on Ms. Krabappel's best fit line, about how many hours would a student need to study, per week, to average a perfect 10 on their quizzes?

   A. 8
   B. 10
   C. 13
   D. 15
   E. 17

52. Which of the following equations is an equivalent form of Ms. Krabappel's best fit line?

   F. $10y - 3x - 50 = 0$
   G. $y = \frac{3x+5}{10}$
   H. $3y = 10x + 50$
   J. $x = \frac{10y}{3} - 5$
   K. $\frac{y}{0.3} + 5 = x$

53. A residual (used to determine how well data in a set are correlated) is the vertical distance from a data point to the line of best fit. Based on the data, what were Bart and Lisa's combined residual?

   A. 0
   B. 1.2
   C. 2.4
   D. 6.2
   E. 6.8

GO ON TO THE NEXT PAGE.

54. On a certain golf hole, the probability of a golfer carding 2, 3, 4, 5, or 6 strokes is shown in the table below (the probability of getting less than a 2 or more than a 7 is negligible). If a tournament features 60 golfers, how many total strokes can be expected on the hole on any given day?

Score	Probability
2	0.03
3	0.24
4	0.46
5	0.19
6	0.08

F. 4.05
G. 60
H. 240
J. 243
K. 926

55. In the figure below, $\overline{AB}\|\overline{DC}$, $\overline{AB}$ is 5 feet long, $\overline{DC}$ is 16 feet long, and $\overline{AC}$, 12 feet long, represents the height of trapezoid $ABCD$. What is the *perimeter*, in feet, of trapezoid $ABCD$?

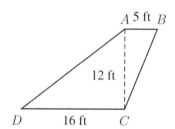

A. 33
B. 54
C. 66
D. 78
E. 126

56. for what values of x such that $0 \le x < 2\pi$ is $\sin^2 x + \cos^2 x < 1$?

F. $\{\ \}$
G. $\{0 < x < \pi\}$
H. $\{0 \le x \le \frac{\pi}{2}\}$
J. $\{\pi \le x < \frac{3\pi}{2}\}$
K. $\{\pi < x \le 2\pi\}$

57. A perfect number is a number whose factors, excluding for the number itself, add up to that number (eg. 6 is a perfect number, since its other factors, 1, 2, and 3, add up to 6). Which of the following numbers is a perfect number?

A. 11

B. 15

C. 24

D. 28

E. 36

58. In the figure below, all angles are right angles. In terms of x, what is the area of the shaded region?

F. $6x^2 - 44x + 70$

G. $6x^2 - 41x + 70$

H. $70 - 6x^2$

J. $5x^2 - 21x + 17$

K. $5x^2 - 70$

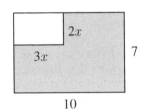

59. Kris' doctor gave him a prescription that contained 30 pills and instructed him to take 1 pill every 3 hours (even at night) until they were all gone, warning him not to miss a single dose if he wanted to get healthy. If he takes the first pill at 10:00 am on Monday, at what time will he take his LAST pill?

A. 1:00 pm on Tuesday

B. 1:00 pm on Thursday

C. 4:00 pm on Thursday

D. 1:00 am on Friday

E. 4:00 am on Friday

60. If $a = b$ for all positive integers a and b, which of the following expressions will result in a *real* number?

F. $\dfrac{a + b}{a - b}$

G. $\sqrt{a - 2b}$

H. $(-4a + b)^{1/2}$

J. $(a^2 - b^2)^{-1}$

K. $\sqrt[3]{-|a^2 + b^2|}$

END OF TEST 2.
STOP! DO NOT TURN THE PAGE UNTIL TOLD TO DO SO.
DO NOT RETURN TO THE PREVIOUS TEST.

READING TEST

35 Minutes — 40 Questions

DIRECTIONS: There are four passages in this test. Each passage is followed by several questions. Choose the best answer to each question and fill in the corresponding oval on your answer document. You may refer to the passages as often as necessary.

Passage I

LITERARY NARRATIVE: This passage is adapted from the short story *A Man Apart* by Alice Willoughby (©2014 by Alice Willoughby National Press).

Now that the sun had set over Pine Ridge, trying to estimate the size of the opposing army's losses wasn't only futile and disheartening, but dangerous. Field Commander Forrest ordered his battalion to douse their fires, even
5 though they'd barely just gotten them lit. It would have to be hardtack and salted pork again tonight, leaving two, maybe three nights' worth left. He did his best to ignore the sidelong looks of disapproval from his subordinates as he made his way back to his tent.

10 They'd wanted to engage the enemy two days earlier, when the element of surprise was still on their side and they had the higher ground between the hills and the river. But Forrest, expecting the reinforcements Lee had promised him, had advocated caution and patience, the
15 two traits, which more than any others, had given him many a victory and established his reputation as a skilled tactician and trusted leader.

Now, of course, with the fallen bodies of so many of his men between here and the enemy camp—one of the
20 last sights he'd been able to see before nightfall came was the blue devils carousing victoriously around the dancing flames of campfires—he knew that he had been wrong to trust in his superiors, and that his men's trust had been misplaced in him.

25 Stories had come to him from up North, too many to discount, of the harsh conditions of the prison camps there, where men's wounds went untreated, little food was given out, and the men were often worked to death repairing the enemy's uniforms and left to fend for themselves with no
30 shelter against the elements. To get better treatment, the men would often inform on one another. Forrest would rather face certain death, and willingly submit all his men to it as well, rather than surrender and enter into such a place.

35 And from the look of things, that was exactly what was going to happen. At the most optimistic count, they had lost over half of their men—and, with the enemy re-ceiving reinforcements in the late afternoon, they were now outnumbered at least two to one. Low on food, am-
40 munition, and morale, they had no practical chance of sur-viving the next morning's engagement, let alone obtaining victory.

Forrest sat at his desk, barely looking over the bat-tle plans that his men had prepared for him. They all
45 knew that it was a useless exercise. He read more than disappointment in so many eyes as he walked up the hill, and it was more than for the point to which his decisions had brought them—it was the knowledge, well-established among all the men, that Forrest would never surrender.
50 That their lives were forfeit to his unbending pride.

He managed to smile a little bit at that. Partially be-cause it was true—he was certainly a proud man, but also because it covered a deeper truth: He was also a spiteful man. He'd give his own life and that of a dozen of his men
55 just to wipe that conceited look, the one he'd seen more and more of late, off the face of one of those Yanks. He supposed, when it came right down to it, that this was the real reason he was fighting. He knew others talked about protecting and preserving the Southern Way of Life, but he
60 didn't hold much truck with that. And as for slavery, well, he himself was opposed to it. It was the nature of a man, not the color of skin, that dictated his true quality. And unlike so many of his fellow officers, he hadn't come from money either; there was no big white mansion just waiting
65 for him to return. No, what set him apart was what some might see as a flaw, but which he held to be a virtue—an unbending will to never forgive an offense that was know-ingly given until a proper reparation or apology had been made.

70 And these Northerners, who were they to think that they knew better than he the proper way to live life? The hypocrisy enraged him: with one breath they'd talk about freedom for all men, and in the next they'd be calling the South treasonous. And why? Simply because they had se-
75 ceded, had taken for themselves the very freedom that the Northerners seemed to so highly prize—but in theory only, it would seem. And why was that? Well, there was no se-cret there. It was the same desire that had led Judas astray, with many a man long before and since: money. The North
80 needed the Southern fields, the tobacco, the cotton. And

GO ON TO THE NEXT PAGE.

if the South decided they didn't need the North, well, then a different version of freedom would have to be laid upon the necks of the former.

He laughed a little at himself. Here he was, working
85 himself into a frenzy over something that come morning, he would have no power to change. He knew he ought to be enjoying, or trying to enjoy, his supper.

1. Which of the following events mentioned in the passage happened first chronologically?

A. The enemy received reinforcements.
B. The sun set over the pine ridge.
C. Forrest settled down to his supper.
D. Forrest's men were between the hills and river.

2. According to the passage, Forrest's men were unlikely to survive the next morning's engagement because:

F. they were fighting for the Southern Way of Life.
G. they were low on supplies and morale.
H. Lee had asked them to ambush the enemy.
J. they were plotting to disobey Forrest's orders.

3. Based on the passage, Forrest's attitude toward Northerners can best be described as:

A. hostile.
B. tolerant.
C. optimistic.
D. impartial.

4. Which of the following best captures the narrator's comments in lines 44–49?

F. The soldiers were unhappy that Forrest would risk their lives.
G. Forrest secretly debated forfeiting the upcoming battle.
H. Forrest felt pity for the soldiers who had volunteered to fight.
J. The soldiers felt proud to fight for a cause that they believed in.

5. The passage indicates that Forrest is different from many of his fellow officers because:

A. he disobeys orders from his superiors.
B. he is more forgiving of Northerners.
C. he believes in slavery.
D. he does not have a rich family.

6. In the passage, all of the following are described as conditions in Northern prison camps EXCEPT:

F. men being worked to death.
G. poorly built barracks.
H. untreated wounds.
J. a lack of food for prisoners.

7. The main purpose of the last paragraph is to:

A. illustrate the feelings of soldiers in the battalion.
B. explain Forrest's strategy to win the war.
C. capture Forrest's emotions the night before a difficult battle.
D. identify the meal that Forrest would eat for supper.

8. As it is used in line 62, *quality* most nearly means:

F. mood.
G. advantage.
H. character.
J. action.

9. The main idea of the seventh paragraph (lines 51–69) is that Forrest:

A. inspired both his superiors and those under him to fight for glory.
B. considered slavery to be an important part of the Southern Way of Life.
C. was a vindictive person who sought revenge against enemies.
D. resented his fellow officers because he did not have a mansion.

10. It can most reasonably be inferred from the passage that after the battle, Northern soldiers:

F. surrendered and were taken to prison camps.
G. retreated from the battlefield because of their loss.
H. pressured their leaders to secede from the nation.
J. celebrated their victory in battle.

Passage II

SOCIAL SCIENCE: Passage A is adapted from "The March of Progress" by Mattie Ortega (©2010 by Mattie Ortega). Passage B is adapted from "The Ecology of a Society" by Sonya Robinson (©2015 by Sonya Robinson).

Passage A by Mattie Ortega

Progress is a dense, multi-sided concept, but its characteristic trait is a certainty that when people use their inborn gift of reason to address society's problems, the result will be a steady and universal improvement in that
5 society's standard of living. In both the material and the moral sense, the lives of human beings improve with every passing generation. Progress means railroads and religious tolerance, indoor plumbing and liberal democracy.

Society believes that Progress, once started, can't be
10 stopped, that the really important improvements are permanent. Once roving bands of hunters and scavengers developed agriculture, farming became the default way of life wherever it was introduced. The more recent Industrial Revolution is following the same path. Technologically
15 sophisticated production and organization, once it reaches a society, is never rejected. Thus, we can expect our extremely comfortable way of life to become, over generations, the new normal for all of humanity.

But a critical look at the record of the human past
20 paints a very different picture of the human condition. One overriding lesson to emerge from this examination is that the core assumptions underlying the idea of Progress are false. Paleontologists and anthropologists have found that the average human being who lived before the invention
25 of agriculture was four inches taller, and twenty pounds heavier, than the average agricultural laborer. Peasants lived shorter, poorer, sicker lives than their hunter-gatherer ancestors; their diets were less nutritious and varied, and they worked nearly three times as many hours per week as
30 hunter-gatherers. And peasants were, until three decades ago, the majority of the human species. Seen from this perspective, the modern expansion of technologically driven economic development that raised so many poor farmers into middle class lifestyles has, in fact, only restored a
35 standard of living that our pre-literate, pre-urban ancestors took for granted.

If history warns us not to take for granted the constant improvement of our condition, how should we think about our society, where it has been and where it is going? What
40 kind of story should we tell ourselves?

Passage B by Sonya Robinson

In recent years, a new wave of scholarship has challenged the way we think about how human societies thrive. One of the most striking metaphors of this new school of thought conceives of society as an organism—that is, as
45 a complex, dynamic system that lives or dies depending upon its successful adaptation to its environment. Society is not a static structure, not a clockwork machine with regular rhythms. Instead, it is constantly changing, fine-tuning its adaptation to its environment as it pursues its
50 own reproduction. This is the central insight that informs the study of social ecology.

Social ecology seeks to understand human institutions and behavior as more or less successful practices for coping with the environment. Not surprisingly, the prac-
55 tice of social ecology has evolved under the shadow of the developing climate crisis. The paradox at that crisis's heart—that industrial society, in the course of improving living standards for large swathes of the human population, did serious damage to the environment that sustained those
60 improvements—is one of the key questions that motivates scholars working in the field.

Consider the well-documented perils of ecological homogenization. As the species diversity of an ecosystem falls, the more susceptible the remaining species become
65 to illness or other natural disaster. Monocultures, in which only one species predominates, are more vulnerable still. Modern agriculture, for example, relies on monoculture to produce massive quantities of staple grains, like corn. But this involves the risk that a single parasite or infec-
70 tion could wipe out an entire harvest, and this vulnerability has led to the development of toxic pesticides to protect crops, though at an unknown and potentially steep cost to the health of consumers.

By contrast, a more diverse and interlinked collection
75 of species is more resilient, a benefit for both individual species and the larger ecosystemic whole. On the other hand, the more diverse an ecosystem, the more complex it is to understand. The processes that determine the health or sickness of the whole are thus much harder to identify,
80 track, and predict.

In short, social ecology amounts to a drastic revision of our idea of progress, one that requires us to think of ourselves as an inseparable part of the natural world, rather than its overlord.

Questions 11–13 ask about Passage A.

---

11. The author of Passage A uses the list in lines 7–8 to refer to the way that Progress:

A. can improve physical goods and ethical ideas in society.

B. is not as related to technology as people once thought.

C. has declined over recent centuries.

D. happened most rapidly during the Industrial Revolution.

12. Passage A most strongly suggests that a critical look at history has which of the following effects on the idea of Progress?

F. Progress has improved the lives of all average human beings.
G. Technology most benefits the poorest people in a society.
H. Assumptions made by historians are usually correct.
J. Changes to society have not always been completely positive.

13. The author's use of the phrases "less nutritious and varied" and "three times as many" (lines 28–29) in Passage A most nearly serves to emphasize which of the following points?

A. Hunter-gatherers lived healthier lives than the peasants that came after them.
B. Peasants were the majority of the human species until recently.
C. Peasants were significantly happier than hunter-gatherers.
D. Hunter-gatherers survived because of their more advanced technologies.

Questions 14–17 ask about Passage B.

14. Passage B makes which of the following claims about monocultures in agriculture?

F. Production of single-species crops has caused more natural disasters in recent years.
G. Monocultures are so dominant that they cannot fail.
H. Staple crops have the potential to be wiped out by a single event.
J. Pesticides can harm the crops themselves.

15. As it is used in line 47, *static* most nearly means:

A. constant.
B. adaptable.
C. electric.
D. dynamic.

16. According to Passage B, the paradox of the climate crisis is that:

F. the majority of society disputes the need to adapt to the environment.
G. natural disasters are caused by ecological homogenization.
H. social ecology scholars disagree with most human institutions.
J. improving human living conditions caused harm to the environment.

17. The main purpose of the paragraph in lines 74–80 of Passage B is primarily to:

A. explain the author's opinion about social ecology.
B. introduce positives and negatives of complex and diverse ecosystems.
C. discuss the changes that must be made to improve monocultures.
D. provide examples of simple and complex ecosystems.

Questions 18–20 ask about both passages.

18. The authors of both passages would most likely agree that:

F. modern agriculture is in danger of collapsing.
G. human progress has both positive and negative consequences.
H. societies should attempt to resist further changes.
J. experts should focus more on environmental than social change.

19. Compared to the author of Passage B, the author of Passage A provides more information about:

A. the lives of people in different eras.
B. the risks of ecological homogenization.
C. changes in societies over time.
D. scholars who study societal changes.

20. To support their claims about progress in society, both passage authors:

F. include counterexamples to show negative aspects of progress.
G. quote scholars who study the environment.
H. analyze publications that promote modern technologies.
J. define key concepts from sociological research.

GO ON TO THE NEXT PAGE.

Passage III

HUMANITIES: This passage is adapted from *Frost: the Dark Path Taken* by Tristao Lowe (©2012 by Tristao Lowe).

From Hallmark™ cards to calendars, the poetry of Robert Frost appears in the consciousness of most Americans as gentle—perhaps even beautiful—rural wisdom. It is taken as the home-spun knowledge of the farmer or wall-
5 builder, one who wanders through the wilderness of America using a language that is distinctly American to convey some larger truth about the world. When most people think of Robert Frost, they think of poems such as "The Road Not Taken," which they take to be a statement on the
10 importance of individuality, of literally forging one's own path. Or they think of the poem, "Stopping by a Woods on a Snowy Evening," which they often interpret as moralizing about the importance of hard work despite difficulties, of the desire for rest but the indomitable will (or even the
15 American work ethic) that drives one on to fulfill responsibilities: the "miles to go before I sleep" that repeats in the last stanza.

But the deeper truth of Frost's poems has little to do with any rousing call to action: it's something much darker,
20 much starker. His is a world of isolation, irreparable damage, and death. Why then, are his works so often printed on backgrounds full of sunshine and butterflies or on refrigerator magnets?

One reason is the exclusion of the majority of Frost's
25 poems in which the despair and horror are not, and could not be, covered up with a reference to flowers or rainbows. Consider works such as "Home Burial," which from its title to its topic (the death of a child), to the bitter accusations of the wife against her husband, paints a scene of
30 marriage that has, like the child, passed on. Or of "Out, Out," in which a young man working with a buzzsaw accidentally severs his hand and dies, while the people around him take so little emotional notice that they continue their work. Certainly, there are American literature teachers,
35 both in high schools and universities, who ask their students to read and interpret these works; nevertheless, they remain less famous. It would appear that American students, like most Americans, prefer to dwell on the positive.

But a far more disturbing reason for Frost being held
40 up as a spinner of cheerful rural scenes is the common misinterpretation of even those poems that might appear, at first glance, to espouse what might be termed "American values." Let us consider the poem first mentioned in this piece, "The Road Not Taken," which begins with a state-
45 ment that, while well-written and beautifully rhymed, is so obvious as to make one wonder why it was written at all: "Two roads diverged in a yellow wood / And sorry I could not travel both / And be one traveller, long I stood..." Everyone is well aware that a person cannot be two places at
50 once; what is less obvious is how truly "sorry" the speaker is.

The desire expressed here is not a casual one, but a deep urge to somehow escape from himself, a desire that is impossible to fulfill. The speaker goes on to take the
55 less-used path "because it was grassy and wanted wear," but acknowledges that his using it will render it much like the other ("Though as for that the passing there / Had worn them really about the same."), hinting at the irony that reaches its climax in the conclusion: that it makes no dif-
60 ference which path he takes; that life is a random series of events despite our efforts to attribute meaning to them. In the final stanza, the speaker says, "I shall be telling this with a sigh / Somewhere ages and ages hence: / Two roads diverged in a wood, and I— / I took the one less traveled
65 by, / And that has made all the difference." Most American readers hold onto the last line, but few stop to question the "sigh" in the first.

Why should the speaker be sighing? Some might answer that it's his nostalgia for a remembered youth, but
70 given the dark irony and pessimism present in so much of Frost's work, isn't it far more likely that he feels worn out by life and by the illusions he has carried? That he knows that his choosing of a path in the woods (or, metaphorically, his own path through life), has had no effect what-
75 soever? Even if one were to argue that the speaker believes what he is saying, one might well wonder what kind of "difference" this choice has made; perhaps this nearly random act has, as a flapping of a butterfly's wings in Japan may cause a hurricane in Florida, been the ruin of
80 his life. Either way, the poem deals with the sadness of self-delusion, not the pride of originality.

None of this is to slight Frost in the slightest, given that for many, he is the finest American poet of the twentieth century. The works of this visionary, musical poet
85 should continue to be widely read—but perhaps if we can dispense with the typical American love of positivity, we can begin to stop misreading him and appreciate him not only as a poet of nature, but as a poet willing to explore the darkness of the human soul.

21. The main idea of the passage is that:

  A. Frost's poetry has darker ideas than many readers interpret.
  B. Frost's poetry can only be understood by trained academics.
  C. people should stop reading Frost's poetry.
  D. Frost never wrote poetry about positive images.

22. The author mentions Frost as a "spinner of cheerful rural scenes" (line 40) primarily in order to:

   F. contrast the darker underlying themes in Frost's poems.

   G. establish why the author is a fan of Frost's poetry.

   H. explain why Frost preferred to write about nature.

   J. provide a title of one of Frost's most famous poems.

23. According to the author, Frost's poetry is interpreted by most Americans as being about:

   A. pleasant rural themes.

   B. sunshine and butterflies.

   C. music.

   D. despair and death.

24. According to the passage, the speaker in "The Road Not Taken" is most likely sighing because:

   F. the choice of which path to take is stressful.

   G. he hopes to soon travel to Florida.

   H. he feels most content in nature.

   J. he is feeling worn out by life.

25. The main idea of the last paragraph is that:

   A. Frost is the most important poet in American literature.

   B. Frost is an influential American poet, but his work should be read more critically.

   C. readers should have complete freedom to interpret Frost's poetry as they wish.

   D. Frost avoided exploring deep issues in the majority of his poetry.

26. As it is used in line 26, the phrase *covered up* most nearly means:

   F. enclosed.

   G. masked.

   H. housed.

   J. compensated.

27. One function of the passage author's statement that flapping of butterfly wings in Japan may cause a hurricane in Florida is to:

   A. list the negative emotions that the poem's speaker often feels.

   B. give an example of a random act that has serious consequences.

   C. describe the types of metaphors that Frost used in his poetry.

   D. help support the passage author's assertion that the path Frost walks on is in Europe.

28. The passage author states that a theme in Frost's poetry commonly interpreted by readers is:

   F. forest hikes.

   G. dark irony and pessimism.

   H. hard work in the face of difficulties.

   J. a desire to escape reality.

29. The passage author most strongly implies that works like "Home Burial" and "Out, Out" are less popular because:

   A. topics like rainbows and flowers appear more commonly in these poems.

   B. readers prefer works with lighter, more positive themes.

   C. they have been banned from print in the past.

   D. American teachers refuse to assign these works to classes.

30. As it is used in line 87, *misreading* most nearly refers to reading Frost's poems:

   F. from an overly positive perspective.

   G. in an American Literature class.

   H. with a dark mindset.

   J. for themes of hard-working Americans.

Passage IV

NATURAL SCIENCE: This passage is adapted from *Geoengineering* by Muriel Reid (©2017 by Muriel Reid).

For nearly three decades, the scientists of the UN Intergovernmental Panel on Climate Change (IPCC) have been forecasting the effects of increasing global temperatures. Their models assess the consequences of myriad weather
5 systems that make up the infinitely complex web of global climate.

The IPCC attempts to model what life will be like on a planet that, over the course of the next century, will likely warm between two and four degrees centigrade. It is
10 not a comforting vision. Polar ice will continue to shrink, devastating local ecosystems and raising global sea levels, which in turn will expose tens of millions of people to devastating floods and likely prompt the evacuation of some major population centers. Hurricanes and cyclones will
15 become more frequent and powerful, while disruptions to stable weather patterns like the Atlantic gulf stream could render parts of Europe uninhabitable. Polar warming will also contribute to the melting of permafrost, potentially releasing millions of tons of trapped methane that could
20 rapidly accelerate global warming.

Mountains of evidence suggest that these scenarios are by no means science fiction. They may become reality for our grandchildren. Even if the industrial carbon dioxide emissions that are driving climate change were imme-
25 diately halved—which would a mean drastic drop in living standards for people in industrialized countries—the temperature would still rise two degrees by 2100. Current plans for reducing global carbon dioxide emissions envision a 25% reduction by 2050.

30 Increasingly, scientists are considering the possibility of geoengineering—large scale human interventions in the climate system aimed at reining in or negating the effects of global warming. If the climate change process is too far advanced to be halted by emission reductions, say scien-
35 tists, then we may have no choice but to hack the planet and tinker with its underlying systems of climate regulation.

One such proposal is marine cloud brightening. This is a form of solar radiation management which aims to mit-
40 igate the effects of global warming by slightly reducing the the amount of sunlight absorbed into the atmosphere. The solution may lie in deflecting some sunlight away from the planet, and clouds already do this. Depending on their position and form, clouds can reflect large amounts of sun-
45 light and bounce solar radiation back into space. Cloud formations over oceans and other large bodies of water deflect the most radiation. Like all aerosols, clouds are simply condensed particulate matter suspended in the air. Water vapor latches onto extremely small particles called
50 cloud condensation nuclei (CCN), which catalyze the pro-

cess of condensation and act as the seeds for cloud masses. Dense collections of CCN yield dense cloud formations, and dense cloud formations have a high albedo—a measurement of a surface's ability to reflect solar radiation. In
55 theory, spraying atmospheric regions prone to dense cloud formation with very small CCN could yield high albedo cloud banks that deflect incoming solar radiation and cool off global temperatures.

Another proposal also relies on mimicking and en-
60 hancing natural processes to slow climate change. Stratospheric aerosol injection is based on observations of climate patterns following large-scale volcanic events, which can temporarily lower temperatures by spewing enough particulate matter into the atmosphere to reduce the
65 amount of solar radiation reaching Earth's surface. In this plan, sulfur dioxide and hydrogen sulfide would be dispersed into the stratosphere—the layer of the Earth's atmosphere that most effectively filters radiation from space— where they would act in a manner similar to CCN, drawing
70 in other particles and condensing them into visible form.

Of course, these plans have drawbacks. For one thing, they remain theoretical. Until scientists can test these processes on a sufficient scale, there is no way of knowing if they will work as intended. In addition, using aerosols
75 to deflect solar radiation is not a one-time process. CCN are as subject to gravity as anything else and so continually drift downward toward the planet's surface. Marine cloud brightening and stratospheric injection would have to be conducted constantly in order to keep up the artificial
80 shield deflecting sunlight from the planet. And all of this would be done while the atmosphere remained saturated with billions of tons of carbon dioxide. If the process were to be suspended, or fail for some reason, solar radiation would come flooding back and immediately reactivate the
85 warming process, creating a termination shock that would deliver potentially decades worth of warming in a matter of years.

Even so, it remains unwise to bet against human ingenuity in a situation with stakes as high as these. Scientists
90 remain committed to geoengineering plans to preserve the climate conditions that made our civilization possible.

31. The passage as a whole can best be described as:

    A. a report on the positive impacts of human technologies.
    B. a proposal to stop climate change with marine cloud brightening.
    C. an argument against potential negative side effects of geoengineering.
    D. a discussion of possible methods to combat the results of climate change.

32. Based on the passage, which of the following do both marine cloud brightening and stratospheric aerosol injection seek to reduce?

    F. Hydrogen sulfide and sulfur dioxide
    G. Solar radiation on Earth's surface
    H. Cloud formations in the stratosphere
    J. Cloud condensation nuclei

33. The main purpose of the eighth paragraph (lines 71–87) is to:

    A. present a plan to combat climate change.
    B. explain that climate interventions are not as necessary as the public believes.
    C. acknowledge the disadvantages of geoengineering methods.
    D. provide evidence of how geoengineering has failed in the past.

34. In the passage, all of the following are mentioned as possible climate interventions EXCEPT:

    F. marine cloud brightening.
    G. limiting carbon dioxide emissions.
    H. halting industrialization.
    J. stratospheric aerosol injections.

35. Based on the passage, the UN IPCC has forecasted results of climate change for:

    A. fifteen years.
    B. thirty years.
    C. one hundred years.
    D. three centuries.

36. The author refers to the "artificial shield" in line 79–80 primarily in order to:

    F. prove that marine cloud brightening is necessary for human survival.
    G. compare the layers of Earth's atmosphere to each other.
    H. emphasize the potential negative results if the shield is not maintained.
    J. describe the results of small-scale geoengineering experiments.

37. In the passage, climate change interventions are most nearly compared to:

    A. learning the inner workings of a planet.
    B. hacking and tinkering with a technology.
    C. deflecting sunlight like an umbrella.
    D. turning around a large ship.

38. As it is used in line 21, the phrase *these scenarios* most nearly refers to:

    F. carbon dioxide emissions.
    G. extreme weather events.
    H. geoengineering proposals.
    J. science fiction movies.

39. According to the passage, one possible result of polar warming is:

    A. the release of trapped methane.
    B. refreezing of permafrost.
    C. more frequent hurricanes.
    D. drought conditions.

40. As it is used in lines 52–53, the word *dense* most nearly means:

    F. unintelligent.
    G. overcast.
    H. scattered.
    J. tightly packed.

SCIENCE TEST
35 Minutes—40 Questions

DIRECTIONS: There are six passages in this test. Each passage is followed by several questions. After reading a passage, choose the best answer to each question and fill in the corresponding oval on your answer document. You may refer to the passages as often as necessary. You are NOT permitted to use a calculator on this test.

Passage I

Chemical substances are made of single elements connected together with various chemical bonds. For some substances, when heat is applied those bonds are broken down, resulting in elements escaping from the substance. The energy of the bonds is released as visible light. Each element has a specific bond energy, resulting in specific colors matching to single elements when exposed to an open flame or other heat source. For reference, the frequencies of visible light are shown in Table 1.

Table 1	
Color	Frequency (Hz)
Red	400-480
Orange	480-510
Yellow	510-530
Green	530-600
Blue	600-670
Violet	670-790

Experiment

A classroom of students performed an experiment to identify the elements in substances by analyzing the frequencies of visible light exhibited when the substances were broken down over an open flame. Each student had an apparatus as seen in Figure 1.

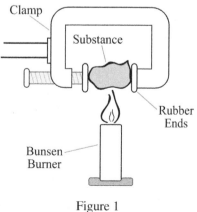

Figure 1

The students took turns placing one of four unknown substances — A, B, C, and D — into the apparatus using the following procedure:

1. An unknown substance was placed into the clamp, and then the clamp was tightened

2. The Bunsen burner was ignited

3. Luminous intensity, measured in candela (the luminous intensity of approximately one common wave candle), was recorded at various frequencies

The results were averaged across all trials and are displayed in Figure 2.

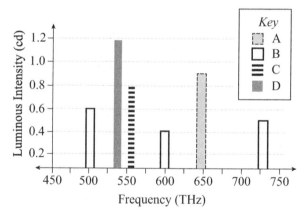

Figure 2

1. According to Figure 2 and and Table 1, what color did Substance C exhibit when broken down by the flame?
   A. Green
   B. Yellow
   C. Red
   D. Blue

---

2. When undergoing a flame test, copper burns blue, boron burns green, lithium burns red, and sodium burns yellow. According to Figure 2 and Table 1, which of the following elements is most similar to Substance A?

F. Copper
G. Boron
H. Lithium
J. Sodium

3. If the heat of the Bunsen burner is significantly increased, will the color of the flames change as a result?

A. Yes, because the color of the flame is dependent on the heat of the reaction
B. Yes, because the color of the flame is dependent on the element exposed to the heat source
C. No, because the color of the flame is dependent on the heat of the reaction
D. No, because the color of the flame is dependent on the element exposed to the heat source

4. The intensity of light measured from a substance is directly related to how bright the resulting color appears. Which of the four unknown substances burned the brightest?

F. Substance A
G. Substance B
H. Substance C
J. Substance D

5. Which of the following is the most likely reason why the students used a clamp in Step 1 of the experimental procedure? The students used the clamp to:

A. insulate the unknown substance from the flame.
B. heat the unknown substance.
C. stabilize the substance over the flame.
D. compress the substance until it began to break down.

6. Which of the following instruments was most likely used to measure the results of the experiment?

F. Ruler
G. Balance
H. Voltmeter
J. Spectrometer

Passage II

A major metropolitan area commissioned a study of traffic patterns. A group of statisticians constructed models based on observations to describe the buildup and release of vehicles in a certain location, in order to visualize the effects of traffic lights and accidents on vehicle accumulation. The statisticians created two models: one for the accumulation of traffic versus time, or $A(t)$, and one for the release of traffic versus time, or $D(t)$. Figure 1 shows an example of $A(t)$ alone, showing how a bottleneck (for example a car accident or construction obstruction) can affect the amount of cars at a certain segment of road. Figure 2 shows an example of $D(t)$, via the stop-and-release action of a traffic light.

Figures 3 and 4 combine the baseline of $D(t)$ with the traffic of $A(t)$ for two case studies. Figure 3 displays the results of light traffic with no incidents. Figure 4 gives an example of heavier traffic with a minor bottleneck.

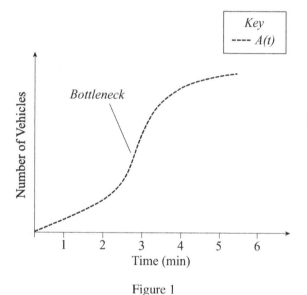

Figure 1

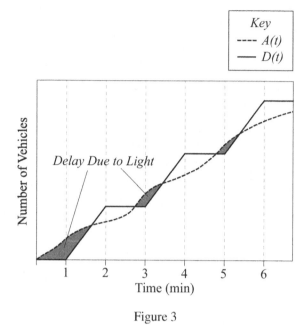

Figure 3

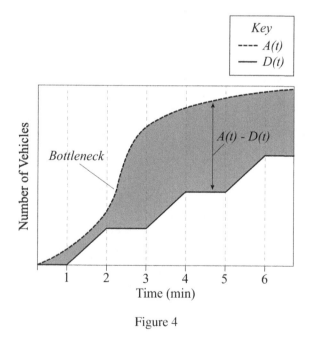

Figure 4

Figure 2

GO ON TO THE NEXT PAGE.

7. Based on Figure 1, during which of the following time intervals did the number of vehicles increase most rapidly?

    A. 0 min to 2 min
    B. 2 min to 4 min
    C. 4 min to 5 min
    D. 5 min to 6 min

8. Which of the following ideal graphs would describe the road in Figure 2 with longer red lights?

    F.
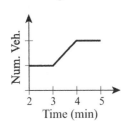

    H.
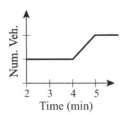

    G.
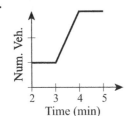

    J.
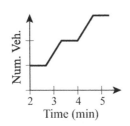

9. Based on Figure 1, for the number of vehicles per minute, a bottleneck results in a:

    A. shallow beginning slope.
    B. shallow middle slope.
    C. steep beginning slope.
    D. steep middle slope.

10. In Figure 4, from 2 min to 3 min, which of the following best explains the growing gap between $A(t)$ and $D(t)$?

    F. Green light, traffic is building slowly
    G. Green light, traffic is building quickly
    H. Red light, traffic is building slowly
    J. Red light, traffic is building quickly

11. Consider the fact that if the $A(t)$ function falls below $D(t)$, then there will be no cars present at a given intersection. Based on Figure 3 and this fact, for which of the following times will the intersection have no cars?

    A. 0.5 min
    B. 1 min
    C. 2 min
    D. 3 min

12. The *total delay* of traffic can be represented by the difference of accumulation of traffic and release of traffic, or $A(t) - D(t)$. Based on Figure 4, for which of the following times is the total delay the greatest?

    F. 1 min
    G. 2 min
    H. 3 min
    J. 4 min

13. Traffic statisticians, when analyzing Figure 4, label the time period from 1.5 min to 2 min as *Segment A*, and the time period from 2.5 min to 3 min as *Segment B*. Which of the following best describes the behavior of Segment A and Segment B?

    A. Segment A and Segment B both have a constant Total Delay
    B. Segment A has an increasing Total Delay, Segment B has a constant Total Delay
    C. Segment A has a constant Total Delay, Segment B has an increasing Total Delay
    D. Segment A has zero Total Delay, Segment B has an increasing Total Delay

Passage III

Birds of different species and genus lay eggs of various shapes, as partially illustrated in Figure 1. Generally the shapes of eggs vary from spherical through two measurements: asymmetry and elliptical distortion (see Figure 1). Four scientists debate the cause of the variation of bird eggs.

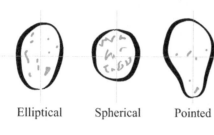

Elliptical   Spherical   Pointed

Figure 1

Scientist 1

The variation in bird eggs is due to the gender of the new bird growing inside the egg. Male birds hatch from pointier eggs, while female birds hatch from more spherical eggs. The egg shape is due to the differing developmental hormones in the growing bird's environment. Just as different chromosome and hormones lead to differing body shapes and development, the chemicals and programming create different egg shapes as well.

Scientist 2

Bird egg shape is based upon how well a bird flies. The shape of the egg is affected largely by the birth canal through the pelvis of female birds, a skeletal structure that is only modified for purposes of improved flight (and thus improved survival, depending on the bird). An aerodynamic bird with great flight ability has narrower pelvis, leading to a more irregular egg shape (high degree of asymmetry and elliptical distortion). Non-flying birds have no need to develop narrow pelvic bones, and their reliance on running stability favors a slightly wider base; these modifications to skeletal structure allow for a fully spherical egg to develop.

Scientist 3

Scientist 2 has noted a strong correlation between high-flying birds versus land birds and egg shape, but this correlation is not due to pelvic structure: it is due to nest height. Bird egg shape is designed for optimum survival of the egg itself. Birds that nest high in trees and on mountains have a much higher probability of egg death due to falling, and as such eggs of asymmetric and elliptical shape have featured a better survival rate thanks to their reduced rolling profile. Spherical eggs are more likely to roll out of the nest and fall. Land-based nesting birds do not have this issue, and thus spherical eggs remain the norm.

Scientist 4

Egg shape is correlated to bird diet. Depending on the iron content, protein content, and vitamin profile of a certain bird's diet, eggs will form with different structural qualities and thus different shapes. Scientists 2 and 3 have noticed a correlation between birds of various heights of living, but this is due to commonalities in diet for land birds with other land birds, tree birds with other tree birds, mountain birds with other mountain birds, and so on.

14. An independent study finds all ostrich eggs look alike. Which scientist's viewpoint is weakened by this study's results?

F. Scientist 1
G. Scientist 2
H. Scientist 3
J. Scientist 4

15. Suppose the prey normally consumed by a bird becomes extinct, forcing the bird to find a different prey. Which of the following scientists would support the idea that, because the prey of the bird changed, the shape of the bird's eggs would also change?

A. Scientist 1
B. Scientist 2
C. Scientist 3
D. Scientist 4

16. If Scientist 3 is correct, which of the eggs from Figure 1 would belong to a land-based nesting bird?

    F. Eliptical
    G. Spherical
    H. Pointed
    J. None of the above

17. An independent third party wants to design an experiment that would help examine the theory of Scientist 4. Which setup would serve this purpose the best?

    A. Comparing low-nesting migrating birds' eggs with high-nesting migrating birds' eggs
    B. Comparing low-nesting carnivorous birds' eggs with low-nesting vegetarian birds' eggs
    C. Comparing low-nesting migrating birds' male eggs with low-nesting migrating birds' female eggs
    D. Comparing high-nesting migrating birds' eggs with low-nesting non-flight birds eggs

18. Suppose a wild bird is captured for a zoo. In captivity, it faces a new diet and is forced to nest at a much lower height than in the wild. According to Scientist 3's viewpoint, how should the eggs of the captive bird compare to examples from a wild bird nest? The eggs would be:

    F. Less spherical
    G. More asymmetric
    H. Less elliptical
    J. There would be no variation

Questions 19 and 20 refer to the following table.

Clade	Example	Diet	Flight	Nest
Paleognathae	Emu	Omnivore	None	Land
Galloanserae	Duck	Herbivore	Low	Land
Telluraves	Hawk	Carnivore	High	High
Strisores	Hummingbird	Herbivore	Medium	Low
Gruiformes	Crane	Omnivore	High	Land

19. If the eggs of Telluraves are all found to be different from Gruiformes, which scientist(s) could be supported?

    A. Scientist 1 only
    B. Scientist 4 only
    C. Scientists 1 and 2
    D. Scientists 3 and 4

20. According to the passage, the theory of Scientist 2 would require which clades of birds to have similar egg shapes?

    F. Paleognathae and Telluraves
    G. Telluraves and Gruiformes
    H. Strisores and Gruiformes
    J. Galloanserae and Gruiformes

Passage IV

A medical lab performing research on diseases and cures conducted pre-experiments to define proper working conditions for bacteria growth in Petri dish cultures. One such experiment examined the effects of changing pH on bacteria population.

Experiment

30 Petri dish cultures were split into three groups of ten cultures each. For bacteria group A, pH was held at a constant neutral value. For bacteria group B, the pH started at a neutral value and then gradually increased by addition of ammonia every 20 minutes. In bacteria group C, the pH started at a value of 5 and increased exponentially by adding increasing amounts of ammonia every 20 minutes. The pH change over time of the three different groups are shown in Figure 1.

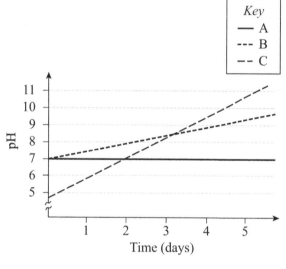

Figure 1

The number of viable bacteria cells in each group was measured in colony-forming units, CFU, by automated computerized systems. The results over time of the bacteria cell count of the three different groups are shown in Figure 2.

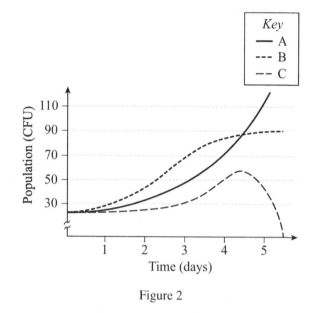

Figure 2

21. According to Figure 2, at which point in time is the population of bacteria group A at least twice as much as the population of bacteria group C?

A. 2 days
B. 3 days
C. 4 days
D. 5 days

22. Based on Figures 1 and 2, at what pH does the population of bacteria group C start to decline?

   F. 7
   G. 8
   H. 9
   J. 10

23. According to Figures 1 and 2, the growth of bacteria group B illustrates that a pH between 8 and 10 leads to:

   A. an exponentially increasing bacteria population.
   B. slowed increasing bacteria population growth.
   C. a static bacteria population.
   D. bacterial elimination.

24. A scientist proposes that bacteria populations flourish in acidic pH environments. Do the data in Figures 1 and 2 support this statement?

   F. Yes, because bacteria group C grows at a faster rate than bacteria group A during the first day of the experiment.
   G. Yes, because bacteria group A grows at a faster rate than bacteria group C during the first day of the experiment.
   H. No, because bacteria group C grows at a faster rate than bacteria group A during the first day of the experiment.
   J. No, because bacteria group A grows at a faster rate than bacteria group C during the first day of the experiment.

25. Based on the results of the experiment, when the pH of bacteria group C was neutral, the population of bacteria group C was:

   A. less than 30 CFU.
   B. between 30 CFU and 40 CFU.
   C. between 40 CFU and 50 CFU.
   D. greater than 50 CFU.

26. To avoid having pH as a variable in future bacteria studies, which of the following conclusions should the scientists consider?

   F. Holding pH carefully at 7 for all dishes will result in optimal growth conditions
   G. Increasing pH as time passes helps maintain bacteria growth at a constant rate
   H. Maintaining pH at an acidic value of 4 will cause wild variation in bacteria reproduction
   J. Highly basic (pH > 10) Petri dish cultures will cause immediate bacteria population decline

GO ON TO THE NEXT PAGE.

Passage V

Carbon, silicon, and germanium are elements that each have an outer layer of four electrons. This atomic structure causes them to form precise crystal structures. The crystalline structures are well-balanced on their own, but, in the case of silicon, scientists can create paths for electrons to move through a process called *doping* (introducing impurities into the original structure). Elements added for the doping effect are highly effective in small quantities: 0.001% of the original mass added creates a 10,000 fold increase in conductivity.

N-type doping involves adding phosphorus to the silicon crystal lattice in small amounts. The 5-electron outer layer of the phosphorous leaves one electron free and ready to move around, giving the N-type structure an overall negative charge. *P-type doping* involves adding boron, which has 3 outer layer electrons, to the crystal lattice silicon. When P-type doped, the silicon now has a missing electron, which is called a *hole*. These differences are illustrated in Figure 1.

A standard silicon crystal lattice is an insulator. P-type or N-type doped silicon lattices are moderately effective conductors, known as semi-conductors. However, combining P-type with N-type silicon creates a *one-way conductor* (electrons flow from N-type to P-type and not backwards). This one-way flow setup is called a diode and is essential to modern electronics. Figure 2 illustrates how a silicon diode restricts voltage, V, attempting to reverse current flow, I, through the circuit, but permits forward flow through the diode once it has reached a certain threshold.

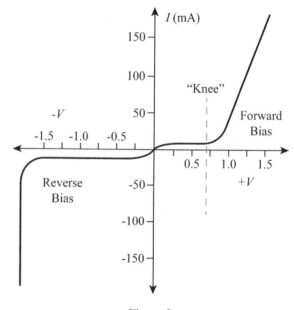

Figure 2

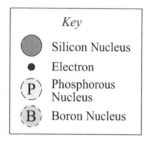

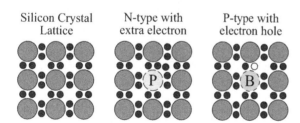

Figure 1

27. Based on Figure 2, when the voltage, V, applied to a silicon diode is -1 V, the current flow, I, is closest to which of the following?

 A. -50 mA
 B. -20 mA
 C. 20 mA
 D. 50 mA

28. Based on the description of Figure 1, which of the following could be the charge of a N-type structure?

 F. -1
 G. 0
 H. $+1$
 J. $+2$

29. Based on Figure 2, at approximately what minimum threshold voltage does forward current flow begin to significantly increase in the silicon diode?

 A. 0.0 V
 B. 0.5 V
 C. 0.7 V
 D. 1.0 V

30. Based on the passage, do pure silicon or doped silicon lattices have better electron movement within their structures?

 F. Pure silicon, because doping helps to create paths for electrons to move
 G. Doped silicon, because doping helps to create paths for electrons to move
 H. Pure silicon, because a neutral lattice structure is best for electron flow
 J. Doped silicon, because a neutral lattice structure is best for electron flow

31. Consider the quantity of outer electrons for the following elements:

Element	Outer electrons
Aluminum	3
Carbon	4
Nitrogen	5
Oxygen	6

Based on the description of Figure 1, which of the above elements would fare the best as a substitute for phosphorous in a N-type lattice?

 A. Aluminum
 B. Carbon
 C. Nitrogen
 D. Oxygen

32. Based on the description of a one-way conductor and Figure 1, which of the following best describes why electrons flow forwards in a silicon diode?

 F. The additional electrons of boron in the N-type flow to fill the electron holes in the P-type
 G. The additional electrons of boron in the P-type flow to fill the electron holes in the N-type
 H. The additional electrons of phosphorous in the N-type flow to fill the electron holes in the P-type
 J. The additional electrons of phosphorous in the P-type flow to fill the electron holes in the N-type

33. According to the information provided, if a certain silicon crystal structure contains 2.8×10^{23} atoms, how many phosphorous atoms would have to be added to increase conductivity by 10,000?

 A. 2.8×10^{18} atoms
 B. 2.8×10^{20} atoms
 C. 2.8×10^{21} atoms
 D. 2.8×10^{28} atoms

GO ON TO THE NEXT PAGE.

Passage VI

A group of scientists set out to study the effect of technology related distraction on productivity in the workplace. Two experiments were designed to examine computer-based and cellphone-based distractions.

Experiment 1

Two computers were placed side by side in a single cubicle. 80 participants were asked to complete a set of simple research-and-summarize typing tasks. Each task required the participant to look up information from a web browser and then summarize it in a few sentences typed into a word processor. The total number of tasks was enough to fill up at least two hours of focused work. The participants were interrupted after two hours, ending the session regardless of total progress.

The 80 participants were equally distributed into 10 groups. Each group faced a different set of distractions. A *neighbor* (a nonparticipant experimenter) was placed in certain groups at two different time intervals: early (0-60 min) and late (60-120 min). The neighbor was instructed either to be distracting and engage the participant in discussion, or to be independently focused on work for the entire duration.

Half of the groups experienced an internet blocker on their computers, preventing access to any sites not deemed necessary for the basic research. The results were measured in tasks completed per 15 minutes by participants. The results for each group were averaged and are shown in Table 1.

Experiment 2

The procedure from Experiment 1 was repeated, except 60 participants were distributed equally into 4 groups where a cell phone was present to cause distraction. In addition, all neighbors were early and independently focused on work for the entire duration. The control group, Group 11, lacked a neighbor. The participants were interrupted after 90 minutes.

The 3 experimental groups had the following differences: in Group 12 there was no cellphone, in Group 13 the neighbor left a cellphone face down, and in Group 14 the neighbor left a cellphone face up. The results were measured in tasks completed per 15 minutes by participants. The results for each group were averaged and are shown in Table 2.

Table 2								
Group	Neighbor	Cell Phone	Tasks completed per 15 min					
			15	30	45	60	75	90
11	No	N/A	13	14	11	7	12	11
12	Yes	None	15	16	14	15	10	9
13	Yes	Face Down	14	13	13	9	12	15
14	Yes	Face Up	10	9	8	9	13	14

Table 1											
Group	Internet	Neighbor	Mode	Tasks completed per 15 min							
				15	30	45	60	75	90	105	120
1	Free	No	N/A	12	14	11	7	12	10	6	10
2	Blocked	No	N/A	13	15	14	11	10	7	6	8
3	Free	Early	Focused	14	16	15	15	8	4	5	9
4	Blocked	Early	Focused	15	15	14	15	11	10	7	6
5	Free	Early	Distracted	10	8	7	9	13	12	14	11
6	Blocked	Early	Distracted	10	9	9	9	13	14	16	15
7	Free	Late	Focused	12	13	13	8	10	14	15	16
8	Blocked	Late	Focused	13	15	13	11	12	10	8	10
9	Free	Late	Distracted	12	11	12	9	7	4	11	12
10	Blocked	Late	Distracted	14	14	14	12	8	7	9	7

34. How many participants, if it can be determined, were placed in each group in Experiment 1?

F. 8
G. 10
H. 80
J. Cannot be determined from the given information

35. To consider the effect of blocked internet on tasks completed per 15 minutes for an early neighbor with distraction, one should compare the results for:

A. Groups 1 and 2.
B. Groups 2 and 3.
C. Groups 5 and 6.
D. Groups 6 and 7.

36. Study 1 differs from Study 2 in which of the following ways?

F. Participants were asked to complete tasks every 15 min in Study 1, but every 30 min in Study 2.
G. Participants were split evenly into several groups in Study 1, but unevenly in Study 2.
H. There were fewer participants utilized in Study 1 than in Study 2
J. Tasks completed were recorded for a longer duration in Study 1 than that of Study 2

37. Which of the following would be considered an independent variable in Experiment 1?

A. Group number
B. Presence of a neighbor
C. Presence of a cellphone
D. Number of participants per group

38. In Experiment 1, Group 2 noticed no major change on average between 60 and 75 minutes. Which of the following, if any, most likely explains the changes in productivity of Groups 5 and 6 from 60-75 minutes?

F. When a distracting coworker leaves, productivity increases
G. When a distracting coworker arrives, productivity increases
H. As time passes, productivity increases
J. None of the above statements explain the changes in productivity

39. In Experiment 2, which group was used as the standard of comparison?

A. Group 11
B. Group 12
C. Group 13
D. Group 14

40. In order to draw a proper conclusion on whether the presence of cell phones affected the productivity of coworkers, which two groups should be compared?

F. Groups 11 and 12
G. Groups 11 and 13
H. Groups 12 and 13
J. Groups 13 and 14

STOP! DO NOT RETURN TO ANY OTHER TEST.

Government Data Collection

Modern governments compile large amounts of data on everyday citizens, including everything from personal spending habits to political affiliations to health records. Supporters of this practice claim that amassing such data is necessary in order to provide vital services to citizens. Moreover, they say, policies informed by comprehensive personal data can improve government efficiency and effectiveness. Critics of this practice say that these efforts violate individuals' right to privacy, including the right to anonymity. In an increasingly data-driven society, new balances must be struck between the practices of the government and the privacy of the individual. Are there limits to the government's right to know details of its citizens' lives?

Read and carefully consider these perspectives. Each suggests a particular way of thinking about government data collection.

Perspective 1	Perspective 2	Perspective 3
The government has a responsibility to defend and promote the welfare of its citizens. It should use whatever means necessary, including the collection of personal information, to fulfill this responsibility.	The individual right to privacy is a vital one. The government cannot infringe upon an individual's right to keep her life private as she sees fit.	A democratic society should not insist on absolute rights or absolute responsibilities. It should encourage compromise over competing legitimate claims.

Essay Task

Write a unified, coherent essay in which you evaluate multiple perspectives on data collection. In your essay, be sure to:

- analyze and evaluate the perspectives given
- state and develop your own perspective on the issue
- explain the relationship between your perspective and those given

Your perspective may be in full agreement with any of the others, in partial agreement, or wholly different. Whatever the case, support your ideas with logical reasoning and detailed, persuasive examples.

ACT1 - A0116

Practice Test

ENGLISH TEST
45 Minutes—75 Questions

DIRECTIONS: In the five passages that follow, certain words and phrases are underlined and numbered. In the right-hand column, you will find alternatives for the underlined part. In most cases, you are to choose the one that best expresses the idea, makes the statement appropriate for standard written English, or is worded most consistently with the style and tone of the passage as a whole. If you think the original version is best, choose "NO CHANGE." In some cases, you will find in the right-hand column a question about the underlined part. You are to choose the best answer to the question.

You will also find questions about a section of the passage, or about the passage as a whole. These questions do not refer to an underlined portion of the passage, but rather are identified by a number or numbers in a box.

For each question, choose the alternative you consider best and fill in the corresponding oval on your answer document. Read each passage through once before you begin to answer the questions that accompany it. For many of the questions, you must read several sentences beyond the question to determine the answer. Be sure that you have read far enough ahead each time you choose an alternative.

PASSAGE I

Finding Refuge in Costa Rica

Reflecting back on my time in Costa Rica, a favorite
    1
memory, meeting my dear friend Rosie, often comes to mind.

While Rosie spent most of her days happily sitting in a swing,

hanging from a branch, or would find leaves to chew on,
                                      2

our first encounter was much less merry.
                                    3

[1] My team and I found Rosie, a three-toed sloth, alone

and starving after she had, we assumed, lost her mother. [2] At

the time, working as a volunteer at the Sloth Sanctuary of
          4

1. A. NO CHANGE
    B. As I reflect
    C. Having reflected back
    D. While reflecting,

2. F. NO CHANGE
    G. would chew leaves,
    H. chewing on leaves,
    J. chews a leaf,

3. Which of the following alternatives to the underlined portion would be LEAST acceptable?
    A. adequate
    B. cheery
    C. jovial
    D. exciting

4. F. NO CHANGE
    G. I had worked
    H. I was working
    J. I have been working

Costa Rica. ⌐5⌐ [3] Every morning, a team of volunteers, myself included, would follow up on calls with reports of abandoned or orphaned sloths. [4] Young sloths cling to their mothers for nearly a year after birth, so separation between the two can prove fatal for the young.

[5] Rosie, however, was a fighter: At three weeks old, this
_____
            6
tough cookie had slowly crawled her way to the side of a road where a passerby reported her to our hotline number. [6] Sloths often resist capture, but Rosie seemed to smile as we picked her up and loaded her into our truck. ⌐7⌐

  Once at the sanctuary, we were able to determine that Rosie was extremely malnourished and suffered

from mange—an annoying, irritating skin infection caused by
              _____
                    8
parasitic mites. I was lucky enough to be assigned to monitor Rosie's transition into the sanctuary, which meant that I'd be the one to give her the mange spa treatment: first, a complete haircut to remove the mites' natural habitat, followed by a soothing massage to balm suffocate any remaining mites.
                   ____
                    9
For the finishing touch, I wrapped Rosie in brightly printed bandages that would keep her skin smooth and protect her from any further damage by the pesky mites. When I'd performed this task before, each and every exasperated critter would let
                                   _____
                                       10
out a cry of protest—but Rosie was different.

5. At this point, the writer is considering adding the following true statement:

  Sanctuaries, which are vital to ecological conservation, have become increasingly prevalent in tropical areas of Central America.

Should the writer make this addition?
- A. Yes, because it provides necessary explanation of the word "sanctuaries."
- B. Yes, because without this addition the goals of the sanctuary would be unclear.
- C. No, because it is only indirectly related to other information in the paragraph.
- D. No, because it focuses environmental protections in Central America, not Costa Rica specifically.

6. F. NO CHANGE
 G. Rosie however was a fighter: at
 H. Rosie, however, was a fighter and at
 J. Rosie, however, was a fighter, being

7. For the sake of the logic and coherence of this paragraph, Sentence 5 should be placed:
- A. where it is now.
- B. after sentence 1.
- C. after sentence 3.
- D. after sentence 6.

8. F. NO CHANGE
 G. annoyingly irritating
 H. irksome, grating
 J. irritating

9. The best placement for the underlined portion would be:
- A. where it is now.
- B. before the word "massage."
- C. before the word "soothing."
- D. before the word "mites'."

10. F. NO CHANGE
 G. pleased
 H. ambivalent
 J. contented

Before falling asleep, her kind eyes and silly smile made
<u>her look at me</u> in what looked like a fancy pajama onesie of
11
bandages.

From that moment on, Rosie thrived <u>among</u> her many
12
new sloth friends. She fattened up on a daily regimen of

leaves and eventually <u>shed her pajamas to reveal her sleek
13
brown hair.</u> Unfortunately, scientists have not yet found a way
to release orphaned sloths back into their natural habitats;
most lose their mothers before they're able to learn basic
survival skills. <u>Consequently,</u> they must spend the rest of their
14
days at the sanctuary. Watching Rosie's resiliency was
inspiring. Though she could have given up, she just kept
going...no matter how slowly she actually went.

11. **A.** NO CHANGE
    B. Her silly smile with kind eyes intact, she looked at me throughout the entire process, eventually falling asleep
    C. Her silly smile intact with kind eyes, before falling asleep the process made her look at me
    D. Her silly smile intact, she looked at me with kind eyes throughout the entire process, eventually falling asleep

12. Which of the following alternatives to the underlined portion would be LEAST acceptable?
    F. in the company of
    G. beside
    H. in proximity to
    J. around

13. **A.** NO CHANGE
    B. shed her pajamas, just in the nick of time, to reveal her sleek brown hair.
    C. over an amount of time that we found reasonable, shed her pajamas to reveal her sleek brown hair.
    D. revealed her sleek brown hair to shed her pajamas.

14. **F.** NO CHANGE
    G. Even so,
    H. However,
    J. For example,

Question 15 asks about the preceding passage as a whole.

15. Suppose the writer had chosen to write a brief essay explaining the history and development of sloth sanctuaries in Costa Rica. Would this essay successfully fulfill the writer's goal?
    A. Yes, because the essay describes in detail how these sanctuaries are supporting and preserving local sloth populations.
    B. Yes, because the writer effectively places her work at the sloth sanctuary into a greater national context.
    C. No, because the essay focuses more on the experiences of one volunteer, not on those of sanctuaries in general.
    D. No, because the essay never fully explains the history and development of the term "Sloth Sanctuary."

PASSAGE II

Ballet: Sport or Art?

Athletic sports and performing arts are, more often than not, considered to be <u>completely separately</u> entities. Sports commentators are likely to comment on the merits of a play <u>rather then the aesthetically pleasing nature of the players'</u> <u>movements;</u> a newspaper article reviewing a symphony discusses the emotional journey of the performance, rather

than the dexterity <u>with which the cello player moved his bow.</u> How, then, should society categorize professional

<u>ballet dancers; as artists</u> or as athletes?

Most people quickly classify ballet as an art form, so which aspect is sport? Ballet dancers, like athletes, are constantly pushing the limits of the human body. Most professional dancers have rigorous training schedules <u>kind of like</u> professional athletes.

16. **F.** NO CHANGE
    G. complete separate
    H. completely separate
    J. complete separately

17. **A.** NO CHANGE
    B. rather than the aesthetically pleasing nature of the players' movements;
    C. rather than how the players move and their aesthetic nature,
    D. rather then how the players move and their aesthetic nature,

18. At this point, the writer is considering deleting the underlined portion from the sentence. Should the writer make this deletion?
    F. Yes, because it adds unnecessary information that distracts from the main purpose of the paragraph.
    G. Yes, because it repeats information explained later in the passage.
    H. No, because it provides a clarification to a comparison referenced earlier in the sentence.
    J. No, because it more fully explains what the cello player is intending to accomplish.

19. **A.** NO CHANGE
    B. ballet dancers: as artists
    C. ballet dancers, are they artists
    D. ballet dancers as artists

20. **F.** NO CHANGE
    G. a little bit close to
    H. rivaling those of
    J. that, in this writer's opinion, are almost identical to

This training often starts at a very young age. [21] Having taken classes since the age of four or five, a dancer might eventually train from 10am to 6pm for five or six days a week, attending rehearsals and performances on top of an already exhausting schedule. Ballet requires

many important physical abilities. Most professional dancers
                    22
regularly see chiropractors, physical therapists, and doctors to ensure their physical well-being, as do athletes. Professional

athletes fear having to sit out for injury; a physical injury is
                                          23
just as devastating to a dancer's career.

[1] Perhaps even more interesting, is that many ballet

dancers compete in ballet competitions. [2] At the same time,
                                                        24
dancers from around the globe annually flock to various countries to compete for titles and job opportunities. [3] Representatives, each from an elite ballet institution, scouts
                                                                    25
new talent while judges score dancers' technical and artistic performances. [4] Dancers must stay in step with the music, evoke emotional responses, and show their truest artistic selves while simultaneously showing off their physical
                    26
mastery of the craft. [5] Legs must be perfectly straightened, toes perfectly pointed, and heads perfectly turned. [6] When

judges are able to assign a numerical value to each dancers'
                                                        27
physical fitness and competence, the line between art and

21. At this point, the writer is considering adding the following true statement:

> The concept of training muscles is a crucial component of a myriad of physical endeavors, from athletics to arts performances.

Should the writer make this addition?

A. Yes, because it provides important historical context to the word "training."
B. Yes, because it explains exactly what the dancers are hoping to accomplish.
C. No, because it is not effectively linked to the goals of the athletes referenced earlier in the passage.
D. No, because it adds unnecessary information that distracts from the main idea of the paragraph.

22. Given that all the following are true, which one most specifically describes the skills that ballet dancers are expected to acquire?

F. NO CHANGE
G. a myriad of skills that may take a lifetime to perfect.
H. skills that, in my view, are truly admirable.
J. speed, agility, and extreme power.

23. Which of the following alternatives to the underlined portion would be LEAST acceptable?

A. injury, a
B. injury. A
C. injury, and a
D. injury; however, a

24. F. NO CHANGE
G. Occasionally,
H. Every year,
J. DELETE the underlined portion, fixing any necessary capitalization.

25. A. NO CHANGE
B. scout
C. is scouting
D. has scouted

26. Which of the following alternatives to the underlined portion would be LEAST acceptable?

F. hyperbolically
G. at the same time
H. concurrently
J. also

27. A. NO CHANGE
B. each dancers
C. dancer's
D. dancers'

sport seems <u>still even more blurred then ever.</u> [29]
28

Of course, there is no clean-cut way to decide whether or

not ballet should be categorized as solely sport or art. The

medium lends itself to a mixture of the two, <u>although I highly</u>
30
<u>doubt we'll see sports commentators covering a production</u>
30
<u>of Swan Lake anytime soon.</u>
30

28. **F.** NO CHANGE
  G. increasingly blurred than ever.
  H. blurrier than ever.
  J. blurrier then ever.

29. For the sake of the logic and coherence of Paragraph 3, Sentence 1 should be placed:
  A. where it is now.
  B. after sentence 2.
  C. after sentence 3.
  D. after sentence 5.

30. Given that all the choices are true, which one best concludes the passage?
  F. NO CHANGE
  G. since ballet, although underappreciated for a time, is finally gaining national prominence.
  H. and the last performance I saw of Swan Lake during my senior year was one of the best experiences of my life!
  J. although sports, like baseball, remain a beloved American pastime.

PASSAGE III

Creating Warmth and Jobs for the Homeless

[1]

While attending the College for Creative Studies in

Detroit, Veronika Scott was given an assignment that would

one day change <u>lives, and that was: create</u> something that fills
31

a social need. Looking around the city, <u>abundant were</u> the
32
pervasive poverty and homelessness that plagued her

community. After careful consideration, she decided to create

<u>portable warmth that was easy to carry</u> for homeless
33
individuals.

31. **A.** NO CHANGE
  B. lives: and that was create
  C. lives: create
  D. lives, specifically being: create

32. **F.** NO CHANGE
  G. unfortunate was
  H. Scott was saddened by
  J. it was obvious to everyone that

33. **A.** NO CHANGE
  B. portable warmth
  C. portable warming, easy to carry,
  D. portable warming that was easy to carry

[2]

She quickly went to work, designing a sleek pattern that would allow for cheap, easy manufacturing. The final product

34

was a coat — being complete with a sleeping bag attachment

35

that neatly folded into the back of the garment. To ensure portability, she designed the coat to fold into a backpack for warmer days. After receiving a top-notch grade for her work,

36

Scott pushed her idea one step further, by raising funds to start

a small shop where she could manufactured the coats

37

herself and distribute it to homeless people around the city.

37

Eventually, she began sewing donor's names into the coats to

38

remind homeless citizens that someone was on their side.

[3]

Scott's company—the Empowerment Plan—didn't stop

39

there. One day, a woman in a homeless shelter

confronted Scott and she explained that coats could only go

40

so far; the homeless needed jobs to survive over the long run. Scott immediately realized what she needed to do, and perhaps what she should have been doing all along.

41

---

34. **F.** NO CHANGE
G. would allow for cheaply, easy
H. might allow for cheap easy
J. might allow for cheaply easy

35. **A.** NO CHANGE
B. coat; complete with
C. coat, it was complete when including
D. coat, complete with

36. Which of the following true statements, if added here, would best maintain the focus of the sentence?

F. NO CHANGE
G. A natural entrepeneur,
H. Sitting in her apartment office,
J. However, once her patent was approved,

37. **A.** NO CHANGE
B. manufactured the coats herself and distribute them
C. manufacture the coats herself and distribute it
D. manufacture the coats herself and distribute them

38. **F.** NO CHANGE
G. donors names
H. donors' names
J. donors names'

39. Which of the following alternatives to the underlines portion would be the LEAST acceptable?

A. company, the Empowerment Plan, didn't
B. company (the Empowerment Plan) didn't
C. company, the Empowerment Plan — didn't
D. company, known as the Empowerment Plan, didn't

40. **F.** NO CHANGE
G. Scott, explaining
H. Scott, and explaining
J. Scott, she explained

41. If the writer were to delete the underlined portion, the sentence would primarily lose:

A. an explanation of why Scott created her company.
B. details supporting her move to hiring homeless individuals.
C. a clear timeline of exactly when Scott began hiring homeless individuals.
D. a sense that Scott wished she had performed an action at an earlier point.

[4]

These days, Scott also hires individuals who are often turned away from traditional vocations: those with incarcerations, have low-level educations or no proper skills to compete in an increasingly competitive job market.

[5]

Now, students everywhere are realizing that their class projects could someday lead to tangible changes in our world.

42. F. NO CHANGE
G. those with incarcerations, have low-level educations, and improper skills
H. those who have previously been incarcerated, lack a high school education, or proper skills
J. those who have previously been incarcerated, have low-level educations, or lack the proper skills

43. Which of the following is the most effective conclusion of the passage as a whole?

A. NO CHANGE
B. Scott has since had more than a handful of ideas—I can't wait to see what comes next!
C. With a seemingly novel idea, Scott now actively plays a role in creating a cohesive and caring community.
D. Homelessness is a tragic reality in today's society, and there are many ways to combat this ongoing issue.

Questions 44 and 45 ask about the preceding passage as a whole.

---

44. Upon reviewing the passage and realizing that some information has been left out, the author composes the following sentence:

> Since that moment, the Empowerment Plan has hired homeless members of the community to manufacture these coats, providing many families with much-needed, long-term solutions.

The most logical placement for this sentence would be:

F. At the end of Paragraph 2
G. At the beginning of Paragraph 3
H. At the beginning of Paragraph 4
J. At the end of Paragraph 4

45. Suppose the writer had chosen to write an essay that spotlights various humanitarian efforts in today's society. Would this essay fulfill the writer's goal?

A. Yes, because Scott's fight to end homelessness is clearly indicative of many other humanitarian efforts.
B. Yes, because the author demonstrates Scott's willingness to collaborate with others.
C. No, because Scott's endeavors do not qualify as humanitarian efforts.
D. No, because the passage discusses only one example of humanitarian efforts.

PASSAGE IV

Yummy Science

<u>Walking into the Alinea restaurant of Chicago, Illinois</u>
₄₆ without having done your research might be a jarring

experience. While the menu boasts typical upscale fare,

the presentation and contents <u>of these dishes</u> are anything but
₄₇
average. The restaurant's chef transforms scallops with a sea

of aromatic mist, presents sweetbreads over a miniature

campfire, and <u>dessert is drawn on the table by the chef</u>
₄₈
<u>himself.</u>
₄₈

Molecular <u>gastronomy, a growing trend</u> in restaurants
₄₉
across the nation, merges the seemingly separate worlds

of cuisine and science. Chefs, like those at Alinea,

have abandoned their skillets and spatulas for liquid

nitrogen and centrifuges to create unprecedented,

futuristic dining experiences <u>that are exciting!</u>
₅₀

<u>The term "molecular gastronomy" was first coined in 1988.</u>
₅₁
Prior to this movement, nobody had investigated how science

could be applied to cooking in the home or in restaurants,

rather than for industrial purposes.

46. F. NO CHANGE
   G. If you stroll into the Alinea restaurant of Chicago, Illinois
   H. At first glance, when you walk into the Alinea restaurant of Chicago, Illinois
   J. If you decide to head into the Alinea restaurant of Chicago, Illinois

47. A. NO CHANGE
   B. of them
   C. of it all
   D. of everything included

48. F. NO CHANGE
   G. dessert is presented on the table after having been drawn by the chef.
   H. draws dessert on the table himself.
   J. he drew a masterful dessert on the table.

49. A. NO CHANGE
   B. gastronomy: a growing trend
   C. gastronomy a growing trend
   D. gastronomy—a growing trend

50. F. NO CHANGE
   G. which we often enjoy.
   H. unlike anything you've ever seen.
   J. DELETE the underlined portion and end the sentence with a period after the word "experiences."

51. If the writer were to delete the underlined portion, the passage would primarily lose:
   A. an important detail that helps explain the popularity of the term "molecular gastronomy."
   B. information that shows the historical unrest during the development of molecular gastronomy.
   C. a fact that helps place the phrase "molecular gastronomy" into a historical context.
   D. a counterexample to the preceding sentence.

Chefs and scientists meeting began sometime between 1992 and 2004 in conferences that made the discipline popular to discuss a plethora of topics including applying heat, and obtaining flavor, textures, and interactions between solid and liquid food.

Now, the field of molecular gastronomy has quite a few normalized cooking techniques that explore those topics. Spherification for example, uses the calcium content of everyday liquids to form small jelly-like balls that resemble fish eggs. Balls of ice, injected with beverages, are shattered, they release the cool liquids. Dishes traditionally accompanied by a lemon are now often served with

"lemon air," a seemingly weightless and tasty lemon-flavored foam. Perhaps most intriguing, are those practices that aren't directly eaten; "aromatic accompaniment" describes the process of trapping gasses in bags that are then presented to patrons as a garnish, proving that smell indeed effects taste.

[1] They argue that emphasizing the science behind cooking takes away from the artistic liberties of chefs, who before now had relied on being spontaneous and personal, rather than strictly regulated scientific processes.

52. F. NO CHANGE
    G. Conferences held between 1992 and 2004 further popularized the discipline and brought together chefs and scientists alike
    H. Chef and scientists alike, sometime between 1992 and 2004, met in conferences that helped make the discipline popular
    J. Between 1992 and 2004, conferences were held and chefs and scientists met and this helped popularize the discipline

53. A. NO CHANGE
    B. Spherification for example
    C. Spherification, for example
    D. Spherification, for example,

54. F. NO CHANGE
    G. shattered they release
    H. shattered to release
    J. shattered, to release

55. The best placement for the underlined portion would be:
    A. where it is now.
    B. before the word "are."
    C. before the word "often."
    D. after the word "weightless."

56. F. NO CHANGE
    G. effects
    H. affected
    J. does indeed affect

57. A. NO CHANGE
    B. spontaneity and personal attention,
    C. naturally spontaneous natures and personal affection,
    D. having spontaneously and personal attention,

[2] Regardless of its artistic merits, however, molecular gastronomy is a culinary trend that offers patrons an experience completely different from that of all preceding cuisine. [3] Where else can you find transparent ravioli that dissolves instantly once you've taken a bite? 59

58. F. NO CHANGE
G. completely separated
H. extremely differently
J. DELETE the underlined portion.

59. The writer is considering adding the following true statement to this paragraph:

> Although more and more molecular gastronomy restaurants are popping up in various cities nationwide, many culinary traditionalists take offense at the field's rising popularity.

Should the sentence be added to this paragraph, and if so, where should it be placed?

A. Yes before sentence 1.
B. Yes, before sentence 2.
C. Yes, before sentence 3.
D. The sentence should NOT be added.

Questions 60 asks about the preceding passage as a whole.

---

60. Suppose the writer had chosen to write a brief essay explaining the history and characteristics of molecular gastronomy. Would this essay successfully fulfill the writer's goal?

F. Yes, because the essay gives a detailed explanation of the scientists behind the creation of the molecular gastronomy.
G. Yes, because the essay discusses the initial stages of molecular gastronomy to its current form.
H. No, because it focuses more on the popularity and history of the restaurant Alinea, rather than molecular gastronomy in general.
J. No, because the essay only discusses the current state of molecular gastronomy, not its history.

PASSAGE V

Fashion Fortune Telling

[1]

Running a fashion blog is no easy feat. Three years ago, when I first decided pursuing my love of fashion, I started the blog for my friends and family. I was living far from home and thought doing so might be a fun and easy way for my loved ones to see what I had been up to. A million followers, and ten employees later, my job is still fun, but it is much more difficult than I had originally anticipated.

[2]

Each season marks a fresh start. [A] My team works tirelessly to predict trends, push aesthetic boundaries, and adding twists to everyday market pieces. The

fashion in any given season has been dictated by the designer shows held anually in New York, Paris, Milan, and London. Before designers' collections go public, however, my job seems similar to that of a fortuneteller: using what I've divined from the winter collections, for example, I must look into my crystal ball to decide which fashions will stay for spring, which ones will go, and which new trends from previous years might pop up again.

61. **A.** NO CHANGE
B. that I first decided pursuing
C. when I first decided to pursue
D. that I first decided to pursue

62. **F.** NO CHANGE
G. it is much more difficult then
H. doing so is much more difficult than
J. doing so is much more difficult then

63. **A.** NO CHANGE
B. to predict trends, push aesthetic boundaries, and add twists
C. to predict trends, to pushing aesthetic boundaries, and to add twisting
D. to predicting trends, pushing aesthetic boundaries, and to adding twists

64. **F.** NO CHANGE
G. is being
H. are
J. was

65. The writer is considering deleting the underlined portion, ending the sentence with a period after the word "fortuneteller." Should they make this edit?

A. Yes, because the explanation given is redundant.
B. Yes, because the explanation strays too far from the main topic of the passage.
C. No, because it explains a comparison mentioned earlier in the sentence.
D. No, because it adds a specific example from the author's past as a fortune teller.

[3]

[B] Leading up to New York's Spring Fashion Week, I sleepily stumble into the office every morning at 6am sharp, in search of inspiration. The most recent pages of our fashion-forward website were filled with dark tones of blue
66
and black. How could I possibly use those somber looks to predict the light and colorful innovations that were to come for spring? I sat in that same spot, day after day, ferocious searching through magazines, clothing websites,
67
and other fashion blogs, for a blip of inspiration. [C] Every year, I post a photo of my outfit at Spring Fashion Week's grand opening ceremony to showcase my prediction of the fashions to come, but this time I felt lost. One day, I gave up. I send everyone home early and rode my bike through the park
68
feeling frustrated and defeated.

[4]

At that moment, something caught my eye, it was: a
69
playground covered in snow with bright bits of blue, yellow, and purple metal pieces sticking out of the snow. My mind was immediately flooded with visions of the muted tones from last year's summer collection brightened to welcome the spring. [D] I pedaled back as quickly to the office as my legs
70
would allow and posted a photo of the playground on the blog.

[5]

That photo not only correctly predicted the trend for that spring season, but it was inspiring my own Fashion Week
71
outfit. In a nice white dress covered with specks of bright
72

66. **F.** NO CHANGE
    G. has been
    H. was
    J. will be

67. **A.** NO CHANGE
    B. ferociously searching
    C. I ferocious searched
    D. I ferociously searching

68. **F.** NO CHANGE
    G. sent
    H. am sending
    J. was sending

69. **A.** NO CHANGE
    B. At that moment, I found myself looking at:
    C. Suddenly, something caught my eye:
    D. Suddenly, something caught my eye that was:

70. The best placement for the underlined portion would be:
    F. where it is now.
    G. after the word "playground."
    H. after the word "and."
    J. after the word "office."

71. **A.** NO CHANGE
    B. but it also inspired
    C. however it was also inspiring
    D. however inspired

72. Which choice would most effectively describes the fit and quality of the author's dress?
    F. NO CHANGE
    G. Draped in a crisp white dress
    H. Wearing a unique dress
    J. Clothed in a beautiful dress

GO ON TO THE NEXT PAGE.

blue, yellow, and purple, the talk of the town was my
_____
73
look — and I couldn't have been more proud.
_____
73

73. **A.** NO CHANGE
    B. I felt like the belle of the ball — the crystal ball, that is.
    C. my look was the talk of the town.
    D. not a single person walked by without complimenting my dress.

Questions 74 and 75 ask about the preceding passage as a whole.

---

74. Upon reviewing the passage and realizing that some information has been left out, the author composes the following sentence:

> Last spring proved to be an especially difficult season.

The most logical placement for this sentence would be:

    F. Point A in Paragraph 2
    G. Point B in Paragraph 3
    H. Point C in Paragraph 3
    J. Point D in Paragraph 4

75. Suppose the writer had chosen to write an essay highlighting the highs and lows of being the boss of one's own company. Would this essay fulfill the writer's goal?

    A. Yes, because the author highlighted a variety of occupations.
    B. Yes, because the author gave examples of both good and bad experiences.
    C. No, because the author only gave examples of good experiences.
    D. No, because the author was not the boss of a company.

END OF TEST 1.
STOP! DO NOT TURN THE PAGE UNTIL TOLD TO DO SO.

MATHEMATICS TEST
60 Minutes — 60 Questions

DIRECTIONS: Solve each problem, choose the correct answer, and then fill in the corresponding oval on your answer document.

Do not linger over problems that take too much time. Solve as many as you can; then return to the others in the time you have left for this test.

You are permitted to use a calculator on this test. You may use your calculator for any problems you choose, but some of the problems may be best done without using a calculator.

Note: Unless otherwise stated, all of the following should be assumed:
1. Figures are NOT necessarily drawn to scale.
2. Geometric figures lie in a plane.
3. The word *line* indicates a striaght line.
4. The word *average* indicates arithmetic mean.

---

1. Eliza sells cars. She receives 4% of the sale price of each car she sells. What does Eliza earn for a car that she sells for $18,300?
    A. $ 457
    B. $ 732
    C. $ 4,575
    D. $ 7,320
    E. $73,200

2. If $y^3 + 7 = 22$, then $36 - y^3 = ?$
    F. $\sqrt{15}$
    G. 7
    H. 12
    J. 21
    K. 51

3. Given that $3z + 4 = 10$, what is the value of $(3 + z)^3$?
    A. 2
    B. 5
    C. 27
    D. 125
    E. 216

74

GO ON TO THE NEXT PAGE.

4. The accompanying table shows the income earned by 4 students selling wrapping paper for a school fundraiser.

Student	Number of Rolls Sold	Total Income
Julia	5	$16.25
Dean	13	$42.25
Denise	22	$71.50
Joe	8	$26.00

Each student earned the same amount for each roll sold. What did the students charge per roll of wrapping paper?

F. $2.25
G. $2.75
H. $3.00
J. $3.25
K. $3.50

5. Gail has $200 available to buy centerpieces for her school's prom. Each centerpiece costs $14. Gail pays a 7% sales tax on the entire purchase. What is the maximum number of centerpieces that Gail can buy?

A. 10
B. 11
C. 12
D. 13
E. 14

6. The cube root of some value Z is approximately 2.061. Which two integers does Z lie between?

F. 4 and 5
G. 7 and 8
H. 8 and 9
J. 9 and 10
K. 18 and 19

7. The Observatory on Mountain Peak recorded the daily temperatures, during the second week in January, in Fahrenheit (°F). The results were 12°, −2°, −10°, 7°, 3°, −13°, and 18°. To the nearest °F, what was the mean temperature for that week?

A. 0°F
B. 2°F
C. 3°F
D. 5°F
E. 9°F

GO ON TO THE NEXT PAGE.

8. Arthur is eating at a restaurant and will order an appetizer, a main course, and a dessert. The restaurant serves 3 appetizers, 5 main courses, and 2 desserts. How many different meals could Arthur order?

    F. 10
    G. 20
    H. 30
    J. 96
    K. 225

9. Steve runs a company which currently has 72 employees, which is three less than five times the number of employees he hired in his first year of business. How many employees did Steve hire in his first year of business?

    A. 5
    B. 10
    C. 14
    D. 15
    E. 24

10. One leg of a right triangle is 3 meters long. The hypotenuse of the triangle is 5 meters long. How long is the other leg?

    F. 2 m
    G. 4 m
    H. $\sqrt{34}$ m
    J. 9 m
    K. 16 m

11. A system of equations is given below.

    $$t = 5s - 3$$
    $$s = t - 1$$

    What is the value of s in the (s,t) solution to the system?

    A. -1
    B. $-1/2$
    C. $1/2$
    D. 1
    E. 2

12. Given that $7 - \sqrt{2x} = 1$, $x = ?$

    F. 18
    G. 36
    H. 6
    J. $\sqrt{6}$
    K. -36

13. A high school chess league has 12 competitors. League rules state that each player must play at least once against each other player, each season. For n players in the conference, there must then be at least $\dfrac{n^2 - n}{2}$ games in the season. What is the minimum number of games that must be played in a season for the members of this league?

   A. 33
   B. 60
   C. 66
   D. 72
   E. 132

14. A company ships Rubik's Cubes in boxes that are 8 inches by 12 inches by 16 inches. The Rubik's Cubes are 4 inches on a side. What is the maximum number of Rubik's Cubes that will fit into a single closed box?

   F. 6
   G. 9
   H. 12
   J. 18
   K. 24

15. In the figure below, XW and UZ intersect at Y, and UW is parallel to XZ. Which of the following angles must be congruent to $\angle ZXY$?

   A. $\angle UWY$
   B. $\angle UYW$
   C. $\angle YUW$
   D. $\angle XYZ$
   E. $\angle ZYW$

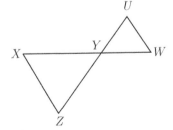

16. In the standard (x,y) coordinate plane, the point $(2, 1)$ is the midpoint of the line segment with endpoints $(10, 4)$ and:

   F. $(-6, -2)$
   G. $(-3, -8)$
   H. $(\ 3,\ \ 8)$
   J. $(\ 6,\ \ 2.5)$
   K. $(\ 8,\ 15)$

Use the following information to answer questions 17-19.

Elmo's Cupcake Emporium and Carl's Cupcake Castle both sell cupcakes in prearranged boxes. The table below lists the number of cupcakes per box, and the price (the total amount the customer pays) for each of the shops. For each shop there is a linear relationship between the number of cupcakes per box and the price of the box. Customers can only buy cupcakes in prearranged boxes.

Cupcakes per Box	Price at Elmo's	Price at Carl's
2	$2.50	$3.25
4	$4.00	$4.00
6	$5.50	$4.75
8	$7.00	$5.50
10	$8.50	$6.25
12	$10.00	$7.00

17. Kevin has $7.00 in quarters. What is the maximum number of quarters Kevin would have left over after paying for a box of 6 cupcakes at Carl's?
(Note: a quarter is $0.25.)

   A. 6
   B. 8
   C. 9
   D. 12
   E. 16

18. At Elmo's what is the price per cupcake (to the nearest $0.01) in a box of 10 cupcakes?

   F. $0.09
   G. $0.63
   H. $0.80
   J. $0.85
   K. $1.00

19. Which of the following gives the relationship between the price in dollars, c, and the number of cupcakes, n, at Carl's?

   A. $c = \dfrac{0.75n}{2} + 4$

   B. $c = 0.75n - 3.25$

   C. $c = \dfrac{0.75n}{2} + 3.25$

   D. $c = 0.75n + 3.25$

   E. $c = \dfrac{0.75n}{2} + 2.50$

GO ON TO THE NEXT PAGE.

20. The floor plan of Henry's attic bedroom is shown below. He is going to install baseboard along the bottom of each wall (shown by solid lines in the floor plan). Assuming the floor plan is accurate, which of the following is closest to the number of feet of baseboard he will need?

F. 36
G. 42
H. 53
J. 66
K. 84

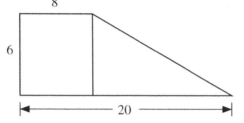

21. The Ferris wheel at a county fair has a radius of 40 feet, rotates at a constant speed, and completes one full rotation every 3 minutes. How many degrees does it rotate in 20 seconds?

A. 20°
B. 30°
C. 40°
D. 54°
E. 120°

22. Noemi threw darts in three games for her darts team. In the second game, she scored 15 more points than in the first game; in the third game, she scored 15 more points than in the second game. Her average score was 100 points for the three games. How many points did Noemi score in the third game?

F. 70
G. 85
H. 100
J. 115
K. 130

23. Given that $a \leq 2$ and $a + b \geq 10$, what is the LEAST value that b can have?

A. 7
B. 8
C. 8.5
D. 9
E. 12

GO ON TO THE NEXT PAGE.

24. Malachi told Annie, "If I spend up to 20 dollars from savings, my account will have at least two thirds of its current value." What is the least amount Malachi can have in his savings?

F. $20
G. $30
H. $40
J. $60
K. $90

25. Dale baked dog treats for 5 hours and 45 minutes on Sunday. It took him 30 minutes to bake a dozen treats, which is one batch, and 45 minutes to bake a double batch. In total, Dale baked 168 dog treats. How many double batches did Dale bake?

A. 0
B. 4
C. 5
D. 6
E. 7

26. For all nonzero a and b, which of the following is always positive?

F. $-|-a-b|$
G. $-|a+b|$
H. $|a|-|b|$
J. $|a|+|b|$
K. $-|-a|-|-b|$

27. Suzerain's goal for the summer was to save an average of $6.00 per week for 12 weeks. She saved an average of $5.00 per week for 10 weeks, then saved $9.50 for *each* of the last two weeks. She was still short of her goal, however. How much *more* should she have saved for each of the 12 weeks, on average, to meet her goal?

A. 15 cents
B. 25 cents
C. 35 cents
D. 45 cents
E. 60 cents

28. The dimensions of a picture is currently 4 inches in length by 8 inches in width. The owner increases the size of the picture using a computer program, and increases both dimensions by the same amount. The new picture has 3 times the area of the old one. What is the length, in inches, of the new picture?

F. 6
G. 8
H. 12
J. 16
K. 24

PP-ACT1

GO ON TO THE NEXT PAGE.

29. Which inequality is equivalent to
$3x - 9y < 3y + 6$?

   A. $x > -4y - 2$

   B. $x < -4y - 2$

   C. $x < 4y + 2$

   D. $x > 4y - 2$

   E. $x < -4y + 2$

30. An organism contains roughly 4.2×10^7 nerve cells, out of 2.1×10^{10} cells total. If a cell is selected at random from the organism, what is the probability that it will be a nerve cell?

   F. 0.0002

   G. 0.002

   H. 0.005

   J. 0.02

   K. 0.05

31. Which of the following equations has an integer solution?

   I. $2n + 7 = 43$
   II. $7n + 2 = 47$
   III. $7(n + 2) = 49$

   A. I only

   B. II only

   C. III only

   D. I and II only

   E. I and III only

32. For all nonzero x and y, $\dfrac{(9x^6y^9)(8x^9y^8)}{18x^{10}y^{20}} = ?$

   F. $\dfrac{4}{x^5y^3}$

   G. $\dfrac{x^5}{4y^3}$

   H. $\dfrac{4x^5}{y^3}$

   J. $4x^5y^3$

   K. $4x^{53}y^{52}$

Use the following information to answer questions 33-36.

A parents' association is building a sandbox for neighborhood kids to play in, at the corner of Neighbor Street and Friend Way, which meet at a right angle as shown in the diagram. The sandbox is 24 feet long and 10 feet wide. The parents purchase 1 bag of sand for $21.00, 20 toys for $1.10 each, and 4 buckets for $2.25 each. There is a 9% sales tax on the items. They also plant a flagpole in the sandbox such that it is equidistant from all three corners of the sandbox.

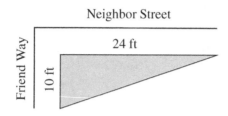

Neighbor Street

Friend Way

10 ft

24 ft

33. The parents calculated the area of the sandbox before purchasing the sand as well as the other supplies. What is the area, in square feet, of the sandbox?

A. 34
B. 60
C. 120
D. 240
E. 576

34. What was the total price, including sales tax, of the sand, toys, and buckets purchased by the parents?

F. $ 26.54
G. $ 52.00
H. $ 56.68
J. $ 57.77
K. $100.70

35. The plan of the sandbox will be placed on the standard (x, y) coordinate plane so that the right angle is at the origin, and the other 2 vertices are at $(24, 0)$ and $(0, -10)$. What coordinates give the location of the flagpole?

A. $(6, -2.5)$
B. $(6, -5)$
C. $(9, -3.75)$
D. $(12, -2.5)$
E. $(12, -5)$

36. The parents realize they forgot to purchase wood to make the border of the sandbox. What length of wooden beams is required to enclose the entire sandbox?

F. 30

G. 34

H. 60

J. 68

K. 78

37. What is the length, in coordinate units, of the altitude from X to $\overline{YZ}$ in $\triangle XYZ$ shown below?

A. 3

B. 4

C. 5

D. $\sqrt{26}$

E. $\sqrt{34}$

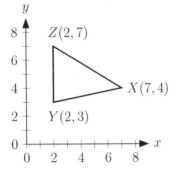

38. A regular hexagon is inscribed in a circle of radius r and center O as shown in the figure below. Point A lies on both the circle and a vertex of the hexagon. Suppose the figure was placed on the standard (x, y) coordinate plane such that the center of the circle was at the origin. What would be the x-coordinate of Point A?

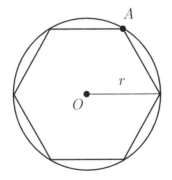

F. $\dfrac{r}{3}$

G. $\dfrac{r}{2}$

H. r

J. $r\sqrt{2}$

K. $r\sqrt{3}$

GO ON TO THE NEXT PAGE.

39. What is the amplitude of $y = -3\sin\left(2x - \dfrac{\pi}{4}\right)$?

   A. -3

   B. $\dfrac{1}{3}$

   C. $\dfrac{3}{2}$

   D. 2

   E. 3

40. The angle of elevation to the top of a nearby building, from a spot on level ground 60 feet from the base of the building, is $35°$. Which of the following is closest to the height of the building, in feet?

   F. 30

   G. 34

   H. 42

   J. 49

   K. 61

41. The graphs of the linear equations $y = -x + 8$ and $y = 4x - 12$ intersect at the point $(4, 4)$ as shown in the standard (x,y) coordinate plane below. The shaded region is bounded by these 2 lines, the x-axis, and the y-axis. What is the area of the shaded region, in square coordinate units?

   A. 22

   B. 24

   C. 26

   D. 28

   E. 32

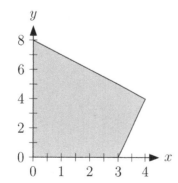

42. The table, below, gives the birth weights and the weights at 1 year, of five puppies. A veterinary student models these weights as a linear function where the weight at 1 year is dependent on the weight at birth. Among the following models, which one best fits the data?

Names	Weight at birth (x pounds)	Weight at 1 year (y pounds)
Buddy	2	6
Fido	3	8.5
Lassie	3.5	9.5
Ralph	2.5	7
Rex	4	12

F. $y = x + 5$

G. $y = x + 7$

H. $y = 2x$

J. $y = 2x - 1$

K. $y = 3x - 1$

43. Three linear equations are given below:

$$y = 2x - 1$$
$$y = 2x + 1$$
$$y = -\frac{1}{2}x + 2$$

In terms of being perpendicular, being parallel, or intersecting, how are the graphs of these equations related in the standard (x, y) coordinate plane?

A. All 3 lines are parallel.

B. All 3 lines are perpendicular.

C. All 3 lines meet in a common point.

D. Exactly 2 of the lines are parallel.

E. None of the lines are parallel or perpendicular.

44. In the standard (x,y) coordinate plane, consider the set of points equidistant from the origin and the line $y = 2$. When graphed, what shape is formed by this set of points?

F. A circle

G. An ellipse

H. A hyperbola

J. A parabola

K. Cannot be determined based on the information given

45. The domain of $f(x) = \dfrac{7}{x^3 - 16x}$ is the set of all real

numbers EXCEPT:

A. 0
B. 0 and 4
C. −4 and 4
D. −7 and 4
E. −4, 0, and 4

46. During a rainstorm, the relationship between the depth of water in a barrel, y inches, and the elapsed time, x hours, was modeled by the equation $2x - 3y = 0$. Which of the following graphs in the standard (x,y) coordinate plane models the equation for positive values of x and y?

F.

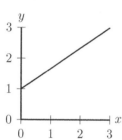

J.

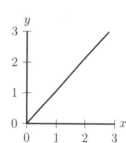

G.

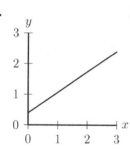

K.

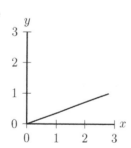

H.

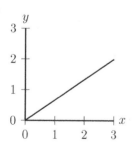

47. Each of 24 students in a class took a test and received a whole number score. The median of the scores was 84. None of the students received a score of 84 and 25% received a score of 88 or above. How many students received a score of 85, 86, or 87?

   A. 4

   B. 5

   C. 6

   D. 7

   E. 12

48. Two events are independent if the outcome of one event does not affect the outcome of the other. One of the following does NOT describe independent events. Which one?

   F. A queen is drawn from a deck of cards, then without replacing the card, a 2 is drawn

   G. A coin lands tails up, then a 5 is drawn from a deck of cards

   H. A single 6 sided die rolls a 3 face up, then a coin lands heads up

   J. A jack is drawn from a deck of cards, then after replacing the card, a jack is drawn

   K. A 6-sided die rolls a 5 face up, it is then rolled again and lands with a 2 faceup

49. Four matrices are given below.

$$L = \begin{bmatrix} 2 & 7 \\ 13 & 4 \end{bmatrix} \qquad M = \begin{bmatrix} 4 & 6 \\ 1 & 19 \end{bmatrix}$$

$$N = \begin{bmatrix} 22 & 4 & 17 \\ 8 & 5 & 3 \end{bmatrix} \qquad O = \begin{bmatrix} 8 & 2 \\ 7 & 0 \\ 12 & 5 \end{bmatrix}$$

Which of the following matrix products is undefined?

   A. LM

   B. LN

   C. NO

   D. ML

   E. MO

GO ON TO THE NEXT PAGE.

50. What is the 7th term in a geometric sequence whose third term is -2 and whose 8th term is $\frac{1}{16}$?

   F. $-\frac{1}{8}$

   G. $\frac{15}{64}$

   H. $\frac{1}{8}$

   J. $\frac{1}{4}$

   K. 8

51. If 4 fair coins are flipped, what is the probability that *exactly* 2 of the coins land heads up?

   A. $1/16$
   B. $1/4$
   C. $1/2$
   D. $5/8$
   E. $3/8$

52. Let z be a positive odd integer. The expression zy^5 is a negative even integer whenever y is any member of which of the following sets?

   F. All integers
   G. Negative integers
   H. Negative odd integers
   J. Negative even integers
   K. Positive even integers

53. The height above the ground, h units, of a pumpkin t seconds after being thrown from the top of a building in the Halloween Pumpkin Smash is given by the equation $h = -3t^2 - 6t + 24$. An equivalent factored form of this equation shows that the pumpkin:

   A. starts at a height 6 units off the ground.
   B. reaches a maximum height of 14 units.
   C. reaches the ground in 2 seconds.
   D. reaches the ground in 4 seconds.
   E. reaches a maximum height of 4 units.

54. Point K lies on $\overline{LN}$ and point L lies on $\overline{JM}$. Right triangle MLN has right angle L and $\angle MNL$ measures $30°$. What is the value of $\sin(a + b)$?

F. 1

G. $\dfrac{1}{2}$

H. $\dfrac{\sqrt{3}}{2}$

J. $\dfrac{\sqrt{2}}{2}$

K. 0

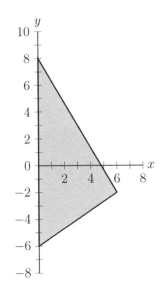

55. The shaded portion of the graph in the standard (x, y) coordinate plane represents the solution set of which of the following systems of linear inequalities?

A. $y < -\dfrac{8x}{5} + 8$ and $y > \dfrac{2x}{3} - 6$

B. $y > -\dfrac{8x}{5} + 8$ and $y < \dfrac{2x}{3} + 6$

C. $y \le -\dfrac{8x}{5} + 8$ and $y \ge \dfrac{2x}{3} - 6$

D. $y \ge -\dfrac{8x}{5} + 8$ and $y \le \dfrac{2x}{3} - 6$

E. $y \le -\dfrac{8x}{5} + 8$ and $y \le \dfrac{2x}{3} - 6$

56. Which of the following inequalities is equivalent to

$$\left(|x| + \frac{3}{2}\right)^3 \leq 27 \text{?}$$

F. $-\dfrac{3}{2} \leq x \leq \dfrac{3}{2}$

G. $-3 \leq x \leq 3$

H. $-\dfrac{5}{2} \leq x \leq \dfrac{3}{2}$

J. $-\dfrac{5}{2} \leq x \leq \dfrac{5}{2}$

K. $-1 \leq x \leq 1$

57. For how many integers, x, is the equation
$2^{x+2} = 4^{2x-1}$ true?

A. 0

B. 1

C. 2

D. 3

E. An infinite number of integers

58. One of the following equations determines the graph in the standard (x, y) coordinate plane below. Which one?

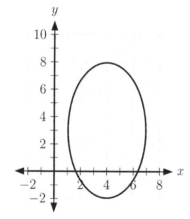

F. $\dfrac{(x-4)^2}{25} + \dfrac{(y-3)^2}{9} = 1$

G. $\dfrac{(x-4)^2}{25} + \dfrac{(y+3)^2}{9} = 1$

H. $\dfrac{(x-4)^2}{9} + \dfrac{(y-3)^2}{25} = 1$

J. $\dfrac{(x+4)^2}{25} + \dfrac{(y+3)^2}{9} = 1$

K. $\dfrac{(x+4)^2}{9} + \dfrac{(y+3)^2}{25} = 1$

59. Which of the following polar coordinates represents the same location as $(4, 55°)$?

    A. $(4, -55°)$

    B. $(4, -305°)$

    C. $(4, 305°)$

    D. $(4, 110°)$

    E. $(4, 165°)$

60. A rectangular pyramid is intersected by a plane that is not parallel to the base and does not intersect the base or the vertex, as shown in the figure below. Which one of the following figures shows the shape of the intersection?

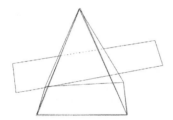

    F.   **J.**

    G.   **K.**

    H.

END OF TEST 2.
STOP! DO NOT TURN THE PAGE UNTIL TOLD TO DO SO.
DO NOT RETURN TO THE PREVIOUS TEST.

READING TEST

35 Minutes — 40 Questions

DIRECTIONS: There are four passages in this test. Each passage is followed by several questions. Choose the best answer to each question and fill in the corresponding oval on your answer document. You may refer to the passages as often as often as necessary.

Passage I

LITERARY NARRATIVE: This passage is adapted from *The Lost Boys* by Paul Ryan (©1915 by Paul Ryan).

But let us retreat to the early eighties, when Alvina was a baby: or even further back, to the flourishing days of James Houghton. In his flourishing days, James Houghton was the crème de la crème of Woodhouse so-
5　ciety. The house of Houghton had always been well-to-do. Tradespeople, we must admit, but after a few generations of affluence, tradespeople acquire a distinct cachet. Now James Houghton, at the age of twenty-eight, inherited a splendid business in Manchester goods, in Woodhouse.
10　He was a tall, thin, elegant young man with side-whiskers, genuinely refined. He had a taste for elegant conversation, elegant literature, and elegant Christianity: a tall, thin, brittle young man, rather fluttering in his manner, full of facile ideas, and with a speaking voice, most beautiful. Withal,
15　of course, a tradesman. He courted a small, dark woman, older than himself, daughter of a Derbyshire squire. He expected to get at least ten thousand pounds with her. In that he was disappointed, for he got only eight hundred. Being of a romantic-commercial nature, he never forgave her,
20　but always treated her with the most elegant courtesy. To see him peel and prepare an apple for her was an exquisite sight. But that peeled and quartered apple was her portion. This elegant Adam of commerce gave Eve her own back, nicely cored, and had no more to do with her. Meanwhile
25　Alvina was born.

Before all this, however, before his marriage, James Houghton had built Manchester House. It was a vast square building standing on the main street and highroad of the small, but growing town. The lower front consisted
30　of two fine shops, one for Manchester goods, one for silk and wools. This was James Houghton's commercial poem.

For James Houghton was a dreamer, and something of a poet: commercial, be it understood. He wove one continual fantasy for himself, a fantasy of commerce. He
35　dreamed of silks and poplins, luscious in texture and of unforeseen exquisiteness. He dreamed of exquisite women ruffling charmed, entranced to his counter. And charming, entrancing, he served them his lovely fabrics, which only he and they could sufficiently appreciate. His fame
40　spread, until Alexandra, Princess of Wales, and Elizabeth, Empress of Austria, the two best-dressed women in Europe, floated down from heaven to the shop in Woodhouse, and sallied forth to show what could be done by purchasing from James Houghton.

45　In those early days when he brought his wife to her new home, his window on the Manchester side was a foam and a may-blossom of muslins and prints, his window on the London side was an autumn evening of silks and rich fabrics. What wife could fail to be dazzled! But she, poor
50　darling, from her stone hall in stony Derbyshire, was a little bit repulsed by the man's dancing in front of his stock. The little child was born in the second year. And then James Houghton decamped to a small, half-furnished bedroom at the other end of the house, where he slept on a
55　rough board. His wife was left alone with her baby and the built-in furniture. She developed heart disease, as a result of a nervous condition.

But like a butterfly, James fluttered over his fabrics. He was a tyrant to his shop-girls. The girls detested him.
60　And yet, his curious refinement and enthusiasm entranced them. They submitted to him. The shop attracted much curiosity. But the poor-spirited Woodhouse people were weak buyers. They wearied James Houghton with their demand for common zephyrs, for red flannel, which they
65　would scallop with black wools, for black alpacas and merinos. He fluffed out his silk-striped muslins, his India cotton-prints. But the natives shied off as if he had offered them the poisoned robes of Herakles.

There was a sale. These sales contributed a good
70　deal to Mrs. Houghton's nervous heart-disease. They brought the first signs of wear-and-tear into the face of James Houghton. At first, of course, he merely marked down, with discretion, his less-expensive stock of prints and muslins with a few fancy braidings and trimmings.
75　And Woodhouse bought cautiously.

After the sale, however, James Houghton felt himself at liberty to plunge into an orgy of new stock and huge bundles, bales and boxes arrived in Woodhouse, and were dumped on the pavement of the shop. Friday evening
80　came, and with it a revelation in Houghton's window: the first piques, the first strangely-woven and honey-combed toilet covers and bed quilts, the first frill-caps and aprons

for maid-servants: a wonder in white. That was how James advertised it. "A Wonder in White."

1. The passage as a whole can primarily be characterized as:

A. details about the garment industry in English society.
B. the narrator's concern over time for Mrs. Houghton's health.
C. a description of day-to-day life in Woodhouse.
D. background information about Alvina's family.

2. The passage indicates that the reason for Mrs. Houghton's heart disease was:

F. a difficult childbirth.
G. an unhappy marriage.
H. a nervous condition.
J. her hard work as a seamstress.

3. According to the passage, the people of the house of Houghton were known as:

A. fabric store owners.
B. tradespeople.
C. squires.
D. servants.

4. As it is used in line 53, *decamped* most nearly means:

F. lived in a tent.
G. locked.
H. moved suddenly.
J. stored fabric.

5. In the context of the passage, lines 20–25 are most likely meant to suggest that:

A. Mrs. Houghton must eat fruit to relieve her nervous condition.
B. Mr. Houghton gives his wife what he feels she is due, but little else.
C. Mr. and Mrs. Houghton have a romantic relationship.
D. Mr. Houghton thinks that his wife is as exquisite as an apple.

6. According to the passage, how does James Houghton feel about the townspeople of Woodhouse?

F. Pleased to sell them his fine silks and wools
G. Disgusted by their preference for poisoned robes
H. Ecstatic that they wanted to copy the fashion of the Princess of Wales
J. Frustrated by their demand for plain clothing

7. The main purpose of the third paragraph (lines 32–44) is to show Mr. Houghton's:

A. close friendships with important women in society.
B. aspirations of becoming a poet.
C. desire to run a highly successful shop.
D. devotion to his wife and to his daughter.

8. The passage most strongly implies that the employees of Mr. Houghton's shop were:

F. hateful; they were thoroughly opposed to working for him.
G. compliant; they disliked him but were charmed by him.
H. enthusiastic; they completely enjoyed working in the shop.
J. irate; they were angry about his treatment of the shop-girls.

9. The passage suggests that Mrs. Houghton is disgusted by her husband because of:

A. his enthusiasm for the fabrics of his shop.
B. his close friendship with Elizabeth, Empress of Austria.
C. the poorly furnished conditions of his home.
D. his insistence on dressing her in fine clothing.

10. It can most reasonably be inferred from the passage that the sale at Mr. Houghton's shop:

F. allowed space and funds to purchase a fresh stock of fabric.
G. was intended to help servants acquire uniforms.
H. was a major success among the townspeople.
J. caused such unhappiness among the family that it would not be repeated.

Passage II

SOCIAL SCIENCE: This passage is adapted from *Movable Type and the Printing Press* by John Guta (©1955 by John Guta).

Writing is synonymous with civilization. Modern scholars associate the rise of urban societies with the invention of writing, which allowed civilizations to not just communicate more effectively but to chronicle their history
5 more precisely. But literacy had traditionally been the preserve of social elites, who controlled both the costly process of hand-copying texts and the skilled scribes who did the work. Books and scrolls were precious and rare items that were almost exclusively the property of rulers. This
10 changed with the invention of the movable type printing press in late-Renaissance Europe.

Printing technology was first developed in East Asia, where it was under the control of the central government. The earliest form was woodblock printing, which used
15 hand-carved wood to print official documents and currency in large quantities. This method was of limited use, since each block had to be carved painstakingly by hand. It was only in 11th century China that diversified large-scale printing became possible with the invention of movable type. Thousands of ceramic or metal tiles, each bearing a different character, could be arranged in whatever order desired and printed. But this too involved tremendous amounts of labor, since Chinese writing makes uses of tens of thousands of distinct characters. Setting a document re-
25 quired hundreds of hours of labor, though the result was a text that could be rapidly mass produced.

These movable type presses were also restricted to government use. This only changed when news of the technology diffused through the trade routes that linked Eu-
30 rope and Asia together in the 15th century. Until that time, written texts in Europe were copied by hand. The ancient Greeks and Romans had access to whole libraries of texts in thousands of copies. But the armies of slave-scribes that produced copies of the epics, poems, treatises, and official
35 documents under the Roman Empire vanished in the early Middle Ages and were replaced by small communities of Christian monks who laboriously copied small numbers of classic texts. It was these anonymous scribes who transmitted the legacy of the ancient world through the darkest of
40 the dark ages and laid the groundwork for the Renaissance. Movable type provided the means to mass produce texts once again, but without the need for thousands of scribes to copy those texts by hand.

In 1450, in the German city of Mainz, an obscure
45 goldsmith named Johannes Gutenberg became aware of the technique and spent several years secretly assembling a metal type set of the 26 characters of the Latin alphabet (the basis of most European written languages) and converting a wine press into a printing press. Because the
50 Latin alphabet contained only a tiny fraction of the thousands of characters used in Chinese writing, the potential to quickly print a variety of texts was much greater in Europe than in China.

Gutenberg demonstrated the power of his movable
55 type press in 1455, when he set and printed an edition of the Bible. Traditionally, it took multiple scribes several years to produce a single copy of the Bible. Gutenberg's movable type press could print a complete edition in weeks. The revolutionary potential of Gutenberg's press
60 was readily apparent. Within decades, 300 printing shops had sprung up in the cities of Western Europe. It has been estimated that when Gutenberg was surreptitiously assembling his type in 1450, there were 30,000 books in Europe. By 1500 there were more than 20 million printed books
65 circulating far and wide.

The social effects were immediately apparent as well. News of the early Spanish voyages to the New World spread rapidly via cheaply printed pamphlets in a dozen languages. The mass production of Bibles gave new impe-
70 tus to the movement to reduce the power of the Catholic Church by translating the Bible from Latin (a language known only by the clergy and other learned elites) into vernacular languages. This movement took form with the outbreak of the Reformation, and in the 1520s Martin Luther
75 contributed to the 'printing revolution' by publishing his own translation of the Bible into German. Hundreds of thousands of copies were created within a few years of the first publication. Later in the 16th century, when the Polish astronomer Nicolaus Copernicus wrote a single
80 manuscript of his theory that the earth revolved around the sun, the Catholic Church was unable to suppress the dangerous theory of heliocentrism, which was swiftly disseminated through mass produced copies of Copernicus' text.

The scientific knowledge and political radicalism of
85 early modern Europe only survived because it could spread out of the control of authorities who wished to suppress it. The movable type printing press made this possible by flooding the continent with mass produced texts. The rapid proliferation of books and the rise in literacy that it sparked
90 made both democracy and capitalism possible—and with them, the modern world itself.

11. The main purpose of the passage is to:

   A. describe the origins and impact of a technology that has helped shape the modern world.
   B. compare and contrast the purpose and use of movable type in both China and Europe.
   C. explain the revolutionary social outcomes that occurred after the invention of the printing press by a single man, Johannes Gutenberg.
   D. give proof that the written word spread much more quickly during the 15th and 16th centuries than in the past.

GO ON TO THE NEXT PAGE.

12. Which of the following events mentioned in the passage occurred last chronologically?

F. Wood block printing was first developed in East Asia.

G. Martin Luther published his German translation of the Bible.

H. The Catholic Church found itself unable to stop the dissemination of Copernicus' theory of heliocentrism.

J. Johannes Gutenberg printed the first complete Latin edition of the Bible.

13. In line 72–73, the word *vernacular* most nearly means:

A. commonly understood.

B. widely distributed.

C. simple and unsophisticated.

D. creative but unusual.

14. The author most likely includes the information provided in the last paragraph in order to:

F. suggest that during unstable periods, leaders will always try to stop revolutionary thinking.

G. imply that the invention of the printing press had revolutionary effects that led to modern democracy.

H. provide evidence of the number of books mass produced in early modern Europe.

J. offer proof of the link between printing in 11th century China and 16th century Europe.

15. In lines 38–40, the author implies that the monks during the Middle Ages did all of the following EXCEPT:

A. created works that provided a crucial conceptual foundation for the Renaissance.

B. showed painstaking dedication to their craft.

C. worked collaboratively to accomplish a goal.

D. labored in a way that made literary knowledge more widely available.

16. According to the passage, large-scale printing in China was challenging primarily due to the:

F. materials needed to print official documents.

G. unrealistic expectations about the amount of work involved in typesetting.

H. complexity of the Chinese language.

J. variations in the types of tiles used.

17. The author most likely included the reference to woodblock printing in the second paragraph (lines 12–16) in order to provide an example of the:

A. great influence that ancient elites and rulers often possessed.

B. admired prominence of the Mesopotamian and Egyptian civilizations.

C. extreme simplicity of early forms of printing.

D. very early origins of the printing process.

18. The statistics quoted in the fifth paragraph (lines 54–65) were likely included by the author to suggest which of the following?

F. After the invention of the movable type press by Gutenberg, ordinary citizens were finally unafraid to express their ideas in public.

G. After the invention of the movable type press by Gutenberg, mass printing became much easier for larger groups of people.

H. One individual can create enough books for an entire continent.

J. There was great hunger for knowledge in Western Europe during the 15th century, which could be met by the dedication of monks copying texts.

19. As it is used in lines 5–6, the word *preserve* most nearly means:

A. savings.

B. expense.

C. domain.

D. commonality.

20. According to the passage, mass production of Bibles affected the power of the Catholic Church by:

F. keeping it in the hands of the clergy.

G. allowing it to be translated from Latin to other languages.

H. translating it from German into Latin.

J. allowing it to be sent to Asia.

Passage III

HUMANITIES: This passage is adapted from *Who Was Shakespeare?* by Taylor Anne (©2001 by Taylor Anne).

Standing on her famous balcony, Juliet sought to justify her love for Romeo, son of her father's great enemy. 'What's in a name?' she said, 'That which we call a rose by any other name would smell as sweet.' A name is noth-
5 ing. What really matters is the character that lies beneath a name. There is much wisdom in these lines, some of Shakespeare's most famous. But according to a long scholarly tradition, he may have been hinting at a deeper, hidden truth.

10 Ever since Shakespeare's death in 1616, a persistent line of critics have found it simply unbelievable that the indifferently educated son of a rural leather worker could have written the most extraordinary poetry ever to grace the English language. How could a man with no social
15 connections or university education have produced dozens of plays that flawlessly recreate aristocratic society and are teeming with historical and literary allusions? To these critics, the answer is simple: he didn't write them.

To be sure, there was a such a man as William Shake-
20 speare. His life is meagerly but reliably recorded. Born in the village of Stratford in 1564, married to Anne Hathaway in 1582, he vanishes from historical sight until the mid-1590s when his name appears in lists of actors in London stage productions. About this time he also begins to appear
25 in official registers as the author of several plays. Subsequent records describe a man with an interest in property, who purchased homes and land in both London and Stratford. His will of 1616, shows that he had amassed some wealth, enough to buy a handsome burial plot in Stratford's
30 Church of the Holy Trinity. And this, say the skeptical critics, is all we know of William Shakespeare. There's no contemporary evidence of the towering genius from whose mind sprang *Hamlet*, *Twelfth Night*, and *The Tempest*. No signed written drafts, no praise from enraptured audiences,
35 no public recognition at all of the man responsible for the most successful plays staged in London. Surely an artist of such talent would leave behind stronger traces than this.

So who did write the plays? The critics have many candidates. Operating on the assumption that the author of
40 Shakespeare's plays must have been educated and knowledgeable of court politics, critics have put forward the names of many courtiers and aristocrats. The most popular candidate is Edward de Vere (1550–1604), Earl of Oxford, and benefactor of several theatre companies. De Vere
45 had a reputation among the members of Queen Elizabeth's court as a poet, and indeed many of his contemporaries suspected him of being the author of several well-regarded, anonymously published literary works. Supporters of this theory say that de Vere had the qualifications necessary
50 to be the true Shakespeare, and have pointed to supposed stylistic similarities between de Vere's surviving poems and several of the canonical plays and poems attributed to William Shakespeare.

But if de Vere was the real author, why hide behind a
55 pen name? There was nothing to stop de Vere from publishing plays under his own name. Might there have been a political reason for the true author to hide behind the name of William Shakespeare? That is the argument made by those who say that Sir Francis Bacon (1561–1626) was
60 the true author. Bacon was a lawyer, scientist, and philosopher who served as counsel to Queen Elizabeth, and proponents of Bacon's authorship point to the many legal expressions and metaphors in Shakespeare's plays as circumstantial evidence. But Bacon's legal theories were of a radical
65 sort, and he was a member of a secret circle of disaffected courtiers that sought to bring republican ideas to England as a prelude to the eventual replacement of the monarchy. Supporters of this theory claim that Bacon wrote plays under the name of William Shakespeare that included several
70 anti-royal plots, characters, and speeches meant to gradually plant the seeds of democracy in the minds of the common people. If this was so, then obviously the Queen's counsel could not publish such inflammatory material under his own name.

75 This account strains believability, but it does get at a problem that has vexed the majority of scholars who believe the Stratford leather worker's son was the true poet: Why is there so little trace of Shakespeare in the abundant records of the period? Those who suspect a coverup be-
80 lieve that this was no accident. All of the theories of alternate authorship suppose that the man William Shakespeare was a willing mask for whomever wrote the works attributed to him. The fact that some of the few records we have stated that Shakespeare died a wealthy man suggest
85 that he was well paid by whichever nobleman was the true author of his works. All that was needed was his silence, which lasted not just until the end of his life, but into posterity as well.

It says much about the mystery of Shakespeare's ge-
90 nius, that, for four hundred years devotees of his work have been looking behind the plain man from Stratford for a more comprehensible image of artistic brilliance. Surely, the creator of Lear, Viola, Prospero, and a universe of other beloved characters must have been born of noble blood
95 and immersed in the opulent pageantry of the royal court. For the critics in search of the hidden truth behind Shakespeare's identity, such splendor is the only conceivable cradle for a poet who possessed a matchless understanding of his fellow man. But this search overlooks the most
100 fascinating aspect of Shakespeare's art: that a man of obscure birth and a smattering of schooling could, through his unique sensitivity to emotion and language, conjure on the stage and on the page, the limitless breadth of the human experience.

GO ON TO THE NEXT PAGE.

21. In line 25, the word *registers* most nearly means:

   A. records.
   B. machines.
   C. opinions.
   D. impressions.

22. Which of the following best describes the "deeper, hidden truth" mentioned in lines 8–9?

   F. It does not make sense that Shakespeare, who came from humble beginnings, could have possessed personal knowledge of the royal court.
   G. Scholars cannot comprehend how Shakespeare produced plays and poems of such tremendous complexity, given his lack of education.
   H. It is difficult to understand why there is relatively little written and eyewitness evidence about the life of Shakespeare.
   J. There is a significant debate around who actually created plays and poems attributed to "Shakespeare."

23. In lines 14–18, the statement about the critics most nearly means that:

   A. Shakespeare had a gift that allowed him to write about aristocratic society.
   B. poets benefit from understanding the lives of common people.
   C. Shakespeare was likely more educated than history led them to believe.
   D. they do not believe an uneducated person could write at the level of Shakespeare's works.

24. The passage includes all of the following pieces of evidence for why Francis Bacon was a likely candidate for the true author of works attributed to Shakespeare EXCEPT:

   F. As a member of the court, Bacon would have had an intimate knowledge of its inner workings.
   G. Bacon was attempting to overthrow the monarchy and wrote under the pen name "Shakespeare" in order to inflame public opinion.
   H. The references to anti-royal plots, characters, and speeches in Shakespeare's works make sense, given Bacon's often controversial views of the monarchy.
   J. The legal language and metaphors in Shakespeare's plays reflect Bacon's position as legal counsel to the Queen.

25. In lines 30–37, the author's attitude can best be characterized as:

   A. forceful.
   B. annoyed.
   C. uncertain.
   D. angry.

26. According to the passage, what are the principal attributes of the theories of alternate authorship?

   F. Two writers took turns producing Shakespeare's plays, and both split the profits afterwards.
   G. Shakespeare was embarrassed by the content of his plays and changed his name in order to protect his true identity.
   H. Shakespeare was not the true author of his plays and poems, and instead was paid to take on that role by the wealthy nobleman who actually wrote them.
   J. A wealthy nobleman paid Shakespeare to write, which eventually made Shakespeare rich.

27. The passage suggests that "critics in search of the hidden truth" (line 96) believe:

   A. Shakespeare was able to write about the court despite never seeing it himself.
   B. was secretly a man named Lear.
   C. Shakespeare was unable to understand other people's personalities.
   D. the creator of Shakespeare's works was a member of the nobility.

28. In line 103, the phrase "limitless breadth" refers to the:

   F. restrictions on language that Shakespeare had to overcome as an author.
   G. struggles that all humans must go through at some point during their lives.
   H. scope of people's lives represented in Shakespeare's plays and poems.
   J. energy and creativity that Shakespeare often brought to his writing.

29. According to the passage, why do critics consider de Vere to be a likely candidate for the true author of Shakespeare's works?

   A. The content of several of his poems is similar to the canonical works of Shakespeare.
   B. de Vere was a member of the royal court of Queen Elizabeth.
   C. de Vere was apparently hesitant about publishing works under his own name.
   D. de Vere was not focused enough on politics in his writing.

30. In line 12, the phrase "indifferently educated" implies that Shakespeare:

   F. did not receive a formal education, and instead was self-taught.
   G. was educated, but only to a limited degree.
   H. did not study as hard as he could have in school.
   J. was taught by instructors who sometimes made fun of him.

Passage IV

NATURAL SCIENCE: This passage is adapted from *The Tunguska Event* by Vladimir Klichkov (©2011 by Vladimir Klichkov).

At 7:17 AM on the morning of June 30, 1908, local tribes and Russian settlers in the remote Lake Baikal region of Siberia, near the Tunguska River, reported seeing a bluish light as bright as the sun moving across the sky. Soon after,
5 there was a bright flash and a sound that witnesses compared to artillery fire. Seconds later a shock wave knocked people to the ground and shattered windows across a radius of three hundred kilometers. People closer to the epicenter of the blast reported that the sky seemed to split
10 open, and that a wave of intense heat preceded the shock wave that flattened whole swathes of forest. The blast was so strong that it was registered by seismic stations across Europe and Asia and measured 5.0 on the Richter scale—equivalent to a moderate earthquake. For several nights
15 after the event, observers through the northern hemisphere reported strange glowing patterns in the sky.

For over a decade after the mysterious blast, no scientists were able to investigate the event. The Tunguska River area was remote, a lightly populated wilderness hun-
20 dreds of miles from any major settlement. Moreover, the chaos of World War I and the Russian Revolution made investigation of the curious incident a low priority. The first expedition to the region was mounted in 1927. At the supposed center of the blast site was a zone eight kilo-
25 meters across of scorched trees—all standing but shorn of branches and leaves. Around this lay a zone of 2100 square kilometers of felled trees, all lying away from the epicenter.

In 1908, there was no human technology capable of
30 creating devastation of this scale. The scientists' conjecture was that a meteorite—a fragment of rock or iron that fell to earth—caused what was referred to as the 'Tunguska event.' But if it was a meteorite impact it was unlike any previously recorded incident. For one thing, there
35 was no crater. The central zone of scorched but standing trees made little sense: why weren't they too knocked over, facing away from the center of the explosion?

Further evidence that the Tunguska event was caused by a meteorite only deepened the mystery. Scientists exam-
40 ined the trees and soil in the blast zone and found microscopic spheres of silicate and magnetite, compounds commonly found together in meteorite fragments. Analysis found a high level of nickel relative to iron in the spheres, another feature usually associated with meteorites.

45 It was only in the period following World War II, and the development of nuclear weapons and atmospheric monitoring technology, that it became possible for scientists to offer more definitive explanations. In the 1950s, both Russia and the United States conducted atmospheric tests of
50 nuclear weapons. Some of these tests involved air bursts—the detonation of bombs hundreds or thousands of feet above the ground. The blast wave traveled downward, but then bounced back from the surface and expanded horizontally, its force flattening everything at ground level begin-
55 ning some distance from the epicenter. These effects were strikingly similar to the evidence found at the Tunguska blast site.

Atmospheric monitoring technology in the 1950s and 1960s confirmed for the first time that meteorite airbursts
60 were very common occurrences. Meteorites striking the atmosphere at a speed of 11 meters per second compress the air in their path, generating tremendous amounts of heat. The intensifying heat triggers an explosion in the meteorite before it can strike the surface of the earth. An
65 air burst of a meteorite between 5 and 15 meters in diameter, can generate an explosive force in the range of 20 kilotons—the same size of the atomic bomb blasts that destroyed Hiroshima and Nagasaki. Based on the amount of land damaged by the Tunguska blast, the meteorite that
70 struck there was many times larger, generating an explosion in the megaton range.

Some scientists have hypothesized that the Tunguska object was not a meteorite but rather a comet. Comets are composed of a stone core surrounded by layers of
75 ice and dust. When comets strike the atmosphere, the compression-generated heat vaporizes the ice and dust prior to the explosion of the rocky core. The dispersion of these vaporized particles in the atmosphere reflect incoming sunlight and produce glowing effects like those
80 observed after the Tunguska event.

Comet strikes are even rarer occurrences than meteorite strikes, but just as dangerous. Objects the size of the one at Tunguska are estimated to strike every 300 years. Indeed, had an object of similar size struck a city or other
85 heavily settled area, the damage and loss of life would been unrivalled in human history. Since 1908, human population growth has led to expanded settlement across the globe and raised the likelihood that an impact event would occur over an urban area. The eventuality of another
90 such event has prompted space agencies and governments around the world to develop plans to deflect incoming objects.

31. The primary purpose of the passage is to:

   A. compare and contrast two theories around what created the Tunguska event, which scientists speculate was most likely caused by either a meteoroid or comet.
   B. provide support for the argument that scientists need more monitoring of meteoric events in general, including their impact on human activities.
   C. describe the history of the Tunguska region from prehistory to the present day.
   D. describe the impact of the Tunguska event on the settlement and people living near the Tunguska River in 1908.

32. According to the passage, meteor strikes:

   F. are more lethal than comet strikes.
   G. were the definitive cause of the Tunguska event.
   H. are more common than comet strikes, and are equally dangerous.
   J. leave no visible crater.

33. Which of the following does NOT support the claim that the Tunguska event was caused by a meteor?

   A. A high level of nickel relative to iron in microscopic spheres left behind
   B. The lack of a crater at the impact site
   C. Microscopic spheres of silicate and magnetite found by scientists at the blast site
   D. The discovery that meteoric airbursts are common occurrences

34. In line 88, the word *likelihood* most nearly means:

   F. failure.
   G. certainty.
   H. proof.
   J. possibility.

35. The main purpose of paragraph seven (lines 72–80) is to:

   A. describe in detail the concept of meteoric airbursts and the impact that airbursts of varying speeds and size can have.
   B. draw comparisons between the power and outcomes of the Tunguska event and the bombs dropped on Hiroshima and Nagasaki.
   C. provide proof that the meteoroid that caused the Tunguska event was exceptional in both size and effect.
   D. introduce a scientific concept that helps support one theory behind the Tunguska event.

36. According to the passage, the air burst theory best explains the:

   F. vertical heat wave after the event.
   G. glowing patterns in the sky.
   H. presence of silicate and magnetite at the blast site.
   J. pattern of scorched trees around the epicenter.

37. According to the passage, meteoric air bursts are caused by:

   A. meteorites exploding as they hit the atmosphere.
   B. atomic bomb blasts on Earth.
   C. comet strikes outside of Earth's atmosphere.
   D. meteorites striking other planets in the solar system.

38. The main purpose of the statement in lines 45–48 is to:

   F. explain why no crater was left behind after the Tunguska event.
   G. illustrate the development of nuclear weapons in the period following World War II.
   H. transition between pieces of information supporting theories about the Tunguska event.
   J. prove that World War II was part of the cause of the Tunguska event.

39. The passage states that the shockwave from the Tunguska event took place:

   A. minutes before the event.
   B. a decade after the mysterious blast.
   C. seconds after a flash of light.
   D. directly before the sound of artillery fire.

40. All of the following are facts about the Tunguska event EXCEPT:

   F. The blast was equal to a moderate earthquake.
   G. The damage and loss of life was unrivaled.
   H. The shockwave had a radius of 300 kilometers.
   J. Scientists found a high level of nickel relative to iron.

99

STOP! END OF TEST 3.

SCIENCE TEST
35 Minutes—40 Questions

DIRECTIONS: There are six passages in this test. Each passage is followed by several questions. After reading a passage, choose the best answer to each question and fill in the corresponding oval on your answer document. You may refer to the passages as often as necessary. You are NOT permitted to use a calculator on this test.

Passage I

A team of researchers aim to study the aerodynamics of different shapes under different conditions. Two experiments are conducted and outlined below.

Experiment 1

In this experiment, the researchers choose various rods of uniform cross-sectional shape to be used in the wind tunnel. For each shape, three trials are conducted in which the wind velocity is held constant at 50 meters per second for each trial. Using a force gauge, the drag force for each trial in calculated is Newtons (N). The researchers then use this drag force to calculate the drag coefficient. This coefficient is an inherent quality of the shape at a certain set of conditions. The data from Experiment 1 is shown in Table 1 below.

Table 1			
Shape	Trial	Drag Coefficient	Drag Force (N)
Circle	1	1.27	102.2
	2	1.32	110.5
	3	1.29	105.8
Square	4	2.03	134.5
	5	1.89	132.3
	6	1.93	133.9
Triangle	7	1.51	122.6
	8	1.47	123.3
	9	1.53	120.0
Ellipse	10	0.62	74.3
	11	0.57	76.7
	12	0.55	77.6

Experiment 2

In this experiment, the researchers aim to study how changing the dimensions of a certain shape, and changing the wind conditions, affect the drag coefficient. The researchers modify the dimensions of the ellipse by varying its length (L) and diameter (D) in accordance with the image below.

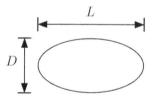

Figure 1

The researchers also run experiments under *laminar air flows* (characterized by an ordered, slower air flow) and *turbulent air flows* (characterized by a chaotic, faster air flow). The data from Experiment 2 is shown in Table 2 below.

Table 2		
$\frac{L}{D}$	Laminar flow drag coefficient	Turbulent flow drag coefficient
0.5	0.70	0.40
1.0	0.35	0.35
2.0	0.20	0.25
4.0	0.10	0.20
8.0	0.05	0.15

1. According to the results of Experiments 1 and 2, the highest drag coefficient recorded was:

   A. 0.70.
   B. 1.32.
   C. 1.53.
   D. 2.03.

2. One of the researchers proposes that any shape will possess an innate *critical* $\frac{L}{D}$ *number*, in which both the laminar flow coefficient and turbulent flow coefficient are equal. Based on the results of Experiment 2, the ellipse's critical $\frac{L}{D}$ number is most likely:

   F. 0.5.
   G. 1.0.
   H. 2.0.
   J. 8.0.

3. The drag coefficient is an inherent quality of the shape at a certain set of conditions. Based on the results of the experiments, the drag coefficients were recorded to the nearest:

   A. hundredths place.
   B. tenths place.
   C. ones place.
   D. tens place.

4. Do the results in Experiment 1 support the hypothesis that, at a given set of environmental conditions, ellipses result in the smallest drag coefficient of the four shapes tested?

   F. Yes, because ellipses resulted in the largest drag coefficients over the three trials.
   G. Yes, because ellipses resulted in the smallest drag coefficients over the three trials.
   H. No, because ellipses resulted in the largest drag coefficients over the three trials.
   J. No, because ellipses resulted in the smallest drag coefficients over the three trials.

5. The results of Experiment 2 support the conclusion that as $\frac{L}{D}$ increases:

   A. The laminar flow drag coefficient increased while the turbulent flow drag coefficient decreased.
   B. The laminar flow drag coefficient decreased while the turbulent flow drag coefficient increased.
   C. The laminar flow drag coefficient and the turbulent flow drag coefficient both decreased.
   D. The laminar flow drag coefficient and the turbulent flow drag coefficient both increased.

6. The researchers conducted the experiment in a wind tunnel that had been shielded on all sides from ambient weather conditions. Which of the following is the most likely reason why the researchers chose to conduct the experiment in this wind tunnel?

   F. To ensure the shapes used in the experiment would not deteriorate from the weather
   G. To control the wind velocity inside the wind tunnel
   H. To block incoming solar radiation from disturbing the experimental setup
   J. To keep the moisture level inside the wind tunnel at a minimum

7. Suppose the *Lift Coefficient* is defined as the lift force divided by the drag force. Based on the data, would one be justified in concluding that the square rod has the highest Lift Coefficient?

   A. Yes, because the lift force provided by the square rod was the highest of all the shapes.
   B. Yes, because the drag force provided by the square rod was the lowest of all the shapes.
   C. No, because the drag force provided by the square rod was the highest of all the shapes.
   D. No, because the information provided is insufficient to determine the lift coefficient.

Passage II

A *pegmatite* is a crystalline igneous rock formation composed of phaneritic igneous rock. A pegmatite rock formation consists of igneous rocks that are composed of many different crystals ranging from 2.5 cm to 10 m.

A pegmatite rock formation was mined to find the ranges of valuable crystal composition and size. Figure 1 shows the percent by mass of the crystals by size. Figure 2 shows the percent by mass of the crystals by depth below the surface. Table 1 shows relative data of the crystals normally found.

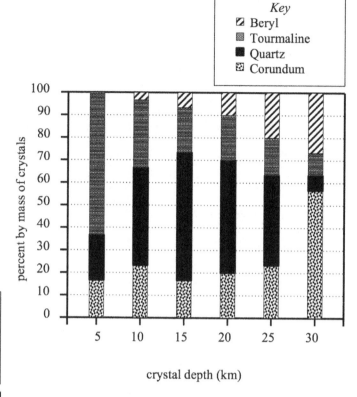

crystal depth (km)

Figure 2

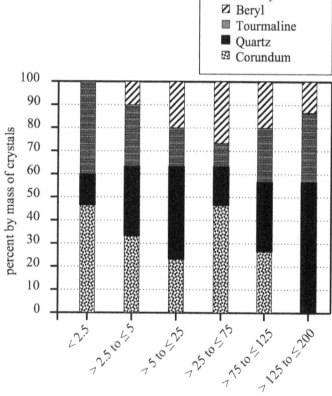

crystal diameter size (cm)

Figure 1

Table 1			
Name	Mohs Hardness	Crystal system	Chemical Formula
Beryl	7.5-8	Hexagonal	$Be_3Al_2(SiO_3)_6$
Corundum	8	Trigonal	Al_2O_3
Tourmaline	7.5-8	Trigonal	SiO_2
Quartz	7.5-8	Trigonal	$Na(Al)_3(BO_3)(OH)_4$

In contrast to the Mohs Hardness rating in Table 1, the *Brinell Hardness Number* (BHN) may be used. The BHN is determined by manually indenting the material of interest with a material of known quantities. The equation for BHN is given below:

$$BHN = \frac{2F}{\pi D(D - \sqrt{D^2 - d^2})}$$

where F is the applied force (N), D is the diameter of indenter (mm), and d is the diameter of the indentation (mm).

8. According to Figure 1, as the crystal diameter size increases, the percent by mass of Tourmaline:

F. increased only.
G. decreased only.
H. increased, then decreased.
J. decreased, then increased.

9. Gemstones with trigonal crystal systems often allow for useful optical properties. Optical properties are important because they are responsible for, but not limited to, luster, brilliance, and color. Which crystal would NOT be a good candidate for these properties?

A. Beryl
B. Corundum
C. Quartz
D. Tourmaline

10. Based on the results of the study, at which depth did Tourmaline exist at the majority of the percent mass of crystals?

F. 5 km
G. 10 km
H. 15 km
J. 20 km

11. Based on the results of the study, at what crystal diameter size was Beryl NOT discovered?

A. < 2.5 cm
B. > 2.5 to ≤ 5 cm
C. > 5 to ≤ 25 cm
D. > 25 to ≤ 75 cm

12. Consider the information in Figures 1 and 2 regarding the crystals with diameters ranging from > 125 to ≤ 200 cm and existing at a depth of 30 km. Crystals of what kind accounted for more than 50 percent by mass of the crystals in diameter and depth, respectively?

F. Quartz and Beryl
G. Quartz and Tourmaline
H. Quartz and Corundum
J. Beryl and Tourmaline

13. The Brinell Hardness Number classifies the hardness of materials and is widely used for hardness testing in engineering. A mineral with which of the following parameters will yield the largest Brinell Hardness Number?

	$F(N)$	D (mm)	d (mm)
A.	10	3	1
B.	10	3	2
C.	20	3	1
D.	30	2	1

Passage III

Graduate students experimentally determine the unitless quantities μ_s and μ_k, the coefficient of static friction and kinetic friction, for different materials.

Friction acts upon an object when it is placed on an inclined plane both when the object is static and sliding. When the object is in static equilibrium, the force of static friction is equal to the component force of gravity pulling the object down the plane. When the object is moving, the force of kinetic friction will act opposite the component force of gravity. The kinetic friction will always be less than the component force of gravity. The static and kinetic frictional forces may be calculated by multiplying the weight of an object by the constants μ_s and μ_k.

In each experiment, the students place a different object on top of a long board that is attached to a table with a hinge (Figure 1). The object is then placed 1 meter above the attached end of the board. The students slowly began raising the free end of the board.

Figure 1

When the object began to slide down the inclined plane, a sensor would track the object's motion and give the time taken for the object to travel down the 1 meter board. The students also measured the θ at which the board began to move. Using θ, time and distance. the students were able to calculate μ_s and μ_k.

In Figure 2 below, a free-body diagram is shown of the object as it accelerates down the inclined plane. The mass of the object is represented by m and the acceleration due to gravity is represented by g. Arrows indicate the appropriate force vector.

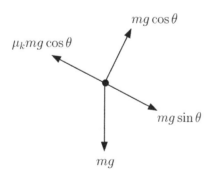

Figure 2

Using Newton's second law, it may be found that the net acceleration of the box moving down the plane is

$$a = g[\sin(\theta)) - \mu_k \cos(\theta)]$$

where $0 \leq \theta \leq 90$.

Experiment 1

The students tested several blocks of 3 different materials: glass, wood, and Teflon. Each block had a mass of 1 kg and the long board used was made of a plane of steel. The blocks were placed on the long board at various angles, θ, and allowed to slide down to the bottom. The duration of the block's slide, t, was recorded and the coefficient of static friction and coefficient of kinetic friction were calculated. The results of their experiment are shown in Table 1.

Table 1				
Object	θ (°)	μ_s	μ_k	t (s)
Glass	32	0.62	0.41	0.65
Wood	21	0.39	0.26	0.79
Teflon	10	0.14	0.05	1.45

Experiment 2

The procedure from Experiment 1 was repeated, except the long board used was made of a plane of glass. The results of the experiment are shown in Table 2.

Table 2				
Object	θ (°)	μ_s	μ_k	t (s)
Glass	32	0.82	0.78	0.60
Wood	21	0.49	0.34	0.69
Teflon	10	0.33	0.30	0.87

Experiment 3

The procedure from Experiment 1 was repeated, except three wooden blocks of different masses were tested and the angle of the board was held constant at 25°. The results of the experiment are shown in Table 3.

Table 3				
Mass (kg)	θ (°)	μ_s	μ_k	t (s)
0.5	25	0.52	0.33	0.69
1.0	25	0.52	0.33	0.69
1.5	25	0.52	0.33	0.70

104

GO ON TO THE NEXT PAGE.

14. Suppose a student stated that objects of the same material but different masses will yield different values of μ_s and μ_k. Do the results of Experiment 3 verify this statement?

    F. Yes, because as mass increases the values of μ_s and μ_k both increase.

    G. Yes, because as mass increases the values of μ_s and μ_k both decrease.

    H. No, because as mass increases the value of μ_s increases while the value of μ_k decreases.

    J. No, because as mass increases the values of μ_s and μ_k remain constant.

15. Based on Experiments 1-2, which of the following graphs best represents the relationship between θ and μ_s?

A.
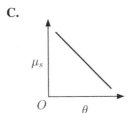

C.

B.
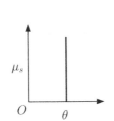

D.

16. If, in Experiment 1, an additional trial had been completed with an object that moved at an angle of 26°, μ_s would have most likely been:

    F. less than 0.14.
    G. between 0.14 and 0.39.
    H. between 0.39 and 0.62.
    J. greater than 0.62.

17. For all block-board material interactions tested in Experiments 1-3, which two materials yielded the smallest value of μ_k?

    A. A glass block on a steel board
    B. A Teflon block on a steel board
    C. A wooden block on a glass board
    D. A glass block on a glass board

18. As the object is sliding down the plane, two forces act on the object: the force due to gravity and the force due to kinetic friction. Which of these forces must have been stronger?

    F. The force due to gravity, because the object moved down the plane

    G. The force due to gravity, because the object moved up the plane

    H. The force due to kinetic friction, because the object moved down the plane

    J. The force due to kinetic friction, because the object moved up the plane

19. According to Figure 2, Experiments 1-3, and the equation for acceleration a, which of the following would lead to the greatest acceleration of the block down the plane?

    A. Increasing mass (m) and decreasing θ
    B. Increasing mass (m) and decreasing μ_k
    C. Increasing θ and decreasing μ_k
    D. Increasing μ_k and decreasing θ

20. Based on Experiments 1-3 and information provided in the passage, which force will be largest for a given object sliding down a plane?

    F. The force of inertia
    G. The force of static friction
    H. The force of kinetic friction
    J. The force of the weight of the object

Passage IV

Glycated hemoglobin (known as HbA1C), is a form of the blood carrying protein hemoglobin (Hb). Two studies, one with humans and one with rats, examined the effect of sugar consumption on HbA1C.

Hemoglobin is a four subunit protein present in red blood cells that is responsible for the transport of molecular oxygen (O_2) throughout the body. Due to Hb's quaternary structure, there are many functional groups that are vulnerable to oxidation by plasma glucose. An example of this reaction is shown below.

$$C_6H_{12}O_6 + H_2N-Hb \rightarrow HbA1C + H_2O$$

Each molecule of Hemoglobin may be oxidized by up to 20 molecules of glucose ($C_6H_{12}O_6$). The oxidized Hb is HbA1C.

Study 1

A food-and-drink questionnaire was given to 1,213 adult men who had an average age of 57.3 yr. Each man was assigned to 1 of 5 groups according to his sugar consumption. The average HbA1C for each group is shown in Figure 1.

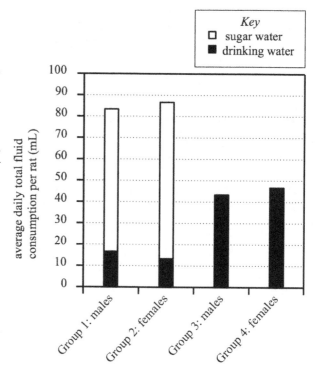

Note: Bars are stacked.

Figure 2

Study 3

At the end of the 50 days, the average HbA1C level was measured for each Group from Study 2. Figure 3 shows, for each group, the average HbA1C on Day 50.

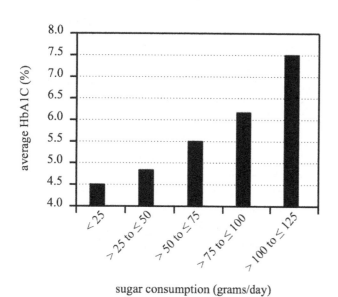

Figure 1

Study 2

Sixty 12-week old rats were divided into 4 groups: Groups 1 and 2 consisted of 20 male and female rats, respectively; Groups 3 and 4 consisted of 10 male and female rats, respectively. Each rat in Groups 1 and 2 was provided with unlimited supplies of solid rat food, drinking water, and sugar water for 50 days. Each rat in groups 3 and 4 was provided with unlimited supplies of the rat food and drinking water, but no sugar water, for 50 days. Figure 2 shows, for each group, the average daily total fluid consumption per rat.

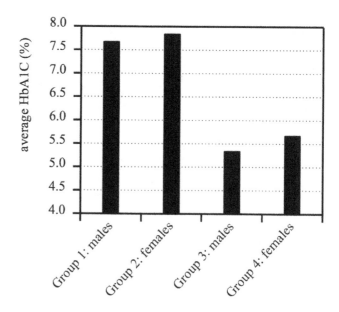

Figure 3

GO ON TO THE NEXT PAGE.

21. Based on the results of Study 2, on average, did male rats or female rats consume more sugar per day?

    A. Male rats; Group 1 rats, on average, consumed more sugar water per day than did Group 2 rats.
    B. Male rats; Group 2 rats, on average, consumed more sugar water per day than did Group 1 rats.
    C. Female rats; Group 2 rats, on average, consumed more sugar water per day than did Group 1 rats.
    D. Female rats; Group 1 rats, on average, consumed more sugar water per day than did Group 2 rats.

22. When unaltered, Hb is an enzyme composed of amino acids. Hb is most likely considered a:

    F. lipid.
    G. carbohydrate.
    H. nucleic acid.
    J. protein.

23. According to Study 2, what is the most likely reason that the average daily fluid consumption per rat in Group 4 was approximately half that of the average daily total fluid consumption per rat in Group 2?

    A. There were half as many rats in Group 2 as were in Group 4.
    B. There were half as many rats in Group 4 as were in Group 2.
    C. The average daily total fluid consumption per rat was lower for Group 4 rats because they were provided sugar water, and rats do not consume sugar water.
    D. The average daily fluid consumption per rat was higher for Group 2 because they preferred sugar water over drinking water.

24. In Study 1, the greatest number of men were assigned to the group that consumed how many servings of sugar per week?

    F. > 25 to ≤ 50
    G. > 50 to ≤ 75
    H. > 100 to ≤ 125
    J. Cannot be determined by the information given

25. Which 2 groups of rats served as the control groups in Study 2?

    A. Groups 1 and 2
    B. Groups 1 and 4
    C. Groups 2 and 3
    D. Groups 3 and 4

26. What is the most appropriate conclusion that may be drawn based on the results of Study 3?

    F. Rats that consume more sugar water have lower levels of HbA1C.
    G. Rats that consume more sugar water have higher levels of HbA1C.
    H. Rats that do not consume sugar water are healthier than rats that do consume sugar water.
    J. Rats will always drink more sugar water than drinking water if they are given both.

27. In a separate experiment, 3 mol of Hb are mixed with 100 mol of glucose in a test tube. According to the balanced chemical equation in the passage, assuming the reaction goes to completion, how many moles of HbA1c are created and how many mole of glucose remain?

    A. 20 mol HbA1c and 80 mol glucose
    B. 40 mol HbA1c and 60 mol glucose
    C. 60 mol HbA1c and 40 mol glucose
    D. 80 mol HbA1c and 20 mol glucose

Passage V

Parkinson's disease is a disorder of the central nervous system characterized by the degeneration of neurons. The cause of Parkinson's disease is generally unknown, but believed to be a product of both genetic and environmental symptoms. Four scientists discuss the possible causes of the disease.

Scientist 1

Parkinson's disease is caused by one or more mutations of specific genes. When a *missense* mutation is apparent in the gene SNCA, the alpha-synuclein protein will be over expressed, leading to the development of Lewy bodies. Significant concentrations of Lewy bodies in nervous tissue is known to be a characteristic feature of neuronal cell death and dementia. While other forms of the mutation may be just as harmful, the *silent* mutation is known to produce a functional form of the protein that does not lead to the production of Lewy bodies.

Scientist 2

Environmental toxins are responsible for causing Parkinson's disease. Organochlorine pesticides, for instance, have been shown to induce missense mutations of the SNCA gene. Individuals who often work in areas where Organochlorine pesticides are frequently sprayed indicate significantly higher levels of Lewy bodies as compared to age matched controls.

Scientist 3

The progression of Parkinson's disease is characterized by exposure to environmental toxins. Frequent exposure to the toxin *beta-Methyamino-L-alanine*, or BMAA, has been shown to lead to the progression of Lewy bodies and thus symptoms of Parkinson's disease. BMAA is an amino acid that may be incorrectly incorporated into human proteins in the place of L-Serine. This incorporation leads to significant concentrations of misfolded proteins that tend to aggregate within nerve cells.

Scientist 4

Parkinson's disease is caused by an overabundance of Reactive Oxygen Species (ROS). Accumulation of ROS in the brain has been noted to damage neurons when present in high concentrations. While the human antioxidant glutathione is known to quench the harmful effects of ROS, exposure to environmental toxins such as BMAA has been shown to decrease glutathione's antioxidant capacity.

28. Both Scientist 1 and 2 would agree that Parkinson's disease is most likely caused by:

    F. decreased levels of glutathione.
    G. exposure to high concentrations of organochlorinated pesticides.
    H. missense mutations of neuronal proteins.
    J. presence of significant concentrations of Lewy Bodies.

29. Recent scientific studies have conclusively shown that significant concentrations of ROS do lead to the progression of Parkinson's disease. These findings would most likely *strengthen* the viewpoint(s) of:

    A. Scientist 3 only.
    B. Scientist 4 only.
    C. both Scientist 3 and Scientist 4.
    D. none of the scientists.

30. Based on Scientist 4's discussion, it is assumed that in healthy individuals the antioxidant glutathione is able to:

    F. increase the levels of BMAA.
    G. decrease the harmful effects of ROS.
    H. increase the concentration of Lewy Bodies.
    J. decrease the total amounts of missense mutations in cells.

31. Thialysine is an environmental toxin that has the ability to be substituted for *L-Lysine* in human proteins. Continual substitution of thialysine for *L-Lysine* has been shown to lead to dangerously high levels of misfolded proteins in nerve cells. This information supports information presented by:

    A. Scientist 1.
    B. Scientist 2.
    C. Scientist 3.
    D. Scientist 4.

32. Two additional environmental toxins are identified: PCBs and CFCs. PCBs have been shown to increase the presence of *missense* mutations, whereas CFCs have been shown to increase the presence of *silent* mutations. Exposure to which toxin is most likely more harmful?

    F. PCBs, because missense mutations lead to production of Lewy bodies.
    G. CFCs, because silent mutations lead to the production of Lewy bodies.
    H. PCBs, because missense mutations lead to the production of ROS.
    J. CFCs, because silent muations lead to the the production of ROS.

33. *Sulforaphane*, a naturally occurring organic molecule found in cruciferous vegetables such as broccoli, has been shown to boost levels of glutathione in both healthy and sick patients. Treating patients with high concentrations of Sulforaphane would most likely cause which of the following to occur?

A. Decrease the effects of ROS
B. Convert missense mutations to silent mutations
C. Incorporate L-Serine into proteins over BMAA
D. Increase the amount of Lewy bodies

34. Which of the following reasons most likely explains why BMAA may be incorporated into human proteins instead of L-Serine?

F. Both BMMA and L-Serine cause the production of Lewy bodies
G. Their concentrations are both increased by ROS
H. BMMA and L-Serine resemble each other structurally as molecules
J. BMAA is a natural by-product of glutathione antioxidant activity

GO ON TO THE NEXT PAGE.

Passage VI

When a gas is enclosed within a specified volume, that gas exerts a specific pressure, P, on the inner walls of its container. P depends on the temperature, T, the volume of the container, V, and the type of gas within the container.

Table 1 below gives P, in atmospheres (atm), under various combinations of T in degrees Celsius (°C), V, in liters (L), and type of gas as either oxygen (O_2), Nitrogen (N_2), Argon (Ar), or Neon (Ne).

Table 1				
Combination	T (°C)	V (L)	Gas	P (kPa)
1	30.0	22.4	O_2	21.3
2	40.0	22.4	O_2	23.8
3	50.0	22.4	O_2	26.4
4	60.0	22.4	O_2	28.9
5	30.0	22.4	O_2	20.9
6	30.0	44.8	O_2	15.6
7	30.0	67.2	O_2	10.3
8	30.0	89.6	O_2	5.6
9	30.0	22.4	O_2	21.2
10	30.0	22.4	N_2	21.4
11	30.0	22.4	Ar	21.2
12	30.0	22.4	Ne	21.3

Gases rarely act ideally. For instance, a gas molecule with bond dipoles has the opportunity to create temporary weak repulsive forces with adjacent molecules. Because the gas molecules would then be pushed farther apart from each other than they would be if acting ideally, the measured pressure would then be greater.

The larger the gas molecule, the more volume it takes up and greater the pressure it exerts as well. Thus, a molecule like Xenon, which has a molecular weight of 131.293 amu, behaves much less ideally than Argon, which has a molecular weight of 39.948 amu.

To account for these deviations for ideal behavior, the ideal gas law may be modified to the following equation:

$$\left(P + \frac{n^2 a}{V^2}\right)(V - nb) = nRT$$

where R is the universal gas constant, n is the amount of moles of gas, a is the corrective factor for intermolecular forces, and b is the corrective factor for the volume.

The assumptions made for a gas to follow *ideal behavior* are:

1. Gas molecules take up no volume

2. The movement of gas molecules is continuous and random

3. All collisions of the gas molecules are completely elastic

4. There are no repulsive forces between gas particles

35. According to Table 1, as the volume of the container increases, the pressure of the gas:

   A. increases only.
   B. decreases only.
   C. varies, but with no general trend.
   D. remains the same.

36. Based on Combinations 1-4, the relationship between T and P is best described by which of the following graphs?

F.

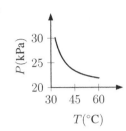

H.

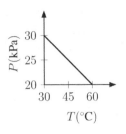

G.

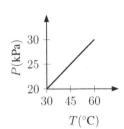

J.

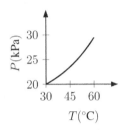

37. A student wanted to create a setup where the pressure of the system will be high. Based on Table 1, the student would choose which of the following values for T and V, and which type of gas, to yield the greatest value for P?

	$T(°)$	V (L)	Gas
A.	30	22.4	Ne
B.	30	89.6	N_2
C.	60	89.6	Ne
D.	60	22.4	N_2

38. If experimental trials were conducted in which Combinations 9-12 were tested, what would be the independent variable?

F. V
G. Gas
H. P
J. T

39. Based on the information provided, which molecule, Xenon (Xe) or Argon (Ar), gives a larger corrective factor b?

A. Xenon, because it has greater volume and thus needs greater correction.
B. Xenon, because it has smaller volume and thus needs less correction.
C. Argon, because it has greater volume and thus needs greater correction.
D. Argon, because it has smaller volume and thus needs less correction.

40. Based on the information provided, what conditions would a gas molecule have the greatest deviation from *ideal behavior*?

F. A small gas molecule with noncontinuous straight-line motion
G. A large gas molecule with noncontinuous straight-line motion
H. A small gas molecule with continuous random motion
J. A large gas molecule with continuous random motion

Energy and the Environment

A technologically and economically advanced society such as ours requires tremendous amounts of energy to function. The forms of fuel presently used to provide this energy come from non-renewable sources that harm the environment. Critics say that the damage caused by these fuels outweighs their importance in powering our society, while others say that it is a necessary price to be paid for the wealth and comfort we enjoy. How should we think about the balance between fuel needs and environmental concerns?

Read and carefully consider these perspectives. Each suggests a particular way of thinking about teaching and expertise.

Perspective 1	Perspective 2	Perspective 3
The environmental damage caused by our energy use threatens the future existence of our society. We must shift to alternative, renewable sources no matter the immediate economic cost.	Our society depends on the uninterrupted availability of energy sources to keep growing. The risks of changing to different sources of energy outweigh the impact of current fuels on the environment.	A society that requires fuels on this scale is unsustainable. Society itself must change and learn to thrive on lower levels of energy altogether.

Essay Task

Write a unified, coherent essay in which you evaluate multiple perspectives on energy and the environment. In your essay, be sure to:

- analyze and evaluate the perspectives given
- state and develop your own perspective on the issue
- explain the relationship between your perspective and those given

Your perspective may be in full agreement with any of the others, in partial agreement, or wholly different. Whatever the case, support your ideas with logical reasoning and detailed, persuasive examples.

ACT2 - A0316

Practice Test

ENGLISH TEST
45 Minutes—75 Questions

DIRECTIONS: In the five passages that follow, certain words and phrases are underlined and numbered. In the right-hand column, you will find alternatives for the underlined part. In most cases, you are to choose the one that best expresses the idea, makes the statement appropriate for standard written English, or is worded most consistently with the style and tone of the passage as a whole. If you think the original version is best, choose "NO CHANGE." In some cases, you will find in the right-hand column a question about the underlined part. You are to choose the best answer to the question.

You will also find questions about a section of the passage, or about the passage as a whole. These questions do not refer to an underlined portion of the passage, but rather are identified by a number or numbers in a box.

For each question, choose the alternative you consider best and fill in the corresponding oval on your answer document. Read each passage through once before you begin to answer the questions that accompany it. For many of the questions, you must read several sentences beyond the question to determine the answer. Be sure that you have read far enough ahead each time you choose an alternative.

PASSAGE I

Tracing the Oldest Trees

<u>Walk</u> through the Inyo National Forest in
1

<u>Inyo California</u>, you can't help but feel a sense of wonder.
2
Trees stretch as far as the eye can see. No two are exactly

<u>alike; being that some are mere saplings</u>, while others have
3

existed for <u>centuries — wow!</u> Hidden within this crush of
4

trees sits the oldest living thing in the <u>world; a</u> Bristlecone
5
Pine.

1. **A.** NO CHANGE
   B. Picture walking
   C. Walking
   D. You walk

2. **F.** NO CHANGE
   G. Inyo California
   H. Inyo, California
   J. Inyo, California,

3. **A.** NO CHANGE
   B. alike; some
   C. alike some
   D. alike, some

4. **F.** NO CHANGE
   G. centuries — that's a long time!
   H. centuries, which is a lengthy amount of time.
   J. centuries.

5. **A.** NO CHANGE
   B. world. A
   C. world: a
   D. world a

GO ON TO THE NEXT PAGE.

[1] Just how old is this tree? [2] The idea behind dendrochronology is: trees grow in ring formations,
                              6

and by counting these rings, scientists were able to determine
                                            7

the age of any tree. [3] Further investigation of a trees' ring's
                                                   8
can reveal stories of climate change, droughts, and

other weather patterns in its surrounding environment.

[4] Originally, scientists had to cut down trees to fully study

these rings, but now the trees reveal their secrets to scientists
             9
in a more environmentally friendly way. [5] The process by
                        9
which scientists determine a tree's age is called

dendrochronology. [6] Once the sample has been obtained,

scientists seal up the hole for preventing disease. | 11 |
                              10

Scientists first assumed that the tallest, best-situated trees

would be the oldest: A mild climate with regular rain should

allow trees to grow without restraint for centuries upon

centuries. However, Edmund Shulman, a well-known
                                   12
dendrochronologist, thought otherwise. He believed that trees
       12
thriving in the most adverse conditions would be more

likely to withstand natural disasters, droughts, and

the testing of times. To prove his hypothesis, Shulman
       13

6. F. NO CHANGE
   G. dendrochronology being:
   H. dendrochronology is simple;
   J. dendrochonology;

7. A. NO CHANGE
   B. are
   C. should of been
   D. would of been

8. F. NO CHANGE
   G. trees' rings
   H. tree's ring's
   J. tree's rings

9. Given all the choices are true, which one most specifically describes the new process used by scientists?
   A. NO CHANGE
   B. but now a modern and less invasive process has been invented.
   C. but now they do so with a specific and localized technique.
   D. but modern scientists are able to take out straw-sized samples from the tree using a tool that resembles a corkscrew.

10. F. NO CHANGE
    G. to prevent disease.
    H. in order to preventing disease.
    J. in order for disease to be prevented.

11. For the sake of the logic and coherence of this paragraph, sentence 5 should be placed:
    A. where it is now.
    B. before sentence 1.
    C. after sentence 1.
    D. after sentence 3.

12. F. NO CHANGE
    G. Shulman, a well-known dendrochronologist
    H. Shulman a well-known dendrochronologist,
    J. Shulman; a well-known dendrochronologist

13. A. NO CHANGE
    B. the testing of time.
    C. the test of time.
    D. the time that is tested.

sampled trees from all across the driest forests in the United States. |14| Eventually, he landed at the Inyo National Forest. There, he found one tree that clocked in at 4,832 years old, the oldest known tree at that time. Years later, he found an even older one, more than 5,000 years old.

Today, while you can visit the vast array of Bristlecone Pines—including the oldest ones—at the Inyo National Forest, you won't find a fancy plaque identifying the oldest living tree. It hides anonymously, among the others, to protect it from harm. Then, you might stumble upon the oldest living
 15
tree—until somebody else discovers an older one, that is.

14. If the writer were to delete the word "driest" from the preceding sentence, the sentence would primarily lose:

    F. a detail that relates the sentence to the hypothesis mentioned elsewhere in the paragraph.
    G. an indication of how dry the Inyo National Forest is.
    H. an example of the species of trees Shulman tested.
    J. an unnecessary detail that distracts from the main point of the passage.

15. A. NO CHANGE
    B. In essence,
    C. Consequently,
    D. Nevertheless,

PASSAGE II

Amateur Night at the Apollo

Up in Harlem, past Central Park and Columbia University, sits a New York City landmark: the Apollo
                                                        16
Theater. Many have heard of this great theater, few realize
                  17
just how instrumental it, and its famous Amateur Night, have been to the last century of American pop culture.

[1] Today, the Apollo is best known for showcasing
     18

African-American comedians and musicians, but it's origins
                                                  19
were quite different. [2] The building opened in 1914 as Hutig & Seamon's New Burlesque Theater, and, like many of its time, the theater banned African-American patrons and

16. F. NO CHANGE
    G. landmark
    H. landmark, it is
    J. landmark;

17. A. NO CHANGE
    B. Many having heard of this great theater, although,
    C. While many have heard of this great theater,
    D. Many have heard of this great theater; but,

18. F. NO CHANGE
    G. In fact,
    H. However,
    J. Indeed,

19. A. NO CHANGE
    B. their
    C. its'
    D. its

performers. [20] [3] Rather than close shop for good, the

theater's owner decided to change tactics and <u>instead</u> fill a
21
much-needed entertainment gap. [4] He reopened the theater

as the 125th Street Apollo Theater, producing variety shows

directly marketed towards Harlem's growing

African-American community. [5] In 1933, however, a

citywide campaign against burlesque theaters forced the

theater to close its doors. [6] The Apollo featured a large

variety of performers, <u>being</u> comedians, musicians, and tap
22
dancers, all of whom aided in making the 125th Street Apollo

Theater the premiere spot for entertainment in Harlem.

[7] <u>The Apollo became the largest employer of</u>
23
<u>African-American theater workers in 1937 and</u>
23
<u>backstage positions in the nation.</u> [24]
23

20. If the writer were to delete the phrase 'African-American' from the preceding sentence, the sentence would primarily lose

F. a phrase that distracts from the passage's meaning.
G. information necessary to understanding the problematic origins of the Apollo Theater.
H. information clarifying that African-Americans were not the only people banned from the theater.
J. information about the only people who lived in Harlem in 1914.

21. All of the following would be acceptable placements for the underlined portion EXCEPT

A. where it is now.
B. after the word *theater's*.
C. after the word *change*.
D. after the word *entertainment*.

22. F. NO CHANGE
G. including
H. including,
J. such as:

23. A. NO CHANGE
B. The Apollo was the largest African-American employer of theater workers and the only theater to hire African-American backstage workers in the nation by 1937.
C. Then, in 1937, the Apollo had the largest employer of African-American theater and backstage workers in the nation.
D. By 1937, the Apollo was the largest employer of African-American theater workers and the only theater to hire African-Americans for backstage positions.

24. For the sake of the logic and coherence of this paragraph, Sentence 5 should be placed:

F. where it is now.
G. before Sentence 2.
H. before Sentence 3.
J. after sentence 6.

What makes the Apollo so enduringly popular? One
<u> </u>
25

of the theater's main draws is <u>it's</u> famous Amateur Night.
26
Every Wednesday, amateur performers take to the stage for a

distinctly vaudevillian audience: Audience members are

encouraged <u>to cheer for acts they enjoy and heckling</u> those
27
that disappoint. The performers who draw "boos" from the

audience are then literally swept off of the stage by a man with

a broom. Regular open auditions for amateur night <u>ensures</u>
28

that the Amateur Night audiences <u>always gets the opportunity</u>
29
<u>to put the newest and freshest talent to the test.</u> Past winners
29
of Amateur Night include such American legends as Ella

Fitzgerald, Jimi Hendrix, and James Brown. The number of

careers that have been launched or celebrated at the Apollo

Theater seems endless. Names like Aretha Franklin, Michael

Jackson, Stevie Wonder, and Hall & Oates grace the walls of

the theater's Legends Hall of Fame. <u>Today, young hopefuls</u>
30
<u>can still put their skills to the test every Wednesday by taking</u>
30
<u>to the Apollo's stage, where cheers can make a career, and</u>
30
<u>heckling can end one.</u>
30

25. Which choice most effectively introduces the following paragraph?
  A. NO CHANGE
  B. How many famous people have gotten their start at the Apollo?
  C. Where is the Apollo?
  D. What does the Apollo look like?

26. F. NO CHANGE
  G. one's
  H. their
  J. its

27. A. NO CHANGE
  B. by cheering for the acts they enjoy and heckling
  C. to cheer for the acts they enjoy, thereby heckling
  D. to cheer for the acts they enjoy and heckle

28. F. NO CHANGE
  G. ensure
  H. will ensure
  J. has ensured

29. Given that all the choices are true, which one is most relevant to the focus of the paragraph?
  A. NO CHANGE
  B. always goes home having seen many varying acts.
  C. is constantly challenged by performers.
  D. gets the chance to see veteran performers live.

30. Which of the following choices best concludes the essay?
  F. NO CHANGE
  G. Now, the Apollo is still located in the same historic building in Harlem.
  H. Anybody can sign up for Amateur Night, even now.
  J. These people are famous now, but at one time they weren't.

PASSAGE III

Podcasts: News and Stories on Demand

[1]

Walking out of my house this morning, my headphones
immersed me in a captivating story with the push of a button.
                    31
However, I wasn't listening to a book on tape or to my favorite

musical soundtrack. I was listening to a podcast.
                                        32
Podcasts are audio shows that are available in digital

format. The word "podcast" is a portmanteau or a mash-up,
                                        33

of the words "iPod" and "broadcast," which make sense since
                                                    34
most people listen to podcasts on portable devices like iPods

or smartphones.

Many podcasts are just repurposed radio shows

which they package for distribution online. Broadcasters like
            35

National Public Radio (NPR) recognizing that more people
                              36
are unavailable to tune into their shows during the allotted

air–times. Therefore, they offer their radio programs in
            37
podcast form, usually at no cost, in an effort to gain a wider

audience. They gave programs like "Radiolab" and
                    38
"This American Life" huge followings because of that.
                            38

Other shows are created explicitly for the podcast

31. A. NO CHANGE
B. my headphones suddenly immersed me,
C. I was suddenly immersed
D. I was suddenly immersed,

32. Which of the following alternatives to the underlined portion would NOT be acceptable?

F. soundtrack: I was listening to a podcast.
G. soundtrack, I was listening to a podcast.
H. soundtrack; I was listening to a podcast.
J. soundtrack—I was listening to a podcast.

33. A. NO CHANGE
B. portmanteau, or, a mash-up
C. portmanteau, or a mash-up
D. portmanteau, or a mash-up,

34. F. NO CHANGE
G. makes scents
H. make scents
J. makes sense

35. A. NO CHANGE
B. who are packaged for distribution online.
C. and they are packaged for distribution online.
D. packaged for distribution online.

36. F. NO CHANGE
G. recognize that most
H. recognizes that most
J. recognizes that more

37. A. NO CHANGE
B. Additionally,
C. Moreover,
D. However, consequently,

38. F. NO CHANGE
G. Huge followings have been gotten by "Radiolab" and "This American Life" because of this practice.
H. Programs like "Radiolab" and "This American Life" have gotten huge followings because of this practice.
J. Practices like this have gotten huge followings for programs, and those include "Radiolab" and "This American Life".

medium. The variety of these podcasts <u>seem endless.</u> Some
³⁹
tell a story over the course of several episodes. Others invite

people to tell their own stories. <u>There is such plethora of</u>
⁴⁰
<u>topics that the options seem infinite.</u> The medium has grown
⁴⁰
so quickly that today, over 100,000 different English-language

podcasts are produced. With that amount of choice, I

sometimes feel like I find a new favorite podcast every day!

[1] It's hard to say exactly why podcasting has become

so <u>popular, part of it must be</u> the ease and accessibility that
⁴¹
streaming affords. [2] Another part is that it's inexpensive. [3]

The only expense to podcast producers is the recording

equipment. [4] This makes it easy for one to create a podcast,

even with a small budget. [5] Almost everybody in the United

States has access to the Internet, so <u>its very easy</u> for podcast
⁴²
producers to distribute their shows to a wide

audience. [43]

Clearly, the accessibility and diversity of podcasts

<u>bodes well</u> for the new medium. We listeners are lucky to be
⁴⁴
living in an age of such creativity. Every day, I wake up

excited to plug in my headphones and to find a new favorite

podcast.

39. **A.** NO CHANGE
    B. seems endless.
    C. seemingly endless.
    D. seemed endless.

40. Which of the following choices most specifically describes the vast array of podcast topics?

    F. NO CHANGE
    G. Podcasts come in all lengths, from sixty minute interviews to five minute snippets.
    H. Some podcasts have regular hosts, while others play with even the most basic rules of the medium and opt for more creative structures.
    J. There are interview and discussion podcasts about science, finance, movies, comedy, parenting, technology, and any other topic you can think of.

41. **A.** NO CHANGE
    B. popular; part of it being
    C. popular. Part of it must be
    D. popular: partially being

42. **F.** NO CHANGE
    G. it's very easy
    H. its' very easy
    J. it's very easily

43. What is the most logical placement for sentence 5?

    A. Where it is now
    B. Before sentence 2
    C. After sentence 2
    D. Before sentence 4

44. **F.** NO CHANGE
    G. bode good
    H. bodes good
    J. bode well

Question 45 asks about the preceding passage as a whole.

45. Suppose the writer's goal had been to write an essay describing how podcasts have changed the world of media. Would this essay accomplish that goal?

    A. Yes, because it focuses on a variety of changes within mainstream media.
    B. Yes, because it dispels the notion that podcasts are a fad.
    C. No, because it doesn't discuss podcasts in the greater context of media.
    D. No, because it doesn't give enough detail about how podcasts are created.

PASSAGE IV

A Sisters' Weekend in the Coolest Borough

When people think of New York City, their thoughts usually turn first to the sights of Manhattan, including: the
Empire State Building, Central Park, Broadway, and Wall
Street. Thusly, when I visit New York, I prefer to hang out in Brooklyn.

My sister Petra moved to Brooklyn after she graduated from college. 48 She wanted to live in New York City and work in the book publishing industry, but found she couldn't afford Manhattan rents on her salary. Now that

she lives in Brooklyn, however, she says she can't imagine living in elsewhere; she much prefers the southeast borough to the bustling streets of Manhattan neighborhoods.

On my spring break last year, I went to visit Petra and seeing the borough for myself. Elaborately planning out

each and every second, some of Petra's favorite spots were included in our itinerary.

The first place we went was Prospect Park. Petra picked up sandwiches from her favorite Italian deli, which specializes in creative versions of classic sandwiches. Once in the park,

46. F. NO CHANGE
    G. to the magnificent sights of Manhattan, including:
    H. to the sights of Manhattan,
    J. to the sights of Manhattan:

47. A. NO CHANGE
    B. However,
    C. For example,
    D. Moreover,

48. The writer is thinking of adding the following sentence:

> From Williamsburg to Far Rockaway, each and every Brooklyn neighborhood has its own sense of self.

Should the writer make this addition there?

    F. Yes, because it adds pertinent information.
    G. Yes, because it gives specific details about the main topic.
    H. No, because it digresses from the main point of the paragraph.
    J. No, because it doesn't mention any Manhattan neighborhoods.

49. A. NO CHANGE
    B. Brooklyn, however
    C. Brooklyn however,
    D. Brooklyn however

50. F. NO CHANGE
    G. and I saw it
    H. but also I went to see
    J. to see the borough

51. A. NO CHANGE
    B. Petra's schedule included some of her favorite spots.
    C. Petra scheduled a myriad of surprises to showcase some her favorite spots.
    D. surprise visits to all of Petra's favorite spots were showcased in our itinerary.

52. F. NO CHANGE
    G. who specializes
    H. whom specializes
    J. where specializing

we had a picnic and people-watched. To our left, a group of five-year-olds were having a birthday party while their parents looked on and kept order. Across the field, a group of
53
older men were playing a lively game of soccer. On the

sidelines of the game, their family's cheered them on as they
54
set up the most elaborate barbecue I had ever seen. A few yards away from us, a young couple sat reading on a blanket on the grass. Petra told me that she comes to hang out in the park whenever she can.

After we left the park, we headed to the Brooklyn Flea Market. The market was basically a schoolyard crammed full of booths. ⸢55⸣ Those booths were filled with everything imaginable: rugs, handmade furniture, vintage clothes, jewelry, and weird knick-knacks. Petra and I strolled from

booth to booth, admiring owners' wares and modeling clothes
56
and jewelry for each other. When Petra tried on a particularly ridiculous jacket, neither of us

was keeping a straight face.
57
At the end of our day, we walked across the Brooklyn

Bridge. The sight of the intricately woven cables and beams
58
silhouetted against the fiery orange sunset took my breath
58
away. As we walked toward the Manhattan side of the river, I
58
started to feel sad. We were walking away from Brooklyn, the

trendiest and coolest part of New York City, and I was going
59
to miss it.

53. Which of the following alternatives to the underlined portion would NOT be acceptable?
  A. parents looking on and kept order.
  B. parents, looking on, kept order.
  C. parents were looking on and keeping order.
  D. parents made sure to look on and keep order.

54. F. NO CHANGE
  G. their families
  H. they're families
  J. they're family's

55. If the writer were to delete the preceding sentence, the essay would primarily lose:
  A. an introduction to a topic that is then discussed more fully.
  B. an off-topic detail that takes away from the main idea.
  C. a reason for the narrator's interest in the market.
  D. a detail that emphasizes the variety of things available for purchase at the market.

56. F. NO CHANGE
  G. admiring owner's
  H. we admired owner's
  J. we admired owners

57. A. NO CHANGE
  B. was able to keep a straight face.
  C. were keeping a straight face.
  D. were able to keep a straight face.

58. Given that all the choices are true, which one gives the most detailed description of the natural and structural beauty of the locale?
  F. NO CHANGE
  G. The colorful sun light of the sunset made me feel at home — even in such a bustling city.
  H. Standing on that bridge with my favorite sister, I wondered at the grandness of it all.
  J. I stood there in wonder, staring intently at the beautiful sunset that welcomed me with warmth.

59. A. NO CHANGE
  B. but most coolest
  C. and the most cool
  D. OMIT the underlined portion

Question 60 asks about the preceding passage as a whole.

60. Suppose the writer's goal had been to write an essay detailing a mix of attractions throughout Brooklyn. Would this essay accomplish that goal?

   F. No, because the author's sister is the main focus of the essay.

   G. Yes, because the essay's tone gives a first-impression encounter of each location.

   H. No, because the essay fails to relate each attraction to Brooklyn's history.

   J. Yes, because the author mentions a wide range of attractions throughout Brooklyn.

PASSAGE V

Abigail Fillmore: First Lady of Education

[1]

The White House, <u>which has been</u> the home and
⁶¹
workplace of over 40 presidents and their families, is a

building steeped in tradition. [A] The <u>building itself, is a</u>
⁶²
thriving representation of history. How could a single

individual leave his or her mark on such an illustrious

building? [B] Just ask Abigail Fillmore, First Lady to

President Millard Fillmore.

[2]

Abigail Fillmore was born to Reverend Lemuel Powers,

a Baptist minister, in New York. [63] Her mother instilled in

Abigail and her brother, their father's love of learning. As she

grew up, Abigail feverishly devoured each and every volume

in her father's personal library.

61. **A.** NO CHANGE
   B. being
   C. has been
   D. which will be

62. **F.** NO CHANGE
   G. building itself
   H. building, itself,
   J. building, being itself,

63. At this point, the writer is considering adding the following phrase (and making the word "Her" lowercase):

> Although Abigail's father died soon after her birth,

Should the writer make this addition there?

   A. Yes, because it clarifies what follows in the sentence.

   B. Yes, because it explains Abigail's motivations later in life.

   C. No, because it distracts from the main focus of the paragraph.

   D. No, because it contradicts information stated earlier in the passage.

She eventually had become a teacher at the New Hope
                    64
Academy in New York. There, she taught an ambitious young

man who had just finished a cloth-making apprenticeship: the
                                           65
soon-to-be President Millard Fillmore. She was his teacher for

six months—though he was only two years her junior—until
                                        66
they married in 1826.

[3]

[1] Abigail continued to teach, which making her the
                                67
first, future First Lady to continue working after marriage.
[2] Meanwhile, Millard's career was evolving to new

heights: he rose swiftly through the political ranks, from
68
attorney to congressional representative and finally to Vice

President of the United States under President Zachary Taylor.

[3] Taylor dying in 1850, Millard Fillmore was sworn in as
             69
the 13th president of the United States, and Abigail became

the First Lady. [4] While her daughter took on these

ceremonial duties, Abigail worked on her own legacy: the

White House Library. [C] [5] Consequently, her poor health
                                     70
made it difficult for her to fulfill many duties of the

position, which were at that time mainly social

obligations. [6] During multiple sessions, Abigail
                    71
would hand-pick and arrange books in the

brand new library, slowly growing it from
                          72

64. F. NO CHANGE
    G. will become
    H. becoming
    J. became

65. A. NO CHANGE
    B. apprenticeship, the
    C. apprenticeship the
    D. apprenticeship; the

66. If the writer were to delete the underlined portion, the
    sentence would primarily lose:
    F. a reference to how long Abigail and Millard
       were married before he became President.
    G. a fact that is later contradicted in the passage.
    H. information that explains a perhaps unexpected
       closeness in age.
    J. a detail that foreshadows the trouble that their
       age difference would cause later in their mar-
       riage.

67. A. NO CHANGE
    B. making her into
    C. letting her be
    D. which made her

68. Which of the following alternatives to the underlined
    portion would be LEAST acceptable?
    F. NO CHANGE
    G. heights; he
    H. heights, he
    J. heights. He

69. A. NO CHANGE
    B. After Taylor's abruptly death in 1850,
    C. In 1850, Taylor abruptly died, the result was that
    D. When Taylor abruptly died in 1850,

70. F. NO CHANGE
    G. Unfortunately,
    H. Indeed,
    J. On the other hand,

71. Given that all of the choices are true, which one most
    specifically demonstrates the amount of time Abigail
    dedicated to building the library?
    A. NO CHANGE
    B. By herself,
    C. From sunset to sunrise,
    D. To achieve her goals,

72. F. NO CHANGE
    G. grew
    H. she grew
    J. growing with

just a couple of volumes, to an impressive collection. [73]

[4]

The library was later relocated and expanded, but the thirst for knowledge that Abigail Fillmore institutionalized within the White House remains strong. [D] Today, the
                                                                74
library includes thousands of volumes.
                    74

73. For the sake of the logic and coherence of this paragraph, Sentence 5 should be placed:

   A. where it is now.
   B. after sentence 1.
   C. after sentence 3.
   D. after sentence 6.

74. Given that all the choices are true, which one best concludes the passage?

   F. NO CHANGE
   G. A lifelong learner and teacher, Abigail Fillmore will be remembered as the first First Lady of education.
   H. When Abigail Fillmore moved to the White House, everything changed.
   J. The room where the White House Library is today used to be filled with buckets and tubs.

Question 75 asks about the preceding passage as a whole.

---

75. Upon reviewing this essay and realizing that some information has been left out, the writer composes the following sentence, incorporating that information:

   > For nearly two hundred years, its hallowed halls have seen the leaders of the United States make decisions that have changed the course of history.

   The most logical and effective place to add this sentence would be at point:

   A. A in Paragraph 1.
   B. B in Paragraph 1.
   C. C in Paragraph 3.
   D. D in Paragraph 4.

END OF TEST 1.
STOP! DO NOT TURN THE PAGE UNTIL TOLD TO DO SO.

MATHEMATICS TEST
60 Minutes — 60 Questions

DIRECTIONS: Solve each problem, choose the correct answer, and then fill in the corresponding oval on your answer document.

Do not linger over problems that take too much time. Solve as many as you can; then return to the others in the time you have left for this test.

You are permitted to use a calculator on this test. You may use your calculator for any problems you choose, but some of the problems may be best done without using a calculator.

Note: Unless otherwise stated, all of the following should be assumed:
1. Figures are NOT necessarily drawn to scale.
2. Geometric figures lie in a plane.
3. The word *line* indicates a straight line.
4. The word *average* indicates arithmetic mean.

---

1. $|(-4)(-3) - 20| =$
    A. -32
    B. -8
    C. 8
    D. 32
    E. 92

2. Choose the answer which puts the numbers in order from least to greatest.
    F. $0.004, 0.03, 1/2$
    G. $0.004, 1/2, 0.03$
    H. $0.03, 0.004, 1/2$
    J. $1/2, 0.03, 0.004$
    K. $1/2, 0.004, 0.03$

3. The price of a stereo decreased from $120 to $90. By what percent did the price decrease?
    A. 25%
    B. 30%
    C. 33%
    D. 70%
    E. 75%

4. For real numbers x, y, and z, the expression $-xa - ya + za$ can be written as a product of a and:
    F. $x - y + z$
    G. $x - y - z$
    H. $-x + y + z$
    J. $-x - y - z$
    K. $-x - y + z$

5. A line contains the points $(2, -5)$ and $(3, 6)$.
    Its slope is:

    A. composite.
    B. negative.
    C. positive.
    D. undefined.
    E. zero.

6. Solve for b: $\dfrac{9b}{2} - 11 = 7$

    F. -4

    G. $-\dfrac{8}{9}$

    H. $\dfrac{8}{9}$

    J. 1

    K. 4

7. What is the least common multiple of 40, 45, and 60?

    A. 180
    B. 280
    C. 360
    D. 1,080
    E. 108,000

8. On a standard (x, y) coordinate plane, point A has the coordinates $(2, -4)$, and the midpoint of segment AB has coordinates $(-1, 1)$. What are the coordinates of point B?

    F. $(-4, \ \ 6)$
    G. $(-3, \ \ 7)$
    H. $(\ \ 1, -3)$
    J. $(\ \ 1, -2)$
    K. $(\ \ 5, -9)$

9. What is the slope of the line whose equation is $3x - 5y = 12$?

    A. -3

    B. $-\dfrac{5}{3}$

    C. $\dfrac{3}{5}$

    D. $\dfrac{5}{3}$

    E. 3

10. On a number line, Point L has coordinate -10, while point M has coordinate -21. What is the distance between L and M?

 F. -31

 G. -11

 H. 11

 J. $15\frac{1}{2}$

 K. 31

11. What is the product of $(2x - 7)$ and $(4x + 1)$?

 A. $-26x - 7$

 B. $8x^2 - 7$

 C. $8x^2 - 56x - 7$

 D. $8x^2 - 30x - 7$

 E. $8x^2 - 26x - 7$

12. 50 is the same fraction of 40 as 60 is of what number?

 F. 45

 G. 48

 H. 50

 J. 70

 K. 75

13. In the diagram below two rays are drawn from point B to points A and C on a circle with center D. $\overline{EF}$ is a diameter and is perpendicular to $\overline{AD}$. $\overline{EDFB}$ is a line. Which of the following has the largest degree measure?

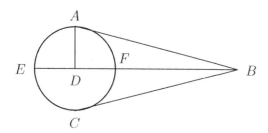

 A. $\overset{\frown}{EA}$

 B. $\overset{\frown}{AC}$

 C. $\angle DAB$

 D. $\angle ABD$

 E. $\angle EBC$

14. When $2(2a - 4b) + c = 0$, which of the following is equivalent to a?

   F. $\dfrac{b}{2} - \dfrac{c}{4}$

   G. $\dfrac{b}{2} - c$

   H. $2b - \dfrac{c}{4}$

   J. $2b - c$

   K. $8b - c$

15. In the figure below, the frame around the shaded picture is of uniform thickness. The width of the frame is 40 centimeters and the width of the picture is 20 centimeters. The length of the frame is 61 centimeters. What is the measure, in centimeters, of the length of the picture?

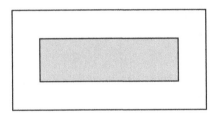

   A. 32
   B. 39
   C. 41
   D. 42
   E. 47

16. In the figure below points E, A, C, and D are colinear. The measures of $\angle EAB$ and $\angle ABC$ are 108° and 62°, respectively. What is the measure of $\angle BCD$?

   F. 46°
   G. 62°
   H. 108°
   J. 134°
   K. 154°

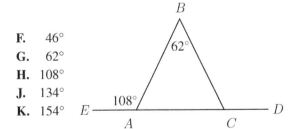

17. An angle θ in a right triangle has a cosine of $\frac{11}{61}$ and a tangent of $\frac{60}{11}$. What is $\sin\theta$?

 A. $\dfrac{11}{\sqrt{3842}}$

 B. $\dfrac{60}{\sqrt{3842}}$

 C. $\dfrac{61}{\sqrt{3842}}$

 D. $\dfrac{11}{60}$

 E. $\dfrac{60}{61}$

18. If $\overline{AB}$ is parallel to $\overline{DE}$, which of the following angles must be congruent to $\angle BAC$?

 F. $\angle AED$
 G. $\angle ECD$
 H. $\angle BCE$
 J. $\angle CDE$
 K. $\angle ABC$

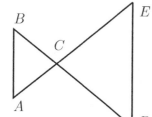

19. Which of the following (x, y) pairs is the solution to the system of equations containing $2x + y = -1$ and $x - 2y = 17$?

 A. $(-4, \quad 7)$
 B. $(-3, \quad 5)$
 C. $(\ 2.8, \quad 6.6)$
 D. $(\ 3, \quad -7)$
 E. $(\ 3.8, -8.6)$

20. Each side of a square is 5 centimeters long. One vertex is at $(-1, 3)$. Which of the following could be another vertex of the square?

 F. $(-5, \quad 3)$
 G. $(-3, \quad 1)$
 H. $(-1, -2)$
 J. $(\ 2, \quad 5)$
 K. $(\ 5, \quad 3)$

21. A set of numbers consists of all of the even integers that are greater than 2 and less than 41. What is the probability that a number picked at random from the set will NOT be divisible by 4?

    A. $\dfrac{1}{4}$

    B. $\dfrac{3}{10}$

    C. $\dfrac{9}{19}$

    D. $\dfrac{10}{19}$

    E. $\dfrac{3}{4}$

22. In the figure given, $\overline{AE} \parallel \overline{DC}$ and B is the intersection point of $\overline{DE}$ and $\overline{AC}$. What is the length of $\overline{AC}$?

    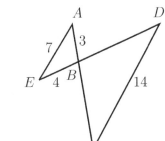

    F. 6
    G. 8
    H. 9
    J. 11
    K. It cannot be determined
        from the information given.

23. The perimeter of a rectangle is 30 cm. and the area of the same rectangle is 36 cm^2. What is the length of the shorter side of the rectangle?

    A. 2 cm
    B. 3 cm
    C. 4 cm
    D. 6 cm
    E. 12 cm

24. Observation of a family of rabbits on Farmer Jim's Rabbit Ranch has shown that the population of rabbits doubles every 6 months. Given an initial population of 6 rabbits, which of the following would be closest to the number of rabbits in the colony after 1.5 years?

    F. 48
    G. 96
    H. 192
    J. 384
    K. 1.78×10^6

25. 36% of 60 is equal to 72% of what?

    A. 15.5

    B. 21.6

    C. 30

    D. 43.2

    E. 120

26. Points A, B, C, and D lie on the real number line below. The coordinate of C is 0. $\overline{BD}$ is 18 units long, $\overline{AC}$ is 12 units long, and $\overline{AD}$ is 24 units long. What is the coordinate of B?

    F. −6

    G. −4

    H. 0

    J. 2

    K. 6

27. For an angle with measure Z in a right triangle, $\tan(Z) = \dfrac{9}{12}$ and $\cos(Z) = \dfrac{12}{15}$. What is the value of $\csc(Z)$?

    A. $\dfrac{9}{15}$

    B. 1

    C. $\dfrac{15}{12}$

    D. $\dfrac{15}{9}$

    E. $\dfrac{17}{9}$

28. The area of rectangle $LMNO$ is 108 in^2. The ratio of the side lengths is 3:4. What is the length of the longer side of the rectangle?

    F. 4

    G. 9

    H. 12

    J. 27

    K. 54

Use the following information to answer questions 29-31.

At Paula's Prancing Feet Dance Academy, each dancer can sell two types of tickets to the Winter Concert: Student and Adult. There are two performances, Friday and Saturday. The price of Student tickets is $3 and the price of Adult tickets is $5. The table below outlines the ticket sales for the performances:

	Friday	Saturday
Student	55	112
Adult	73	86

The stem and leaf plot below shows the number of tickets sold by the 19 cast members, regardless of type or day:

stem	leaf
0	0, 3, 7, 7, 9
1	0, 2, 2, 5, 7, 9
2	1, 1, 3, 6, 7, 8
3	1, 8

The auditorium where the Winter Concert is held has 8 seats in the first row. Each row behind the first has 6 more seats than the row in front of it

29. Suppose 1 cast member is chosen at random to receive a flower bouquet on opening night. What is the probability that she sold more than 20 tickets?

   A. $8/19$
   B. $2/5$
   C. $4/6$
   D. $6/17$
   E. $11/19$

30. For which night did Paula earn more in ticket sales, and by how much?

   F. Saturday by $236
   G. Saturday by $112
   H. Friday by $76
   J. Friday by $36
   K. Friday by $112

31. How many seats are in the seventh row of the auditorium?

   A. 32

   B. 38

   C. 44

   D. 50

   E. 56

---

32. Square ABCD has an area of 64 in². A certain triangle, RST, has the same area. Base $\overline{ST}$ has a length of 16 in. What is the ratio of the length of the side of the square to the height of the triangle?

   F. 2:1

   G. 1:2

   H. 4:1

   J. 1:1

   K. 1:3

33. In a distinct plane, the lines $\overline{AB}$ and $\overline{CE}$ intersect at point D, where D is between A and B. The measure of $\angle CDA$ is 27°. What is the measure of $\angle BDC$?

   A. 27°

   B. 54°

   C. 68°

   D. 117°

   E. 153°

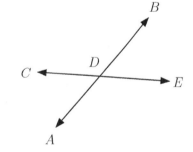

34. Consider a right triangle with angle C, where

$\sin C = \dfrac{15}{25}$ and its hypotenuse is 25 meters in length.

What is the area of the triangle in square meters?

   F. 60

   G. 150

   H. 187.5

   J. 300

   K. Cannot be determined from the information given

35. Shown below are right triangles ABC and ADE, where $\overline{CB} = 36$ cm, $\overline{BA} = 24$ cm, and $\overline{ED} = 6$ cm. What is the length in centimeters of $\overline{AE}$?

A. $2\sqrt{13}$
B. 4
C. $\sqrt{17}$
D. 6
E. $12\sqrt{13}$

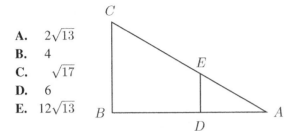

36. Whenever x and y are nonzero, $\dfrac{(6x^{12}y^2)(3xy^2)^2}{18x^8y^3}$ is equivalent to which of the following expressions?

F. $3x^6y^3$

G. $\dfrac{3x^6}{y^3}$

H. $\dfrac{x^5y}{3}$

J. $\dfrac{x^6y^3}{3}$

K. $\dfrac{3x^3}{2y^2}$

37. What is the length of the altitude from A to $\overline{BC}$ in triangle ABC shown below?

A. 4
B. 5
C. 10
D. 11
E. $\sqrt{96}$

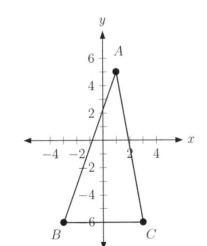

38. If $a + 7 = b$ and $a + 12 = c$, what is the value of $c - b$?

   F.   5

   G. $2a + 5$

   H. $2a + 19$

   J.   19

   K. -5

39. On Saturday, Mary and Sarah opened separate bank accounts with initial deposits of \$56 and \$108 respectively. Every Saturday after opening the accounts, Mary will deposit \$3.25 and Sarah will withdraw \$9.00. Which of the following equations, when solved, gives the number of weeks (w) after opening the accounts that Mary and Sarah will have the same amount of money in their respective accounts?

(Note: They make no other deposits/withdrawals and no interest is applied to the money in the accounts.)

   A. $56 + 3.25w = 108 - 9w$

   B. $56 - 3.25w = 108 + 9w$

   C. $56w + 3.25 = 108w - 9$

   D. $-56 + 3.25w = 108 - 9w$

   E. $56 + 3.25w = 108 + 9w$

40. A sphere with a radius of x has a volume of 18 cubic centimeters. What is the value of x?

(Note: The volume of a sphere with radius r is $\frac{4}{3}\pi r^3$.)

   F.   1.63

   G.   2.38

   H.   3

   J.   4.5

   K.   13.5

41. In the figure below, $\overline{AD}$, $\overline{BE}$, and $\overline{CF}$ all intersect at point O. If the measures of $\angle BOF$ and $\angle AOC$ are $46°$ and $15°$, respectively, what is the measure of $\angle DOE$?

   A. $44°$

   B. $46°$

   C. $75°$

   D. $119°$

   E. $149°$

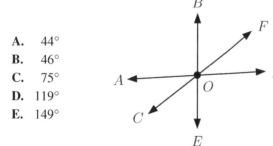

42. In the standard (x,y) coordinate plane, what is the slope of the line perpendicular to the line $6x + 11y = 121$?

F. $-\dfrac{11}{6}$

G. $-\dfrac{6}{11}$

H. $\dfrac{6}{11}$

J. $\dfrac{11}{6}$

K. 11

43. Hannah rents a car to travel around Arkansas for 2 days. She has a total of $275 to spend on the rental. Vinny's Vehicles charges $60 per day and $0.25 per mile driven. Carlie's Cars charges $50 per day and $0.35 per mile driven. Which company allows her to travel more miles in 2 days, and by how many?

A. Vinny's by 120 miles

B. Vinny's by 325 miles

C. Carlie's by 100 miles

D. Carlie's by 45 miles

E. Hannah will get the same maximum number of miles from each company

44. For what value of m would the following system of equations have an infinite number of solutions?

$$2x + 3y = 7$$
$$8x + 12y = 14m$$

F. 1

G. 2

H. 4

J. 14

K. 28

45. Given $3^x = 27$ and $x^y = 81$, what is the value of xy?

A. $3/4$

B. 4

C. 7

D. 12

E. 81

46. Kibo is baking cookies. The cookie recipe calls for $1\frac{1}{4}$ cups of sugar for every 2 cups of flour. Kibo has 5 cups of sugar. How many cups of flour should he use in order to keep the ratio in the recipe constant?

   F. $5\frac{3}{4}$

   G.   6

   H. $6\frac{1}{4}$

   J.   8

   K.   10

47. Which of the following is a factor of $4x^2 - 6x - 18$?

   A. $x - 6$

   B. $2x - 3$

   C. $2x - 6$

   D. $4x - 6$

   E. $4x + 3$

48. Vectors $\overline{AM}$ and $\overline{NT}$ are shown in the standard (x, y) coordinate plane below. Which of the following is the unit vector notation of the vector $\overline{AM} + \overline{NT}$?

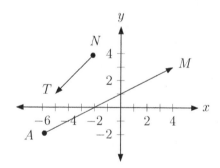

   F. $-7\mathbf{i} + \mathbf{j}$

   G. $-2\mathbf{i} + 3\mathbf{j}$

   H. $2\mathbf{i} - 3\mathbf{j}$

   J. $7\mathbf{i} + \mathbf{j}$

   K. $7\mathbf{i} + 2\mathbf{j}$

49. Two chords intersect inside of a circle. The chords are split into lengths as shown in the diagram below. What is the value of x?

A. $2\frac{2}{5}$

B. $6\frac{2}{3}$

C. 8

D. 12

E. 15

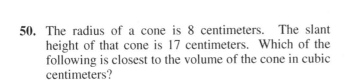

50. The radius of a cone is 8 centimeters. The slant height of that cone is 17 centimeters. Which of the following is closest to the volume of the cone in cubic centimeters?

(Note: For a cone $V = \frac{1}{3}Bh$, where B is the area of the base and h is the height.)

F. 251

G. 754

H. 1,005

J. 1,139

K. 3,418

51. For $0 \le \theta < 2\pi$, $\sec\theta = 2$ when $\theta =$

A. $\dfrac{\pi}{3}, \dfrac{2\pi}{3}$

B. $\dfrac{\pi}{3}, \dfrac{4\pi}{3}$

C. $\dfrac{\pi}{3}, \dfrac{5\pi}{3}$

D. $\dfrac{2\pi}{3}, \dfrac{4\pi}{3}$

E. $\dfrac{4\pi}{3}, \dfrac{5\pi}{3}$

    GO ON TO THE NEXT PAGE.

52. Given that $(x + 2)$ and $(x - 4)$ are factors of $x^2 + (a + 2)x + (a - b)$, what are the values of a and b, respectively?

F. -4 and -4

G. -4 and -2

H. -4 and 4

J. -2 and -4

K. 4 and -2

53. The height of a ball above the ground in meters as a function of time is given by the equation $h = -3t^2 + 6t + 45$. An equivalent, factored form of the equation shows that:

A. The ball hits the ground at $t = 3$

B. The ball hits the ground at $t = 5$

C. The ball reaches maximum height at $t = 2.5$

D. The ball reaches maximum height at $t = 4$

E. The ball starts at a height of 15 meters.

54. Given that $2 \tan \alpha = 2$ and $2 \sin(\pi + \beta) = -2$, which of the following could be the value of $\alpha + \beta$?

F. $\dfrac{2\pi}{3}$

G. $\dfrac{3\pi}{4}$

H. $\dfrac{7\pi}{6}$

J. $\dfrac{5\pi}{4}$

K. $\dfrac{3\pi}{2}$

Questions 55-57 pertain to the following information.

FloorMax is a company that rents office space in its buildings to other businesses. They have a deal right now where anyone who signs a one-year lease with them receives half off their monthly rent for the first month. The chart below shows FloorMax's five size categories of office to rent, the amount of space each category of rental offers, and the monthly rental cost of each.

Size	Floor Space	Rental Cost Per Month
1	20' x 40'	$400
2	40' x 40'	$800
3	40' x 80'	$1,500
4	80' x 80'	$2,900
5	80' x 160'	$5,700

55. LexCo will rent a size 2 office space from FloorMax for 12 months, under the current deal. Which of the following is closest to the percent of the cost without the deal in place that LexCo will pay?
   A. 91.7%
   B. 93.8%
   C. 95.0%
   D. 95.8%
   E. 96.0%

56. Behavorial studies show that each worker in a company needs a minimum of 40 square feet of space for optimum productivity. MadiCorp currently has 300 workers. How many units should they rent from FloorMax to minimize cost but make sure each worker has enough space?
   F. One unit each of sizes 1, 2, 3, and 4.
   G. One size 5 unit
   H. Fifteen size 1 units.
   J. Seven size 2 units and one size 1 unit.
   K. Three size 4 units, one size 1 unit.

57. The prices of the units follow a consistent pattern from sizes 2 through 5. Assuming the pattern continues, what would be the price of a size 8 unit?
   A. $18,300
   B. $22,500
   C. $44,900
   D. $45,500
   E. $89,700

58. Consider a rectangular solid made out of cubes, each with side length 0.75 centimeters. The solid is 16 layers high, and each layer contains 8 of the cubes. What is the volume, in cubic centimeters, of the solid?

    F.   27
    G.   54
    H.   72
    J.   108
    K.   144

59. When $\angle YOW$ is measured in radians, which of the following expressions correctly gives the length of $\overparen{YW}$?

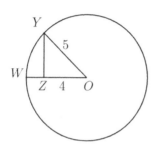

    A. $4\cos^{-1}\left(\dfrac{4}{5}\right)$

    B. $4\sin^{-1}\left(\dfrac{4}{5}\right)$

    C. $4\tan^{-1}\left(\dfrac{4}{5}\right)$

    D. $5\sin^{-1}\left(\dfrac{4}{5}\right)$

    E. $5\cos^{-1}\left(\dfrac{4}{5}\right)$

60. The rational function $y = \dfrac{x^2 - 4}{2x^2 - 18}$ has two vertical asymptotes and one horizontal asymptote. What is the equation of the horizontal asymptote?

    F. $y = \dfrac{1}{2}$
    G. $y = 0$
    H. $y = 2$
    J. $x = 2$
    K. $x = 3$

END OF TEST 2.
STOP! DO NOT TURN THE PAGE UNTIL TOLD TO DO SO.
DO NOT RETURN TO THE PREVIOUS TEST.

THERE ARE NO TESTING MATERIALS ON THIS PAGE.

READING TEST

35 Minutes — 40 Questions

DIRECTIONS: There are four passages in this test. Each passage is followed by several questions. Choose the best answer to each question and fill in the corresponding oval on your answer document. You may refer to the passages as often as often as necessary.

Passage I

LITERARY NARRATIVE: Passage A is adapted from *Desperate Remedies* by Thomas Hardy (©1874 by Thomas Hardy). Passage B is adapted from *The King in Yellow* by Robert William Chambers (©1895 by Robert William Chambers).

Passage A by Thomas Hardy

Eight years later, feeling lonely and depressed—a man without relatives, with many acquaintances but no friends—Ambrose Graye met a young lady of a different kind, fairly endowed with money and good gifts. As to
5 caring very deeply for another woman after the loss of Cytherea, it was an absolute impossibility with him. With all, the beautiful things of the earth become more dear as they elude pursuit; but with some natures, utter elusion is the one special event which will make a passing love per-
10 manent forever.

This second young lady and Graye were married. That he did not, first or last, love his wife as he should have done, was known to all; but few knew that his unmanageable heart could never be weaned from useless repining
15 at the loss of its first idol.

His character to some extent deteriorated, as emotional constitutions will under the long sense of disappointment at having missed their imagined destiny. And thus, though naturally of a gentle and pleasant disposition, he
20 grew to be not so tenderly regarded by his acquaintances as it is the lot of some of those persons to be. The winning and sanguine receptivity of his early life developed by degrees a moody nervousness, and when not picturing prospects drawn from baseless hope, he was the victim
25 of indescribable depression. The practical issue of such a condition was improvidence, originally almost an unconscious improvidence, for every debt incurred had been mentally paid off with a religious exactness from the treasures of expectation before mentioned. But as years re-
30 volved, the same course was continued from the lack of spirit sufficient for shifting out of an old groove when it has been found to lead to disaster.

In the year 1861 his wife died, leaving him a widower with two children. The elder, a son named Owen, now just
35 turned seventeen, was taken from school, and initiated as pupil to the profession of architect in his father's office. The remaining child was a daughter, and Owen's junior by a year.

Her christian name was Cytherea, and it is easy to
40 guess why.

Passage B by Robert William Chambers

In the city of New York the summer of 1899 was signalized by the dismantling of the Elevated Railroads. The summer of 1900 will live in the memories of New York people for many a cycle; the Dodge Statue was removed
45 in that year. In the following winter began that agitation for the repeal of the laws prohibiting suicide which bore its final fruit in the month of April, 1920, when the first Government Lethal Chamber was opened on Washington Square.

50 I had walked down that day from Dr. Archer's house on Madison Avenue, where I had been as a mere formality. Ever since that fall from my horse, four years before, I had been troubled at times with pains in the back of my head and neck, but now for months they had been absent, and
55 the doctor sent me away, that day, saying there was nothing more to be cured in me. It was hardly worth his fee to be told that; I knew it myself. Still I did not grudge him the money. What I minded was the mistake which he made at first. When they picked me up from the pavement where I
60 lay unconscious, and somebody had mercifully sent a bullet through my horse's head, I was carried to Dr. Archer, and he, pronouncing my brain affected, placed me in his private asylum where I was obliged to endure treatment for insanity. At last he decided that I was well, and I, know-
65 ing that my mind had always been as sound as his, if not sounder, "paid my tuition" as he jokingly called it, and left. I told him, smiling, that I would get even with him for his mistake, and he laughed heartily, and asked me to call once in a while. I did so, hoping for a chance to even
70 up accounts, but he gave me none, and I told him I would wait.

The fall from my horse had fortunately left no evil results; on the contrary it had changed my whole character for the better. From a lazy young man about town, I

75　had become active, energetic, temperate, and above all—oh, above all else—ambitious. There was only one thing which troubled me, I laughed at my own uneasiness, and yet it troubled me.

| Questions 1–3 ask about Passage A. |

1. Which of the following statements about Ambrose Graye is best supported by Passage A?

  A. He was incapable of caring for other people, including his family.
  B. His first wife had been his true love, making it difficult for him to love his new wife.
  C. He felt that over time, he would be able to recover from losing his wife.
  D. He was an unpleasant man who severely disliked his children.

2. According to Passage A, Ambrose Graye continued to love his first wife Cytherea because:

  F. she reminded him of his daughter of the same name.
  G. his second marriage was doomed by his new wife's disgust toward him.
  H. he desired to love each of his wives equally.
  J. her death had made his love for her permanent.

3. The main purpose of the second paragraph of Passage A (lines 11–15) is to:

  A. contrast the public view of Ambrose Graye with the reason for his behavior.
  B. establish the benefits of the marriage for both parties.
  C. illustrate the history behind Ambrose Graye's second marriage.
  D. suggest the deep connection between Ambrose Graye and his second wife.

| Questions 4–7 ask about Passage B. |

4. Which of the following events referred to in Passage B occurred first chronologically?

  F. A visit to Dr. Archer's house
  G. The narrator's fall from his horse
  H. A stay in an asylum
  J. A walk down Madison Avenue

5. It can reasonably be inferred from Passage B that Dr. Archer's "mistake" (line 58) was that he:

  A. placed the narrator in an asylum.
  B. chose not to offer treatment to the narrator.
  C. left the narrator lying on the pavement.
  D. caused the accident that injured the narrator.

6. In the passage, the narrator was most likely sent away from Dr. Archer's house because:

  F. Dr. Archer held a grudge against him.
  G. the narrator refused to pay the doctor's fees.
  H. the narrator's mental state was severely deteriorated.
  J. the narrator was already healthy.

7. According to Passage B, the narrator's fall from his horse eventually resulted in:

  A. permanent damage to his brain, causing insanity.
  B. evil results, causing him to become lazy.
  C. positive effects, making him a more active and ambitious person.
  D. him deciding to shoot his own horse.

| Questions 8–10 ask about both passages. |

8. A similarity between the two passages is that they both:

  F. use a first person omniscient narrator to tell a story.
  G. describe the family situation of a character.
  H. examine an event that has profound effects on a character.
  J. include a historical context in which the story is set.

9. An element of Passage B that is not present in Passage A is:

  A. a positive outcome to a difficult situation.
  B. a description of the character's romantic situation.
  C. the loss of a close relationship for the main character.
  D. a discussion of the main character's moods.

10. Which statement provides the most accurate comparison of the tone of each passage?

  F. Passage A is optimistic, whereas passage B is reflective.
  G. Passage A is objective, whereas Passage B is fanciful.
  H. Passage A is critical, whereas Passage B is irate.
  J. Passage A is descriptive, whereas Passage B is personal.

Passage II

SOCIAL SCIENCE: This passage is adapted from *Gentrification Nation* by Schoolhouse Press (©1999 by Schoolhouse Press).

   In the early 1960s, British sociologist Ruth Glass began to notice some peculiar demographic changes in working-class districts of London. Neighborhoods like Islington and Notting Hill, which for decades had been the cul-
5 tural strongholds of factory laborers, longshoremen, and artisans, were now being settled by middle-class professionals. These newcomers brought with them not just their own cultural values and expectations—which differed greatly from that of their neighbors—but also eco-
10 nomic clout superior to anything the existing working-class residents of the neighborhood could muster.

   In short order, the neighborhood's whole character was transformed as working-class families were driven out by rising rents and more affluent families took their place.
15 The thrift shops and pubs that had catered to the blue-collar clientele gave way to cafes and boutiques serving the neighborhood's new majority. The social cohesion that had defined these neighborhoods for generations was disrupted as one class was replaced by another that both con-
20 sciously and unconsciously sought to claim the neighborhood as its own cultural preserve. Professor Glass named the social dynamic that drove these changes *gentrification*.

   At first glance, gentrification seemed a stark reversal from the earlier trend of suburbanization. In both Britain
25 and America, following World War II, middle-class city dwellers moved in great numbers to new suburban communities, leaving behind congested urban cores in favor of open space. Left behind were the working-class enclaves and minority neighborhoods, whose residents were
30 priced out of the new suburban towns. Government policies subsidized this move to the suburbs, offering generous mortgages to new homeowners and building massive highway networks to link suburbanites to their jobs, which remained in the cities.

35   So why, in the 1960s, were middle-class professionals spurning leafy suburbs in favor of gritty urban neighborhoods whose cultural and social norms differed so starkly from their own? To find the answer, Professor Glass developed a profile of the gentrifiers who were transform-
40 ing places like Islington and Notting Hill. She found that many of the so-called pioneers—the first non-working-class newcomers—were the bohemian sons and daughters of London's affluent classes. Rejecting their families' expectations of higher education, professional employment,
45 and marriage, these young non-conformists sought out cheap housing and—in the case of artists—studio space that was unavailable either in their home neighborhoods or in the new suburbs. Despite their bohemian pretensions, these pioneers nevertheless replicated the middle-class cul-
50 ture in which they were raised, and over time this attracted more conventional professionals whose high purchasing

power transformed the neighborhood entirely.

   Simultaneously, Professor Glass found, the industrial jobs upon which the neighborhoods' original working-
55 class residents depended began to vanish, as manufacturing firms relocated overseas. When these reliable, well-paid, unionized jobs began to disappear, working-class residents were left with two options to cope with their steadily rising rents: leave London to find similar work elsewhere
60 or take one of the low-paying service industry jobs that replaced industrial employment. Most working-class families left entirely, either of their own will, or because they could no longer afford to live in the neighborhoods in which they had been born and raised.

65   Using Professor Glass's model, scholars around the world have identified the mechanisms of gentrification and developed numerous case studies of the process at work, especially here in the United States. According to these researchers, the process of gentrification has accelerated in
70 the past generation, a fact which they ascribe to the desire of many well-to-do suburbanites to live the city life. In a sense, gentrification generates its own momentum. As formerly working-class neighborhoods in New York, Los Angeles, Chicago, and elsewhere become more attractive
75 to both the middle class and the wealthy, aspiring urbanites priced out of long-gentrified districts look for new neighborhoods to transform, a process welcomed by landlords looking to rake in higher rents, and city governments eager to grow their tax base.

80   Another factor at work is the contemporary enthusiasm for environmentally-conscious living. According to green advocates, suburbia's lack of mass transit and prodigious demands for energy and water require its residents to leave a large carbon footprint that puts the planet in dan-
85 ger. In an urban core geared around public transportation, however, one can live with a much smaller carbon footprint. Environmentally-friendly living has great appeal for younger generations, who see living in gentrified neighborhoods as an act of social conscience.

90   But what of the people displaced by this process? For Professor Glass, this was an injustice whose impact was often lost on the beneficiaries of gentrification. While proponents of gentrification saw a process of regeneration that brought new life to ailing cities, Glass cautioned such op-
95 timists to remember that gentrifiers could themselves be pushed out as easily as their working-class predecessors. And if a city is affordable only for the wealthy, how can it be expected to thrive culturally and economically? Without a balance of classes, cities lose their vitality. Sadly, it
100 seems that runaway gentrification only adds to the woes it purports to solve.

11. The main purpose of the passage is to:

    A. explore the background of a social dynamic.

    B. provide multiple examples of a phenomenon across the world.

    C. describe the career and personal life of a renowned sociologist.

    D. provide personal anecdotes of working-class people forced out of their homes by gentrification.

12. According to the passage, artists often moved to urban neighborhoods in the 1960s because of:

    F. expectations of their working-class peers.

    G. educational opportunities.

    H. available studio space.

    J. abundant art supply shops.

13. The primary function of the seventh paragraph (lines 80–89) is to:

    A. introduce an additional reason for movement to urban areas.

    B. shift the focus of the passage from urban gentrification to problems taking place in suburbia.

    C. explain the most compelling reason for people to lower their carbon footprint.

    D. describe in detail the history of gentrification.

14. Professor Glass's attitude toward gentrification can best be described as:

    F. wary and adverse.

    G. praising and admiring.

    H. indifferent and apathetic.

    J. amused and appreciative.

15. As it is used in line 36, *spurning* most nearly means:

    A. rejecting.

    B. dwelling in.

    C. accepting.

    D. reducing.

16. It can most reasonably be inferred from the first paragraph that gentrifiers:

    F. wanted to make a neighborhood's culture their own.

    G. purposefully sought to displace the former residents.

    H. existed solely in 1960s London.

    J. began to move to urban areas because of Professor Glass's writings.

17. The main purpose of the information in lines 3–7 is to:

    A. list the professions of most of the citizens in London in the 1960s.

    B. describe in detail the cultural attributes of London neighborhoods.

    C. characterize all neighborhoods that were studied by sociologists.

    D. provide examples of a phenomenon described in the passage.

18. The passage states that the appeal of gentrification for landlords most likely comes from:

    F. support of the city government through tax breaks.

    G. the environmentally friendly aspects of public transportation.

    H. displacement of original neighborhood residents.

    J. more money earned from higher rents.

19. In the passage, the trend of suburbanization describes:

    A. the preference for gritty urban neighborhoods.

    B. movement of middle-class city dwellers to the suburbs.

    C. the displacement of historical residents of city neighborhoods.

    D. purchasing of suburban homes by minorities and working-class people.

20. The passage indicates that relocation of manufacturing firms overseas:

    F. was beneficial for the high paying jobs of working-class people.

    G. hurt citizens of the United States across all social classes.

    H. caused the disappearance of well-paid, unionized jobs for working-class residents of gentrified areas.

    J. created jobs in Islington and Notting Hill.

Passage III

HUMANITIES: This passage is adapted from *The Western Hero* by Arthur Gilchrist (©1975 by Arthur Gilchrist).

Since the late 18th century, when settlers blazed the first trails over the Appalachian Mountains to reach Kentucky and Ohio, American writers, artists, and filmmakers have explored the Western frontier as a crucible for individual
5 and social transformation. What makes the Western so distinctive? Its greatest invention is a character type which has become the model for American bravery: the solitary hero.

The early Western writer James Fenimore Cooper in-
10 vented the lone frontier hero. In "The Leatherstocking Tales," a series of novels and stories, Cooper recounted the adventures of Natty Bumppo, who travelled the New York frontier in the days before and after the American Revolution. Bumppo saved the daughters of a British offi-
15 cer during the French and Indian War and worked to make peace between settlers and Native Americans on the shores of the Great Lakes. In Cooper's stories, Bumppo is honest and blunt, a skilled hunter who understands how to survive and thrive in an unforgiving wilderness. Because of
20 his background (born to English parents but raised in the family of a Native American chief), he is the perfect mediator between peoples whose ways of life are hostile to one another. Bumppo represents an early stage of America's westward expansion, a time when the possibility for
25 some form of peaceful coexistence still remained, before the differences between two alien cultures became insurmountable.

As the pace of Western settlement quickened in the nineteenth century, the frontiersman created by Cooper
30 was transformed. Fictional frontier heroes were no longer able to move between worlds; instead, their heroism was defined by their ability to outfight their Native American opponents. Stories about this new type of hero flourished after the invention of the rotary printing press in 1844,
35 which fueled a boom of cheap dime novels that promised stories of thrilling adventures on the lawless fringes of civilization. Whereas Natty Bumppo could claim the trust of both Native Americans and settlers, the new generation of Western heroes were wandering gunslingers who, unable
40 to fit in with the settled life in the East, went West to find their fortunes. They were violent men who mastered the wilderness by subduing it.

Dime novelists like Karl May helped invent the myth of the "Wild West"—a place between wilderness and civ-
45 ilization, with the vices of both and the virtues of neither, filled with the perennial American hope of individual rebirth and redemption. Despite their thin stories, the works of May and his fellow writers firmly lodged the archetypes of the West in the minds of generations of readers. On their
50 pages, the frontier was a land to be conquered. This was the world of Manifest Destiny and the relentless expansion of American civilization, with all of its attendant dangers. Out of this new world, a new kind of villain emerged: the outlaw corrupted by life out West, where a man was as
55 likely to prosper by violence and fraud, as by cooperation and hard work.

By the end of the nineteenth century, most of the West had been settled. Railroads and telegraph wires crossed the mountains and the deserts, and the memory of the frontier
60 had vanished from the land east of the Mississippi River. Western literature reflected this change. The new hero was no longer the frontiersman facing the wilderness alone. Instead, the action moved to the raw towns and mining camps of the West, and the struggle to build a civilization
65 out of nothing. The solitary gunslinger became a sheriff; his gun now came with a badge that marked him as a champion of order. The enemy was no longer the Native American war band, but the murderous outlaw and the tyrannical cattle baron out to take land from the hard-working, honest
70 townspeople.

In the twentieth century, the Western film genre took up the banner of the solitary sheriff-hero, helping to make him the most recognized American archetype, especially as portrayed by actors like John Wayne and Gary Cooper.
75 The sheriff's heroism resided in his profound sense of right and wrong, and a willingness to fight on behalf of the weak against the strong. Throughout the centuries, the Western hero's fight has always been on behalf of the forces of order against chaos, whether that chaos comes in the form of
80 Native American raiders or greedy frontier landlords and their hired thugs.

21. The main purpose of the passage is to:
   A. describe the career and works of Western trope author Karl May.
   B. provide background information for characters portrayed by John Wayne and Gary Cooper.
   C. explain the origins and development of a literary trope.
   D. illustrate sources of tension between groups living in the American West in the 18th century.

22. All of the following are true about the character Natty Bumppo EXCEPT that he was:
   F. the main character of "The Leatherstocking Tales."
   G. raised by English parents.
   H. a skilled hunter.
   J. a peacemaker between settlers and Native Americans.

23. According to the passage, the invention of the rotary printing press:

A. was the downfall of the Western genre.
B. greatly increased the popularity of writer James Fenimore Cooper.
C. enhanced the desires of Americans to move westward.
D. led to a boom in cheap novels.

24. In the third paragraph (lines 28–42), the author constructs a contrast primarily between the:

F. books created using the rotary printing press and other methods of printing.
G. frontiersmen characters who worked with settlers and Native Americans and later ones who fought against Native Americans.
H. character Natty Bumppo and the writer James Fenimore Cooper.
J. lifestyles of settlers in the nineteenth and twentieth centuries.

25. It can most reasonably be inferred that dime novelists viewed the frontier as:

A. a territory rightly owned by Native Americans that had lived there for years.
B. an area that needed to be controlled.
C. a distant land impossible for people to reach.
D. a beautiful land ready for settlers to visit.

26. As it is used in line 67, *order* most nearly means:

F. sequence.
G. law.
H. request.
J. unruliness.

27. In the passage, the 20th century marked a shift toward:

A. a time of uncertainty in the West.
B. the rise in popularity of Natty Bumppo.
C. the Western hero as a solitary sheriff.
D. settlers traveling to Kentucky and Ohio.

28. It can most reasonable be inferred from lines 23–27 that Bumppo represents:

F. a historical figure who was fictionalized for the purposes of Cooper's novels.
G. an activist who protested the alien cultures of the American West.
H. the twentieth century Western film genre.
J. a time when peace between settlers and Native Americans seemed achievable.

29. The passage states that the most important invention of the Western genre was:

A. the rotary printing press.
B. the solitary hero.
C. the popularity of Westward expansion.
D. a peace agreement between Native Americans and settlers.

30. Which of the following best describes the role of the Western hero over time? The Western Hero:

F. existed only during the 19th century.
G. battled against violence on the frontier.
H. fought against Native Americans.
J. worked to maintain the frontier towns.

Passage IV

NATURAL SCIENCE: This passage is adapted from *Neanderthals* by Henry Smith (©1984 by Henry Smith).

In the spring of 1856, workers in a lime quarry near the German village of Neanderthal called on the local schoolmaster to help explain a puzzling discovery. The workers had unearthed some bones that they initially believed to
5 be a bear's, but upon digging further they came across a skull that looked uncannily human. The schoolmaster forwarded the bones to the University of Berlin, where Doctor Ernst Haeckel, the greatest of the first generation of physical anthropologists, examined them and declared that, de-
10 spite their strange appearance and size, they were in fact the remains of a previously unknown human species.

Dr. Haeckel reached out to colleagues across Europe to see if any other remnants of this strange human relation had been found, and gradually he received reports of sim-
15 ilar bone fragments, often mistaken for animals', that had been unearthed by miners and farmers. At a conference of physical anthropologists in 1864, fierce debate raged over whether or not the bones were in fact a new species or a strange offshoot of *Homo sapiens*. Surely, many of
20 the attendees believed, the hulking brute revealed by skeletal fragments could not possibly be a direct relation to the civilized humanity of the 19th century. The English geologist William King won the day and convinced the assembled scientists that this was, in fact, a new species, not
25 just physically distinct from modern humans, but also presumably lacking the moral conceptions unique to our own species. Thus was *Homo neanderthalis* introduced to the world, and though this cousin of *Homo sapiens* became a symbol of everything primitive and barbaric in the evo-
30 lutionary past of the human race, recent discoveries have radically revised our understanding of the Neanderthals.

For decades, Neanderthals were assumed to be savage cavemen who eked out an existence in the fierce environment of the Eurasian Ice Age. The average Nean-
35 derthal stood between 5 feet 1 inch and 5 feet 5 inches tall, with thick, short forearms and legs, a stocky build that made Neanderthals strong and cold-resistant. Their skulls were longer and flatter than those of modern humans, with broad, protuberant noses. This evidence supported the hy-
40 pothesis that Neanderthals were an offshoot of *Homo erectus*, an ancestor of modern humans and the first hominid to reach what is now Europe and East Asia: as the glaciers advanced and the climate grew colder, *Homo neanderthalis*, with its cold-resistant traits, emerged. Because of the un-
45 forgiving environment and sheer difficulty of survival, scientists assumed that Neanderthals were culturally primitive, without language, art or any kind of social organization.

But skeleton fragments found in 1983 overturned all
50 of these presumptions. That year, a Neanderthal hyoid bone was found in a cave in Israel. In humans, the hyoid bone anchors the muscle clusters of the tongue and larynx, making possible a wide range of coordinated muscular movement in the throat. This in turn expands the
55 possibilities of pitch and tone in vocalization. Since modern humans can manipulate these vocalizing possibilities and create language, Neanderthals could also have done so. Later finds further complicated the common image of the Neanderthal. Cave sites in Spain revealed deliberately laid
60 out skeletons whose bones were coated in flower pollen, indicating that they had been ritually buried, a strong indication that Neanderthals might have had a social structure after all.

If Neanderthals were not a savage, hardy species, as
65 was previously assumed, then where did they come from? Modern genome sequencing has made a definitive answer possible. Sequencing of DNA taken from dozens of Neanderthal bone samples found that Neanderthals shared 99.7% of their genome with *Homo sapiens*. Mitochondrial
70 DNA studies, which yield an even more specific measure of differentiation, found that out of 16,000 base pairs, Neanderthals and modern humans differed by only 202 bases. As the genome sequencing project progressed, scientists identified in Neanderthals, the presence of the FOXP2
75 gene, which in humans is associated with language acquisition.

As more and more of the Neanderthal genome was reconstructed, scientists were able to offer even more large-scale comparisons with humans. Using genetic
80 markers common to both *Homo sapiens* and *Homo neanderthalis*, scientists found that *Homo sapiens* and *Homo neanderthalis* split from their common ancestor 700,000 years ago. This takes us well before the last Ice Age and into the more remote hominid past. It appears that Nean-
85 derthals were not, in fact, sculpted by the rigors of a frigid climate, but evolved in conditions much like those of modern humans, albeit with some modifications due to their different migrations.

The genome sequencing project also uncovered a
90 final, and totally unexpected, discovery. The average genome of a modern European contains a few unique markers that are not found in any other humans, but that are found in the depths of the Neanderthal genome. For modern European humans, the Neanderthals aren't just cousins
95 on another branch of the family tree—instead, they are siblings.

31. The primary purpose of the passage is to discuss the:

  A. discovery and development in scientific understanding of a species.
  B. genetic similarities between *Homo neanderthalis* and *Homo sapiens*.
  C. state of physical anthropology in the 19th century.
  D. importance of genetics in learning about species of animals.

32. In lines 64–65, the author most likely poses a question about the origins of Neanderthals in order to:

  F. explain scientific techniques used to sequence the genome.
  G. confirm previous findings that Neanderthals were distantly related to humans.
  H. transition from previous assumptions to current findings.
  J. conclude an argument supported by physical anthropologists.

33. According to the passage, the discovery of a Neanderthal hyoid bone shows that Neanderthals:

  A. likely took part in ritual singing ceremonies.
  B. were able to create language like modern humans.
  C. were likely unrelated to modern humans in Israel.
  D. communicated in drastically different ways.

34. The passage states that *Homo neanderthalis* and *Homo sapiens* split from their common ancestor:

  F. 150 years ago.
  G. 16,000 years ago.
  H. 100,000 years ago.
  J. 700,000 years ago.

35. In can reasonably be inferred from the passage that many attendees of the 1864 conference:

  A. relied on advances in genetics to study the Neanderthal.
  B. considered Neanderthals to be highly evolved.
  C. believed *Homo neanderthalis* was closely related to *Homo sapiens*.
  D. were unwilling to see a connection between themselves and Neanderthals.

36. According to the passage, Neanderthals were considered to be culturally primitive due to:

  F. the harsh environment they lived in.
  G. their clearly expressed dislike of social organization.
  H. the short, stocky build of members of the species.
  J. genetic differences between *Homo neanderthalis* and *Homo sapiens*.

37. In the passage, the bones that were discovered in Neanderthal were thought to belong to a:

  A. bear.
  B. human.
  C. dinosaur.
  D. Neanderthal.

38. All of the following are facts about Neanderthals EXCEPT:

  F. The skulls were longer and flatter than modern humans.
  G. They share a language acquisition gene with modern humans.
  H. They are considered primitive and barbaric by modern science.
  J. They buried their dead ritualistically.

39. The passage indicates that at the conference in 1864, physical anthropologists debated:

  A. the authenticity of the bones.
  B. whether the bones were a new species or a relation to *Homo sapiens*.
  C. the credentials of Dr. Ernst Haeckel.
  D. when *Homo neanderthalis* and *Homo sapiens* split from their shared ancestor.

40. The fact that *Homo neanderthalis* and *Homo sapiens* split from their common ancestor before the last Ice Age suggests that the two species:

  F. had few genetic markers in common.
  G. developed in similar conditions.
  H. were, in fact, the same species.
  J. followed similar migratory patterns.

SCIENCE TEST
35 Minutes—40 Questions

DIRECTIONS: There are six passages in this test. Each passage is followed by several questions. After reading a passage, choose the best answer to each question and fill in the corresponding oval on your answer document. You may refer to the passages as often as necessary. You are NOT permitted to use a calculator on this test.

Passage I

Fertilizer is a soil amendment that is used to supply essential plant nutrients for optimal growth. Typical fertilizers contain variable amounts of nitrogen, phosphorus, and potassium, with trace amounts of calcium, magnesium, and sulfur. Adding appropriate amounts to fertilizer is crucial to plant health, as an excess of nutrients in fertilizer may cause the plants to dry out and die. To test out the effects of fertilizer concentration on plant growth, a group of students designed an experiment utilizing *Hibiscus rosa-sinensis*, a large, flowering plant native to subtropical regions.

Experiment

The students utilize 24-6-12 fertilizer, an industry standard, for four different garden beds. Each garden bed was treated with a different concentration of 24-6-12 fertilizer, as shown in Table 1 below. 100 *H. rosa-sinensis* seeds were equally dispersed in each garden bed. Six weeks after the initial planting, the average length of the stem and mass per seed were determined for each group (see Figures 1 and 2).

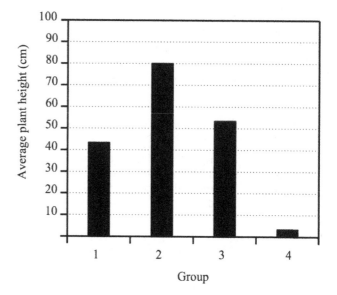

Figure 1

Table 1	
Group	Fertilizer Treatment
1	5 lbs. of 24-6-12 fertilizer added to 1000 sq ft. bed
2	10 lbs. of 24-6-12 fertilizer added to 1000 sq ft. bed
3	15 lbs. of 24-6-12 fertilizer added to 1000 sq ft. bed
4	0 lbs. of 24-6-12 fertilizer added to 1000 sq ft. bed

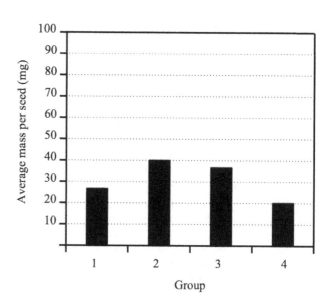

Figure 2

1. In the experiment, which group served as the control?

   A. Group 1
   B. Group 2
   C. Group 3
   D. Group 4

2. To obtain the results shown in Figure 1, which of the following pieces of equipment was most likely used?

   F. Thermometer
   G. Ruler
   H. Balance
   J. Microscope

3. Following the experiment, the students conclude that *H. rosa-sinensis* seed mass is more dependent on fertilizer concentration than *H. rosa-sinensis* plant height. Do the results in Figure 1 and Figure 2 support this conclusion?

   A. Yes, because the average plant heights from each group varied more than the average seed mass for each group.
   B. Yes, because the average plant heights from each group varied less than the average seed mass for each group.
   C. No, because the average plant heights from each group varied more than the average seed mass for each group.
   D. No, because the average plant heights from each group varied less than the average seed mass for each group.

4. For any group, the value shown in Figure 2 was most likely calculated using which of the following expressions?

   F. $\dfrac{\text{total plant height}}{\text{number of plants}}$

   G. $\dfrac{\text{number of plants}}{\text{total plant height}}$

   H. $\dfrac{\text{total seed mass}}{\text{number of seeds}}$

   J. $\dfrac{\text{number of seeds}}{\text{total seed mass}}$

5. The experiment was designed to answer which of the following questions?

   A. Does the location of *H. rosa-sinensis* planting affect growth?
   B. How long after planting do *H. rosa-sinensis* plants reach maturity?
   C. How does fertilizer concentration affect *H. rosa-sinensis* growth and seed mass?
   D. What is the optimal nutrient balance for *H. rosa-sinensis* growth?

6. Despite receiving no fertilizer, *H. rosa-sinensis* plants were still able to grow in Group 4. What is the most reasonable explanation for this?

   F. *H. rosa-sinensis* are not affected by fertilizer concentration
   G. The garden bed possessed some plant nutrients before addition of fertilizer
   H. The height of *H. rosa-sinensis* does not vary with fertilizer concentration
   J. The garden bed possessed no calcium, magnesium or sulfur before addition of fertilizer

153

GO ON TO THE NEXT PAGE.

Passage II

Proteins have significant biological importance in living organisms. These macromolecules are responsible for a variety or tasks ranging from structural support, immunity, cell signaling, and intercellular transport. Proper protein function is entirely dependent on their folded shape. Four students discuss factors that influence protein shape and how mutant, or misfolded, proteins arise.

Student 1

Protein shape is entirely dependent on the amino acid sequence that the protein is composed of. While each amino acid has the same basic structure, they vary through a side chain group. Side chain groups have a tendency to interact with other side chain groups along the sequence. The accumulation of all of these side chain interactions pulls the amino acid sequence into its folded form. Accordingly, a mutant arises when an amino acid is improperly substituted into, or deleted from, the sequence.

Student 2

The driving force behind correct protein folding is a negative change in *Gibbs Free Energy*, ΔG as measured in kJ mol^{-1}. As a measure of free energy change of the protein, ΔG is given by the formula $\Delta G = \Delta H - T\Delta S$, where ΔH is change in enthalpy, T is temperature, and ΔS is a change in entropy. Mutant proteins arise when local energy barriers are too large and the protein must adopt higher energy states to accommodate.

Student 3

The amino acid sequence that determines how a protein folds is entirely dependent on DNA. The nucleotides that make up DNA act as a genetic code for the amino acids that are required to make a certain protein. When a nucleotide is switched for another, an amino acid is also switched out from the correct sequence. Protein mutants are thus created by changes to DNA.

Student 4

The shape of a protein is dependent on the environmental conditions. For instance *albumin*, a protein in human blood plasma, will adopt different shapes depending on if it is immersed in water, alcohol, or acetone. A protein is meant to function properly in a specific environment and will fold into its functional form when exposed to the proper conditions. When a protein is exposed to non ideal conditions it will misfold and adopt mutant shapes.

7. Which of the students would most likely agree that a negative Gibbs free energy is the driving force behind protein folding?

   A. Student 1
   B. Student 2
   C. Student 3
   D. Student 4

8. In further experiments, Student 3 discovers that not all nucleotide substitutions within DNA cause mutant proteins. The most appropriate conclusion is that:

   F. enzymes may correct some nucleotide substitutions.
   G. the amino acid sequence is influenced only by specific nucleotide substitutions.
   H. the protein was able to replace the incorrect amino acid.
   J. a new DNA molecule was created.

9. Sickle cell disease is a genetic disorder in which the Hemoglobin protein folds incorrectly due to a substitution of a valine amino acid for a glutamic acid amino acid. This information *strengthens* the argument of which student(s), if any?

   A. Students 1 and 3 only
   B. Students 2 and 4 only
   C. Student 3 only
   D. None of the students

10. According to Student 1, which of the following most likely defines the amino acid sequence?

   F. Immersion in a alcohol solution
   G. Negative value of ΔG
   H. Order, type, and number of amino acids
   J. Nucleotide sequence of DNA

11. *Pepsin* is a digestive protein that resides in the stomach where the acidity is large. When pepsin is placed in a bicarbonate solution, which has a much lower acidity, it adopts a different protein structure. This information supports the argument of which student?

   A. Student 1
   B. Student 2
   C. Student 3
   D. Student 4

12. Based on Student 2's explanation, which of the following values of ΔG would prompt correct protein folding?

    F. $\Delta G =$ 304.3 kJ mol^{-1}

    G. $\Delta G =$ 26.7 kJ mol^{-1}

    H. $\Delta G =$ 0.0 kJ mol^{-1}

    J. $\Delta G = -705.8$ kJ mol^{-1}

13. The main assumption behind the arguments of Student 1 and Student 3 is that:

    A. protein structure is highly dependent on environmental conditions.

    B. proteins are able to auto correct mutations.

    C. protein structure is dependent on coded information.

    D. all proteins must be at least several thousand amino acids long.

GO ON TO THE NEXT PAGE.

Passage III

A *universal testing machine* (UTM) is used to test the tensile strength of materials. A specimen of the material is loaded between grips positioned on the base and load cell. When initiated, the load cell will move upward with increasing force until the specimen snaps (See Figure 1).

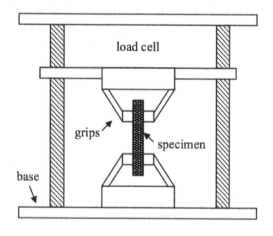

Figure 1

Most UTMs will output a *stress-strain curve* following a test on a given specimen. These graphs will plot the applied tensile stress as a function of the observed strain on the specimen. Tensile stress is defined by the applied pulling force of the load cell over the cross-sectional area of the specimen (MPa), whereas strain is a unitless quantity measured in the change in length of the specimen over the original length ΔL L^{-1}.

A typical stress-strain curve is shown is Figure 2.

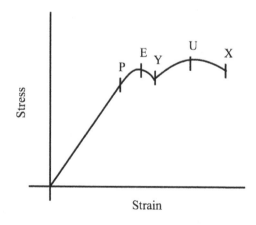

Figure 2

As given from Figure 2:

- **P** is the *limit of proportionality* where the linear relationship between stress and strain ends.

- **E** is the *elastic limit*. Beyond this point the specimen will no longer return to its original shape.

- **Y** is the *yield point* where plastic (nonconservative) deformation begins.

- **U** is the *ultimate tensile stress*, the maximum stress that is applied to the specimen without it snapping.

- **X** is the *failure point*, where the specimen snaps.

For most materials, **P**, **E**, and **Y** are indistinguishable.

Study

A group of physicists test the tensile strengths of four different materials using the universal testing machine. As the specimen is loaded, the tensile stress is graphed against the strain of the material. An X indicates the point of specimen failure. The results are displayed in Figure 2.

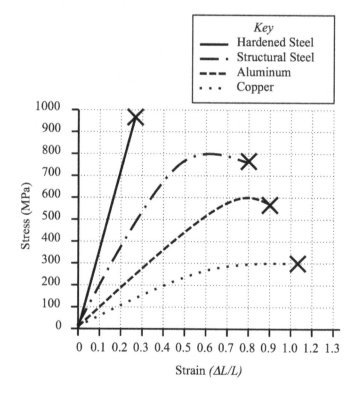

Figure 3

14. According to Figure 3, the maximum value of strain for the structural steel prior to failure is:

    F. 0.3.
    G. 0.8.
    H. 0.9.
    J. 1.0.

15. An architectural engineer must incorporate a material that may endure a strain of 0.7 and still return to its original shape. His colleague recommends structural steel. Based on Figure 2 and Figure 3, is this a good choice?

    A. Yes because at a strain of 0.7, structural steel has passed its elastic limit.
    B. Yes because at a strain of 0.7, structural steel has not yet reached its elastic limit.
    C. No because at a strain of 0.7, structural steel has passed its elastic limit.
    D. No because at a strain of 0.7, structural steel has not yet reached its elastic limit.

16. Based on Figure 3, the material that may endure the largest stress without failure is which of the following?

    F. Hardened Steel
    G. Structural Steel
    H. Aluminum
    J. Copper

17. Based on Figure 3, the ultimate tensile stress (**U**) of Aluminum is:

    A. 900 MPa
    B. 800 MPa
    C. 600 MPa
    D. 300 MPa

18. According to Figure 2, the linear relationship between applied force and strain is maintained if which point is not exceeded?

    F. **P**, limit of proportionality
    G. **E**, elastic limit
    H. **Y**, yield point
    J. **U**, ultimate tensile stress

19. Which of the materials presented in Figure 3 would be still intact following a load of 700 MPa?

    A. Hardened steel only
    B. Hardened steel and structural steel only
    C. Structural steel and aluminum only
    D. Aluminum and copper only

20. *Young's Modulus* is defined by the slope of a given material on a stress-strain curve up to the limit of proportionality. It is thus defined as the linear change in stress/strain and in units of MPa. Large values of the Young's Modulus indicate brittleness, whereas small values indicate malleability. According to Figure 3, which material would be most malleable?

    F. Hardened Steel because it has the highest value of Young's Modulus.
    G. Copper because it has the lowest value of Young's Modulus.
    H. Hardened Steel because it has the lowest value of Young's Modulus.
    J. Copper because it has the highest value of Young's Modulus.

Passage IV

A group of students perform 3 different experiments to understand the physics of music and sound.

Experiment 1

Using a grand piano, the students record the frequencies, f, and wavelengths, λ, of the notes from C of the fourth octave (C_4) to C of the fifth octave (C_5). Then, the students divide the frequency of a given note by the root note to determine the frequency ratio, ϕ. The results are in Table 1 below.

Table 1				
Note	Interval	f (Hz)	λ (cm)	ϕ
C_4	Unison	261.63	131.87	1/1
$C\#_4$	Minor Second	279.07	124.47	16/15
D_4	Major Second	293.33	117.48	9/8
$D\#_4$	Minor Third	311.13	110.89	6/5
E_4	Major Third	329.63	104.66	5/4
F_4	Perfect Fourth	349.23	98.79	4/3
$F\#_4$	Tritone	369.99	93.24	64/45
G_4	Perfect Fifth	392.00	88.01	3/2
$G\#_4$	Minor Sixth	415.00	83.07	8/5
A_4	Major Sixth	440.00	78.41	5/3
$A\#_4$	Minor Seventh	466.16	74.01	16/9
B_4	Major Seventh	493.88	69.85	15/8
C_5	Octave	523.25	65.93	2/1

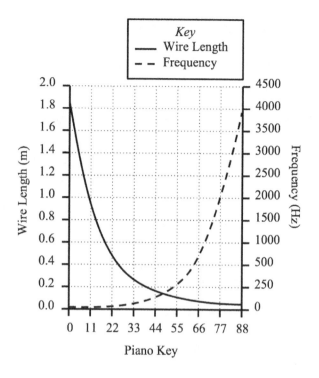

Figure 1

Experiment 3

A 1 m steel piano wire is wound using a piano tuner and the tension recorded. The students pluck the string of a known tension and record the frequency of vibration. Results are shown in Figure 2.

Experiment 2

The students open the piano and measure the length of the steel wire for each of the 88 keys on the piano. The students then record the frequencies of all of the additional keys on the piano. They record and then graph the results which are shown in Figure 1.

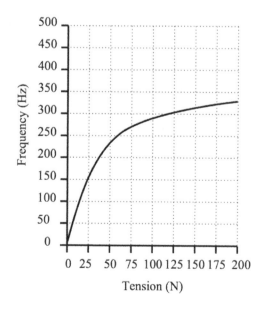

Figure 2

21. According to Figure 1, as wire length increases, f:

    A. increases.
    B. decreases.
    C. increases then decreases.
    D. remains constant.

22. According to Experiment 3, a 1 m wire pulled to a tension of 125 N would give a frequency of:

    F. 150 Hz.
    G. 270 Hz.
    H. 300 Hz.
    J. 325 Hz.

23. Experiments 2 and 3 differed in which of the following ways? In Experiment 2, the students determined how wire length varied with:

    A. wavelength, whereas in Experiment 3 they determined how frequency varied with piano key.
    B. tension, whereas in Experiment 3 they determined how wire length varied with piano key.
    C. frequency, whereas in Experiment 3 they determined how piano key varied with tension.
    D. piano key, whereas in Experiment 3 they determined how frequency varied with tension.

24. Within Experiment 1, a separation of twelve keys defines an octave. According to Experiment 1 and Experiment 2, how many octaves are present on a grand piano?

    F. 4
    G. 6
    H. 7
    J. 8

25. According to the results of Experiment 3, the wire length of piano key 22 is approximately:

    A. greater than 0.8 m.
    B. between 0.8 and 0.6 m.
    C. between 0.6 and 0.4 m.
    D. less than 0.4 m.

26. The relationship between frequencies of different notes within an octave are shown in Experiment 1. To find the frequency of C_6 (the sixth octave of C), the students would have to perform which operation to the frequency of C_4 (the fourth octave of C)?

    F. Divide by 4
    G. Divide by 2
    H. Multiply by 2
    J. Multiply by 4

27. According to music theory, intervals that yield frequency ratios with smaller integers are more *consonant* ("pleasant sounding"), whereas intervals that yield frequency ratios with larger integers are more *dissonant* ("unpleasant sounding"). Which of the following intervals is most dissonant?

    A. Unison
    B. Minor Second
    C. Minor Seventh
    D. Major Seventh

Passage V

The figure below is a pedigree that shows the inheritance of a trait, Trait R, that runs in a family. The likelihood of an individual inheriting Trait R is entirely dependent on Gene R alone. There are two afferent alleles for Gene R: Gene *R*, which is dominant, and Gene *r*, which is recessive.

Each individual in the pedigree was assigned a number (shown below the symbol for an individual) for reference. Geneticists determined that the Gene R genotype for Individual 23 is *Rr* and that the Gene R genotype for Individual 24 is *rr*. Based on these findings, the geneticists concluded that Trait R is a recessive trait.

Pedigree

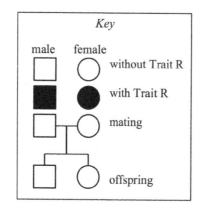

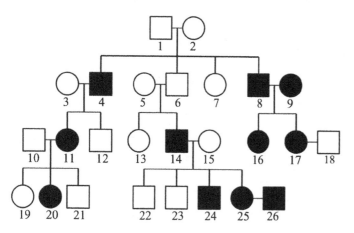

28. How many males are shown in the pedigree?

   F. 7
   G. 13
   H. 14
   J. 26

29. Which individuals are first cousins?

   A. Individual 2 and Individual 4
   B. Individual 8 and Individual 12
   C. Individual 12 and Individual 18
   D. Individual 16 and Individual 24

30. According to the figure, how many individuals in the fourth generation, if any, have Trait R?

   F. 0
   G. 1
   H. 2
   J. 3

31. What are the most likely Gene R genotypes for Individuals 1 and 2?

   A. *RR* and *RR*
   B. *Rr* and *RR*
   C. *Rr* and *Rr*
   D. *Rr* and *rr*

32. If Trait R is a dominant trait instead of recessive, what would a geneticist expect in the pedigree, given that the allelic frequency of Trait R does not change?

   F. Fewer individuals with Trait R
   G. Additional individuals with Trait R
   H. The same number of individuals with Trait R
   J. Additional males only with Trait R

33. What is the probability that offspring from Individual 25 and 26 will have Trait R?

    A.   25%
    B.   50%
    C.   75%
    D. 100%

34. Without knowing that Trait R is a recessive trait, which parents would give evidence that Trait R is indeed recessive?

    F. Individuals 5 and 6
    G. Individuals 8 and 9
    H. Individuals 10 and 11
    J. Individuals 14 and 15

GO ON TO THE NEXT PAGE.

Passage VI

The following experimental setup was used in 12 trials to determine how different factors affect the period (P) and maximum velocity (Vmax) of a pendulum. As shown in Figure 1 below, L represents the length of the string to which a ball is connected. The ball may also vary in mass (M). The pendulum is pulled back to a angle θ and then released. The entire pendulum is enclosed in a sealed box so that the pendulum system may be tested in different mediums. The equilibrium point of the pendulum system is shown by the dotted line.

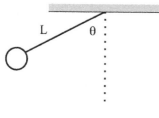

Figure 3

The results of period and maximum velocity are shown in Table 1 below.

Table 1						
Trial	L	M	Medium	Angle	P	Vmax
	(m)	(kg)		(θ)	(s)	(m/s)
1	1.0	0.2	Air	45 °	1.65	3.16
2	1.0	0.3	Air	45 °	1.63	3.14
3	1.0	0.4	Air	45 °	1.60	3.15
4	1.0	0.2	Air	45 °	1.64	3.15
5	1.5	0.2	Air	45 °	1.98	3.75
6	2.0	0.2	Air	45 °	2.43	4.12
7	1.0	0.2	Water	45 °	1.65	3.14
8	1.0	0.2	Ethanol	45 °	6.54	1.40
9	1.0	0.2	Oil	45 °	10.43	0.74
10	1.0	0.2	Air	60 °	1.66	3.96
11	1.0	0.2	Air	45 °	1.67	3.15
12	1.0	0.2	Air	30 °	1.65	2.74

35. Based on Table 1 and the results of Trials 1-3, as the mass of the ball increased, the maximum velocity:

   A. increased only.
   B. decreased only.
   C. increased, then decreased.
   D. varied, but with no general trend.

36. In which trial did the ball experience the smallest maximum velocity?

   F. Trial 3
   G. Trial 6
   H. Trial 9
   J. Trial 12

37. Suppose an additional trial was conducted in which the conditions were identical to trial 4 with the exception that L is equal to 1.2. What would be an appropriate estimate for the period of this new trial?

   A. Less than 1.64 s
   B. Between 1.64 and 1.98 s
   C. Between 1.98 and 2.43 s
   D. Greater than 2.43 s

38. The maximum velocity of the pendulum would be expected to occur:

   F. at the release point.
   G. at 45 degrees to the equilibrium point.
   H. at the equilibrium point.
   J. at the maximum height the pendulum will reach.

GO ON TO THE NEXT PAGE.

39. Suppose in Trial 12 the length had been changed to 3.0 meters and the mass had been changed to 0.3 kg. Our expected value for maximum velocity would most likely be:

A. greater than 3.96.
B. between 3.96 and 3.15.
C. between 3.15 and 2.74.
D. less than 2.74.

40. In order to achieve the greatest maximum velocity, which of the following conditions should be selected?

	Length (m)	Mass (kg)	Medium	Angle (θ)
F.	2.0	0.2	Air	60
G.	1.0	0.2	Air	45
H.	2.0	0.4	Oil	60
J.	1.0	0.4	Oil	45

Law and Freedom

Laws are designed to guide the behavior of citizens and protect them from harm. However, in pursuing this goal, many laws highly regulate citizens' behavior. Laws against loitering, jaywalking, and disturbing the peace with loud music criminalize activities that many critics say should not be considered crimes at all. Arresting and punishing people for harmless offenses limits their freedoms. Others say that strict enforcement encourages respect for the law and promotes equal treatment for all citizens. Are there limits to how far the law should go in regulating personal behavior? How should we think about the tension between the claims of the law and the claims of the individual?

Read and carefully consider these perspectives. Each suggests a particular way of thinking about law and order.

Perspective 1	Perspective 2	Perspective 3
Respect for the law holds society together, and no one should be immune to the law's regulations. If a law is properly passed, then it must be obeyed, regardless of the nature of the behavior it regulates.	Petty laws criminalizing activity that harms no one else rob individuals of some of their freedoms. Laws should be limited to penalizing behavior that harms others.	Laws must be constantly evaluated in legislatures and courts in order to prevent abuses. The way to deal with conflicts over the law is through the institutions that make the laws in the first place.

Essay Task

Write a unified, coherent essay in which you evaluate multiple perspectives on the law and freedom. In your essay, be sure to:

- analyze and evaluate the perspectives given
- state and develop your own perspective on the issue
- explain the relationship between your perspective and those given

Your perspective may be in full agreement with any of the others, in partial agreement, or wholly different. Whatever the case, support your ideas with logical reasoning and detailed, persuasive examples.

ACT3 - A0516

Practice Test

ENGLISH TEST

45 Minutes—75 Questions

DIRECTIONS: In the five passages that follow, certain words and phrases are underlined and numbered. In the right-hand column, you will find alternatives for the underlined part. In most cases, you are to choose the one that best expresses the idea, makes the statement appropriate for standard written English, or is worded most consistently with the style and tone of the passage as a whole. If you think the original version is best, choose "NO CHANGE." In some cases, you will find in the right-hand column a question about the underlined part. You are to choose the best answer to the question.

You will also find questions about a section of the passage, or about the passage as a whole. These questions do not refer to an underlined portion of the passage, but rather are identified by a number or numbers in a box.

For each question, choose the alternative you consider best and fill in the corresponding oval on your answer document. Read each passage through once before you begin to answer the questions that accompany it. For many of the questions, you must read several sentences beyond the question to determine the answer. Be sure that you have read far enough ahead each time you choose an alternative.

PASSAGE I

The Mighty Atom of the Ring

When asked to name the best boxers of all time, most individuals go with the men of highly publicized fights: Muhammad Ali, Sugar Ray Robinson, or perhaps even Mike Tyson, all of whom weighed over 160 lbs with physiques
　　　1
rivaling those of Greek Gods. But what about the women?

A rich historical tradition, Barbara Buttrick was an
　　　2

unlikely candidate for the sport. Even so, this tiny
　　　　　　　　　　　　　　　3

terror known as, "The Mighty Atom of the Ring," played an
　　　　　　　　　　　　　　　4
integral role in putting women's boxing on the map.

1. **A.** NO CHANGE
   B. of who
   C. for whom
   D. for who

2. **F.** NO CHANGE
   G. Though originally an ancient game,
   H. At 4'11" and less than 120 lbs,
   J. A maximum of twelve rounds,

3. **A.** NO CHANGE
   B. Consequently,
   C. After all,
   D. Correspondingly,

4. **F.** NO CHANGE
   G. terror, known as, "The Mighty Atom of the Ring"
   H. terror, known as "The Mighty Atom of the Ring,"
   J. terror, known as "The Mighty Atom of the Ring"

GO ON TO THE NEXT PAGE.

Born in 1930, Buttrick spent most of her early years in Cottingham, Yorkshire. Though she would often spar with boys in the backyard, the inkling that she might become a female boxer wasn't realized until she was 15 years old. At that time, Buttrick read an article <u>fixating on</u> the career of

5

Polly Burns, a woman <u>whose said to be</u> the first ever

6
Women's World Boxing Champion. Buttrick was

inspired by the <u>womans' enthralling stories</u> and

7

<u>begun</u> training on her own. A mere three years later,

8
she was invited to train in London.

[1] Buttrick worked tirelessly for her big break. [2] While in London, she worked as a typist by day, and trained for over three hours each night. [3] As she began to gain success, however, critics arose. [4] <u>Words of hate plastered</u>

9
<u>local newspapers, spreading the word of Buttrick's negative</u>

9
<u>connotations.</u> [5] Buttrick paid the critics no mind and

9

continued to fight in the carnival circuit, <u>which then</u>

10
<u>served as the main arena for women's boxing in the UK.</u>

10

5. **A.** NO CHANGE
   B. pushing
   C. accentuating
   D. highlighting

6. **F.** NO CHANGE
   G. whose been
   H. who's said to be
   J. who's been

7. **A.** NO CHANGE
   B. womans enthralling story's
   C. woman's enthralling stories
   D. woman's enthralling story's

8. **F.** NO CHANGE
   G. began
   H. had began
   J. begins

9. Given that all the following are true, which one provides specific information about the criticism that Buttrick faced?
   A. NO CHANGE
   B. Ridicule seemed to lurk in every corner, waiting to strike.
   C. Finding one's own drive is only made more difficult by unsolicited negative comments.
   D. Newspapers published that Buttrick was "degrading," "monstrous," and an "insult to womanhood."

10. The writer is considering deleting the underlined portion, ending the sentence with a period after the word "circuit." This portion should NOT be deleted because it:
    F. explains why the sport was more popular in the United States than in the United Kingdom.
    G. clarifies a potentially unfamiliar concept.
    H. emphasizes the poor working conditions of female boxers during that period.
    J. creates a clear contrast within the paragraph.

[6] Among the most extreme actors in this attack against Buttrick was the mayor of Dewsbury, who banned her from ever fighting in his town again. [7] Her work began to pay off in 1952, when she was invited to train in Miami, Florida, a city known for <u>one's</u> top-tier training facilities. [8] Two years
11
later, the Mighty Atom of the Ring participated in the first ever nationally televised female fight. [9] Though Buttrick lost the fight to Joann Hagen, who outweighed Buttrick by over thirty pounds, the televised event marked a serious shift in women's <u>boxing; which</u> had validated the popularity of their sport
12
through syndication, by showcasing an alternative definition of womanhood to the entire nation. ☐13

That loss was the last for Buttrick, who continued winning matches until she was named world champion of her weight class in 1957. Now, the Mighty Atom of the Ring is immortalized in the Florida Boxing Hall of Fame; with <u>perseverance and a steadfast nature,</u> Barbara Buttrick
14

helped to change the face of boxing forever. ☐15

11. **A.** NO CHANGE
    B. their
    C. its
    D. it's

12. **F.** NO CHANGE
    G. boxing: which
    H. boxing: The world
    J. boxing, the world

13. For the sake of the logic and coherence of this paragraph, Sentence 6 should be placed:

    A. where it is now.
    B. after sentence 2.
    C. after sentence 4.
    D. after sentence 5.

14. **F.** NO CHANGE
    G. a never-give-up attitude.
    H. a tenacious perseverance.
    J. perseverance.

15. The writer is considering ending the essay with the following statement:

    > Watching sporting events featuring female athletes is an easy and effective way to further this cause.

    Should the writer add this sentence here?

    A. Yes, because it captures the resiliency that Buttrick epitomized.
    B. Yes, because it follows the general chronology of the essay.
    C. No, because it detracts from Buttrick's grueling journey to fame.
    D. No, because it strays too far from the focus of the essay.

PASSAGE II

Europa: The Water Moon

[1]

Within our solar system, Earth is considered paramount in terms of H_2O. Countless space explorations and endless research is dedicated to finding traces of water on other
16

planets—Mars being perhaps most noteworthy. It may
17
come as a surprise, then, that Europa—one of Jupiter's sixty-two known moons—might have us earthlings

beat; scientists speculating that under its top layer of ice
18

lies a vast liquid ocean containing more water than does the
19
entirety of our small planet.

[2]

[A] Europa is cold. Often clocking in around 350 degrees below freezing, this moon is colder than anything earth-dwellers could even begin to comprehend. A massive shell of ice, estimated to be 10 to 15 miles deep, surrounding
20
the entirety of the moon and covers any trace of liquid water
20
from the naked eye. Space exploration isn't yet prepared for a manned spacecraft to travel as far as Jupiter, but if it were, a
21
trip to Europa in a rocket ship would take over two years'

time. [B] For example, Europa is located in a vacuum,
22
meaning the planet completely lacks an atmosphere. Without the protection of an atmosphere, any living being on Europa's surface would be subjected to intense radiation.

16. **F.** NO CHANGE
    G. have been
    H. has been
    J. was

17. If the writer were to delete the underlined portion, the passage would primarily lose:
    A. a foreshadowing the essay's main topic.
    B. an example to contextualize what precedes the underlined portion.
    C. a useful contrast to what precedes the underlined portion.
    D. a transition into discussing many celestial bodies.

18. **F.** NO CHANGE
    G. beat; scientists speculate
    H. beat, scientists speculating
    J. beat, scientists speculate

19. **A.** NO CHANGE
    B. lays a vast liquid ocean containing more water than
    C. lies a vast liquid ocean containing more water then
    D. lays a vast liquid ocean containing more water then

20. **F.** NO CHANGE
    G. surrounding the entire
    H. that surrounds the entirety of the
    J. surrounds the entire

21. **A.** NO CHANGE
    B. Jupiter but
    C. Jupiter, however,
    D. Jupiter however

22. **F.** NO CHANGE
    G. To illustrate,
    H. Consequently,
    J. OMIT the underlined portion.

[3]

[C] Still, recent studies reveal that Europa may be the second best suited place for life within our solar system—after earth, of course. That same ice that made Europa so clearly
23

uninhabitable for humans may act as a protective barrier
24
against radiation for any life underneath. [D] Some speculate

that tides from Jupiter's gravitational pull works to keep the
25

water at habitable temperatures, others believe active
26
volcanoes underneath the moon's surface might do the same.

[4]

[1] While those plans are in the works, don't count on reading the results anytime soon. [2] With all of the
27

excitement surrounding Jupiter's most popular moon,
28
scientists are hungry to explore Europa with an unmanned spacecraft. [3] Until then, the general public will have to settle for fanciful daydreams of extraterrestrials catching some sweet Europa waves. [4] In fact, NASA estimates that such a mission won't come into play until the 2020's. 29

23. A. NO CHANGE
    B. makes
    C. will make
    D. will have made

24. Which choice most clearly emphasizes Europa's climate as it relates to human beings?
    F. NO CHANGE
    G. deserted
    H. barren
    J. unoccupied

25. A. NO CHANGE
    B. works to ensure
    C. work to keep
    D. work to ensure

26. F. NO CHANGE
    G. still others
    H. many others
    J. while others

27. Which of the following alternatives to the underlined portion would be LEAST acceptable?
    A. their
    B. those
    C. its
    D. official

28. Which of the following alternatives to the underlined portion would be LEAST acceptable?
    F. famed
    G. notorious
    H. most noteworthy
    J. renowned

29. Which of the following sequences of sentences makes the final paragraph most logical?
    A. NO CHANGE
    B. 1, 3, 2, 4
    C. 2, 3, 4, 1
    D. 2, 1, 4, 3

Questions 30 asks about the preceding passage as a whole.

30. Upon reviewing the passage and realizing that a transition has been left out, the author composes the following sentence:

> But don't pack your bathing suit into the spaceship just yet.

The most logical placement for this sentence would be:

F. Point A in Paragraph 2
G. Point B in Paragraph 2
H. Point C in Paragraph 3
J. Point D in Paragraph 3

PASSAGE III

Life in Colonial Village

[1]

"This job requires an unwavering passion for reading historical documents, embodying characters, and to interact
                                                          31
with the general public," have stated the classified ad.
                        32
"Employees work arduous hours, almost always

they've foregone the luxuries of modern life. The work
        33
will be physically and academically demanding, so be

prepared to sweat and study."

[2]

[1] An outsider reading this ad might assume its author
                                                     34

had used extreme exaggeration or hyperbole. [2] Known to
                          35
the patrons of Colonial Village as "Susanna Proctor,"

31. A. NO CHANGE
B. embodying characters and to interact
C. embodying characters, and interacting
D. to embody characters and to interact

32. F. NO CHANGE
G. states
H. were stating
J. state

33. A. NO CHANGE
B. they'll forgo
C. forgo
D. foregoing

34. F. NO CHANGE
G. it's
H. they're
J. their

35. A. NO CHANGE
B. extreme exaggeration with hyperbole.
C. exaggerated hyperbole.
D. hyperbole.

my daily work consists of being what many visitors refer to as
36

a "historical reenactor." [3] I myself however, have
37

experienced these conditions firsthand. [4] We village
38
employees refer to ourselves as "colonial interpreters,"
but our tireless summers have encapsulated some of my
fondest memories – irrespective of its official job title. [39]

[3]

So what exactly does the job entail? Colonial

interpreters study and embody real individuals from Colonial

America, later interacting with visitors as if they were those

people. [A] Some cites assigned interpreters to specific
40

historical figures upon employment, others—like Pilgrim
41
Village—allow you to find a character that fits your own

unique sense of self. Though that may sound simple enough, a

keen attention to detail is key. I've read countless colonial

diaries and memoirs, trained in colonial dialects, and studied

up on local history. I sometimes get lost in the menial tasks
42
of the day, finding comfort in using my hands to make useful
42
materials for the village. [B] Susanna Proctor's gender and
42
socioeconomic position in Colonial America dictate my every

move on a daily basis—like an adaptable puzzle that can only

be solved through improvisation.

[4]

Though I relish nearly every moment at Colonial Village,

the most rewarding aspect of my job has remained constant:

fielding questions from patrons. [C] With such an extreme
43
variety of patrons, I must always be prepared to answer any

question, from what my favorite color might be to whether

36. F. NO CHANGE
    G. I spend my days working as
    H. my job's official title is
    J. this is

37. A. NO CHANGE
    B. I, myself, however
    C. I myself, however,
    D. I myself, however

38. F. NO CHANGE
    G. Us
    H. Those
    J. These

39. For the sake of the logic and coherence of this paragraph, Sentence 3 should be placed:
    A. where it is now.
    B. before sentence 1.
    C. before sentence 2.
    D. after sentence 4.

40. F. NO CHANGE
    G. cites assign
    H. sites assigned
    J. sites assign

41. A. NO CHANGE
    B. employment, while others
    C. employment; while others
    D. employment but others

42. Given that all the choices are accurate, which one most specifically illustrates the narrator's work duties?
    F. NO CHANGE
    G. I do a variety of both physically and mentally demanding work for hours on end.
    H. My hands are now instinctively able to cook Yorkshire pie over a fire, weave cloth on a loom, and fashion soaps from raw materials.
    J. Colonial women were required to master many talents, and true to form, I've done just that.

43. A. NO CHANGE
    B. acquiring and then answering patrons' questions.
    C. answering questions from patrons to the best of my knowledge.
    D. dispersing learned knowledge by answering patrons' questions.

GO ON TO THE NEXT PAGE.

or not I knew someone's great-great-great-grandfather who lived down the street. [D] I always prepare to the best of my ability, but an impeccable dialect and a smile can go quite far when you're caught off guard!

Questions 44 and 45 ask about the preceding passage as a whole.

---

44. Upon reviewing the passage and realizing that some information has been left out, the author composes the following sentence:

> In a single day, I might interact with a rambunctious kindergarten field trip immediately after having spoken to a colonial historian.

The most logical placement for this sentence would be:

F. Point A in Paragraph 3
G. Point B in Paragraph 3
H. Point C in Paragraph 4
J. Point D in Paragraph 4

45. Suppose the writer's primary purpose had been to describe a rewarding and enjoyable occupation. Would this essay accomplish that purpose?

A. Yes, because the writer describes activities in a tone denoting fulfillment.
B. Yes, because the writer indicates her preference for this work over previous employment.
C. No, because the author clearly distinguishes between work and leisure times.
D. No, because the author's neutral tone indicates ambivalence.

PASSAGE IV

The Burj Khalifa: Extravagance by Design

In 2004, a team of architects at Skidmore, Owings, and Merril set out to create the tallest building in the world. Six years and $1.5 billion later, the Burj Khalifa <u>was</u> born. All
46

2,716.5 feet of the building tower over the city of Dubai <u>to</u>
47
<u>the architectural prowess of modern man as a true testament.</u>
47

<u>Featuring a three-pronged, Y-shaped floorplan designed to</u>
48

46. F. NO CHANGE
G. will have been
H. is
J. had been

47. A. NO CHANGE
B. to the architectural prowess as a true testament to modern man.
C. as a true testament of modern man to the architectural prowess.
D. as a true testament to the architectural prowess of modern man.

48. F. NO CHANGE
G. The building features
H. With features like
J. While featuring

abstractly mimic a regional desert flower, the hymenocallis.
                                    ‾‾‾‾‾‾‾‾‾‾‾‾‾‾‾‾‾‾‾‾‾‾‾‾
                                              49
This distinct floor plan not only pays homage to cultural

tradition, but also maximizes sprawling views of the

Arabian Gulf. In fact, many of the building's architectural
              ‾‾
                                            50
aspects have artistic undertones. The 162-story tower spirals
‾‾‾‾‾‾‾‾‾‾‾‾‾‾‾‾‾‾‾‾‾‾‾‾‾‾‾‾‾‾‾‾
        50

towards the sky reducing the mass of its reinforced concrete
                                          ‾‾‾‾‾‾‾‾‾
                                             51
frame with increasing altitude. Sky-sourced ventilation

technology takes in chillingly cool, more dry, less humid air
                    ‾‾‾‾‾‾‾‾‾‾‾‾‾‾‾‾‾‾‾‾‾‾‾‾‾‾‾‾‾‾‾‾‾‾‾‾‾‾
                                      52
from the top of the building to help offset the intense desert

climate, and one of the largest condensate recovery systems

recycles outdoor condensation for indoor use.

   The Burj Khalifa's interior design may rival the
   ‾‾
                                     53
extravagance of its exterior. The building's mixed-use layout
‾‾‾‾‾‾‾‾‾‾‾‾‾‾‾‾‾‾‾‾‾‾‾‾‾‾‾‾‾‾‾
        53
includes offices, retail space, residential units, and even the

Giorgio Armani Hotel. In less than a minute's time, an

elevator whisking visitors up to the 124th floor of the building
         ‾‾‾‾‾‾‾‾
           54
to a 360 degree view of the city below. Every corner of the

building, clad in glass and decorative finishings, reflects a

melding of Dubai's rich cultural history with modern design.

49. Which of the following alternatives to the underlined portion would be LEAST acceptable?

   A. flower: the hymenocallis.
   B. flower called the hymenocallis.
   C. flower; called the hymenocallis.
   D. flower—the hymenocallis.

50. Which of the following best transitions from previous topic into remainder of paragraph?

   F. NO CHANGE
   G. Some of the best architecture contains abstract imagery.
   H. In fact, many of the Burj Khalifa's most interesting attributes have practical purposes.
   J. One would be hard pressed to find a floor plan as elaborate.

51. If the writer were to delete the underlined portion, the passage would primarily lose:

   A. a redundant detail.
   B. a reason as to why the building is so tall.
   C. a useful comparison.
   D. a descriptor that emphasizes the need for mass reduction.

52. F. NO CHANGE
   G. cooler, more dry, less humid
   H. chillingly cool, less humid
   J. cooler, less humid

53. If the writer were to delete the underlined portion, the passage would primarily lose:

   A. examples of interior decor.
   B. the logical reasoning behind the interior design.
   C. a clear change in the writer's tone.
   D. a useful transition in subject matter.

54. F. NO CHANGE
   G. when whisking
   H. whisks
   J. for whisking

Though I've never visited myself, I bet it's even better than
$\underline{\text{the Empire State Building! Tourists can even walk through}}$
$_{55}$

an exhibition that details the building's complete construction

and design process. An intensely popular destination,

the Burj Khalifa $\underline{\text{sees}}$ 1.87 million visitors—composed of
$_{56}$

$\underline{\text{tourists and architectural buffs, alike—just}}$ in the year 2013.
$_{57}$

Of course, in time, another development somewhere in

the world may $\underline{\text{someday}}$ overshadow the extreme stature of the
$_{58}$

Burj Khalifa. Regardless of its ranking in size, $\underline{\text{accordingly,}}$
$_{59}$

the Burj Khalifa has retained a spot in architectural

$\underline{\text{history, it also does so}}$ in the minds of its visitors.
$_{60}$

Not sure where to find the building in Dubai? Just look up!

55. A. NO CHANGE
  B. Dubai is home to a plethora of interesting architecture.
  C. Tourism accounts for a sizable portion of Dubai's earnings.
  D. OMIT the underlined portion

56. F. NO CHANGE
  G. having seen
  H. saw
  J. is seeing

57. A. NO CHANGE
  B. tourists and architectural buffs alike—just
  C. tourists and architectural buffs, alike, just
  D. tourists, and architectural buffs alike, just

58. F. NO CHANGE
  G. in some time
  H. eventually
  J. OMIT the underlined portion

59. A. NO CHANGE
  B. moreover,
  C. in addition,
  D. however,

60. F. NO CHANGE
  G. history as well as
  H. history; while also doing so
  J. history; as well as

PASSAGE V

Deaf West and the Rise of Deaf Theater

[1]

In recent years, deaf theater has hurtled into mainstream

culture with a swiftness that cannot be ignored. While

large-scale productions in New York City have widely

popularized the art form, $\underline{\text{small grassroots productions}}$
$_{61}$
$\underline{\text{in the early 1900s can be traced back in the United States.}}$
$_{61}$

61. A. NO CHANGE
  B. the early 1900s can trace back small grassroots productions in the United States.
  C. small grassroots productions can be traced back to the early 1900s in the United States.
  D. in the United States back to the early 1900s, small grassroots productions can be traced.

175

GO ON TO THE NEXT PAGE.

The National Theatre for the Deaf (NTD), founded in 1967,

was the first organization to formally institutionalize

deaf theater as a legitimate, and unique art form,
                  _____
                         62

they toured the nation with productions that enhance spoken
_____
     63
English dialogue with beautiful signing. A former member of

that theatre, however, had a different vision for the future of

the medium.

[2]

As a child, Ed Waterstreet attended countless theater
                                      _____
                                          64
productions with his family. He was the only deaf member of

an otherwise hearing family and although Waterstreet enjoyed
                       _____
                              65
the productions immensely, something was missing. He

dreamed of creating a theater in which patrons—
                     _____
                            66

each one a unique individual—could all share in an inclusive
_____
          67
experience. His journey to doing so began when he joined the

NTD. As a member of the touring company, Waterstreet

felt the medium was lacking. In showing beautiful

interpretations of American Sign Language (ASL),

the company restricted itself from using raw,

intense aspects of ASL that might enhance the
                        _____
                              68

company's storytelling abilities.
_____
    69

62. F. NO CHANGE
G. as a legitimate and
H. being a legitimate and
J. having been a legitimate and

63. A. NO CHANGE
B. touring
C. with tours around
D. with a tour around

64. Which of the following alternatives to the underlines portion would be the LEAST acceptable?

F. bountiful
G. many
H. numerous
J. a myriad of

65. A. NO CHANGE
B. family, and, although
C. family and although,
D. family, and, although,

66. F. NO CHANGE
G. theater: in which
H. theater. In which
J. theater, in it

67. Given that all the following are true, which one most specifically describes the composition of Waterstreet's desired audience members?

A. NO CHANGE
B. deaf, hard-of-hearing, hearing, or otherwise
C. all diverse in background
D. representative of a broader population

68. F. NO CHANGE
G. should of been enhancing
H. would of been enhancing
J. could of surely enhanced

69. A. NO CHANGE
B. companys'
C. companies
D. companies'

[3]

In 1991, Waterstreet took matters into his own hands.
He founded Deaf West Theatre in Los Angeles, California
in so doing exposing the full range of ASL and the
_____
70

richly potential of what deaf theater could become. [72]
_____
71
Since then, the company has incorporated voice and music
with signing and light to adaptations of classical,
contemporary, and original works.

[4]

While that is great news for Waterstreet, it's even better
news for theatergoers: as the visibility of differently abled

people grow on the national stage, there's no stopping this
_____
73
movement for inclusion.

70. F. NO CHANGE
G. on purpose by
H. with the intention of
J. for the reason of

71. A. NO CHANGE
B. rich potential,
C. richly potential,
D. rich potential

72. At this point, the writer is considering adding the following true statement:

> His first productions incorporated no auditory elements at all until Waterstreet noticed that the majority of his audience members were hearing individuals.

Should the writer make this addition here?

F. Yes, because it further describes a technology utilized at the theater.
G. Yes, because it explains the reasoning behind a concept in the following sentence.
H. No, because it is only tangentially related to the topic at hand.
J. No, because it repeats information stated elsewhere in the passage.

73. A. NO CHANGE
B. grows
C. are growing
D. have grown

Questions 74 and 75 ask about the preceding passage as a whole.

---

74. Upon reviewing the passage and realizing that some information has been left out, the author composes the following sentence:

> Two critically acclaimed Broadway musical productions and over eighty prestigious awards later, Deaf West has redefined deaf theater in the United States.

The most logical placement for this sentence would be:

F. At the end of paragraph 2
G. At the beginning of paragraph 3
H. At the beginning of paragraph 4
J. At the end of paragraph 4

75. Suppose the writer had chosen to write an essay that explores deaf culture in various art forms. Would this essay fulfill the writer's goal?

A. Yes, because the essay indicates that deaf theater is becoming more popular.
B. Yes, because deaf theater's success is indicative of the same throughout various art forms.
C. No, because the essay is limited to deaf theater within the United States.
D. No, because the essay focuses too heavily on a single individual.

END OF TEST 1.
STOP! DO NOT TURN THE PAGE UNTIL TOLD TO DO SO.

MATHEMATICS TEST
60 Minutes — 60 Questions

DIRECTIONS: Solve each problem, choose the correct answer, and then fill in the corresponding oval on your answer document.

Do not linger over problems that take too much time. Solve as many as you can; then return to the others in the time you have left for this test.

You are permitted to use a calculator on this test. You may use your calculator for any problems you choose, but some of the problems may be best done without using a calculator.

Note: Unless otherwise stated, all of the following should be assumed:
1. Figures are NOT necessarily drawn to scale.
2. Geometric figures lie in a plane.
3. The word *line* indicates a striaght line.
4. The word *average* indicates arithmetic mean.

1. Tony's last 6 monthly paychecks were $470, $430, $420, $510, $480, and $370. What is the mean of his earnings to the nearest dollar?
   A. $ 432
   B. $ 447
   C. $ 450
   D. $ 465
   E. $2,680

2. For what values is $(x + 1)(x - 2) = 0$ true?
   F. -1 and -2
   G. -1 and 2
   H. 1 and -2
   J. -1 only
   K. 2 only

3. What is $8\sqrt{x - 7r} + 1$ when $x = 8$ and $r = 1$?
   A. 7
   B. 9
   C. 13
   D. 25
   E. 64

4. A store buys desks wholesale for $80 each. To make a profit, the store increases the price of each desk by 8%. How much does the store charge for each desk?
   F. $ 6.40
   G. $ 64.00
   H. $ 86.00
   J. $ 86.40
   K. $144.00

5. Which of the following vectors results from adding the vectors $< 8, 0 >$, $< 1, 1 >$, and $< -3, -4 >$?

   A. $< -24, -4 >$
   B. $< \;\;\; 6, -3 >$
   C. $< \;\;\; 3, -3 >$
   D. $< \;\;\; 6, \;\; 5 >$
   E. $< \;\; 24, \;\; 0 >$

6. The legs of a right triangle are 8 yards and 10 yards, respectively. Which of the following lengths, in yards, is closest to the length of the hypotenuse?

   F. 6.0
   G. 9.0
   H. 12.8
   J. 13.0
   K. 13.6

7. Orlando Meat's online store has various costs for types of meat and a fixed cost for shipping, shown in the table below.

Meat	Shipping	Price per pound
Organic Chicken	$4.00	$1.15
Salted Ham	$6.00	$2.85
Baby Back Ribs	$6.00	$3.50

   Jeffrey wants to ship 6 pounds of baby back ribs to his home. What is his total expenditure?

   A. $ 6.90
   B. $ 9.50
   C. $21.00
   D. $27.00
   E. $57.00

8. Assume j, k, and l are all real numbers. If $j < k$, and $jl > kl$, then what *must* be true of l?

   F. l is larger than j
   G. l is negative
   H. l is between j and k
   J. l is a fraction
   K. l is any real number

GO ON TO THE NEXT PAGE.

9. In the figure below, $\overline{AF}$, $\overline{BE}$, and $\overline{CD}$ are all parallel. If it can be determined, what is the ratio of the perimeter of $ABEF$ to $EBCD$?

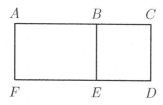

A. $1:4$

B. $1:2$

C. $2:1$

D. $3:1$

E. Cannot be determined from the given information

10. If $x - \dfrac{9}{7} = \dfrac{3}{14}$, then $x =$?

F. 1.5

G. $\dfrac{12}{7}$

H. 3

J. 9

K. 21

11. A pit crew at a race tracked the speed of their driver's car during a 5 second window

t	0	1	2	3	4	5
v	108	112	116	120	124	128

Which of the following equations represents the relationship between v and t?

A. $v = 108t$

B. $v = 4t + 104$

C. $v = 4t + 108$

D. $v = 10t + 98$

E. $v = t + 108$

GO ON TO THE NEXT PAGE.

12. Two shipping companies charge different amounts to ship packages. A partial list of their prices is shown below.

Pounds	UPR	Redex
5	$17	$5
10	$19	$10
15	$21	$15
20	$23	$20

Assuming the pricing trends in the table continue, beyond what weight, in pounds, is UPR the cheaper shipping option?

F. 0

G. 20

H. 22

J. 25

K. 30

13. A bag contains 5 white, 4 red, 2 green, and 4 gold marbles. Antoinette removes a marble, writes down the colour, and then returns it to the bag. If she does this 30 times, how many times should she expect to record a marble that is NOT gold?

A. 20

B. 21

C. 22

D. 25

E. 26

14. A box contains 15 quarters, 11 dimes, and a number of nickels. After experimenting, Pablo estimates the probability of grabbing a nickel is 1 out of 3. If Pablo is correct, approximately how many nickels are in the box?

F. 5

G. 8

H. 13

J. 15

K. 24

15. Rohan went on a road trip and tracked his expenses. He made a pie chart of his results. Rohan's friend Daniel said his numbers were correct, but his graph was not proportional. To fix his pie chart, what measure should Rohan make the central angle for Souvenirs?

A. $\dfrac{\pi}{9}$

B. $\dfrac{\pi}{5}$

C. $\dfrac{2\pi}{5}$

D. $\dfrac{\pi}{2}$

E. $\dfrac{2\pi}{3}$

16. A High School Ultimate Frisbee conference consists of 12 teams. It requires that each team play each other at least once in a season. For x teams in the conference, the number of conference games must then be at least $\dfrac{x(x-1)}{2}$. What is the minimum number of games played in this conference in one season?

F. 33
G. 60
H. 66
J. 71.5
K. 132

17. A certain bacteria population doubles 3 times every second. If the population is initially 12 cells, how many cells will there be in 6 seconds?

A. 9.6×10^1
B. 7.7×10^2
C. 3.1×10^6
D. 1.2×10^7
E. 9.5×10^7

18. The function, f, is defined as $f(x) = 2x - 7x^3$. What is $f(-3)$?

F. -195
G. -183
H. -15
J. 75
K. 183

GO ON TO THE NEXT PAGE.

19. The formula $d = a\left(\dfrac{t+1}{24}\right)$ uses a child's age, t, and the adult dosage of a medication, a, to calculate the child's appropriate dosage, d. Dave and his dad take the same medication. His dad is 47 years old and Dave is 39 years younger than his dad. If his dad takes 250 milligrams, how much should Dave take?

   A.   72.9
   B.   83.3
   C.   93.8
   D.   211
   E. 9,761

20. The product of 2 positive prime integers is 34. Which is the larger integer?

   F.   1
   G.   2
   H.   7
   J.   17
   K.   34

21. Tim creates a frame for his garden which is 10 feet by 3 feet. His existing garden is 7 feet by 2 feet. What area of garden, in square feet, must he add to completely fill his new garden frame?

   A. 14 ft^2
   B. 16 ft^2
   C. 30 ft^2
   D. 34 ft^2
   E. 64 ft^2

22. For what two values of x is the equation $x^2 - 7x + 12 = 0$ true?

   F.   −3 and −4
   G.   4 and 3
   H.   6 and 2
   J.   12 and −7
   K.   12 and 1

23. Susan spends $12.75, before tax, on pens and pencils for her senior year. She buys 3 packs of pens and 4 packs of pencils. Packs of pens are each P dollars each and packs of pencils are C dollars each. A pack of pencils cost half as much as a pack of pens. Which of the following systems of equations, when solved, gives the price, P, of pens and the price, C, of pencils?

A. $\dfrac{1}{2}P = C$

   $4C + 3P = 12.75$

B. $4C = 3P$

   $\dfrac{1}{2}C + P = 12.75$

C. $\dfrac{1}{2}C = P$

   $4C + 3P = 12.75$

D. $\dfrac{1}{2}P = C$

   $3C + 4P = 12.75$

E. $\dfrac{1}{2}P = C$

   $4C - 3P = 12.75$

24. The circle below has diameter $\overline{LM}$ and points N and Q lie on the circle. Arc $\overset{\frown}{MQ}$ measures 50° and minor arc $\overset{\frown}{NQ}$ measures 170°. What is the measure of arc $\overset{\frown}{LN}$?

F. 60°
G. 70°
H. 120°
J. 180°
K. 220°

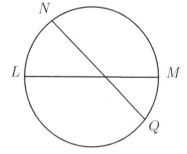

25. One alarm goes off every 90 seconds. A second alarm goes off every 2 minutes. At a certain moment both alarms go off at the same time. How much time elapses from that moment until both alarms go off simultaneously again?

    A.   90 seconds
    B.   120 seconds
    C.   3 minutes
    D.   6 minutes
    E.   12 minutes

26. What value of x satisfies the matrix equation?

$$\begin{bmatrix} 7 & 4 \\ 2 & 3 \end{bmatrix} + \begin{bmatrix} x & 5 \\ -1 & 13 \end{bmatrix} = \begin{bmatrix} 5 & 9 \\ 1 & 16 \end{bmatrix}$$

    F. -2
    G.   0
    H.   1
    J.   2
    K.   5

27. A circle with center $(0, 0)$ and radius 4 is graphed in the standard (x, y) coordinate plane. A line with slope of 1 and x-intercept $(7, 0)$ is graphed in the same plane. At how may points do the line and the circle intersect?

    A.   0
    B.   1
    C.   2
    D.   3
    E.   4

28. In triangle ABC shown below, D lies on $\overline{AB}$ and E lies on $\overline{BC}$ such that triangles ABC and DBE are similar. The length of $\overline{AD}$ is 2, $\overline{DB}$ is 6, and $\overline{AC}$ is 10. What is the length of $\overline{DE}$?

F. 0.625
G. 3.3
H. 4.8
J. 7.5
K. 10

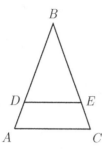

29. Which of the following inequalities is equal to $3x + 6y > -x + 12y - 7$?

A. $x > -\dfrac{3}{2}y + \dfrac{7}{4}$

B. $x > \dfrac{3}{2}y - \dfrac{7}{4}$

C. $x < \dfrac{3}{2}y - \dfrac{7}{4}$

D. $x > 3y + \dfrac{7}{4}$

E. $x > \dfrac{3}{4}x - \dfrac{7}{4}$

30. In a plane, the distinct lines l and m intersect at E. Points A and B are on opposite sides of point E on line l. Point C is on line m. The measure of $\angle CEB$ is $27°$. What is the measure of $\angle AEC$?

F. $27°$
G. $(27 + 90)°$
H. $(90 - 27)°$
J. $(180 - 27)°$
K. $(27 + 27)°$

31. Consider all products ab such that ab is divisible by 6 and b is divisible by 7. Which of the following numbers is not a possible value for ab?

A. 42
B. 86
C. 126
D. 210
E. 294

Questions 32-34 pertain to the following information.

The circle in the standard (x, y) plane below has center $(6, -7)$ and radius 4.

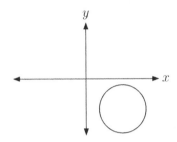

32. Which of the following is the equation of the circle?

   F. $(x - 6)^2 + (y + 7)^2 = 16$

   G. $(x - 6)^2 + (y + 7)^2 = 4$

   H. $(x + 6)^2 + (y - 7)^2 = 16$

   J. $(x - 6)^2 - (y + 7)^2 = 16$

   K. $(x + 6)^2 + (y - 7)^2 = 4$

33. What is the area of the circle in square coordinate units?

   A. 2π

   B. 4π

   C. 16

   D. 16π

   E. 32π

34. The circle will be reflected across the x-axis. What will be the coordinates of the image of this circle's center?

   F. $(\ 6,\ \ 7)$

   G. $(-6, -7)$

   H. $(-6,\ \ 7)$

   J. $(\ 6, -7)$

   K. $(\ 2, -7)$

Questions 35-37 pertain to the following
information.

In the figure below, $ABCD$ is a rectangle with length 6
and height 12, $\overline{CD}$ is the diameter of a semicircle and
$AEFG$ is a square with side lengths 1.5.

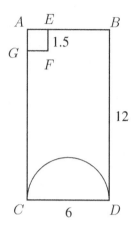

35. The area of square $AEFG$ is what percent of the area
of rectangle $ABCD$?

    A. 2%

    B. 3%

    C. 6%

    D. 18%

    E. 25%

36. What is the perimeter of the semicircular region, which
includes arc $\overset{\frown}{CD}$ and diameter $\overline{CD}$?

    F. 3π

    G. $3\pi + 6$

    H. $6\pi + 6$

    J. $6\pi + 3$

    K. 9π

37. The diagram above is placed on the standard (x, y) coordinate plane with point F at the center $(0, 0)$. What
is the y-coordinate of point D?

    A. -10.5

    B. -4.5

    C. -9

    D. 4.5

    E. 10.5

38. In a certain city people live on average 3 blocks from a bus stop. The probability that someone lives n blocks from the bus stop can be modeled by $P = \dfrac{3^n e^{-3}}{n!}$. Given that $e^{-3} = 0.05$, which of the following values is closest to the probability of someone living 5 blocks from a bus stop?

F. 0.02
G. 0.10
H. 0.16
J. 0.51
K. 2.02

39. In the figure below, lines M and N are parallel and lines R and S intersect M at the same point. If it can be determined, what is the value of x?

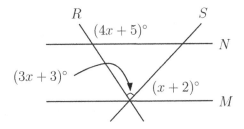

A. 28°
B. 32°
C. 34°
D. 99°
E. Cannot be determined from the given information

40. Let x and y be real numbers such that $x^2 + y = 11$ and $-xy = 14$. What is the value of x?

F. −2
G. −1
H. 2
J. 3
K. 7

41. The table below gives the frequency of scores in a 27 person math class. Which score range contains the median?

Score Interval	Frequency
94 - 100	10
87 - 93	9
80 - 86	3
73 - 79	4
66 - 72	1

  A. 94 - 100

  B. 87 - 93

  C. 80 - 86

  D. 73 - 79

  E. 66 - 72

42. Joe and Mary each swam 20 laps in a 50 meter pool. Mary swam at a rate of 100 meters per minute and Joe swam at a rate of 90 meters per minute. How many more minutes did it take Joe to swim 20 laps than Mary?

  F. 1

  G. 2

  H. 2.5

  J. 10

  K. Joey and Mary finished 20 laps at the same time

43. A square is inscribed in a circle with a diameter of 6 inches as shown below. What is the area, in square inches, of the square?

  A. 4.25

  B. 9

  C. 9π

  D. 18

  E. 18π

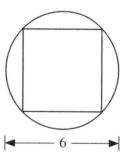

44. Suppose y varies inversely with the square of x. If $y = 12$ when $x = 2$, what is the value of y when $x = 5$?

  F. 1.92

  G. 4.8

  H. 9

  J. 15

  K. 30

45. Given that $x = 7$ when $y = 3$ for the proportion

$\dfrac{4}{x} = \dfrac{k}{y}$, what is the value of y when $x = 28$?

   A. $\dfrac{12}{7}$

   B. 3

   C. 4

   D. $\dfrac{48}{7}$

   E. 12

46. Consider the polynomial $p(x) = \dfrac{5}{6}x + 16$. At what

value of $p(x)$ does $x = p(x)$?

   F. -96

   G. -22

   H. $-\dfrac{96}{5}$

   J. 16

   K. 96

47. $\dfrac{3}{\sqrt{2}} + \dfrac{5}{\sqrt{5}} = ?$

   A. $\dfrac{8}{\sqrt{7}}$

   B. $\dfrac{3\sqrt{5} + 5\sqrt{2}}{\sqrt{7}}$

   C. $\dfrac{3\sqrt{5} + 5\sqrt{2}}{\sqrt{10}}$

   D. $\dfrac{8}{\sqrt{10}}$

   E. $\dfrac{3\sqrt{5} + 5\sqrt{2}}{\sqrt{2} + \sqrt{5}}$

48. A plane begins to descend at an angle of depression of 37°. If the airport the plane is approaching is 240 miles away along the ground, which of the following is closest to the plane's current altitude, in miles?

   F. 120

   G. 150

   H. 160

   J. 180

   K. 320

49. The figure below is constructed of a square, a semi-circle, and a right triangle with side lengths 6 and 8. What is the perimeter of the figure?

   A. $4\pi + 16$

   B. $4\pi + 26$

   C. $4\pi + 32$

   D. $8\pi + 38$

   E. $8\pi + 48$

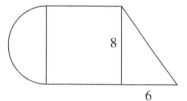

50. On the standard (x, y) coordinate plane, coordinate points $(0, 2)$ and $(3, 4)$ lie on line A and coordinate points $(-3, 4)$ and $(-5, 6)$ lie on line B. What is the point of intersection of lines A and B?

   F. $\left(\dfrac{1}{2}, 2 \right)$

   G. $\left(0, \dfrac{2}{3} \right)$

   H. $\left(-\dfrac{3}{5}, \dfrac{2}{5} \right)$

   J. $(-3, 4)$

   K. $(5, 1)$

51. Which value of x satisfies the equation below?

$$\log_{27} x = -\frac{2}{3}$$

   A. -18

   B. -9

   C. $\dfrac{1}{9}$

   D. $\dfrac{1}{18}$

   E. 9

52. Consider square $ABCD$, with diagonals $\overline{DB}$ and $\overline{AC}$, and shaded rectangle $EFGH$, shown below. Rectangle $EFGH$ intersects the diagonals of square $ABCD$ at points E and F. If both the ratios of $\overline{DE}:\overline{DB}$ and $\overline{CF}:\overline{CA}$ are 1:4, what is the ratio of the area of rectangle $EFGH$ to the area of square $ABCD$?

F. $\dfrac{1}{16}$

G. $\dfrac{1}{10}$

H. $\dfrac{1}{8}$

J. $\dfrac{1}{6}$

K. $\dfrac{1}{3}$

53. The diagram below shows a square of length 3, where each unit length is represented by a pair of dots. Using the same scale, how many dots would a regular polygon with n sides of length q have?

A. nq
B. $nq - 1$
C. $nq - q$
D. $nq - n$
E. $nq + n$

54. Walter mixes 80 mL of Solution A with 20 mL of Solution B. If Solution A is 25% HCl concentrate, and the final mixture is 35% HCl concentrate, what % HCl concentrate is Solution B?

F. 10%
G. 35%
H. 45%
J. 50%
K. 75%

55. The determinant of $\begin{bmatrix} x^2 & -1 \\ -25 & x \end{bmatrix}$ is equal to 2.

What are all possible values of x?

A. -3 only
B. -3 and 3
C. 3 only
D. 9 and 1
E. 9 only

56. Consider the standard (x, y) coordinate plane below with functions $f(x) = x^2$ and $g(x) = A(x - B)^2 + C$. A, B, and C within $g(x)$ are constants. Which of the following statements about A, B, and C is true?

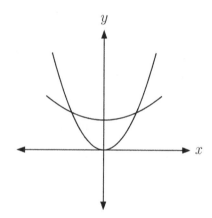

F. $A > 1, B < 0, C = 0$
G. $A > 1, B = 0, C > 0$
H. $A < 1, B = 0, C > 0$
J. $A < 1, B > 0, C = 0$
K. $A < 1, B > 0, C > 0$

57. Which of the following is the solution set to the inequality $|x + 2| < -3$?

A. $\{x \mid -5 < x < 1\}$
B. $\{x \mid x < -5 \bigcup x > 1\}$
C. $\{x \mid x < 1\}$
D. x is an empty set
E. x is the set of all real numbers

GO ON TO THE NEXT PAGE.

58. In the standard coordinate plane (x, y) shown below with origin O, $\angle x = 225°$ and $\overline{RO}$ is 4 coordinate units long. What are the coordinates of point R?

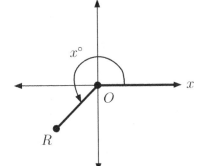

F. $(-2\sqrt{2}, -2\sqrt{2})$

G. $(-2\sqrt{2}, -2)$

H. $\left(-\dfrac{\sqrt{2}}{2}, -\dfrac{\sqrt{2}}{2}\right)$

J. $\left(-\dfrac{3}{2}, -\dfrac{1}{2}\right)$

K. $(-4, -4)$

59. For all values of x where the expression is defined, which of the following expressions is equivalent to the expression below?

$$\frac{\dfrac{2}{x + \frac{1}{2}}}{4 - \dfrac{1}{x + \frac{1}{2}}}$$

A. $\dfrac{2}{3}$

B. $\dfrac{2}{4x + 1}$

C. $\dfrac{8}{4x^2 + 1}$

D. $\dfrac{3}{x + 1}$

E. $\dfrac{2}{3 - x}$

60. Consider the two functions $f(x) = 3x^2 - 1$ and $g(x) = \sqrt{\dfrac{x + n}{3}}$. If $f(g(x)) = g(f(x))$, then $n=$?

F. -1

G. 0

H. 1

J. 3

K. n is not a real number

END OF TEST 2.
STOP! DO NOT TURN THE PAGE UNTIL TOLD TO DO SO.
DO NOT RETURN TO THE PREVIOUS TEST.

READING TEST

35 Minutes — 40 Questions

DIRECTIONS: There are four passages in this test. Each passage is followed by several questions. Choose the best answer to each question and fill in the corresponding oval on your answer document. You may refer to the passages as often as often as necessary.

Passage I

LITERARY NARRATIVE: Passage A is adapted from "The Call of the Wild" by Jack London (©1903 by Jack London). Passage B is adapted from "The Picture of Dorian Gray" by Oscar Wilde (©1890 by Oscar Wilde).

Passage A by Jack London

That night Buck faced the great problem of sleeping. The tent, illumined by a candle, glowed warmly in the midst of the white plain; and when he, as a matter of course, entered it, both Perrault and François bom-
5 barded him with curses and cooking utensils, till he recovered from his consternation and fled ignominiously into the outer cold. A chill wind was blowing that nipped him sharply and bit with especial venom into his wounded shoulder. He lay down on the snow and attempted to sleep,
10 but the frost soon drove him shivering to his feet. Miserable and disconsolate, he wandered about among the many tents, only to find that one place was as cold as another. Here and there savage dogs rushed upon him, but he bristled his neck-hair and snarled (for he was learning fast),
15 and they let him go his way unmolested.

Finally an idea came to him. He would return and see how his own team-mates were making out. To his astonishment, they had disappeared. Again he wandered about through the great camp, looking for them, and again he
20 returned. Were they in the tent? No, that could not be, else he would not have been driven out. Then where could they possibly be? With drooping tail and shivering body, very forlorn indeed, he aimlessly circled the tent. Suddenly the snow gave way beneath his fore legs and he sank
25 down. Something wriggled under his feet. He sprang back, bristling and snarling, fearful of the unseen and unknown. But a friendly little yelp reassured him, and he went back to investigate. A whiff of warm air ascended to his nostrils, and there, curled up under the snow in a snug ball,
30 lay Billee. He whined placatingly, squirmed and wriggled to show his good will and intentions, and even ventured, as a bribe for peace, to lick Buck's face with his warm wet tongue.

Another lesson. So that was the way they did it, eh?
35 Buck confidently selected a spot, and with much fuss and

waste effort proceeded to dig a hole for himself. In a trice the heat from his body filled the confined space and he was asleep. The day had been long and arduous, and he slept soundly and comfortably, though he growled and barked
40 and wrestled with bad dreams.

Passage B by Oscar Wilde

"Stop!" faltered Dorian Gray, "stop! you bewilder me. I don't know what to say. There is some answer to you, but I cannot find it. Don't speak. Let me think. Or, rather, let me try not to think."

45 For nearly ten minutes he stood there, motionless, with parted lips and eyes strangely bright. He was dimly conscious that entirely fresh influences were at work within him. Yet they seemed to him to have come really from himself. The few words that Basil's friend had said
50 to him—words spoken by chance, no doubt, and with wilful paradox in them—had touched some secret chord that had never been touched before, but that he felt was now vibrating and throbbing to curious pulses.

Music had stirred him like that. Music had troubled
55 him many times. But music was not articulate. It was not a new world, but rather another chaos, that it created in us. Words! Mere words! How terrible they were! How clear, and vivid, and cruel! One could not escape from them. And yet what a subtle magic there was in them!
60 They seemed to be able to give a plastic form to formless things, and to have a music of their own as sweet as that of viol or of lute. Mere words! Was there anything so real as words?

Yes; there had been things in his boyhood that he had
65 not understood. He understood them now. Life suddenly became fiery-coloured to him. It seemed to him that he had been walking in fire. Why had he not known it?

With his subtle smile, Lord Henry watched him. He knew the precise psychological moment when to say noth-
70 ing. He felt intensely interested. He was amazed at the sudden impression that his words had produced, and, remembering a book that he had read when he was sixteen, a book which had revealed to him much that he had not known before, he wondered whether Dorian Gray was passing

through a similar experience. He had merely shot an arrow into the air. Had it hit the mark? How fascinating the lad was!

80

Questions 1–3 ask about Passage A.

---

1. Which of the following actions in Passage A is presented as being more figurative than literal?

   A. "glowed warmly in the midst" (lines 2–3)
   B. "bit with especial venom" (line 8)
   C. "aimlessly circled the tent" (line 23)
   D. "whiff of warm air ascended" (line 28)

2. Which of the following best describes Buck's interaction with Billee in Passage A?

   F. Buck interacts with Billee as if they are close allies.
   G. The initial interaction was tense but ultimately became friendly.
   H. Billee and Buck are preparing to fight with each other.
   J. Buck ambushes a sleeping Billee.

3. Passage A indicates that Buck ultimately slept:

   A. in a hole dug under the snow.
   B. inside of a tent used for cooking.
   C. next to his teammate Billee.
   D. outside in the snow.

Questions 4–7 ask about Passage B.

---

4. The author of Passage B most likely includes the information in the third paragraph (lines 54–63) in order to:

   F. describe a character's love for music.
   G. explain Lord Henry's motivation behind the conversation with Dorian Gray.
   H. emphasize the unexpected effect that words can have on a person.
   J. provide an example of vivid and cruel words.

5. Based on Passage B, Lord Henry's reaction toward Dorian Gray can best be described as:

   A. captivated.
   B. shrewd.
   C. bewildered.
   D. annoyed.

6. According to Passage B, the words spoken by Basil's friend:

   F. were paradoxical and spoken by chance.
   G. felt like walking through fire.
   H. were easy to escape from.
   J. sounded completely articulate.

7. As it is used in line 46, the word *dimly* most nearly means:

   A. darkly.
   B. brightly.
   C. clearly.
   D. vaguely.

Questions 8–10 ask about both passages.

---

8. Both passages make use of which of the following?

   F. Direct quotations from a character
   G. Sensory descriptions of the passage's setting
   H. Emotional language to describe a character's inner thoughts
   J. Flashbacks to a character's youth

9. Which of the following statements best captures a main difference in the focus of the two passages?

   A. Passage A focuses on the physical setting of an interaction, while Passage B focuses on the time period of an interaction.
   B. Passage A focuses on a character's feelings and emotions, while Passage B focuses on a character's actions.
   C. Passage A focuses on a character's interaction with others in a group, while Passage B focuses on the relationship between two characters.
   D. Passage A focuses on a transformational experience for a character, while Passage B focuses on a character's unchanging state.

10. The main characters of Passage A and Passage B both:

   F. ultimately become comfortable in their surroundings.
   G. reflect on their feelings after a conversation with another character.
   H. experience an event that changes their perspective.
   J. find complete resolution for their discomfort.

Passage II

SOCIAL SCIENCE: This passage is adapted from *Indo European Languages* by Emily Laar (©1929 by Emily Laar).

In the Celtic languages spoken by the natives of Ireland and Wales, the word for mother is *mathir*. In India, five thousand miles away, the Sanskrit word for mother is *matár*. In the regions between these two extremes, the
5 word for mother is strikingly similar: for Germanic speakers, it's *mutter*, while the speakers of Romance languages say *mère*, *madre*, and *mama*, variations of the original Latin word *mater*.

It is no coincidence that the word sounds so similar
10 in these languages, since they are all members of the Indo-European language family. Over four hundred living languages are part of this family, and its speakers are scattered all over the globe. Though travelers and commentators had noticed similarities in the vocabularies of languages spo-
15 ken in India, Persia, and Europe, it wasn't until 1798 that concrete links were established. In that year, the English philologist William Jones first described deep affinities between Sanskrit, one of the classical languages of India, and ancient Greek and Latin. These languages shared more
20 than just a similar basic vocabulary—they had deep grammatical and syntactic commonalities as well.

How could very different peoples so widely scattered across Eurasia, speak languages that shared so many structural similarities? Two centuries of scholarly investiga-
25 tion have shown a strong genetic relationship among the Indo-European languages. Though the contingencies of history led them to evolve in different directions, they are all rooted in a common source. Just as Latin—which was spread across Europe by the Roman conquest—evolved
30 into French, Spanish, Portuguese, Romanian, and other tongues, so did languages as diverse as Russian and Farsi descend from a common linguistic ancestor. Scholars have dubbed this original language Proto-Indo-European.

No one knows for sure what this language sounded
35 like or where it evolved. No one has heard it spoken. Instead, scholars reconstructed it from the evidence embedded in living and extinct Indo-European languages, tracing the genealogies of words back to their ultimate sources. By sifting through thousands of years of available linguis-
40 tic evidence, scholars can find the earliest form of a given word in a number of languages and from this can infer which form was the earliest of them all, that is, which one is the Proto-Indo-European form of the word. Take mother, for example. By tracing the oldest forms of the
45 word in the oldest Indo-European languages (in this case, Sanskrit, Avestan, Proto-Germanic, and Anatolian), scholars hypothesized that the original form of the word was *méhter*. This process does more than than just suggest the original forms of words. By tracing core vocabularies re-
50 lated to kinship, bodily functions, activities, animals, and natural phenomena, scholars can also infer the nature of Proto-Indo-European culture.

To be sure, this is a controversial field of study, and several hypotheses about this ancient culture have been
55 advanced and are hotly debated today. The two most prominent explanations are the Kurgan and the Anatolian hypotheses. Both hypotheses share one core conclusion long accepted by the scholarly community. Since there is no Proto-Indo-European word for ocean—this word ap-
60 pears in a wide variety of distinct forms in descendent languages—the original culture was an inland one that grew up far away from the sea. Otherwise, the two explanations differ dramatically.

The Kurgan hypothesis argues that the Proto-Indo-
65 European homeland was on the wide plains of what is now Ukraine, approximately five thousand years ago. Proponents focus on the fact that two of the best attested Proto-Indo-European words are those for horse and sheep, which suggest that the first Indo-European speakers were herders
70 whose domestication of the horse gave them a military advantage over neighboring tribes. Archaeological evidence from the region has uncovered remnants of a culture that measured wealth in herds of animals and used chariots in warfare. If this was the culture associated with Proto-Indo-
75 European, it suggests that the language was spread by conquerors who wandered farther and farther from their ancestral homeland in a series of migrations that took culture in every direction.

The Anatolian hypothesis, by contrast, locates the
80 Indo-European homeland in the heart of what is now Turkey, in fertile valleys where archaeologists have found evidence of the first sustained use of agriculture. This hypothesis relies on the common root of words related to farming, such as wheat and sickle, and argues that the
85 Proto-Indo-European speakers were the first farmers, who spread their language along with their revolutionary form of food production. In this view, the broad range of Indo-European languages is due to the spread of farming and the culture that first introduced it. Instead of coming as con-
90 querors, Indo-Europeans came as bearers of new ideas.

Given the conjectural nature of the field, there is as yet no definitive proof for either of these hypotheses. One promising new tool, though, is the science of genetics. If the spread of Indo-European languages can be correlated
95 with the presence of certain genetic markers, we may be able to definitively identify the source of hundreds of the world's languages.

11. In the context of the passage, lines 79–82 primarily serve to:

   A. explain the geographical importance of Turkey to language development.
   B. build on and support the logic put forth in the Kurgan hypothesis.
   C. illustrate the role of archaeologists in agriculture.
   D. introduce a new theory and compare it to another theory.

12. In the passage, modern-day Ukraine is significant to the Kurgan hypothesis because:

   F. it is likely the homeland of the Proto-Indo-European language.
   G. its inhabitants five thousand years ago were sheep herders.
   H. its modern language is a close relative to Greek and Sanskrit.
   J. its cultural features disprove the Anatolian hypothesis.

13. The references to the word "mother" most directly support which of the following points made in the passage?

   A. Tracing word origins gives information about cultural values in addition to language.
   B. Modern languages should transition to using the Proto-Indo-European forms of words.
   C. The differences between word forms make origins impossible to trace.
   D. Scholars are now able to accurately speak Proto-Indo-European.

14. According to the passage, the number of living languages in the Indo-European family is:

   F. more than 400.
   G. approximately 1,000.
   H. approximately 5,000.
   J. less than 1,000,000.

15. The passage states that the shared conclusion of the Kurgan and Anatolian hypotheses is that the Proto-Indo-European society:

   A. had a military advantage, because they used chariots for warfare.
   B. lived inland, because they had no word for ocean.
   C. were farmers, because they had words for 'wheat' and 'sickle'.
   D. shared language traits with Sanskrit- and Latin-speaking neighbors.

16. The author most likely includes the last paragraph (lines 91–97) in order to:

   F. introduce a potential path for continued study of language origin hypotheses.
   G. prove the merit of one hypothesis about language origins.
   H. diminish the importance of a branch of linguistics.
   J. supply evidence that disproves two prominent explanations about the Proto-Indo-European language.

17. According to the passage, the similarities between Sanskrit, Greek, and Latin include:

   A. cultural and linguistic ties.
   B. basic vocabulary only.
   C. vocabulary as well as grammar and syntax.
   D. the exact same grammatical structure.

18. As it is used in line 28, the phrase "rooted in" most nearly means:

   F. planted from.
   G. based on.
   H. will become.
   J. conclude at.

19. The author speculates that a potential future direction for the study of languages is:

   A. the spread of languages through agricultural techniques.
   B. the use of genetic markers to identify where language groups come from.
   C. a focus on differences, rather than similarities, between language groups.
   D. an emphasis on speculation about groups who speak similar languages.

20. Based on the passage, the field of study about Proto-Indo-European languages would best be characterized as:

   F. unerring.
   G. calm.
   H. contentious.
   J. unconcerned.

Passage III

HUMANITIES: This passage is adapted from *Famous Writers' Routines* by Nicholas Reyn (©2011 by Nicholas Reyn).

The celebrated English novelist Graham Greene wrote five hundred words a day. No more, no less. If Greene reached his daily quota of words in the middle of a climactic scene, or even in the middle of a sentence, he would
5 stop. Resolution would have to wait for the next day. If, as was often the case, Greene was under financial pressure, he would split the work and assign two hundred and fifty words to whatever potboiler thriller he was writing to pay the bills and the other two hundred and fifty to a long-term
10 writing project. Greene was noted for his peculiar discipline by friends and colleagues, and though it may seem rigid, one can hardly argue with the results: twenty-four novels and dozens of short stories, some of which—like *The Power and the Glory* and *Brighton Rock*—are regarded
15 as among the best English fiction of the twentieth century.

Ask one hundred fiction writers to describe their creative routines and you will receive one hundred distinct answers. Writing fiction is both an art and a craft. Like any other art, it draws on the deep and obscure wellsprings of
20 the imagination, but so long as a story stays in the writer's head it remains formless. Just as a sculptor sees in a marble block the shape she wishes to carve out of it, so a writer draws upon a vastness of her inner life to give shape to a story. But do writers cultivate the discipline necessary to
25 craft a work of art? Is their art influenced, or even altered, by their individual habits?

Haruki Murakami made his daily routine an integral part of his craft. Arising at four A.M. daily, he would work for five or six hours, then exercise vigorously and read be-
30 fore retiring at nine P.M. During the months—sometimes years—it took him to write a novel, he never deviated from this regimen. The repetition, he said, became a form of mesmerism, a way of inducing a waking trance that helped him reached the state of mind needed for sustained cre-
35 ative work. This, some critics have suggested, may help explain the languid, dreamlike tone of Murakami's novels, which often read as if they were conjured whole out of the writer's subconscious.

Murakami's monk-like discipline contrasts sharply
40 with the method of Vladimir Nabokov. Never one for solitude, Nabokov wrote in the spaces between social engagements and teaching responsibilities. A garrulous man, Nabokov's days were consumed by meals with friends, family excursions, and virtuoso lectures at a variety of col-
45 leges and universities. This daily schedule was frequently punctuated by naps and correspondence. Yet in the midst of it all, Nabokov wrote novels, stories, and essays of exquisite quality. Novels like *Lolita* and *Pale Fire* are often mentioned as some of the very best of recent decades—
50 an extraordinary feat for a loquacious academic who only learned English in his twenties.

Perhaps, then, routine is an incidental element of the writer's craft compared to innate talent. But if this is so, how to explain the habits of Ernest Hemingway? Whereas
55 a writer like Graham Greene set himself a rigorous word limit, Hemingway wrote exhaustively, pouring out words until he felt empty. Depending on the day, he might have set down one hundred words, or three thousand. But as soon as the frenzy of writing was finished, the patient
60 work of editing began. Hemingway would spend the latter parts of the day laboriously reworking his morning's output, mostly by striking out many of the words, sentences, and paragraphs he had written. The result was Hemingway's signature minimalism, a staccato form of English
65 that infused each terse word with a universe of human emotion.

While Nabokov could take thirty minutes of the day and turn out a fully crafted page, Hemingway spent hours polishing his work, reducing his verbose early drafts into
70 finely wrought, exceptionally clear English prose. Between Nabokov's inspired sessions and Hemingway's patient labors, it is impossible to judge which method is "better": what matters is the quality of the art ultimately produced.

75 Creative routines are as unique as the artists who follow them. Perhaps they are, in the final analysis, the idiosyncratic reflections of the inner reality that writers struggle to translate into our shared world. Inevitably, they leave their traces in the completed work which, read care-
80 fully, discloses every ounce of effort that went into its creation.

21. The main purpose of the passage is to:

   A. identify the optimal method for a writer's creative process.
   B. provide details about English novelist Graham Greene's daily routine.
   C. compare the diverse creative routines of writers.
   D. explain why literature is the most important artistic medium.

22. It can reasonably be inferred from lines 5–10 that Graham Greene split up his daily quota of word because he:

   F. did not want to stop his train of thought in an inconvenient place.
   G. wanted to continue a project, but needed to finish a potentially better-paying novel.
   H. was afraid to spend too much time on his writing.
   J. wanted to focus on short stories more than novels.

200

GO ON TO THE NEXT PAGE.

23. Based on the passage, Ernest Hemingway's signature style most likely came from his:

  A. complete lack of routine and structure.
  B. frantic writing followed by strenuous editing.
  C. innate talent, despite his lack of hard work.
  D. distractions in the form of teaching and social engagements.

24. According to the passage, novelist Graham Greene wrote exactly:

  F. 30 minutes per day.
  G. 40 novels in his career.
  H. 250 words per book.
  J. 500 words per day.

25. As it is used in line 46, *punctuated* most nearly means:

  A. combined.
  B. interrupted.
  C. emphasized.
  D. stressed.

26. The passage most strongly suggests that the creative routines of writers:

  F. work better for some authors than others.
  G. should be standardized to become more effective.
  H. do not have any effect on the finished product.
  J. are evident in their works, if read closely.

27. The author characterizes the daily routine of Haruki Murakami as:

  A. rigid; Murakami never strayed from his strict routine.
  B. varied; Murakami sometimes worked and sometimes exercised.
  C. fluid; Murakami did whatever he needed to achieve a dreamlike tone.
  D. lazy; Murakami wrote subconsciously without any daily effort.

28. The main idea of the second paragraph (lines 16–26) is that:

  F. sculptors are the model for the writing process.
  G. fiction writing requires technique and artistry.
  H. all writers follow a similar process to create.
  J. a disciplined routine is more important to writers than artists.

29. In the passage, which of the following activities is NOT mentioned as part of a writer's routine?

  A. Lecturing at colleges and universities
  B. Vigorously exercising and reading
  C. Establishing a word quota and trying to surpass it
  D. Editing work from earlier in the day

30. According to the passage, Vladimir Nabokov's novels are impressive because he:

  F. was overly stressed about the quality of his work.
  G. was an unhappy and withdrawn man.
  H. did not learn English until he was in his twenties.
  J. wrote books while at restaurants with friends.

Passage IV

NATURAL SCIENCE: This passage is adapted from *Bee Colony Collapse* by Tanya Boller (©2009 by Tanya Boller).

We live in an era of ecological disasters. Many of them are grand and dramatic: the melting of polar ice, the surge of unprecedentedly powerful hurricanes, and the onset of severe, years-long droughts. But one of the most omi-
5 nous natural disasters of our time has been happening has been happening quietly and inconspicuously all around us. Over the last several years, honey bee colonies have mysteriously collapsed, leading to the death of approximately 25% of the world's bee population. While this trend has
10 been occurring for decades—there were 5.9 million active hives in the United States in 1947, compared to 2.44 million in 2008—the pace has quickened in recent years. During the winter of 2001 in Pennsylvania, nearly half of all active honey bee hives collapsed.

15   Scientists do not understand why this is happening. Without warning, worker bees desert their colonies, leaving behind the queen, eggs and larvae, and abundant food stores. In most cases, the queen is still healthy and capable of laying eggs and capped brood—bee larvae undergoing
20 the transformation into mature adults—are present. But without the workers, the hive dies. The effect, according to apiologists, is comparable to seeing a thriving, life-filled city abruptly empty out.

Theories as to the causes of colony collapse disorder
25 (CCD) abound. One possible cause is disease. In 2006, Israeli scientists announced the discovery of a virus transmitted by tiny parasites that attacks the RNA of honey bees, resulting in paralysis and death. The virus has been detected in some collapsed colonies, suggesting that a plague
30 caused the masses of worker bees to flee the hive. In one case, the worker bees of a virus-infected colony were observed depositing the dead as far away from the hive as their flight range allowed, offering a glimpse of how CCD might look in its early stages, before abandonment.

35   A second theory is that the use of pesticides to control crop-attacking pests may also be harming bees. Neonicotinoid pesticides are neurotoxic, and either kill or drive away pests by destroying nervous system function. The paralytic feature of this pesticide may account for the fact that
40 stray worker bees found near collapsed hives demonstrate impaired and erratic movement, suggesting a nervous system disorder. However, some bees found in these circumstances were found to only have trace amounts of neonicotinoids in their systems.

45   Finally, some researchers have suggested that CCD is related to increased stress levels in honey bees. Commercial honey producing companies—which have been hit hard by collapses—have progressively lengthened their pollination seasons to increase production, which
50 means that bees have less time to rest during the winter.

Also, drought conditions in honey-producing regions have forced bees to hunt farther and longer to find adequate supplies of nectar to feed the hive. These stressors could contribute to weakening bees' immune systems, leaving them
55 more vulnerable to infection or poisoning.

This troubling phenomenon has engaged widespread attention because it has the potential to damage food production networks. Bees play an essential, if unobtrusive, role in pollinating a huge variety of plants, including many
60 staple foodstuffs. Pollinating these crops, mainly fruits and vegetables, is part of the larger role bees play in pollinating the plant life of various ecosystems. The rising rates of CCD means there are fewer bees to perform these vital functions. In effect, the collapses slow down ecologi-
65 cal circulatory systems. Plants that aren't pollinated do not reproduce, produce fruit, or store the energy necessary to survive winter. As bees die, plants that human civilization relies upon for its own survival begin to die as well.

Authorities have taken steps to address the crisis.
70 Many countries have banned neonicotinoids, and others are crafting new regulations to shorten pollinating seasons for commercial honey producers. But CCD may in part be caused by a larger problem: the ongoing transformations wrought by climate change. As temperatures become ei-
75 ther hotter or colder in a given ecosystem, some plants die while others adapt. Increased rain, or the greater likelihood of drought, makes nectar harder to find and pollination more difficult. Changes to a region's average humidity may impair bees' ability to travel as far as they once
80 did, resulting in a smaller foraging range. This, in turn, leaves the plants outside of that range unpollinated, creating a negative feedback loop that puts bee hives at risk of starvation.

The fate of honey bees, then, may be a warning to
85 the rest of us. Shifting climate patterns may disrupt long established, well-balanced ecosystems, disrupting the delicate cycle of life for all species.

31. The author cites the statistics in lines 9–14 to introduce the passage's argument that:

A. most people are aware of the problems affecting bees.

B. climate change is a nuisance for humans.

C. bees will likely be extinct within 50 years.

D. honey bee colonies are in rapid decline.

32. According to the passage, one possible cause for CCD advanced by Israeli scientists is:

F. a virus that attacks the RNA of honey bees.

G. pesticides that contain neurotoxins.

H. worker bees killing and disposing of other bees.

J. high stress levels among bee populations.

33. Which of the following questions is directly answered in the passage?

- **A.** What happens to plants when they are not pollinated?
- **B.** What is the definitive cause of CCD?
- **C.** How does banning neonicotinoids affect bee populations?
- **D.** Why do bees abandon their colonies when the queen is healthy?

34. In lines 21–23, the author most likely compares a hive to a city in order to:

- **F.** show the benefits of urban beekeeping.
- **G.** illustrate a phenomenon with an example.
- **H.** give one researcher's theory about colony collapse.
- **J.** put into perspective that human disasters are more drastic than those of bees.

35. The passage states that changes to average humidity in a region can cause:

- **A.** changes in the types of crops bees can pollinate.
- **B.** an increase in honey production by local hives.
- **C.** a reduction in the use of neonicotinoids for farming.
- **D.** a decreased foraging range for bees.

36. The main purpose of the fifth paragraph (lines 45–55) is to:

- **F.** conclude the discussion about the problems facing bee hives.
- **G.** introduce one theory about the cause of CCD.
- **H.** contrast the author's opinion with the findings of researchers.
- **J.** use CCD as an example of diseases affecting other animal species.

37. All of the following are related to the stress level of honey bees EXCEPT:

- **A.** a weakened immune system.
- **B.** longer pollination seasons.
- **C.** viruses transmitted by tiny parasites.
- **D.** drought conditions in honey-producing regions.

38. As it is used in line 37, *drive* most nearly means:

- **F.** commute.
- **G.** inspire.
- **H.** force.
- **J.** encourage.

39. According to the passage, when worker bees desert their colonies, they leave behind:

- **A.** other bees, who take over as the workers.
- **B.** sufficient food stores and a healthy queen and larvae.
- **C.** large stores of honey that go untouched.
- **D.** supplies of neurotoxins that they created.

40. Based on the passage, the efforts of countries to ban neonicotinoids and shorten pollinating seasons are likely:

- **F.** not enough to combat the larger problems caused by climate change.
- **G.** proven methods to eradicate CCD in honey bee populations.
- **H.** applauded by the general public, who care deeply about the needs of bees.
- **J.** the final step in winning the war against CCD.

SCIENCE TEST
35 Minutes—40 Questions

DIRECTIONS: There are six passages in this test. Each passage is followed by several questions. After reading a passage, choose the best answer to each question and fill in the corresponding oval on your answer document. You may refer to the passages as often as necessary. You are NOT permitted to use a calculator on this test.

Passage I

A group of biologists conduct a yearlong study of two different terrestrial biomes to observe differences in climate and productivity. Two separate biomes are chosen from two distinct terrestrial regions. The biomes to be studied are *Tropical Wet Forest* and *Temperate Grasslands*.

Study 1

The biologists took monthly temperature readings, in degrees Celsius, using 15 thermometers at various locations within each biome. The average temperature recording was calculated. The biologists measured precipitation using 15 hydrometers at various locations within each biome. The average precipitation was calculated. The results for the tropical wet forest can be seen in Figure 1 and the results for the temperate grasslands can be seen in Figure 2.

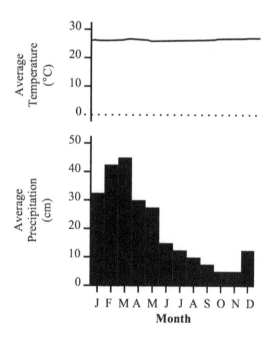

Figure 1

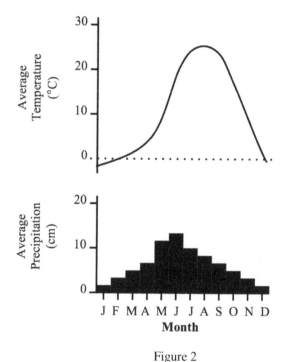

Figure 2

Study 2

The biologists calculated the *Net Primary Productivity* of each biome by measuring carbon dioxide emissions in milligrams of carbon dioxide per square meter per day. The results are shown in Figure 3.

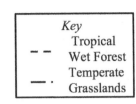

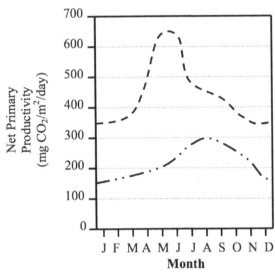

Figure 3

3. From the months of January to June, the average temperature for the temperate grassland:

A. increased, whereas the average precipitation for the temperate grassland decreased.

B. decreased, whereas the average precipitation for the temperate grassland increased.

C. increased, whereas the average precipitation for the temperate grassland increased.

D. decreased, whereas the average precipitation for the temperate grassland decreased.

4. A researcher is attempting to identify the most likely habitat of a tree-dwelling bird. The bird prefers an annual temperature range that stays within 10 °C and an annual precipitation that stays above 20 cm each month. Based on the results of Studies 1 and 2, the preferred habitat of this bird is:

F. a tropical wet forest.

G. a temperate grassland.

H. both a tropical west forest and a temperate grassland.

J. neither a tropical wet forest nor a temperate grassland.

5. Because the biologists recorded their measurements and performed calculations once a month, they were able to determine how:

A. the average precipitation in a biome is dependent on its average temperature.

B. the average temperature in a biome is dependent on its net primary productivity.

C. environmental factors are dependent on the month of the year.

D. the net primary productivity in a biome is dependent on its average precipitation.

1. According to Study 1, the month with the highest recorded average precipitation for the tropical wet forest was:

A. January.

B. March.

C. May.

D. July.

2. According to Figure 1, in the month of October for the tropical wet forest, the average precipitation was:

F. 5 cm.

G. 10 cm.

H. 15 cm.

J. 20 cm.

6. A researcher observes that the maximum value of net primary productivity for both the temperate grassland and tropical wet forest biomes occurs approximately 3–5 months after the highest average precipitation recording. The most likely explanation for this is that:

F. warm weather is necessary for maximum net primary productivity.

G. a delay in measurements is required after the maximum precipitation value for maximum net primary productivity is recorded.

H. the maximum net primary productivity may only occur following a drought.

J. the net primary productivity must stay constant year-round.

Passage II

A group of students use the setup below to understand how forces and energy are distributed depending on the location of a mass on a horizontal beam. A block of mass M is set upon a beam of total length 8 meters. The length of the beam was held constant in both studies.

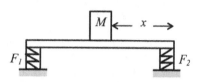

Figure 1

The beam rests upon two springs which will give a force reading in Newtons (N), which are expressed as F_1 and F_2. The students also may place the mass a distance x meters from the right most end of the beam.

Study 1

The students use a mass of 10 kg and place it at several different locations of x. In addition to measuring F_1 and F_2, the students also will measure the amount each spring was compressed by in meters as x_{c1} and x_{c2}. Utilizing the spring compression, and the spring constants of the two springs, the students then calculate the potential energy stored in each spring which is expressed as U_1 and U_2 respectively. Potential energy is measured in Joules (J) and the spring constant for spring 1 and 2 is 600 (N/m) and 450 (N/m). The results are shown in Table 1.

Table 1						
x	F_1	F_2	x_{c1}	x_{c2}	U_1	U_2
(m)	(N)	(N)	(m)	(m)	(J)	(J)
4.0	49	49	0.08	0.11	2.00	2.66
3.5	43	55	0.07	0.12	1.53	3.37
3.0	37	61	0.06	0.14	1.12	4.17
2.5	31	67	0.05	0.15	0.78	5.04
2.0	24	74	0.04	0.16	0.50	6.00
1.5	18	80	0.03	0.18	0.28	7.04

Study 2

The students repeats the same procedure that was used in Study 1 expect that the x value is held constant at 2 m and the mass is varied. The results are shown in Table 2.

Table 2						
M	F_1	F_2	x_{c1}	x_{c2}	U_1	U_2
(kg)	(N)	(N)	(m)	(m)	(J)	(J)
5	12	37	0.02	0.08	0.12	1.50
10	24	74	0.04	0.16	0.50	6.00
15	37	110	0.06	0.25	1.12	13.5
20	49	147	0.08	0.33	2.00	24.0
25	61	184	0.10	0.41	3.13	37.5
30	73	221	0.12	0.49	4.50	54.0

7. The data shown in Tables 1 and 2 for x_{c1} and x_{c2} were most likely collected using which of the following pieces of equipment?

 A. Telescope
 B. Balance
 C. Ruler
 D. Stopwatch

8. The procedures for Study 1 and Study 2 were similar in which of the following ways? Both studies had the same:

 F. mass of the block of 10 kg.
 G. location of the block on the beam at 2 m.
 H. length of the beam of 8 m.
 J. force upon the springs of 49 N.

GO ON TO THE NEXT PAGE.

9. According to the results of Study 1, if an additional test had been done at an x value of 1.0, the U_1 value would have most likely been:

    A. Between 1.12 J and 0.78 J
    B. Between 0.78 J and 0.50 J
    C. Between 0.50 J and 0.28 J
    D. Less than 0.28 J

10. The students want to repeat the procedure of Study 2, but with a different beam. This new beam, however, may only hold up to 200 N of weight. According to the data in Table 2, what is the largest mass that may be placed upon the beam?

    F. 10 kg
    G. 15 kg
    H. 20 kg
    J. 25 kg

11. According to the results of Study 1, as the block is moved towards the right end of the beam, what happens to the forces in the springs?

    A. F_1 increases and F_2 decreases
    B. F_1 increases and F_2 increases
    C. F_1 decreases and F_2 increases
    D. F_1 decreases and F_2 decreases

12. According to the results of Studies 1 and 2, which of the following best explains the relationship between x and the force of each spring and x and the potential energy stored in each springs?

    F. There is both a linear relationship between x and the force of each spring and x and the potential energy stored in each spring.
    G. There is a linear relationship between x and the force of each spring, but an exponential relationship between x and the potential energy stored in each spring.
    H. There is an exponential relationship between x and the force of each spring, but a linear relationship between x and the potential energy stored in each spring.
    J. There is both an exponential relationship between x and the force of each spring and x and the potential energy stored in each spring.

13. The sum of F_1 and F_2 for Study 1 is constant for all values of x, whereas the sum of F_1 and F_2 increases for increasing values of M in Study 2. What is the most likely explanation for this?

    A. Increasing the value of x increases the total load that F_1 and F_2 must bear
    B. Increasing the value of M increases the total load that F_1 and F_2 must bear
    C. Decreasing the value of x increases the total load that F_1 and F_2 must bear
    D. Decreasing the value of M increases the total load that F_1 and F_2 must bear

Passage III

Solvation is the process of dissolution of a solute within a solvent. A commonly studied solute/solvent example is the salt NaCl dissolved in water. Figure 1 below shows how water molecules may solvate a chloride anion. Three students discuss the mechanism of solvation of NaCl in water.

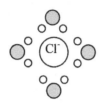

Figure 1

Student 1

Solvation is achieved due to the summation of electrostatic forces that occur between the charged ions and the polar end of water. When NaCl is dissolved into water, it separates into a positively charged sodium cation, and a negatively charged chloride anion. Water, being a polar molecule, will then orient itself around the ion with either its positive hydrogens or negative oxygen facing towards the ion. These opposite charges are then electrostatically attached to each other, and drive the process of solvation.

Student 2

Solvation of NaCl is achieved due to nature's tendency to increase *entropy* (ΔS). Entropy is the measure of randomness, or disorder within a system and processes that act to increase disorder (positive ΔS) are favored in nature. When NaCl is added to water, NaCl will separate into two moles of particles from one initial mole as an ionic solid. The more particles a solute may break up into, the greater tendency it will have to dissolve. Thus, solvation is the reaction of water to allow the increase in entropy of the solute/solvent system.

Student 3

Solvation of NaCl occurs due to a solution's preference to create *coordination complexes*. Coordination complexes are complex structures defined by a central atom or ion surrounded by electron donating *ligands*. Water may act as a ligand due to the fact that its central oxygen atom is surrounded by two pairs of electrons. These coordination complexes are often stable structures and their formation drives the dissolution of NaCl and the Na cation and Cl anion may act as the central atom of the complex.

14. Which of the students would most likely agree that increased electrostatic interactions is the driving force behind solvation?

F. Student 1
G. Student 2
H. Student 3
J. All three students would agree that increased electrostatic interactions is the driving force behind solvation.

15. Figure 1 depicts a negatively charged chloride ion being surrounded by water molecules. According to the argument of Student 1, the grey circles must represent:

A. hydrogen atoms.
B. oxygen atoms.
C. sodium atoms.
D. chloride ions.

16. Based on the viewpoint of Student 2, which of the following values of ΔS would indicate an increase in entropy?

F. −50.0
G. −12.5
H. 0.0
J. 25.0

17. According to Student 3, what is required of the water to dissolve the NaCl? For proper dissolving, water must:

A. act as a central metal for a coordination complex.
B. act as a ligand in a coordination complex.
C. participate in electrostatic interactions with NaCl.
D. increase the disorder of the system.

18. Another student, Student 4, suggests that some solutes become more ordered when they dissolve in solution. This finding would most likely *weaken* the argument of which student(s), if any?

F. Student 1 and 2
G. Student 1 only
H. Student 2 only
J. Cannot be determined from the given information

19. What conclusion would Student 2 most likely make regarding the ease of dissolution of solutes?

   A. Solutes that break up into more moles of particles dissolve easier.
   B. Solutes that break up into fewer moles of particles dissolve easier.
   C. The number of moles a solute breaks up into is independent of its ability to dissolve.
   D. Entropy is the measure of energy contained within a system.

20. A crucial assumption behind the argument of Student 1 is that:

   F. a positive ΔS is required for solvation.
   G. coordination complexes require a central metal and surrounding ligands.
   H. only NaCl is capable of being dissolved in water.
   J. the solute and solvent must both be polar or charged.

Passage IV

A plot of land is used to evaluate the preferred soil conditions for a variety of different tree species. The plot is a 500 m^2 plot of farmland that is evenly split into two plots labeled *Plot A* and *Plot B*. Plot A and Plot B are each treated with different levels of soil amendments, as shown in Table 1 below. Nitrogen is indicated by N, Potassium by K, and Phosphorus by P.

<table>
<tr><td colspan="4" align="center">Table 1</td></tr>
<tr><td>Plot</td><td>N
(g/m^2)</td><td>K
(g/m^2)</td><td>P
(g/m^2)</td></tr>
<tr><td>A</td><td>12</td><td>36</td><td>12</td></tr>
<tr><td>B</td><td>10</td><td>24</td><td>10</td></tr>
</table>

Study

To prepare Plot A and Plot B for the experiment, both plots are treated with an herbicide to kill any pre-existing plants. Once all plants were killed, the plots were treated with the appropriate concentrations of fertilizer.

After each plot is treated, a mixture containing equal amounts of the seeds of five different trees is evenly distributed across the plots. To ensure that the trees will have enough room to grow, adjacent seeds are placed a minimum of 1 meter apart. The trees to be studied are *English Oak*, *Paper Birch*, *White Ash*, *Box Elder*, and *American Elm*. All areas of the plots were controlled from amount of sunlight, water, and humidity. After three years of growth, the emerged seedlings are uprooted. The trees of each seedling are measured for height and mass. The results are shown in Figure 1 and 2 below.

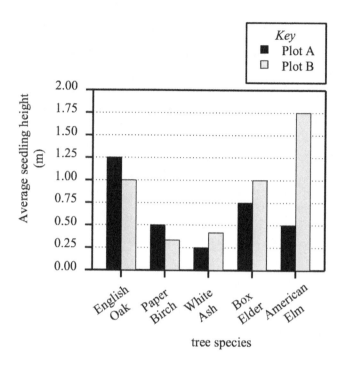

Figure 1

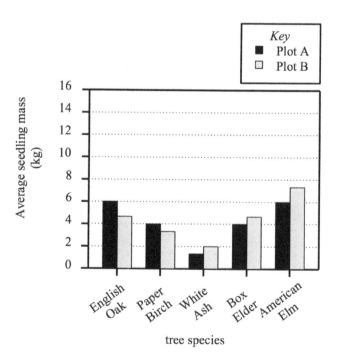

Figure 2

21. According to Figures 1 and 2, which of the following tree and plot combinations gave the tree with the highest average seedling height?

   A. English Oak in Plot A
   B. White Ash in Plot B
   C. Box Elder in Plot A
   D. American Elm in Plot B

22. If 20 total Paper Birch seedlings were collected from Plot A, what is the combined total mass of all Paper Birch seedlings from Plot A?

   F. 4 kg
   G. 20 kg
   H. 60 kg
   J. 80 kg

23. According to the information provided, which variables were intentionally varied in order to determine the effect on the average seedling height and mass?

   A. Soil amendments and seedling height
   B. Seedling mass and seedling height
   C. Seedling mass and tree species
   D. Soil amendments and tree species

24. Suppose that seedlings with a mass less than 4 kg after three years will not produce flower buds. Which seedlings in Plot B will most likely not give flower buds?

   F. English Oak and Paper Birch
   G. White Ash and American Elm
   H. Box Elder and Paper Birch
   J. Paper Birch and White Ash

25. According to the results of the study, which tree had the greatest difference in average seedling height in Plot A and Plot B?

   A. American Elm
   B. Box Elder
   C. White Ash
   D. Paper Birch

26. An ecologist suggests that the conditions in Plot A are most optimal for flowering plants. Do the results of the study support this conclusion?

   F. Yes, because trees in Plot A grew the tallest.
   G. No, because trees in Plot A grew the shortest.
   H. Yes, because Plot A contains the largest amount of potassium.
   J. No, because flowering plants are not studied in the experiment.

27. According to the information provided, the total mass, in grams, of phosphorus that was spread across Plot B was:

   A. 1,200.
   B. 2,500.
   C. 5,000.
   D. 12,000.

GO ON TO THE NEXT PAGE.

Passage V

A group of students work together to understand what variables affect projectile motion. The students utilize a setup as shown in Figure 1. A projectile launcher is set up to fire a projectile at a given velocity and angle above the horizon. The students may set the initial velocity (V_0) in (m/s) and the angle (θ) and will measure the maximum height H in meters (m), maximum distance D in meters (m), and time of flight t in seconds (sec).

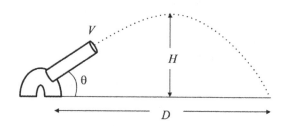

Figure 1

Experiment 1

The students used a projectile ball of mass 1 kg and fired it at an initial velocity of 50 m/s. The angle above the horizon, θ, was varied from 15°C to 75°. The maximum height, maximum horizontal distance, and time of flight were measured and the results are shown in Table 1.

Table 1			
Theta	D	H	t
(θ)	(m)	(m)	(sec)
15	63.77	8.544	1.32
30	110.4	31.88	2.55
45	127.5	63.77	3.61
60	110.6	95.66	4.42
75	63.65	119.0	4.93

Experiment 2

The procedure from Experiment 1 was repeated except the students used a projectile ball of mass 10 kg and kept the angle above the horizon constant at 45°. The initial projectile velocity was varied from 20 m/s to 100 m/s. The maximum height, maximum horizontal distance, and time of flight were measured and the results are shown in Table 2.

Table 2			
V_0	D	H	t
(m/s)	(m)	(m)	(sec)
20	20.41	10.20	1.44
40	81.63	40.81	2.88
60	183.7	91.83	4.33
80	326.5	163.2	5.77
100	510.2	255.1	7.21

Experiment 3

The procedure from Experiment 1 was repeated, except the students fired the projectile at a constant angle of 45°. The initial projectile velocity was kept constant at 50 m/s. The mass of the projectile was varied from 1 kg to 5 kg. The maximum height, maximum horizontal distance, and time of flight were measured and the results are shown in Table 3.

Table 3			
M	D	H	t
(kg)	(m)	(m)	(sec)
1	127.5	63.78	3.61
2	127.3	63.65	3.60
3	127.4	63.75	3.68
4	127.5	63.92	3.65
5	128.0	63.77	3.64

28. According to Experiment 2, which of the following values for V_0 would yield the largest time of flight, t?

    F. 40 m/s
    G. 60 m/s
    H. 80 m/s
    J. 100 m/s

29. Which of the following statements regarding initial projectile velocity and angle above the horizon best described the difference between Experiment 1 and Experiment 2? In Experiment 1, the:

    A. angle above the horizon was varied, whereas in Experiment 2 the initial projectile velocity was varied.
    B. angle above the horizon was held constant, whereas in Experiment 2 the initial projectile velocity was varied.
    C. angle above the horizon was varied, whereas in Experiment 2 the initial projectile velocity was held constant.
    D. angle above the horizon was held constant, whereas in Experiment 2 the initial projectile velocity was held constant.

30. According to the results of Experiment 1, if the students had fired the projectile at an angle of 70°, the time of flight would have most likely been:

    F. less than 2.55 seconds.
    G. between 2.55 seconds and 3.61 seconds.
    H. between 3.61 seconds and 4.42 seconds.
    J. between 4.42 seconds and 4.93 seconds.

31. According to Experiment 3, the relationship between the mass of the projectile and the maximum height is described as:

    A. directly proportional.
    B. inversely proportional.
    C. exponentially related.
    D. independent of one another.

32. According to the results of Experiment 1, as θ increased from 15° to 75°, the maximum distance D:

    F. increased only.
    G. decreased only.
    H. increased, then decreased.
    J. decreased, then increased.

33. Which combination of angle above the horizon and initial velocity would give the largest D?

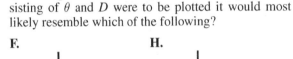

	θ	V_0
A.	30	20
B.	45	60
C.	45	80
D.	60	80

34. According to data from Experiment 1, if a graph consisting of θ and D were to be plotted it would most likely resemble which of the following?

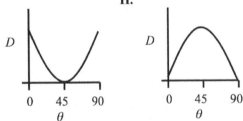

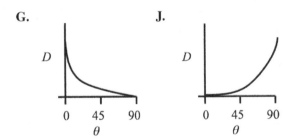

Passage VI

The phenomenon known as the *Doppler effect* is the change in frequency of a wave from an observer who is moving relative to the wave source. It is commonly experienced in the change of pitch heard when a vehicle sounding a horn approaches, passes, and recedes from an observer. A group of physics students designed an experiment to investigate the influence of various parameters on Doppler shifting.

Setup

The students construct a setup where two blocks are placed on a track where they may slide left or right at a set velocity (see Figure 1).

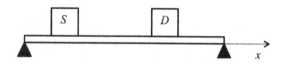

Figure 1

Block S emits a source frequency of 300 Hz and Block D is outfitted with a detector that can perceive the frequency emitted from Block S. The velocity that Block S is set to is expressed as v_s (m/s), and the velocity that Block D is set to is expressed as v_d (m/s). The source frequency is defined at f whereas the perceived frequency is defined as f'. The students define the velocity to the right as the positive direction, and velocity to the left as negative.

Experiment 1

Trials were performed at varying values from 0 m/s to 30 m/s for the velocity of Block D. The velocity of Block S was held constant at 0 m/s. The perceived frequency was measured for each trial and the results are shown in Table 1.

Table 1				
Trial	f	v_d	v_s	f'
	(Hz)	(m/s)	(m/s)	(Hz)
1	300	0	0	300
2	300	10	0	309
3	300	20	0	318
4	300	30	0	327

Experiment 2

Experiment 1 was repeated, except the velocity of Block D was held constant at 0 m/s and the velocity of Block S varied from −10 m/s to −30 m/s. The perceived frequency was measured for each trial and the results are shown in Table 2.

Table 2				
Trial	f	v_d	v_s	f'
	(Hz)	(m/s)	(m/s)	(Hz)
5	300	0	−10	309
6	300	0	−20	319
7	300	0	−30	330

Experiment 3

Experiment 1 was repeated, except the velocity of Block D was varied in the negative direction. The perceived frequency was measured for each trial and the results are shown in Table 3.

Table 3				
Trial	f	v_d	v_s	f'
	(Hz)	(m/s)	(m/s)	(Hz)
8	300	−10	0	291
9	300	−20	0	281
10	300	−30	0	273

Experiment 4

Experiment 1 was repeated, except the velocity of Block S was varied in the negative direction. The perceived frequency was measured for each trial and the results are shown in Table 4.

Table 4				
Trial	f	v_d	v_s	f'
	(Hz)	(m/s)	(m/s)	(Hz)
11	300	10	−10	318
12	300	20	−20	339
13	300	30	−30	360

Experiment 5

Experiment 4 was repeated, except the velocity of Block D was varied in the negative direction and the source frequency was varied from 300 Hz to 340 Hz. The perceived frequency was measured for each trial and the results are shown in Table 5.

Table 5				
Trial	f (Hz)	v_d (m/s)	v_s (m/s)	f' (Hz)
14	300	−10	−10	300
15	320	−20	−20	320
16	340	−30	−30	340

35. Based on Experiments 1–4, in which trial did the perceived frequency differ the most from the source frequency?

   A. Trial 4
   B. Trial 7
   C. Trial 10
   D. Trial 13

36. Based on Table 5, as the source frequency was varied by the students, which variable was directly affected?

   F. The source frequency
   G. The perceived frequency
   H. The velocity of Block D
   J. The velocity of Block S

37. In order for the students to move forward with the experiment knowing their data was accurate, they conducted Trial 1 where both blocks were stationary. The purpose of Trial 1 was most likely to:

   A. verify the track was functioning properly.
   B. ensure the detector was calibrated correctly.
   C. set the initial velocity of Block D.
   D. establish the positive x direction.

38. One of the students stated that when the blocks were moving at the same speed in the same direction, the perceived frequency was the same as the source frequency. Was this student correct?

   F. Yes, because in Trials 11–13 the perceived frequency is NOT equivalent to the source frequency.
   G. Yes, because in Trials 14–16 the perceived frequency is equivalent to the source frequency.
   H. No, because in Trials 11–13 the perceived frequency is NOT equivalent to the source frequency.
   J. No, because in Trials 14–16 the perceived frequency is equivalent to the source frequency.

39. Based on Experiment 3 and other information provided, the direction of the velocity component for Block S and Block D is which of the following?

   A. Block S was moving to the right and Block D was stationary.
   B. Block S was stationary and Block D was moving to the left.
   C. Block S was moving to the right and Block D was moving to the left.
   D. Block S was stationary and Block D was stationary.

40. Based on the results of Experiments 2 and 3, which of the following equations correctly relates f' to the velocity of Block D and the velocity of Block S?
(Note: k is a constant)

   F. $f' = k\, v_d\, v_s$

   G. $f' = \dfrac{k}{v_d\, v_s}$

   H. $f' = k\dfrac{v_s}{v_d}$

   J. $f' = k\dfrac{v_d}{v_s}$

Government Surveillance

Modern surveillance technology has the ability to fully monitor the activities of a targeted person. Governments around the world have eagerly embraced this technology, often citing the threats of terrorism, corruption, or other criminal activity as justification for widespread surveillance. This, in turn, has given governments very broad powers over their citizens. Critiques argue that such surveillance is unacceptable in a democracy where citizens enjoy a right to privacy free of unwarranted observation. Should there be a limit to the government's ability to monitor whomever it chooses? Is such surveillance compatible with democracy?

Read and carefully consider these perspectives. Each suggests a particular way of thinking about government surveillance.

Perspective 1	Perspective 2	Perspective 3
The government's first job is to protect the safety of its citizens. Surveillance is a necessary tool to prevent terrorist violence and other crimes against people and property.	Governments that possess powers like this are likely to abuse them. Mass surveillance will erode citizens' right to privacy and eventually other basic freedoms as well.	Laws must be established to oversee the government's use of surveillance technology. This will help ensure that no abuses occur.

Essay Task

Write a unified, coherent essay in which you evaluate multiple perspectives on government surveillance. In your essay, be sure to:

- analyze and evaluate the perspectives given
- state and develop your own perspective on the issue
- explain the relationship between your perspective and those given

Your perspective may be in full agreement with any of the others, in partial agreement, or wholly different. Whatever the case, support your ideas with logical reasoning and detailed, persuasive examples.

ACT4 - A0117

Practice Test

ENGLISH TEST
45 Minutes—75 Questions

DIRECTIONS: In the five passages that follow, certain words and phrases are underlined and numbered. In the right-hand column, you will find alternatives for the underlined part. In most cases, you are to choose the one that best expresses the idea, makes the statement appropriate for standard written English, or is worded most consistently with the style and tone of the passage as a whole. If you think the original version is best, choose "NO CHANGE." In some cases, you will find in the right-hand column a question about the underlined part. You are to choose the best answer to the question.

You will also find questions about a section of the passage, or about the passage as a whole. These questions do not refer to an underlined portion of the passage, but rather are identified by a number or numbers in a box.

For each question, choose the alternative you consider best and fill in the corresponding oval on your answer document. Read each passage through once before you begin to answer the questions that accompany it. For many of the questions, you must read several sentences beyond the question to determine the answer. Be sure that you have read far enough ahead each time you choose an alternative.

PASSAGE I

Singers of the Sea

> The following paragraphs may or may not be in the most logical order. Each paragraph is numbered in brackets, and question 14 will ask you to choose the most logical paragraph order.

[1]

Though all whales make noises, only the males of certain whale species sing. Cetologists aren't sure exactly why that is, but a few theories dominating the field, some believe
₁
the songs are used for mating purposes, but cetologists

haven't even once spotted yet a female responding to a
₂

song. Others, however believe that whales sing to discover
₃

1. **A.** NO CHANGE
   B. dominate the field,
   C. dominating the field;
   D. dominate the field;

2. **F.** NO CHANGE
   G. haven't ever yet spotted
   H. haven't yet to spot
   J. have yet to spot

3. **A.** NO CHANGE
   B. Others, however, believe
   C. Others however, believed
   D. Others, however, believed

creatures within the surrounded area by utilizing their sonar
4
capabilities.

[2]

Cetologists — scientists who study dolphins, porpoises, and whales—have just began to piece together the mysteries
5
of these giant mammals' songs. The term "whale songs"
6
doesn't refer to a concerto, but rather to a predictable pattern of whale noises that sound similar to human singing. A single song can last up to twenty minutes, and some researchers believe these noises can travel over 10,000 miles. 7

[3]

Although early mariners often told tales of eerie low
8
sounds emanating from the depths below, the exact origin of
8
these ocean groans will remain a mystery for quite some time.
9
It wasn't until 1952 that the sounds were first recorded by a

U.S. Naval hydrophone—an underwater microphone that has
10
since become a modern staple for oceanographers. Fifteen years later, scientists Roger Payne and Scott McVay identified the mystical sounds as the songs of humpback whales.

4. **F.** NO CHANGE
   G. the surrounding area by utilizing their
   H. the surrounded area by utilizing its
   J. the surrounding area by utilizing its

5. **A.** NO CHANGE
   B. will have just began
   C. just begun
   D. have just begun

6. **F.** NO CHANGE
   G. mammal's
   H. mammals
   J. mammal

7. At this point, the writer is considering adding the following true statement:

   Water acts as a much better conductor for sound than air, though aluminum ranks even higher with speeds up to 6,320 meters per second.

   Should the writer make this addition here?

   A. Yes, because it provides a necessary link between whale songs and the scientific community.
   B. Yes, because it contextualizes a detail within the greater context of the science behind it.
   C. No, because it adds information that is tangentially related to the essay but blurs the focus of this paragraph.
   D. No, because it contradicts information provided later in the passage.

8. **F.** NO CHANGE
   G. eerie low sounds ascertaining
   H. eerie, low sounds emanating
   J. eerie, low sounds ascertaining

9. **A.** NO CHANGE
   B. remained
   C. is remaining
   D. remaining

10. Which of the following alternatives to the underlined portion would NOT be acceptable?

    F. hydrophone; an underwater microphone
    G. hydrophone, an underwater microphone
    H. hydrophone, which is an underwater microphone
    J. hydrophone, or underwater microphone,

GO ON TO THE NEXT PAGE.

[4]

It is fascinating to think about how many people study whales. Whales lack many of the mechanisms that humans use to produce sounds, including vocal chords. The beasts need not inhale nor exhale to create their songs, and their mouths remain stationary throughout the process. All of this leads cetologists to believe that these giants of the ocean circulates air through the tubes and chambers of their respiratory systems. A recent study using imaging technologies with fetal whales, suggested that some species of whales develop hearing differently than others, which may help scientists bring to like why and how some species sing while others do not. With so many mysteries to still solve, cetologists surely have their work cut out for them.

11. Which choice effectively introduces the topic of this paragraph?
   A. NO CHANGE
   B. Faced with so many unanswered questions, scientists can research a myriad of whale-related topics.
   C. Various water-bound animals have physical mechanisms different from our own.
   D. Exactly how whales make these incredible noises is yet another unknown within the scientific community.

12. F. NO CHANGE
   G. circulate
   H. is circulating
   J. has circulated

13. A. NO CHANGE
   B. bring likeness to
   C. bring to light
   D. bring to life

Questions 14 and 15 ask about the preceding passage as a whole.

14. For the sake of coherence, the most logical paragraph order is:
   F. 1, 2, 3, 4
   G. 2, 3, 1, 4
   H. 3, 1, 4, 2
   J. 3, 2, 1, 4

15. Suppose the writer's primary purpose had been to offer a general overview of the significant strides and remaining mysteries of whale sound research. Would this essay accomplish that purpose?

   A. Yes, because the author offers personal anecdotes to accompany each example.
   B. Yes, because it presents both discoveries and unanswered questions throughout.
   C. No, because the author does not explicitly explain the significance of each discovery.
   D. No, because it focuses too heavily on differences between whale species.

PASSAGE II

Nellie Bly, Looking to the Future of Journalism

[1]

"Never having failed, I could not picture what failure meant," boasted, famous journalist, Nellie Bly after her
<u>   </u>
16
ground-breaking trip around the world. As one might assume, a woman born into the oppressive gender biases of nineteenth-century America <u>requires</u> a fierce drive and
17
unrelenting will to match the career accomplishments of her male peers; Nellie Bly was no exception.

[2]

Born Elizabeth Jane Cochran, <u>the journalist didn't go by</u>
18
<u>her widely known pen name "Nellie Bly" until the advent</u>
18
<u>of her writing career.</u> Her tumultuous childhood began at age
18
six with the death of her father—a man who had fathered eleven children and left her family without any inheritance. By the age of fifteen, Bly was in school to become a teacher, <u>a career that challenged her keen mind.</u> [A] She was forced to
19
drop out of the program after only one semester, due to finances, and instead aided her mother with keeping an inn to provide for her siblings.

[3]

Everything changed, one day, when Bly wrote a scathing letter to a Pittsburgh publication, responding to a then famous columnist who asserted that a woman's place was in the home, not the workplace. [B] However, after a short period of time, Bly <u>all of a sudden</u> left the publication; her employers allowed
20
her to write only for the <u>womens'</u> page, though she dreamed
21
of covering topics like poverty, corruption, and disenfranchised populations.

16. **F.** NO CHANGE
    G. boasted famous journalist, Nellie Bly
    H. boasted, famous journalist Nellie Bly
    J. boasted famous journalist Nellie Bly

17. **A.** NO CHANGE
    B. will require
    C. requiring
    D. required

18. **F.** NO CHANGE
    G. Nellie Bly's writing career was the reason for her pen name.
    H. a pen name was created for Nellie Bly with the advent of her writing career.
    J. the advent of a writing career gave Nellie Bly her pen name.

19. Given that all of the following are true, which choice best contextualizes Bly's career choice within the given time period?
    A. NO CHANGE
    B. which was one of the few careers deemed suitable for women at the time.
    C. a true testament to her love of words.
    D. a career that has been available since ancient times.

20. **F.** NO CHANGE
    G. soon after
    H. promptly
    J. DELETE the underlined portion

21. **A.** NO CHANGE
    B. women's
    C. womans'
    D. womans

[4]

Bly left Pittsburgh, for the bustling streets of New
York City, landing a job at New York World. [C] One of her
first exposés was also one of her most notable contributions to

journalism; posed as a mad woman, and checked herself
into Blackwell Island, an asylum for the mentally ill.

When all said activities were ceased, she not only exposed
the harsh cruelties perpetrated by the institution's staff against
their patients, but she also created a new form of journalism.
[D] Conversely, "stunt reporting," has become a common
practice, refers to undercover work in which journalists fully
immerse themselves in whatever subject they are covering.

[5]

However, Bly went on to uncover countless atrocities

against otherwise ignored populations, successful business
creation, and various humanitarian efforts were promoted.
She even broke a world record, traveling around the world in

72 days, 6 hours, and 11 minutes to beat the "record" of a
fictional character from Jules Verne's *Around the World in
Eighty Days.* Though she only lived until the age of
fifty-seven, Nellie Bly's contributions to journalism and

society endures the test of time. ☐30

22. **F.** NO CHANGE
    G. Bly left Pittsburgh for the bustling streets of New York City, landing a job at New York World.
    H. Bly left Pittsburgh for the bustling streets, of New York City, landing a job at New York World.
    J. Bly left Pittsburgh, for the bustling streets of New York City landing a job at New York World.

23. **A.** NO CHANGE
    B. journalism, Bly
    C. journalism and Bly
    D. journalism: Bly

24. **F.** NO CHANGE
    G. In so doing,
    H. With doing all of that,
    J. Having done,

25. **A.** NO CHANGE
    B. Instead,
    C. For instance,
    D. Today,

26. **F.** NO CHANGE
    G. Still, Bly
    H. One time, Bly
    J. Bly

27. **A.** NO CHANGE
    B. successful business creation, and promote various humanitarian efforts.
    C. run a successful business, and promote various humanitarian efforts.
    D. run a successful business, and various humanitarian efforts were promoted.

28. The purpose of the quotation marks around the underlined portion is most likely:
    F. to note the fictitious nature of the previous record.
    G. to directly quote Nellie Bly.
    H. to imply the sarcastic nature of Jules Verne.
    J. to clarify the definition of an antiquated term.

29. **A.** NO CHANGE
    B. is enduring
    C. has endured
    D. have endured

GO ON TO THE NEXT PAGE.

30. Upon reviewing the passage and realizing that some information has been left out, the author composes the following sentence:

> The publication was so impressed with Bly's writing that they offered her a position and jokingly donned her with the pen name Nellie Bly after a song in which a character by the same name dreams of the joys in domesticity.

The most logical placement for this sentence would be:

F. Point A in Paragraph 2.
G. Point B in Paragraph 3.
H. Point C in Paragraph 4.
J. Point D in Paragraph 4.

PASSAGE III

Sand Sculptors: The Forgotten Artists

[1]

Many people have constructed casual sandcastles, but only a small portion of that overall sand castle-making population daringly dream to call themselves sand sculptors.

That title is reserved for the eccentrics, all of them have spent countless hours experimenting to hone their craftsmanship

and artistry, like me. From ornate delicate human figures to gargantuan architectural abstracts, sand sculptures

come in an infinite array of sizes and forms—each with their own lesson in planning and flexibility.

[2]

As foreign as it may sound, sand sculpture is a fairly popular medium that spans across various facets with life.

31. **A.** NO CHANGE
B. but few in actuality dare to
C. but only a few of those people
D. but few

32. **F.** NO CHANGE
G. all of whom
H. we all
J. all of us

33. **A.** NO CHANGE
B. ornate delicately human
C. ornate, delicate human
D. ornate, delicately human

34. **F.** NO CHANGE
G. his or her
H. one's
J. its

35. **A.** NO CHANGE
B. various facets of
C. variety facets of
D. variety facets with

[A] One part competition and one part performance art, the medium falls under the category of "sand art," which includes sand brushing, sand painting, and sand bottling. Competitions and festivals across the world gather sand sculptors together to show off their skills and compete for prizes and titles. A single sculpture can take as long as two months to create and, with the proper environment, the masterpiece will last just as long once completed. [B] The largest recorded sand sculpture castle was created by a team in 2007, taking ten days to complete and standing just under fifty feet tall. Creating such a weighty piece of artwork that is not meant to last is quite an endeavor. I consider sand sculpture to fall under the

category of performance art not only due to its temporary, brief nature, but also because spectators love to watch the process of creation.

Upon seeing a massive sand sculpture, you might assume that glue and beams hold up the weighty beach material. However, the science of surface tension and

nature's own sand and water are sole responsibility for keeping these heavy sculptures in one piece.

36. F. NO CHANGE
     G. create and, with the proper environment the masterpiece
     H. create, and with the proper environment, the masterpiece
     J. create and with the proper environment, the masterpiece

37. Which choice best expresses the fleeting nature of sand sculptures?
     A. NO CHANGE
     B. The creation process is often more arduous than spectators might expect.
     C. Creating an exact likeness of any given subject is an imperative aspect of the art.
     D. Errors often occur during the sculpting process, but most can be easily remedied.

38. F. NO CHANGE
     G. nonpermanent, momentary
     H. short-term, temporary
     J. temporary

39. A. NO CHANGE
     B. Likewise,
     C. Subsequently,
     D. Therefore,

40. F. NO CHANGE
     G. solely responsibility
     H. solely responsible
     J. sole responsible

[3]

[C] Just how do you create such sound, large-scale forms?
41
Unlike traditional sculptors, who utilize a solid block of

material, we sand sculptors must first mix the sand and water
42

to create the base for our art. A few techniques dominates the
43
field, but the general idea behind each is to mix proper

proportions of water with sand to create solid forms, adding

pressure to compact the materials.

[4]

[D] A variety of tools, including various household

items, can be used to carve out any three-dimensional figure

that you could possibly imagine. My favorite sculpture to

date? A five-foot tall resemblance of the Mona Lisa. Who
44
says art belongs in a museum? 45

41. If the writer were to delete the underlined sentence, the passage would primarily lose:

A. a contradictory and unrelated statement.
B. a transition to a new but related subject.
C. an unanswerable question.
D. a clear change in the author's tone.

42. F. NO CHANGE
G. us
H. those
J. them

43. A. NO CHANGE
B. dominate
C. have dominated
D. dominating

44. F. NO CHANGE
G. reincarnation
H. ratification
J. recreation

45. Upon reviewing the passage and realizing that some information has been left out, the author composes the following sentence:

> Once the base has been created, that's when the real fun starts.

The most logical placement for this sentence would be:

A. Point A in Paragraph 2.
B. Point B in Paragraph 2.
C. Point C in Paragraph 3.
D. Point D in Paragraph 4.

GO ON TO THE NEXT PAGE.

PASSAGE IV

The Delicate Dance of Political Polling

Turn on any televised news program today, and you'll hear a bevy of statistics, nearly all of which are the products of polling. Although polling—recording a small sample of opinions from a general population, is often our best metric for measuring the intricate facets of a political system that even experts sometimes have difficulty understanding, they are by no means a perfect system. Polling is a delicate

science, the potential for bias lurks around every corner.

The keystone of any accurate polling system resting within its sampled population. The goal is to represent a large, often diverse population of people, by asking the opinions of only a small subset. Nevertheless, these smaller, sampled populations should maintain the same balance of various diversities as does the general population, assuming that different kinds of people have different opinions. In addition, a news program might use polling to report on Pleasantville

locals' reactions to a recent election; rather than ask all 20,000 Pleasantville residents, the news program might decide to target only 500 citizens. If forty-five percent of Pleasantville's citizens are female, the news program should attempt to target 225 females, or forty-five percent of their total 500 participants. The potential for bias not only depends on gender but a myriad of other factors as well: income, race, age, and political affiliations, just to name a few.

46. F. NO CHANGE
   G. opinions, from a general population,
   H. opinions from a general population—
   J. opinions, from a general population—

47. A. NO CHANGE
   B. it is by no means
   C. they haven't any means to
   D. it hasn't any means to

48. F. NO CHANGE
   G. science which potential
   H. science, and the potential
   J. science and the potential

49. A. NO CHANGE
   B. rests
   C. with resting
   D. of the rest

50. F. NO CHANGE
   G. Lest,
   H. On the other hand,
   J. Therefore,

51. A. NO CHANGE
   B. To reiterate,
   C. For example,
   D. Granted,

52. F. NO CHANGE
   G. local's reactions
   H. locals reaction's
   J. locals reactions

53. A. NO CHANGE
   B. recent election, rather than
   C. recent election, to
   D. recent election to

[1] Internet polls are more likely to have younger participants, while targeting landline telephones with those polls are more likely to own only cellphones that might leave out that younger population. [2] The difficulties of accurate polling don't end with sample populations. [3] Polling companies must now also consider how they carry out their polls. [4] People who choose to participate in political polls, then, are likely to be more educationally political and active than other sects of the population. [5] Most polling is self-selecting, meaning that individuals decide of their own evaluation to participate in polls. 57

Exploring the full breadth of polling pitfalls is far beyond the scope of this essay. 58 Many academics and private sector businesses have dedicated their time to the study

of polling, hoping to find newer, more accurate methods to employ. While the average citizen can only understand a fraction of the nuances involved with polling, the moral is this: next time you see a political statistic on a news program, be wary of the pitfalls of polling.

54. F. NO CHANGE
G. polls that target landline telephones might leave out that younger population who are more likely to own only cellphones.
H. polls target younger populations who are more likely to own only cellphones with landline telephones.
J. landline telephones target younger populations for polls who are more likely to own only cellphones.

55. A. NO CHANGE
B. politically active and educated
C. actively political but educated
D. politically educated but active

56. F. NO CHANGE
G. attrition
H. volition
J. submission

57. For the sake of coherence, the most logical sentence order for the preceding paragraph is:
A. 1, 2, 3, 4, 5
B. 3, 2, 1, 5, 4
C. 5, 1, 3, 2, 4
D. 2, 1, 3, 5, 4

58. If the writer were to delete the preceding sentence, the passage would primarily lose:
F. a concession of the essay's limitations.
G. a specific example of a previously mentioned concept.
H. a comparison between this essay and similar publications.
J. a recommendation for future studies concerning polling.

59. A. NO CHANGE
B. newer, most accurate
C. newest, more accurate
D. newest, most accurate

Question 60 asks about the preceding passage as a whole.

60. Suppose the writer's goal had been to write a brief essay focusing on a particular instance of polling bias. Would this essay accomplish that goal?

F. Yes, because the essay relates each point back to a single event.
G. Yes, because the author creates a clear narrative throughout the essay.
H. No, because the author mentions multiple instances of polling bias.
J. No, because the essay focuses on generalizations rather than on a single event.

PASSAGE V

Native Americans of the Four Corners

Deep in the southwestern quadrant of the United States <u>sit</u> an inhospitable patch of land that we now call the Four
61

Corners. Every year, tourists flock here to <u>annually</u> see the
62

only spot in the <u>nation, they are standing</u> in four separate
63
states at one time: Utah to the northwest, Colorado to the northeast, Arizona to the southwest, and New Mexico to the southeast. Unknown to most, however, is the <u>converging unlikely spot of Native American populations cultural intersection.</u>
64

61. A. NO CHANGE
    B. sits
    C. have sat
    D. has sat

62. F. NO CHANGE
    G. over and over
    H. at normal time intervals
    J. DELETE the underlined portion

63. A. NO CHANGE
    B. nation, where they can stand
    C. nation where they can stand
    D. nation when they can stand

64. F. NO CHANGE
    G. cultural intersection of Native American populations that likewise converge at this unlikely spot.
    H. Native American population likewise at this unlikely spot of converging cultural intersection.
    J. cultural intersection converging of Native American populations at this likewise unlikely spot.

GO ON TO THE NEXT PAGE.

Perhaps the most widely recognized Native American population in the area is the Navajo Nation. The Navajo Nation has a separated jurisdiction with the state where its peoples inhabit, a separate capital city within the state of Arizona, and administrative power over the Four Corners site. They are believed to have originally migrated from western Canada, finding ready-made dwellings upon their arrival to the Four Corners. [66] Those dwellings were constructed by a previously collapsed Native American population, the Anasazi.

Navajo land does not cross into Utah but its territory extends into the other three states. Today, the Navajo Tribe is the largest within the United States and relays on craftsmanship and coal mining for economic stability.

The Hopi, a branch of the vast Pueblo Peoples, consider the Four Corners area to be sacred. The arid climate creates various challenges that the Hopi have overcome for centuries. Oraibi, the Hopi [A] settlement near the Four Corners, is located in Arizona and was settled in 1150, making it one of the oldest [B] occupied settlements [C] within the continuously nation. Today, many Hopi people continue to rely on farming the crops of their ancestry including corn, beans, squash, and melons.

65. A. NO CHANGE
B. separated jurisdiction from
C. separate jurisdiction with
D. separate jurisdiction from

66. The author is considering deleting the preceding sentence. Should the sentence be kept or deleted?

F. Kept, because it makes clear the relationship between two Native American populations.
G. Kept, because it introduces a topic that is then further discussed.
H. Deleted, because it blurs the paragraph's focus on a single Native American population.
J. Deleted, because it contradicts a previously stated fact.

67. A. NO CHANGE
B. Utah but its territory, extends into
C. Utah, but its territory extends into
D. Utah, but its territory, extends into

68. F. NO CHANGE
G. relayed with
H. relies on tourism,
J. relied on tourism,

69. A. NO CHANGE
B. for economic stability to ensure its continuation.
C. to gain the funds needed for everyday life.
D. to support itself both economically and financially.

70. Given that all of the following are true, which one most specifically describes cultural significance of the land to the Hopi people?

F. NO CHANGE
G. Countless generations of Hopi people have called this land home.
H. The area is believed to house Mother Earth's most important organs, and according to legend, any disruption to the area would prove catastrophic to the state of the earth as a whole.
J. The Hopi people have a rich cultural history passed down through folklore and ceremony.

71. The most logical placement for the underlined portion is:

A. Point A.
B. Point B.
C. Point C.
D. Where it is now.

GO ON TO THE NEXT PAGE.

Although tourists may be unlikely <u>having had a full</u>
<u>72</u>
understanding of the cultural exchanges happening at the Four

Corners, the Native American influence at the site remains

strong. Flags of the four states as well as the two Native

American nations surround the location, and Native American

artisans and craftsmen <u>sell their</u> wares to tourists passing
<u>73</u>

through <u>who buy the wares.</u>
<u>74</u>

72. F. NO CHANGE
   G. having completely
   H. to have a
   J. to having a

73. A. NO CHANGE
   B. sells their
   C. sell they're
   D. sells they're

74. F. NO CHANGE
   G. who find the pieces visually appealing.
   H. who feel as if they need to take a piece of the site home with them.
   J. DELETE the underlined portion, ending the sentence with a period after the word "through."

Questions 75 asks about the preceding passage as a whole.

---

75. Suppose the writer's primary purpose had been to describe the economic consequences of tourism within the Four Corners. Would this essay accomplish that purpose?

   A. Yes, because it describes various products that tourists purchase at the site.
   B. Yes, because statistical evidence supports the author's claims throughout.
   C. No, because it focuses primarily on a historical overview of the site.
   D. No, because it lacks nuanced critique of the statistics mentioned throughout.

END OF TEST 1.
STOP! DO NOT TURN THE PAGE UNTIL TOLD TO DO SO.

THERE ARE NO TESTING MATERIALS ON THIS PAGE.

MATHEMATICS TEST
60 Minutes — 60 Questions

DIRECTIONS: Solve each problem, choose the correct answer, and then fill in the corresponding oval on your answer document.

Do not linger over problems that take too much time. Solve as many as you can; then return to the others in the time you have left for this test.

You are permitted to use a calculator on this test. You may use your calculator for any problems you choose,

but some of the problems may be best done without using a calculator.

Note: Unless otherwise stated, all of the following should be assumed:
1. Figures are NOT necessarily drawn to scale.
2. Geometric figures lie in a plane.
3. The word *line* indicates a striaght line.
4. The word *average* indicates arithmetic mean.

---

1. Cora works two jobs. Her job at the snack bar pays her \$8.50 an hour, while her babysitting job pays her \$15.00 an hour. Last week Cora worked for a total of 20 hours, 12 of which were at the snack bar, the rest babysitting. How much money did Cora earn last week?

   A. \$170
   B. \$222
   C. \$235
   D. \$248
   E. \$300

2. The expression $a(b - c) + d$ is equivalent to which of the following expressions?

   F. $ab - c + d$
   G. $ab - c - d$
   H. $ab - ac - d$
   J. $ab - ac + d$
   K. $ab - ac - ad$

3. Which value of x is the solution for the following equation: $3(x + 5) = 9x - 4$?

   A. $1/6$
   B. $3/2$
   C. $11/65$
   D. $19/6$
   E. $19/3$

4. A restaurant offers 3 types of bread, 4 types of meat, and 5 types of cheese. How many different sandwiches can the restaurant make using one type of bread, one type of meat, and one type of cheese?

   F. 3
   G. 12
   H. 15
   J. 20
   K. 60

PP-ACT4

232

GO ON TO THE NEXT PAGE.

5. A metal rod measures $32\frac{1}{8}$ inches in length. Barbara is attempting to fit the rod in a window frame that is $29\frac{3}{4}$ inches wide. How many inches will Barbara will need to cut off the metal rod to fit it in the window frame?

A. $2\frac{3}{8}$

B. $2\frac{5}{8}$

C. $3\frac{1}{8}$

D. $3\frac{3}{8}$

E. $3\frac{5}{8}$

6. There are currently 28 countries in the European Union. If 6 of the countries leave the European Union, to the nearest tenth, what percent of the current membership will remain?

F. 21.4%

G. 28.6%

H. 71.4%

J. 72.7%

K. 78.6%

7. The diameter of a circle has endpoints at $(3, 10)$ and $(7, 2)$. What are the coordinates of the center of this circle?

A. $(2, 4)$

B. $(5, 6)$

C. $(11, -6)$

D. $(-1, 18)$

E. $(10, 12)$

8. $(2xy^2)(4x^2y)(5x^3y^4)$ is equivalent to which of the following expressions?

F. $11x^6y^7$

G. $11x^6y^8$

H. $40x^5y^6$

J. $40x^6y^7$

K. $40x^6y^8$

9. Points A, B, C, and D lie on a straight line in that order. If $AC = 12$, $BD = 17$, and $BC = 8$, how long is AD?

    A. 5
    B. 13
    C. 21
    D. 29
    E. 37

10. The distance, d, to the ground of an object dropped from an initial height of 100 feet is modeled by the equation $d = -16t^2 + 100$, where t is the time in seconds since the ball was dropped. How far from the ground will the object be 2 seconds after it is dropped?

    F. 16 feet
    G. 36 feet
    H. 64 feet
    J. 68 feet
    K. 84 feet

11. Which of the following expressions is equivalent to $\sqrt{72} + \sqrt{98} - \sqrt{200}$?

    A. $\sqrt{-30}$
    B. $-3\sqrt{2}$
    C. $\sqrt{2}$
    D. $3\sqrt{2}$
    E. $23\sqrt{2}$

12. The probability that it rains on Saturday is $3/4$. The probability that it rains on Sunday is $2/3$. What is the probability that it rains on both days?

    F. $\dfrac{1}{12}$

    G. $\dfrac{5}{12}$

    H. $\dfrac{1}{2}$

    J. $\dfrac{5}{7}$

    K. $\dfrac{17}{12}$

13. If $a = b - 3$, what is the value, if it can be determined, of the expression $(b - a)^3$?

    A. -27

    B. -3

    C. 3

    D. 27

    E. Cannot be determined from the given information

14. Which of the following would best describe the graph of the function $f(x) = \dfrac{x^2 + 7x}{-x}$?

    F. An upward opening parabola

    G. A line with a positive slope

    H. A downward opening parabola

    J. A line with a negative slope

    K. A horizontal line passing through point $(0, 7)$

15. Consider the following true statements regarding quadrilaterals:

    All rhombi are kites
    All rhombi are parallelograms
    Some parallelograms are kites

Logically, which of the following statements *must* also be true?

    A. If a quadrilateral is a parallelogram, then it is *not* a kite

    B. If a parallelogram is a rhombus, then it is a kite

    C. If a kite is a rhombus, then it is *not* a parallelogram

    D. If a quadrilateral is a kite, then it is a rhombus

    E. If a parallelogram is a kite, then it is *not* a rhombus

16. Given that $\sqrt{-4x} - 11 = -5$, $x = ?$

    F. 9

    G. 4

    H. -1

    J. -4

    K. -9

17. What is the slope of the line modeled by the equation $5x - 3y - 10 = 0$?

A. $\dfrac{3}{5}$

B. $-\dfrac{3}{5}$

C. $\dfrac{5}{3}$

D. $-\dfrac{5}{3}$

E. $\dfrac{1}{2}$

18. Annie needs to average at least an 85 on a series of seven tests to qualify for a trip to London. She has scored 73, 87, 79, 91, and 81 on her first five tests. What must she average on her *remaining* two tests in order to qualify for her trip?

F. 82.2

G. 82.7

H. 87.8

J. 92

K. 99

19. A scientist who tracks changes in weather patterns measured the average daily temperature in a region over a period of 15 days. After realizing that her equipment erroneously records temperature 5 degrees colder than the actual temperature, she adjusted her numbers accordingly. What effect will her adjustment have on the median of her initial data set?

A. The median will increase by 5 degrees

B. The median would remain the same

C. The median will decrease by 5 degrees

D. The median will increase by 75 degrees

E. Cannot be determined from the given information

20. In the figure below, all angles are right angles. What is the perimeter of the figure below?

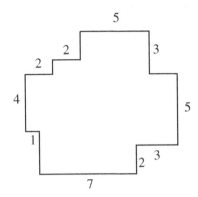

F. 21
G. 34
H. 42
J. 64
K. 110

21. The surface area, A, of a rectangular solid is modeled by the equation $A = 2lw + 2lh + 2wh$ where l represents the length, w represents the width, and h represents the height. Which of the following expressions represents the height in terms of the surface area, length, and width?

A. $h = \dfrac{A + 2lw}{2l + 2w}$

B. $h = \dfrac{A - 2lw}{l + w}$

C. $h = \dfrac{A + 2lw}{l - w}$

D. $h = \dfrac{A - 2lw}{2l - 2w}$

E. $h = \dfrac{A - 2lw}{2l + 2w}$

22. Leo is installing a circular putting green in his backyard, with a diameter of 30 ft. The sod for his putting green costs $120 for each 10 yd^2 palate of sod and he cannot buy partial pallets. How much will it cost Leo to cover his putting green with sod?

(Note: 1 yd^2 = 9 ft^2)

F. $480
G. $960
H. $1,200
J. $3,840
K. $8,520

23. In the right triangle below, what is the value of $\cos B$?

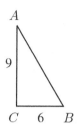

A. $\dfrac{6}{9}$

B. $\dfrac{6}{\sqrt{117}}$

C. $\dfrac{\sqrt{117}}{6}$

D. $\dfrac{9}{\sqrt{117}}$

E. $\dfrac{\sqrt{117}}{9}$

24. Quadrilateral $ABCD$ shown below is an isosceles trapezoid, where $m\angle C = 115°$ and $m\angle BDC = 30°$. What is $m\angle ABD$?

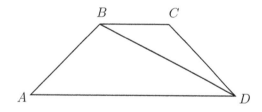

F. $35°$

G. $65°$

H. $80°$

J. $115°$

K. $150°$

25. If the length of a rectangle is $2x - 5$ and the width of the rectangle is $x + 3$, which expression represents the area of the rectangle?

A. $2x^2 - x - 15$

B. $2x^2 + x - 15$

C. $2x^2 - 11x + 15$

D. $2x^2 - 11x - 15$

E. $2x^2 + 11x + 15$

26. A cable 40 feet long is secured from the top of a flag-pole to the ground 15 feet from the base of the flagpole. To the nearest foot, how tall is the flagpole?

   F. 15 feet
   G. 25 feet
   H. 37 feet
   J. 43 feet
   K. 55 feet

27. Keara and Meg own a store where they make and sell charm bracelets. Keara can make 5 bracelets in 20 minutes. Meg can make 6 bracelets in 15 minutes. To-gether, how many bracelets can Keara and Meg make in an hour?

   A. 11
   B. 15
   C. 19.5
   D. 24
   E. 39

28. Two trains are on parallel tracks, 500 miles apart, trav-eling towards each other. If the first train is traveling east at 30 miles per hour and the second train is travel-ing west at 20 miles per hour, which of the following equations could be used to determine how many hours, t, until the two trains meet?

   F. $30t = 500 - 20t$
   G. $30t - 500 = 20t$
   H. $30t = 500 + 20t$
   J. $30t - 20t = 500$
   K. $30t + 500 = 20t$

29. For which value(s) of x would the expression
   $f(x) = \dfrac{x}{x^2 - 9}$ be undefined?

   A. 0 only
   B. 3 only
   C. $3, -3$
   D. $0, 3$
   E. $0, -3, 3$

30. In how many different ways can the letters in the word FACTOR be arranged?

   F. 1
   G. 6
   H. 21
   J. 36
   K. 720

GO ON TO THE NEXT PAGE.

31. What is the 6th term of the geometric sequence $-16, 4, -1, {}^{1}/{4} \ldots$?

A. $\dfrac{1}{64}$

B. $\dfrac{1}{32}$

C. $\dfrac{1}{8}$

D. $-\dfrac{1}{32}$

E. $-\dfrac{1}{64}$

32. If $AC = 10$, $AB = 11$, $DE = 5$, and AD is an altitude, what is the area of the parallelogram?

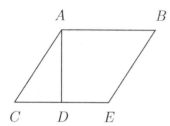

F. 42
G. 55
H. 80
J. 88
K. 110

33. What value of b would make following system of equations have a solution set represented by the equation $2x - y = 6$?

$$6x - 3y = 18$$
$$10x - 5y = 10b$$

A. -3
B. 3
C. 10
D. 15
E. 30

34. In the right triangle below, where $\angle C = 90°$, if $\tan A = 5/12$ and $BC = 15$, what is the length of hypotenuse AB?

   F. 13
   G. 27
   H. 32
   J. 36
   K. 39

35. What is the equation of a circle whose center is at $(-3, 4)$ and passes through the origin?

   A. $x^2 + y^2 = 5$
   B. $x^2 + y^2 = 25$
   C. $(x + 3)^2 + (y - 4)^2 = 5$
   D. $(x - 3)^2 + (y + 4)^2 = 25$
   E. $(x + 3)^2 + (y - 4)^2 = 25$

36. Factored completely, which of the following expressions is equivalent to $3x^5 - 48x$?

   F. $3x(x^4 - 16)$
   G. $x(3x^2 + 12)(x - 2)(x + 2)$
   H. $3x(x^2 + 4)(x - 2)(x + 2)$
   J. $x(3x^2 + 12)(x^2 - 4)$
   K. $3x(x + 2)^2(x - 2)^2$

Questions 37-39 pertain to the following information.

Amanda's garden is 30 feet long, 6 feet wide, and 8 inches deep. She must cover the lateral sides of the garden with a permeable liner and fill the garden with potting soil. Each bag of potting soil costs $20 and contains 3 cubic feet of potting soil.

37. How many square feet of liner must Amanda purchase to cover the sides of her garden?

   A. 44
   B. 48
   C. 168
   D. 288
   E. 408

38. How much money will Amanda spend to completely fill the garden with potting soil?

   F. $450
   G. $800
   H. $1,440
   J. $2,400
   K. $3,600

39. If Amanda wants to plant each flower 8 inches apart in all directions (including from the edges of the garden) on the top layer of the potting soil, how many flowers will her garden hold?

   A. 145
   B. 180
   C. 352
   D. 405
   E. 460

40. What value of x would make the determinant of the matrix $\begin{bmatrix} (x+2) & (x-8) \\ (x+3) & (x-5) \end{bmatrix} = 0$?

   F. -7
   G. $-1/4$
   H. $17/9$
   J. 2
   K. $17/4$

41. A town has 8 men and 12 women running for town council. If the council will consist of 3 men and 3 women, which of the following expressions gives the number of different councils that could be selected from these 20 people?

A. $_{20}P_6$

B. $(_8P_3)(_{12}P_3)$

C. $_{20}C_6$

D. $(_{20}C_3)(_{20}C_3)$

E. $(_8C_3)(_{12}C_3)$

42. The ratio of the surface area of Cube A to the surface area of Cube B is 9:4. If Cube B has a volume of 8 units, what is the volume of Cube A?

F. 27

G. 18

H. 13

J. $3.\overline{5}$

K. 2

43. Jack and Conor attend the same school. To get home from school, Jack bikes 3 miles south and 6 miles east while Conor bikes 9 miles west and 5 miles north. To the nearest mile, what is the straight-line distance between the homes of Jack and Conor?

A. 5 miles

B. 13 miles

C. 17 miles

D. 20 miles

E. 23 miles

44. If $x(1 + 7i) = 100$, which of the following complex numbers represents x?

F. $1 - 7i$

G. $7i - 1$

H. $2 - 14i$

J. $2 + 14i$

K. $14i - 2$

45. Which of the following expressions is equivalent to $x^4 \sqrt[3]{x^7} y^2 \sqrt{y^5}$?

A. $x^{\frac{28}{3}} y^{\frac{7}{2}}$

B. $xy^{\frac{4}{5}}$

C. $x^{\frac{11}{3}} y^5$

D. $x^{\frac{19}{3}} y^{\frac{9}{2}}$

E. $x^{\frac{12}{7}} y^{\frac{5}{4}}$

GO ON TO THE NEXT PAGE.

46. What is the solution set of the inequality
$-3|x - 2| > 6$?

    F. Empty set

    G. $0 < x < 4$

    H. $-2 < x < 2$

    J. $x < 0 \bigcup x > 4$

    K. $x < -2 \bigcup x > 4$

47. If $f(x) = 3x^2 - 15$ and $g(x) = |x| + 3$, what is the value of $g(f(-2))$?

    A. 0

    B. 3

    C. 6

    D. 30

    E. 60

48. The table below shows the results of a survey which asked 50 children how many siblings they have. Based on the results, what is the average number of siblings for the students in the survey?

Number of Siblings	Frequency
0	7
1	10
2	13
3	8
4	5
5	3
6	3
7	1

    F.   2

    G.   2.4

    H.   3.5

    J.   6.25

    K. 120

49. What is the solution set to the equation $4x^3 = 25x$?

    A. $\{0\}$

    B. $\{5/2\}$

    C. $\{0, 5/2\}$

    D. $\{\pm 5/2\}$

    E. $\{0, \pm 5/2\}$

50. What is the equation of the horizontal asymptote of the function $f(x) = \dfrac{3x^2 + 9x}{x^2 - 9}$?

F. $y = 0$

G. $y = 3$

H. $y = -3$

J. $x = 3$

K. $x = -3$

51. Which of the following expressions is defined for all nonzero real values of a and b?

A. $\dfrac{b - a}{b + a}$

B. $\dfrac{b + a}{b - a}$

C. $\dfrac{1}{b + a}$

D. $\dfrac{1}{a^2 + b^2}$

E. $\dfrac{a^2 - b^2}{a + b}$

52. A restaurant has 75 tables. For the last 6 months, the manager has tracked how full the restaurant is during dinner service by counting the proportions of tables full and determined the probability of each proportion. The results are shown in the table below. Based on the results, approximately how many tables can the restaurant expect to have occupied on any given night?

Proportion Full	Probability
1	0.05
0.9	0.15
0.8	0.3
0.7	0.25
0.6	0.2
0.5	0.05

F. 13

G. 23

H. 56

J. 60

K. 75

Questions 53-55 pertain to the following information

At Bank Alpha, interest is calculated annually using the formula: $A_t = A_0(1 + r)^t$. The interest rate is 7%.

At Bank Omega, interest is calculated continuously using the formula: $A_t = A_0 e^{rt}$. The interest rate is 5%.

The formulas above are true where t is the time in years, A_0 is the initial deposit amount, A_t is the amount of money in an account after t years, r is the interest rate in decimal form, and e is Euler's constant (valued at approximately 2.72).

Billy will deposit $1,000 into each account with no additional deposits or withdrawals for the next 30 years.

53. To the nearest cent, how much money will Billy have in his Bank Alpha account after two years?

   A. $1,070.00

   B. $1,105.17

   C. $1,144.90

   D. $1,150.27

   E. $2,890.00

54. In 120 months, to the nearest dollar, which account will have more money and by how much?

   F. Bank Alpha by $318

   G. Bank Alpha by $47

   H. Bank Alpha by $20

   J. Bank Omega by $47

   K. Bank Omega by $318

55. How long will it take, to the nearest tenth of a year, for the amount of money in Billy's Bank Omega account to increase by 100%?

   A. 9.9 years

   B. 10.3 years

   C. 13.9 years

   D. 14.3 years

   E. 20.0 years

56. Which of the following equations, when graphed in the standard (x, y) coordinate plane, would represent an ellipse whose center lies in quadrant II and whose major axis is horizontal?

F. $\dfrac{(x-6)^2}{64} + \dfrac{(y+11)^2}{49} = 1$

G. $\dfrac{(x+7)^2}{9} + \dfrac{(y-5)^2}{64} = 1$

H. $\dfrac{(x-1)^2}{25} + \dfrac{(y+3)^2}{36} = 1$

J. $\dfrac{(x+4)^2}{36} + \dfrac{(y-7)^2}{25} = 1$

K. $\dfrac{(x+8)^2}{49} - \dfrac{(y-9)^2}{16} = 1$

57. Triangle LMN is drawn below, where $LM = 8$, $MN = 11$, and $LN = 15$. Which of the following equations could be used to determine the measure of angle N?

(Note: for any triangle with side lengths of a, b, and c that are opposite angles A, B, and C respectively,

$$c^2 = a^2 + b^2 - 2ab \cos C \text{ and } \frac{\sin A}{a} = \frac{\sin B}{b} = \frac{\sin C}{c})$$

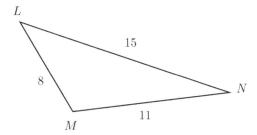

A. $8^2 = 15^2 + 11^2 - 2(15)(11) \cos N$

B. $11^2 = 15^2 + 8^2 - 2(15)(8) \cos N$

C. $15^2 = 11^2 + 8^2 - 2(11)(8) \cos N$

D. $\dfrac{\sin 90°}{15} = \dfrac{\sin C}{8}$

E. $\dfrac{\sin 90°}{8} = \dfrac{\sin C}{11}$

58. Each iteration, N, of a sequence is shown below. How many dots will be in the $N = 10$ arrangement?

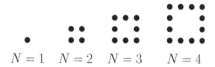

$N = 1 \quad N = 2 \quad N = 3 \quad N = 4$

   F. 385
   G. 217
   H. 100
   J. 40
   K. 36

59. A right cylindrical can of soda has a height of 5 inches and a diameter of 2.5 inches. To the nearest cubic inch, what volume of soda would be contained in a pack of twelve cans?

   A. 25 in^3
   B. 31 in^3
   C. 94 in^3
   D. 295 in^3
   E. 1178 in^3

60. Given that $\sin x = \cos x$ and $0 < x < \dfrac{\pi}{2}$, what is the value of: $[\sin x + \cos x]^2$?

   F. 0
   G. 1
   H. 2
   J. $\sqrt{2}$
   K. $2\sqrt{2}$

END OF TEST 2.
STOP! DO NOT TURN THE PAGE UNTIL TOLD TO DO SO.
DO NOT RETURN TO THE PREVIOUS TEST.

THERE ARE NO TESTING MATERIALS ON THIS PAGE.

READING TEST

35 Minutes — 40 Questions

DIRECTIONS: There are four passages in this test. Each passage is followed by several questions. Choose the best answer to each question and fill in the corresponding oval on your answer document. You may refer to the passages as often as often as necessary.

Passage I

LITERARY NARRATIVE: This passage is adapted from *Arenberg Forest* by Kathleen O'Hanlon (©2009 by Kathleen O'Hanlon).

She was folding laundry when he came home. She heard the clump of the car door and then the crunch of the small, white stones in the driveway.

"Hello?" he called from the echoing front hall. She
5 peeked out from the utility room, filled not just with a surprisingly large washer and dryer, but also with a bright brick floor and an assortment of slickers and coats, and odd bits of footwear that looked ready for the deep mud she guessed was coming.

10 "Hi," she said, wiping her hands dry on the front of her sweatpants.

"How was the trip?" she asked.

He was still looking down at the two bags he had struggled through the door.

15 "The trip?" He looked confused. "Oh, fine. Just two flights from Bilbao."

He stopped fiddling with the bags and straightened up. He looked taller, broader than when she'd seen him a few weeks ago. Had those few weeks of training al-
20 ready taken off his winter weight? Those few extra kilos of well-needed Christmas cheer that had to then come off first thing in the pre-season, so he could best judge what he might be able to do in the Spring Classics.

"Do you want a glass of wine or something? There's
25 some in the kitchen." She took a few steps toward the kitchen, aware that she was making busy, welcoming work here in his house that he should know much better than she did.

"No," he said, following her. "But maybe a little
30 beer."

"I got the Maredsous you like," she offered, again feeling too hospitable.

He stopped in the hallway and slipped off his shoes. He entered the kitchen in white socks that seemed at odds
35 with the slick, brown Italian loafers he had left at the doorway, impervious to the rain spots beaded on the smooth leather.

"It's weird to actually see food in the kitchen," he said, reaching in for the cheerful, red labeled bottle.

40 He opened it and poured a half glass, then capped the bottle and put it back in the refrigerator. She had spent enough time with cyclists now to be able to predict the discipline of keeping track of every stray carbohydrate consumed, but it still surprised her to see it here on this rainy
45 Sunday evening in a warm, quiet home outside Antwerp, with no trainers or team managers around to take notice of whether Kristof had four or six ounces of beer after a hard few weeks in the mountains. But she knew it had little to do with trainers and team managers. It had everything to
50 do with those April dates coming up sooner than any of them would expect. She imagined that even as he stood in his newly redesigned kitchen, slick and perfect in the old manor house, he was mentally picturing himself on the slippery moss of the Arenberg Forest.

55 He paused, as he drank his beer. "Is something wrong?" she asked.

"No." He paused, as if searching for the right words. "It's just that I've never come home and had the house be so warm."

60 She felt a rush of stupidity, her American concern for her own comfort forever trumping the pared down northern European sensibility she was not yet accustomed to. She rushed into her next sentence.

"I'm so sorry." She looked into the hallway, trying to
65 remember where the control was for the newly refurbished heating system, ready to rush and turn it off.

He smiled, as if amused at her discomfort.

"No, don't worry. It's good." He took the last sip of beer and placed the empty glass in the sink. "My mother's
70 always been good about coming over to open the shutters

GO ON TO THE NEXT PAGE.

and turn the heat up when I'm coming home, but she always leaves it dark and a little cold. I feel like I spend my first night home shivering, especially when I come from Spain in the winter. This is good."

75   He looked around the kitchen, with its new stainless steel appliances set against the old stone floor and the newly reglazed two hundred year old windows.

"This is good," he repeated.

1. The point of view from which the passage is told is best described as:

    A. First person, narrated by a main character
    B. First person, narrated by a minor character
    C. Third person, narrated by a voice outside the action of the story
    D. Third person, narrated through the perspective of one character

2. It can most reasonably be inferred from that passage that Kristof's profession is that of a(n):

    F. trainer.
    G. architect.
    H. athlete.
    J. manager.

3. The contrast between "American concern" and "European sensibility" in lines 60–63 can best be described as:

    A. excess and moderation.
    B. sensitivity and resilience.
    C. prosperity and hardship.
    D. hospitality and frigidity.

4. Which of the following points is NOT supported by the paragraph in lines 40–54?

    F. Kristof is typically disciplined about his food intake.
    G. Kristof's moderation is fueled by a future goal.
    H. The female protagonist is accustomed to Kristof's physical training regimen.
    J. Kristof requires the presence of managers to stay focused on his training.

5. According to the passage, where is Kristof's home located?

    A. Outside of Antwerp
    B. Bilbao
    C. The Arenberg Forest
    D. Maredsous

6. The information in lines 25–28 most strongly suggests that the female protagonist feels:

    F. nervous to confront Kristof after his long-awaited return.
    G. uneasy in a space that is not her own.
    H. eager to finish her household chores.
    J. excited to question Kristof about the details of his trip.

7. The main point made in lines 67–74 is that:

    A. Kristof is pleased with his home upon his return.
    B. Kristof's mother is physically unable to take care of his home.
    C. the home tends to be dark and gloomy.
    D. Kristof is always cold when he returns from cycling trips to Spain.

8. In the passage, each of the following is used to describe aspects of Kristof's house EXCEPT that it:

    F. has two hundred year old windows.
    G. has beaded spots from the rain.
    H. was once a manor house.
    J. is newly refurbished.

9. Which of the following events referred to in the passage occurs first chronologically?

    A. The female character was folding laundry.
    B. Kristof returned on two flights from Bilbao.
    C. Kristof participated in the spring classics.
    D. Kristof trained in the mountains.

10. In the passage, the narrator describes Kristof after his return from Bilbao as:

    F. unprepared for the upcoming cycling season.
    G. more muscular than when he left.
    H. unhappy to return home.
    J. heavier from the Christmas holiday.

Passage II

SOCIAL SCIENCE: This passage is adapted from *Nudge* by Mark Harris (©2008 by Mark Harris).

Why do people act in ways that seem contrary to their own interests? This question goes to the heart of what it means to be human, and for thousands of years philosophers, artists, and theologians have pondered its implica-
[5] tions. In recent years, political scientists and economists have tackled the question as well. This inquiry has led social scientists to ask an entirely different question: how can people be persuaded to behave more rationally?

Rationality is the defining attribute of human behav-
[10] ior, and economists place it at the heart of their thinking. If you remove all the layers of cultural conditioning and individual idiosyncrasy that make up a human being, they say, what you'll find is an innate tendency for individuals to seek out and maximize their own best interests. We are,
[15] in effect, all looking out for number one. The whole teeming global economy can be understood if we assume that every individual is a rational actor whose only goal is to advance his or her own best interests.

Using this model, social scientists have sought to ex-
[20] plain how international financial markets sustain long periods of growth, or why communally-farmed land is less productive than privately-farmed land, or even the logic behind the shifting, short-lived political coalitions formed by the members of the United States Congress. Once these
[25] researchers assume that every person involved is motivated by the desire to secure direct personal advantages, it is easy to generate models that explain economic growth and decline, or political victory and defeat, on a grand scale.

But there are problems with this approach. Time and
[30] again researchers find instances of individual and group behavior that does not seem rational. In fact, it is often self-defeating: markets quake as irrationally overvalued companies collapse, leading investors to sell their stock in a blind panic; legislators impulsively react to unforeseen
[35] events and pass laws that anger the electorate and ensure the legislators' defeat at the polls. How can these lapses of logic be explained, and how can more rational alternatives be encouraged?

Recent work by Richard Thaler and Cass Sunstein
[40] sheds some light on this puzzle. According to their research, human beings are not rational actors who are always impartially weighing the pros and cons of each decision they face. Rather, human decision making is always torn between two related but competing systems of
[45] thought: the 'reflective' system and the 'automatic' system.

The reflective system is what we usually think of as the 'rational' mind. It is the system of thought humans use to make deliberate decisions. Choosing which career to pursue, which partner to marry, or which path to follow
[50] to a mountain summit, are all functions of the reflective system. But alongside the reflective system is the automatic system, an older and more deeply hard-wired faculty. Thaler and Sunstein see this system as our primary evolu-
[55] tionary inheritance, built over millions of years of trial and error in the struggle for survival. It determines our basic responses to stimuli, whether it's our impulse to smile when we see a loved one or to feel fear when our plane hits turbulence. This system of mainly unconscious actions carries
[60] us through far more of our lives than we generally realize.

The system's power derives from the hodge-podge of evolved assumptions that drive our behavior. Consider the status quo bias. If a course of action is considered traditionally appropriate, people are highly unlikely to change
[65] course even if it would be in their best interest to do so. This innate fear of change outweighs the rational assessment of pros and cons. Or take the herd phenomenon in which individuals will unconsciously mimic the behavior of those around them, especially if that behavior is com-
[70] mon to a large group. It does not matter if this behavior has good or bad consequences for individuals. Most people will eventually conform to common behavior, regardless of its utility.

We have a built-in system of responses and motiva-
[75] tions meant for semi-lingual apes living in small bands on the savannah; it is emphatically not ideal for bankers hoping to sell at the highest price, or politicians eager to pass a bill with overwhelming support. So how can these systems be harmonized?

[80] For Thaler and Sunstein, the solution is to self-consciously design policies that will 'nudge' individual choices in a specific direction, one that short-circuits the automatic system's preference for short-term immediate gratification. By framing choices in certain ways, individ-
[85] ual behavior can be subtly altered in favor of more rational behavior. For example, in order to instill better eating habits for school children, healthy foods should be placed at eye-level in the school cafeteria, while unhealthy items should be placed in inconvenient spots.

[90] Policies like this would, by no means, inhibit the automatic system. People will still act irrationally and contrary to their own interests. But a society of small 'nudges' would put the reflective system in charge by privileging long-term rational decision making.

252

11. The main idea of the passage is that:

   A. humans are incapable of thinking rationally.
   B. Thaler and Sunstein's theory will radically change the way people behave.
   C. international financial markets are good predictors of human behavior.
   D. human behavior is influenced by two competing systems.

12. Which of the following statements best describes the organization of the passage?

   F. Two systems of thought are introduced, then a solution is given to balance them.
   G. Summaries of behavioral research studies are presented in chronological order.
   H. Multiple scholarly perspectives about human behavior are compared and contrasted.
   J. Two systems are examined, followed by evidence that one is superior.

13. According to the passage, Thaler and Sunstein believe the reflective and automatic systems:

   A. are entirely separate from each other.
   B. compete but function together.
   C. are outdated and do not apply to the present day.
   D. are the only factors behind human decision-making.

14. As it is used in line 10, *heart* most nearly means:

   F. periphery.
   G. understanding.
   H. core.
   J. beginning.

15. According to the passage, people's tendency to follow a course of action that is traditionally appropriate is referred to as the:

   A. reflective system.
   B. nudge hypothesis.
   C. status quo bias.
   D. automatic system.

16. It can most reasonably be inferred from the passage that the author considers rationality to be:

   F. a central motivator to human behavior.
   G. an outdated construct.
   H. a drain on human creativity.
   J. irrelevant to the subject of the passage.

17. The primary function of the statement in lines 80–84 is to:

   A. offer evidence of the effectiveness of a theory.
   B. introduce one solution to a stated question.
   C. signal a shift from a discussion of economics to politics.
   D. refute an argument made earlier in the passage.

18. The passage indicates that the herd phenomenon causes:

   F. humans to imitate people around them.
   G. irrational feelings of isolation.
   H. negative consequences for behavior.
   J. the status quo bias.

19. The main idea of the second paragraph (lines 9–18) is that:

   A. humans are driven by their own needs.
   B. the heart of people's desires is to help others.
   C. people consciously choose to be selfish.
   D. economists have no regard for human desires.

20. According to the passage, the reflective system allows people to make decisions about:

   F. which politicians to vote for.
   G. solutions to puzzles.
   H. what career path to follow.
   J. which land is best for farming.

Passage III

HUMANITIES: This passage is adapted from *Molecular Gastronomies* by Benson Irvine (©2013 by Benson Irvine).

Ferran Adrià walks through aisles of fresh fish, paying particular attention to the scents that spill from the day's catch of cod, mackerel, and grouper. Over the years, he has come to learn the importance of smell in determining the
5 flavor profile of an ingredient. Though the aroma will inevitably go through a thousand translations before it ends up on a diner's plate, the first olfactory impression can be the starting point for a new dish.

Adrià is the head chef of elBulli, which has been
10 called the "most imaginative generator of haute-cuisine on the planet." The restaurant is equal parts kitchen and lab; there, Adrià deconstructs chemical compounds in meats; extracts essences from rare vegetables; and brings together previously unimagined flavor combinations with a sense of
15 humor, surprise, and curiosity.

This approach is typical of molecular gastronomy, a discipline of food science championed by Adrià that investigates the physical and chemical transformations that occur in the process of cooking. The field is highly mod-
20 ern, dependent on and inspired by technological innovation. In molecular gastronomy—also called modernist cuisine, haute-cuisine, or avant-garde cuisine—cooking becomes a mix of magic and science. Cooking times are determined by ultrasound, aromatic gases are trapped in
25 bags, and ingredients are flash-frozen in liquid nitrogen and shattered at the dinner table.

Loaded with today's fresh mackerel, Adrià begins the complex process of de- and reconstruction central to every elBulli dish. Should he turn the fish into a foam? Should
30 he make it look like caviar through "spherification"? Or should he leave it intact, instead using a syringe to inject an unexpected filling?

The mystery and intricacy of these transformations (along with Adrià's masterful execution) are what keeps
35 the waitlist at elBulli numbering in the hundreds of thousands. The dining experience is a true exercise in openmindedness: when nothing is as it appears, and expectation can only betray, the only thing to do is to take a bite, taste, and experience.

40 One of the signature dishes invented in his kitchen (where other than elBulli can a dish also be called an invention?) is a spherified "liquid" olive. This feat of imagination and technical genius requires the syringe insertion of an olive-based liquid into a sphere of green gelatin,
45 made to look like a true olive. When it arrives at the table, the diner sees and tastes "olive," but the form and texture are completely unfamiliar. Another major technique developed in his kitchen, is the creation of culinary foam, which he allegedly discovered as a by-product

50 when he used a bicycle pump to inflate a tomato. A friend then suggested that he use a nitrous oxide canister, which he filled with mixtures of various ingredients and then sprayed. This resulted in an altogether new texture— foam—as yet unseen in the world of gastronomy. This
55 accident-turned-experiment-turned-recipe would come to characterize many of his future creations.

And while many predicted that this level of ingenuity would slow once he reached a certain level of commercial and critical success, Adrià has continually forgone the
60 typical sell-out schemes of celebrity-chefdom in favor of enduring innovation. In 2001, he decided to close down the restaurant for lunch, closing the door on a likely one million euros of yearly revenue for him and his partners. Instead, he decided to dedicate his own time and resources
65 (roughly 20 percent of the restaurant's profits) to opening a culinary research center, focused on educating young chefs and furthering scientific discovery in the field of gastronomy. So, Adrià purchased an 18th-century townhouse in Barcelona and turned it into a workshop, the first of its
70 kind, where he and a team of elBulli cooks could spend months at a time dreaming up and perfecting new techniques for his unique brand of food preparation. In his own words, he wanted to establish a place "at the forefront of seeking out the best conditions to nurture creativity."

75 Perhaps this is what makes Adrià so singularly creative: not only has he invented some of the most novel cooking techniques of the last century, but he has asked questions that inspire others to invent alongside him. He throws conceptions of taste, sight, smell, touch, and mem-
80 ory into a state of chaos, a state in which we can discover food (and even our senses) anew. And it is this ability to disrupt and abandon tradition that itself creates "conditions to nurture creativity." In other words, his is not creativity unto itself; it is a creativity that begets more of
85 its kind.

21. According to the passage, which of the following senses does Ferran Adrià consider to be important when first encountering an ingredient?

A. Touch
B. Smell
C. Taste
D. Sight

22. As it is used in line 6, "a thousand translations" most likely refers to:

F. transforming ingredients through inventive preparation techniques.

G. the inclusion of recipes from other countries.

H. the process of haggling with a fisherman who speaks a different language.

J. determining the flavor profile of an ingredient.

23. According to the passage, each of the following is a tool or technology regularly used by molecular gastronomists to prepare food EXCEPT:

A. a syringe.

B. an ultrasound.

C. liquid nitrogen.

D. a bicycle pump.

24. It can most reasonably be inferred that Ferran Adrià purchases which of the following at the fish market?

F. Cod

G. Mackerel

H. Grouper

J. Not enough information provided

25. Based on lines 57–61, it is reasonable to infer that most successful chefs:

A. maintain a commitment to culinary innovation.

B. establish teaching institutions to educate future generations of chefs.

C. shift their focus to commercial ventures.

D. collapse under the pressures of being a internationally recognized celebrity.

26. As it is used in line 38, *betray* most nearly means:

F. mislead.

G. abandon.

H. provide.

J. support.

27. The main purpose of the seventh paragraph (lines 57–74) is to:

A. introduce the next generation of young chefs being taught by Adrià.

B. object to Adrià's poor financial decisions.

C. prove that Adrià is the most creative chef in the world.

D. illustrate Adrià's committment to culinary creativity.

28. According to the passage, a major technique developed by Ferran Adrià is:

F. culinary foam.

G. liquid nitrogen.

H. spherical caviar.

J. syringe filling.

29. Based on the passage, Ferran Adrià can best be described as:

A. materialistic and radical.

B. methodical and traditional.

C. daring and creative.

D. modern and disorganized.

30. In the passage, the field of molecular gastronomy is most directly inspired by:

F. magic.

G. texture.

H. technological innovation.

J. taste and aroma.

Passage IV

NATURAL SCIENCE: Passage A is adapted from "The Asteroid Impact" by Don Sauer (©1987 by Don Sauer). Passage B is adapted from "Volcano Extinction" by Howard James (©2002 by Howard James).

Passage A by Don Sauer

Dinosaurs, by far the most successful group of species in the history of life on Earth, dominated land-based life for 165 million years. But 65 million years ago, these well-adapted animals died off quickly and com-
5 pletely. According to the geological record, within one million years every known dinosaur species was extinct, along with 75% of other known land-based creatures.

What happened? The most commonly held theory is that a planet-wide disaster dramatically altered environ-
10 mental conditions. The changed environment proved incompatible with the adaptations dinosaurs had developed. This set the stage for what scientists call the Cretaceous-Paleogene extinction event, named for its scale and effects that mark the boundary between two very different
15 eras of Earth's biosphere. A disaster of this scale could only be caused by a few known phenomena, and the most likely candidate is an asteroid or comet impact. Two major pieces of evidence support this claim. The first is the presence of a thin layer of sediment in terrestrial and ma-
20 rine rock layers dating to approximately 65 million years ago. This sediment is rich in iridium, a metal rarely found within terrestrial rocks but very common in asteroids. A worldwide layer of iridium suggests that an asteroid struck the planet and vaporized, leaving a layer of evidence.

25 Dr. Luis Alvarez, a champion of this theory, argues that an asteroid six miles in diameter (about the size of Manhattan) struck the planet with a force equivalent to 1×10^8 megatons, two million times more powerful than the largest nuclear weapon ever detonated. This inconceiv-
30 ably massive blast would have sent billions of tons of dust and debris into the atmosphere, more than enough to block out sunlight for years. Burning debris would have ignited forest fires on a continental scale, further adding to the blanket of particulate haze preventing sunlight from reach-
35 ing the planet's surface. As a result, photosynthesis became impossible and most plant life died off, leaving the survivors of the impact with nothing to eat. Life would survive in deep seas and in scattered pockets of the surface, and though the planet would recover over hundreds
40 of thousands of years, the dinosaurs would not recover with it.

The impact theory of dinosaur extinction received a major boost in 1989, when a team led by Dr. Alvarez discovered a 110-mile-long crater off the coast of Mexico's
45 Yucatan peninsula. Called the Chicxulub Crater, many scientists believe that this is the site of the asteroid's impact. This crater provided evidence to support the widely accepted asteroid impact hypothesis.

Passage B by Howard James

The Cretaceous-Paleogene extinction event has long
50 puzzled scientists, who have struggled to explain how so much of life on Earth could have been destroyed within a million years (merely a heartbeat, on a geological scale). The asteroid impact hypothesis offers an attractive explanation, but events other than an external calamity could
55 have caused such extreme devastation.

It is important to remember that this extinction event was not the only one in Earth's history. There have been at least four others of comparable size, in the three billion year history of life on Earth, and none of these were the
60 result of an external event. Instead, events on Earth itself nearly wiped out life. Volcanism, a major factor in these extinctions, may have also played a key role in the decline of the dinosaurs.

Volcanos are essentially vents in the Earth's crust, dis-
65 charging pressurized gases and molten rock from the burning core of the planet onto the surface. Volcanos played a major role in forming the Earth's surface, and their activity has risen and fallen over the eons depending on poorly-understood fluctuations deep in the heart of the world.
70 Large-scale eruptions can eject enough particulate matter into the atmosphere to block out sunlight and disrupt photosynthesis for years at a time, and release enough carbon dioxide and sulfur dioxide to alter the balance of oxygen and nitrogen in the air and oceans.

75 Heavy volcanic activity has been cited as the major cause of the Permian-Triassic extinction event 100 million years before the evolution of the first dinosaurs. Sometimes called "the Great Dying," this catastrophe wiped out 90% of all known species within 200,000 years and has
80 been linked to volcanic eruptions that spewed billions of tons of methane into the atmosphere, causing a rapid period of global warming that most species were unable to withstand.

Scientists investigating the death of the dinosaurs,
85 have found evidence of extensive volcanic activity around 65 million years ago. Significantly, many volcanic eruptions bring up iridium, which is found in substantial quantities near Earth's core. This may explain the iridium layer that coincides with the decline of the dinosaurs. While
90 it is entirely possible an asteroid did strike the planet around this time, creating the Chicxulub Crater, Earth has been subject to numerous such impacts throughout history. None of these impacts, often caused by even larger objects, have had as devastating an effect.

95 The record of life on Earth suggests that the biggest threats to creatures on land and in the seas do not come from asteroids or other external forces; rather, the planet

GO ON TO THE NEXT PAGE.

itself is most often the culprit. Volcanism is a valid hypothesis for what may have caused the extinction of the
100 dinosaurs.

Questions 31–33 ask about Passage A.

---

31. The main function of the last paragraph of Passage A is to:

   A. describe the area that dinosaurs inhabited 65 million years ago.

   B. refute a theory that was formerly assumed to be correct.

   C. introduce an anecdote about the life expectancy of dinosaurs.

   D. present evidence to support a previously introduced theory.

32. Passage A indicates that the presence of iridium in rock layers:

   F. proves that nuclear weapons were used in the past.

   G. deterred plants from undergoing photosynthesis.

   H. suggests an asteroid impact.

   J. caused the extinction of the dinosaurs.

33. Which of the following details from Passage A best supports Dr. Alvarez's asteroid theory?

   A. Asteroids can exist at the size of Manhattan.

   B. Dinosaurs died off 65 million years ago.

   C. Burning debris adds a layer of haze that keeps out sunlight.

   D. The Chicxulub Crater was discovered in Mexico in 1989.

Questions 34–37 ask about Passage B.

---

34. The reference to the Permian-Triassic extinction event in Passage B primarily serves to:

   F. give an example of a phenomenon to support the perspective being discussed.

   G. prove that the asteroid impact hypothesis is impossible.

   H. render a mental image of an extinction.

   J. confirm that global warming led to the extinction of dinosaurs.

35. According to Passage B, volcanos were a likely cause of the Cretaceous-Paleogene extinction event due to the presence of:

   A. dinosaur fossils.

   B. iridium.

   C. the Chicxulub Crater.

   D. sulfur dioxide.

36. As it is used in line 52, the term *heartbeat* most nearly refers to:

   F. a short period of time.

   G. the death of all dinosaur species.

   H. sounds made by dinosaurs.

   J. an extended period of time.

37. It can most reasonably be inferred from the passage that dinosaur extinction was caused by:

   A. severe burns from molten lava.

   B. injuries from falling rocks.

   C. a dimming of the sun.

   D. an imbalance in the air and lack of sunlight.

Questions 38–40 ask about both passages.

---

38. Compared to Passage A's discussion of the Chicxulub Crater, Passage B describes the crater as:

   F. a hoax introduced by followers of Dr. Luis Alvarez.

   G. the direct cause of the extinction of dinosaurs.

   H. unrelated to the Cretaceous-Paleogene extinction.

   J. the reason for a layer of iridium on Earth's surface.

39. The authors of both passages would most likely agree with which statement about the Cretaceous-Paleogene extinction event?

   A. It took place 65 million years ago.

   B. Its cause was similar to that of the Permian-Triassic extinction event.

   C. It was linked to volcanic activity on Earth.

   D. It was a minor event compared to other extinctions in history.

40. Unlike the first paragraph of Passage B, the first paragraph of Passage A:

   F. refutes a commonly held theory.

   G. conveys the author's opinion about a scientific event.

   H. cites statistics to give background about the event.

   J. introduces a scientist who has studied the topic of the passage.

SCIENCE TEST
35 Minutes—40 Questions

DIRECTIONS: There are six passages in this test. Each passage is followed by several questions. After reading a passage, choose the best answer to each question and fill in the corresponding oval on your answer document. You may refer to the passages as often as necessary. You are NOT permitted to use a calculator on this test.

Passage I

The *Bristlenose Pleco* is an algae-eating freshwater fish found in lakes and ponds. Due to this behaviour, they are popular as domestic pets that keep fish tanks clean. Smaller than the *Common Pleco*, the Bristlenose Pleco has a number of whisker-like protrusions around its mouth, allowing it to better harvest algae deposits.

Study

A group of scientists conducted an experiment to examine how *light zones* (the strongest wavelength of light capable of penetrating that depth of water, which is then used for photosynthesis) and food resources affect Bristlenose Pleco population. The light zones tested, and their respective wavelengths and depths, are tabulated in Table 1.

A group of Bristlenose Pleco and two different species of algae — *Algae 1* and *Algae 2* — were placed in a temperature-controlled 60 m glass tank of freshwater. Fluctuations in water disturbance were measured to calculate the population of each species at varying depths. The results of the study are shown in Figure 1.

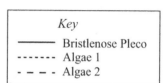

Table 1		
Wavelength of light (nm)	Zone	Depth (m)
50	UV	0-30
570	yellow	30-45
650	red	45-60

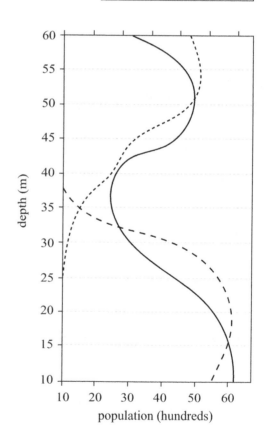

Figure 1

1. At a certain depth in the tank the populations of Algae 1 and Algae 2 are equal. What is the total approximate population of Algae 2 at this depth?

    A.   5
    B.   35
    C.   1,000
    D.   1,500

2. Which of the following questions concerning Bristlenose Pleco does the study attempt to answer?

    F. Does the Bristlenose Pleco consume different types of algae in salt-water containers with similar efficacy as in fresh-water containers?
    G. How does the population of the Bristlenose Pleco depend on the population of different species of algae and wavelength of light?
    H. Do different species of algae compete for the same resources in a controlled environment?
    J. What precisely is the mechanism for which Bristlenose Pleco fish harvest algae deposits?

3. Various types of algae photosynthesize different frequencies of light, causing them to flourish at different depth levels. Based on the results of the study, as the total population of both species of algae, on average, decreases, the population of Bristlenose Pleco:

    A. decreases.
    B. decreases then increases.
    C. increases.
    D. varies, but with no general trend.

4. Which of the following is the most likely reason why the scientists chose to conduct the study with a tank made of glass?

    F. To be able to better see the activity of the Bristlenose Pleco fish and two species of algae
    G. Glass is ideal for controlling the temperature of its contents
    H. To record the procedure of Bristlenose Pleco harvesting algae deposits
    J. To allow light to enter the environment for algae to undergo photosynthesis

5. Suppose the average size of Bristlenose Pleco was 8.1 cm. According to the information provided, which of the following could represent the average size of Common Pleco?

    A. 6.5 cm
    B. 8.1 cm
    C. 10.9 cm
    D. Cannot be determined from the given information

6. Suppose the study were repeated except the temperature-controlled container only contained *Algae 3*, a species which thrives on yellow light, but cannot survive against red light or UV exposure. If the population, p, versus depth, d, data for Algae 3 were plotted, which of the following equations would best represent the resulting population for Bristlenose Pleco?

    F. $p = d$
    G. $p = -d$
    H. $p = d^2$
    J. $p = -d^2$

Passage II

Plants require light and water to grow, bear fruit, and survive. Plants also have the ability to convert solar energy into chemical energy through photosynthesis, which is represented by the chemical equation below:

$$6CO_2 + 6H_2O \rightarrow C_6H_{12}O_6 + 6O_2$$

Experiment 1

The rate of photosynthesis varies due to many factors, two of which are the quantity of water absorbed by the plant, and the frequency of the light received. A team of botanists performed an experiment on a collection of *Lavandula angustifolia* (lavender plants). They recorded the quantity of water absorbed (in mL) each day over the fruit bearing season, which is from the beginning of May to the end of August. They then calculated the rate of photosynthesis each day by measuring the fluctuation of oxygen gas concentration. The results of the study are shown in Figure 1.

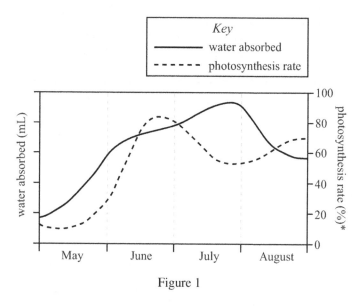

Figure 1

* compared to an ideal value for *Lavendula angustifolia* during the fruit brearing season that was assigned a photosynthesis rate of 100%

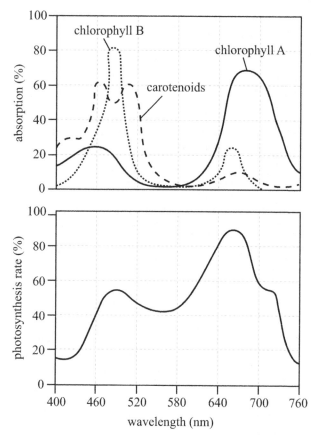

Figure 2

Experiment 2

Leaf material from *Lavandula angustifolia* was collected and passed through a spectrophotometer. The absorption of various wavelengths of light by chlorophyll A, chlorophyll B, and carotenoids were recorded. The team of botanists were then able to calculated the photosynthesis rate at each wavelength, which is shown in Figure 2.

Experiment 3

A collection of 30 *Lavandula angustifolia* was divided evenly and placed in three different controlled locations in a greenhouse — Location A, Location B, and Location C — for 6 months. Botanists controlled the amount of water given to the plants, as well as the wavelengths of light emitted, for each location. One of the three locations was restricted to only violet light (400 nm). The total biomass, in kilograms, produced by the lavender plants each month was measured and displayed in Figure 3.

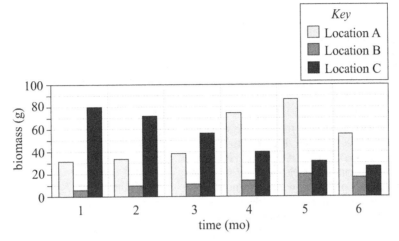

Figure 3

7. Based on the results of Experiment 1, the photosynthesis rate for *Lavandula angustifolia* on August 1st was approximately:

A. 55%
B. 62%
C. 70%
D. 76%

8. Light is a vital energy source for plants and is required to energize the photosynthesis reaction. Not all frequencies are equally effective, however. Consider the average wavelength, λ, of four colors in the visable spectrum shown in the table below:

Color	Blue	Green	Yellow	Red
λ (nm)	420	530	590	680

According to Figure 2, which color of light is most effective for lavender plant growth?

F. Blue
G. Green
H. Yellow
J. Red

9. Light availability causes plant growth, whereas a significant lack of absorptive light energy can lead to plant decay or death. Because lavender plants appear violet and reflect violet light, this wavelength of light is the least efficient energy source for lavender plants. Which location was most likely restricted to only violet light?

A. Location A
B. Location B
C. Location C
D. Cannot be determined from the given information

10. Based on Figure 1, on average, was the photosynthesis rate for lavender plants during the fruit bearing season greater than or less than the ideal value that was used for comparison?

F. Less; the photosynthesis rate during the fruit bearing season was 100%.
G. Less; the photosynthesis rate during the fruit bearing season was less than 100%.
H. Greater; the photosynthesis rate during the fruit bearing season was 100%.
J. Greater; the photosynthesis rate during the fruit bearing season was less than 100%.

11. In Experiment 3, which of the following factors was intentionally varied in order to determine the effect on biomass?

A. The photosynthesis rate of lavender plants for the three greenhouse locations
B. The biomass produced by each collection of lavender plants
C. The quantity of lavender plants in each greenhouse location
D. The amount of water and wavelength(s) of light at each greenhouse location

12. Suppose a lavender plant was placed in a controlled environment with 18 moles of CO_2, 18 moles of H_2O, and sufficient sunlight. Based on the balanced chemical equation in the passage, how many moles of glucose would be produced?

F. 1
G. 3
H. 6
J. 18

GO ON TO THE NEXT PAGE.

Passage III

High school students competing in the Physics Olympics competition are tasked with protecting an egg dropped off a ledge from breaking. Teams in the competition are allowed 10 trials of varying parameters.

After observing maple tree seeds float slowly to the ground while spinning, the students decided to slow the egg down by converting downward acceleration into rotational acceleration using an *egg protection device*. After observing crash test dummy videos, the students added a *crushable impact zone* to the device to collapse on contact with the ground, absorbing the remaining kinetic energy. If the crushable impact zone is too long the apparatus will fail to condense properly and will fall over after impact, causing the egg to roll out and break. This phenomenon is called *posting*. The master design can be seen in Figure 1.

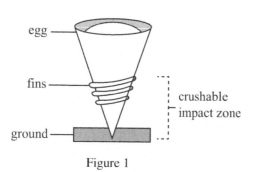

Figure 1

The equation below discusses the drag force, F_d, of a propeller through a substance. C_d represents a fixed drag coefficient, A is the projected area of the protection device, ρ is the fluid density, and ν is the relative velocity. The egg protection device is designed to be a propeller in air, and some of the variations in design can be represented in the equation.

$$F_d = C_d A \frac{1}{2} \rho \nu^2$$

The students completed four experiments to thoroughly examine how to efficiently protect the egg. They measured the angular speed, in radians per second, of their design for each trial, in addition to whether the trial successfully prevented the egg from cracking.

Experiment 1

The students recorded the mass of a paper egg protection device, including the egg, with a mass comparator balance. The egg protection device holding the egg was suspended 100 cm above the landing zone. After instruction by a Physics Olympics supervisor, the students released the egg protection device from suspension and measured the angular speed and success of the trial. They recorded their results in Table 1.

Table 1			
Trial	Mass (g)	Spin (rad/s)	Success
1	120	n/a	no
2	130	0.9	yes
3	140	1.3	no

Experiment 2

The procedure of Trial 1 was repeated except the material of the egg protection device was altered for each trial. The results of experiment are recorded in Table 2.

Table 2			
Trial	Material	Spin (rad/s)	Success
4	paper	1.3	yes
5	styrofoam	1.7	yes
6	cardboard	2.2	no
7	plastic	2.3	yes

Experiment 3

The procedure of Trial 1 was repeated except the height of the egg protection device suspension was altered. The results of the experiment are recorded in Table 3.

Table 3			
Trial	Height (cm)	Spin (rad/s)	Success
8	80	1.1	yes
9	100	1.3	yes
10	120	1.6	no

13. According to the experimental results of the students, what would the spin speed be, in radians per second, of a paper egg protection device containing an egg with a mass of 160 g initially suspended from a height of 100 cm?

   A. Less than 1.1 rad/s
   B. Between 1.1 rad/s and 1.3 rad/s
   C. Between 1.3 rad/s and 1.4 rad/s
   D. Greater than 1.4 rad/s

14. The Physics Olympics requires that contestants use a new egg for each drop during the competition. In addition, the material for the egg protection device must be replaced with a new material for each trial. What is the sum of the total number of eggs and protection device materials that the students used during the Physics Olympics competition?

   F. 3
   G. 10
   H. 12
   J. 20

15. If the egg protection device is made from a highly dense material, the force of impact will transfer to the egg and cause it to crack. Which of the following trials did the students use to investigate how material density would affect the success of the egg protection device?

   A. Trials 1-3 and Trial 10
   B. Trial 2 and Trials 8-10
   C. Trials 5-7
   D. Trials 10-12

16. During one of the Physics Olympics trials, the egg protection device unexpectedly disassembled while descending. The results of this trial, therefore, were immeasurable. In which of the following trials did the egg protection device of the students disassemble?

   F. Trial 1
   G. Trial 3
   H. Trial 5
   J. Trial 8

17. When an object is in free fall, increasing the drag force, F_d, reduces the landing velocity of the object and improves its chances of a successful landing. According to the information provided, which change will help to improve the chances of an object having a successful landing?

   A. Increasing the area of the fins
   B. Increasing the density of the object
   C. Increasing the initial velocity of the object
   D. Increasing the mass of the object

18. The winning design of the Physics Olympics competition is the egg protection device that successfully protects the egg, with the first tiebreaker rewarded for minimizing the mass of the egg protection device, and the second tiebreaker rewarded for maximizing the height of the drop. Suppose a different team of students received second place with the following successful trial:

Mass (g)	Material	Height (cm)
130	Paper	120

Did the students in Experiments 1-3 receive first place in the Physics Olympics competition?

   F. Yes; According to Trial 2, the students successfully landed the egg with an equivalent egg protection device mass, but from a lower height.
   G. No; According to Trial 2, the students successfully landed the egg with an equivalent egg protection device mass, but from a lower height.
   H. Yes; According to Trial 10, the students successfully landed the egg with a lighter egg protection device mass at an equivalent height.
   J. No; According to Trial 10, the students successfully landed the egg with a lighter egg protection device mass at an equivalent height

19. Suppose the Physics Olympics competition took place in Mount Washington, New Hampshire (altitude 1918 m). Based on the study, how would the results of the competition be affected by the change in location?

   A. The egg drop protection device would have a greater chance of success for Trial 1.
   B. The egg drop protection device would have a lower chance of success for Trial 5.
   C. The egg drop protection device would have a greater chance of success for Trials 8-10.
   D. Cannot be determined from the given information.

Passage IV

WAV is an audio file type that is *lossless* (a file that has the same file size per millisecond independent of the information encoded). Common audio file terminiology is defined below.

- *Bit depth* is the amount of information in an audio file at each point in time and is calculated by the following equation:

$$\log_2 b = d$$

  where b is the amount of bits and d is the bit depth.

- *Sample rate* is the amount of information dedicated to representing a sound occurring over time and is measured in kilobytes per second (kB/s). The sample rate and file size of an audio file are directly related.

- *Compression ratio* is the ratio of initial file size to final file size.

WAV files are typically larger in size than other audio file types. In order to save space and bandwidth, MP3 compression is often used to reduce the required storage space without drastically changing the represented audio. Four students debate how MP3 file compression works.

Student 1

MP3 compression reduces the sample rate by cutting out frequencies below 60 Hz and above 16 kHz. Since the human ear can only detect frequencies from 20 Hz to 20 kHz, MP3 compression does not severely affect the music one hears. Because bass frequencies (< 60 Hz) require more voltage to be reproduced than most other frequencies, this results in a significant reduction in file size.

Student 2

MP3 compression works by reducing the compression ratio through a procedure called *quoting*, where repeating chords or sounds are reproduced using one parent reference. Therefore, a song that has an abundance of similar sounds can be compressed well and the file size reduced significantly, while a song that has a random collection of different sounds cannot be compressed well.

Student 3

MP3 compression reduces the bit depth by splitting the audio into two different channels: Mid and Side. The Mid channel contains most of the important instruments, such as voice and drums, and the Side channel contains peripheral information. During MP3 compression, the fidelity of the Side channel is reduced significantly, while the Mid channel is untouched. This reduces file size while preserving essential information, giving the impression of high quality.

Student 4

MP3 compression lowers the maximum ceiling of volume, clipping loud segments and helping to avoid distortion. The distortion of sound occurs from *digital clipping* (smooth sound waves are chopped into inaccurate pieces, resulting in a step function rather than a smooth curve). These edges save space by requiring less information per second.

20. The file size of three WAV files are compared. According to the information provided, which of the following wave files would result in the largest file size?

    F. 5 minutes of silence
    G. 5 minutes of intense drumming
    H. 5 minutes of footsteps
    J. All three WAV files have equal file sizes

21. A high bit depth allows for a larger gradient of volume change between loud and soft sounds. A high sample rate captures high and low frequency information more accurately by dedicating more information per second. Which best describes the differences between Student 1 and Student 4 with respect to bit depth and sample rate?

    A. Student 1 argues MP3 compression reduces bit depth, while Student 4 argues MP3 compression reduces sample rate
    B. Student 1 argues MP3 compression reduces sample rate, while Student 4 argues MP3 compression reduces bit depth
    C. Both Students 1 and 4 argue MP3 compression reduces bit depth
    D. Both Students 1 and 4 argue MP3 compression reduces sample rate

GO ON TO THE NEXT PAGE.

22. Suppose a certain audio file, after MP3 compression, achieved a compression ratio of 10:1 by reducing the sample rate from $1,400$ kB/s to 128 kB/s with no change in bit depth. This compression would strengthen the viewpoints of which student(s)?

   F. Students 1, 3, and 4
   G. Students 1 and 3
   H. Student 1 only
   J. None of the students

23. Consider the smooth sound wave shown below:

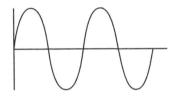

   Which of the following sound waves would Student 4 agree would be the result of the above sound wave undergoing digital clipping?

A.

C.
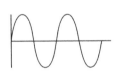

B.
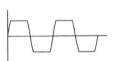

D.

24. When an audio file is compressed by decreasing the sample rate, transient information (large spikes in volume) are spread out over time, causing pre-echo and ringing. *Variable bit rate* compression minimizes these artifacts by examining the transient information, and then compressing the sample rate. The fewer sharp transients, the lower the sample rate and thus the smaller the resulting file size. Which of these recordings would achieve the smallest file size after variable bit rate compression?

   F. 5 minutes of distant ocean waves
   G. 5 minutes of intense drumming
   H. 5 minutes of footsteps
   J. 5 minutes of bird calls

25. For photo files, *JPEG image compression* reduces the pixel depth in areas of repeating colour. JPEG compression does not function well in high contrast and high detail photography. Which students believes MP3 compression works similarly to JPEG compression?

   A. Student 1
   B. Student 2
   C. Student 3
   D. Student 4

26. According to the information provided, if the quantity of bits of an audio file is reduced from 8 bits to 4 bits, what is the resulting bit depth compression ratio?

   F. 1:2
   G. 2:1
   H. 2:3
   J. 3:2

GO ON TO THE NEXT PAGE.

Passage V

Lenses are devices that change the path of light rays. The light rays bend either towards or away from one another depending on which device is used. A *converging lens* manipulates light rays passing through it to bend towards each other. If parallel light rays approach a converging lens, the light rays will converge at a focal point a distance f from the lens as shown in Figure 1.

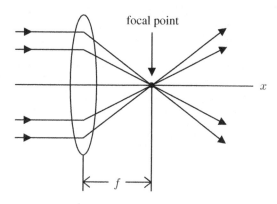

Figure 1

A *diverging lens* manipulates light rays passing through it to bend away from each other. If parallel light rays approach a diverging lens, the light rays will diverge from the focal point a distance f from the lens as shown in Figure 2.

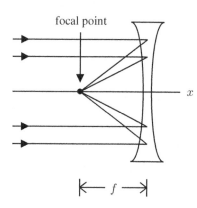

Figure 2

Experiment 1

A team of physics students conducted an experiment to determine the focal length of one converging lens. The lens was placed 10 cm away from five parallel light emitting objects on a laboratory table in a dark room. A screen was placed on the opposite side of the lens and moved along the x axis of the table until the image on the screen came into focus. Table 1 shows the distance each object was from the lens, s_o, and the distance the screen was from the lens, s_i, when a focused picture was obtained.

Table 1			
Object	s_o (cm)	s_i (cm)	f^* (cm)
Candle	10	20	6.67
Pencil	10	22	6.88
Beaker	10	23	6.97
Bottle	10	18	6.43
Phone	10	18	6.43

* The students calculated the focal length (the horizontal distance the object is from the center of the lens at 0 cm) for each object using the following equation:

$$\frac{1}{f} = \frac{1}{s_o} + \frac{1}{s_i}$$

where f is the focal length of the lens, s_o is the distance the object is from the lens, and s_i is the distance the image on the screen is from the lens.

Experiment 2

The procedure from Experiment 1 was repeated except the students calculated the focal length of five different converging lenses for one object. The results of the experiment are shown in Table 2.

Table 2			
Lens	s_o (cm)	s_i (cm)	f (cm)
1	10	20	6.67
2	10	32	7.62
3	10	40	8.00
4	10	55	8.46
5	10	67	8.70

Experiment 3

The procedure from Experiment 1 was repeated except the students calculated the focal length of a single diverging lens. The results of the experiment are shown in Table 3.

Table 3			
Object	s_o (cm)	s_i (cm)	f (cm)
Candle	10	−5.0	−10.0
Pencil	10	−5.1	−10.4
Beaker	10	−5.1	−10.4
Bottle	10	−4.8	−9.2
Phone	10	−4.9	−9.6

27. Based on the results of Experiment 2, as the distance the screen was from the lens increased, the focal length:

    A. increased only.
    B. decreased only.
    C. was constant.
    D. varied, but with no general trend.

28. Which of the following is the most likely reason why the students placed the laboratory table and experiment setup in a dark room?

    F. To minimize ambient noise from affecting the results of the experiment
    G. To better see the focus of the image on the screen
    H. To ensure the experiment setup would not be damaged
    J. To easily identify the difference between a converging lens and diverging lens

29. A student performed an additional trial and recorded the following results:

s_o (cm)	s_i (cm)	f (cm)
10	−7.7	−33.5

    Based on the results of Experiments 1-3 and the information provided, was the student using a converging lens or a diverging lens for the additional trial?

    A. A converging lens, because the focal length recorded was positive.
    B. A converging lens, because the focal length recorded was negative.
    C. A diverging lens, because the focal length recorded was positive.
    D. A diverging lens, because the focal length recorded was negative.

30. Based on Experiments 1 and 2, which lens in Experiment 2 was used for the five trials in Experiment 1?

    F. Lens 1
    G. Lens 2
    H. Lens 3
    J. Lens 4

31. Based on the descriptions of Experiments 1 and 2, how did the procedure of Experiment 1 differ from the procedure of Experiment 2? The procedure of Experiment 1:

    A. tested for the focal length of five different lenses, whereas the procedure of Experiment 2 tested for the focal length of one lens.
    B. tested for the focal length of one lens, whereas the procedure of Experiment 2 tested for the focal length of five different lenses.
    C. tested for the focal length of a diverging lens, whereas the procedure from Experiment 2 tested for the focal length of a converging lens.
    D. tested for the focal length of a converging lens, whereas the procedure from Experiment 2 tested for the focal length of a diverging lens.

32. The lens of the human eye receives light from all angles and consolidates the light rays into a single point on a layer in the back of the eye called the *retina*. Based on Figures 1 and 2, would the lens of the human eye be considered a converging lens or a diverging lens?

    F. A converging lens, because the focal point is located on the opposite side of where light enters the lens.
    G. A converging lens, because the focal point is located on the same side of where light enters the lens.
    H. A diverging lens, because the focal point is located on the opposite side of where light enters the lens.
    J. A diverging lens, because the focal point is located on the same side of where light enters the lens.

33. *Magnification* (m) of a thin lens is defined by the following relationship:

    $$m = -\frac{s_i}{s_o}$$

    Calculations for magnification of each of the 5 lenses used in Experiment 2 were conducted by the team of physics students. The *magnitude* (absolute value) of the magnification calculation of which of the following lenses was the lowest?

    A. Lens 2
    B. Lens 3
    C. Lens 4
    D. Lens 5

267
GO ON TO THE NEXT PAGE.

Passage VI

Infrared spectroscopy (IR spectroscophy) is used frequently in laboratories to identify unknown molecules. An infrared spectrometer measures the percentage of infrared light that is absorbed by the molecule at different *wavenumbers* (the frequencies tested measured in cm^{-1}). The infrared portion of the electromagnetic spectrum is separated into three parts: the near ($> 4,000$ cm^{-1}), middle ($4,000$ cm^{-1} - 2000 cm^{-1}), and far (< 2000 cm^{-1}) ranges.

Organic compounds, a common molecule to test for using IR spectroscopy, have functional groups which absorb IR light at specific wavenumbers (see Table 1). This allows experimenters to deduce which unknown organic compounds are being passed through the IR spectrometer. The higher the absorbance percentage the more likely the molecule has that functional group.

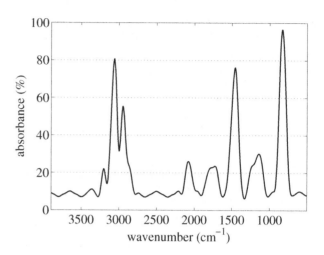

Figure 1

Table 1		
Name	Functional group	wavenumber (cm^{-1})
Alcohol	O-H	3300
Alkane	C-H	3000
Alkene	C=C	850
Halide	C-F	1250
Amine	N-H	1600

Experiment 1

A group of scientists prepared a sample of an unknown organic compound by measuring 2 drops of the unknown using a *pipette* (a thin tube used for transferring small quantities of liquid) onto a dry salt plate. An additional salt plate was placed on top of the unknown. The scientists raised the unknown up to the light to verify that it dispersed evenly between the two salt plates. The sample was placed in the beam entrance of the spectrometer. A spectrum of the unknown organic compound was printed and is shown in Figure 1.

Experiment 2

The scientists repeated the procedure from Experiment 1, except a different unknown organic compound was passed through the IR spectrometer. A spectrum of the unknown organic compound was printed and is shown in Figure 2.

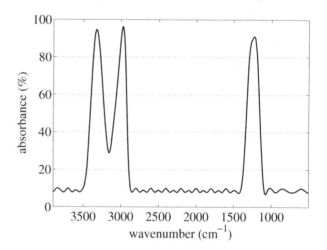

Figure 2

34. Based on the description of Experiment 1, which of the following diagrams best shows the apparatus that was used to obtain the proper quantity of the unknown organic compound?

F.

H.

G.

J.

35. Based on Table 1, and the results of the experiments, which of the following functional groups is most likely present in both unknown organic compounds?

A. Alcohol
B. Alkane
C. Alkene
D. Halide

36. How did the procedure in Experiment 1 differ from the procedure the group of scientists used in Experiment 2? In Experiment 1:

F. one organic compound was passed through the IR spectrometer, whereas in Experiment 2 three organic compounds were passed through the IR spectrometer.
G. one organic compound was passed through the IR spectrometer, whereas in Experiment 2 a different organic compound was passed through the IR spectrometer.
H. the scientists prepared four slides of the unknown compound, whereas in the Experiment 2 the scientists prepared three slides of the unknown compound.
J. the scientists prepared three slides of the unknown compound, whereas in the Experiment 2 the scientists prepared four slides of the unknown compound.

37. The *wavelength* of the vibration of a functional group when hit by IR light is measured in centimeters (cm), the reciprocal of wavenumber. Based on Table 1, which of the following functional groups has the highest wavelength?

A. Alcohol
B. Alkane
C. Halide
D. Amine

38. The three infrared ranges allow scientists to concentrate on a specific region of the infrared spectrum and more efficiently identify unknown organic compounds. Based on the results of Experiment 2 and other information provided, which of the following functional groups is most prevalent in the unknown compound within the IR far range?

F. Alcohol
G. Alkane
H. Halide
J. Cannot be determined from the given information

39. Based on Table 1 and Figure 2, which of the following molecular formulas most likely represents the unknown organic compound used in Experiment 2?

A. CH_3OH
B. CH_3F
C. CH_2NOH
D. CH_2FOH

40. Consider the following molecular structure of the organic compound *Toluene*:

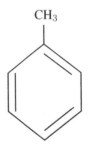

CH_3

Toluene has three carbon-carbon double bonds (C=C) and four carbon-hydrogen single bonds (C-H). Based on Table 1 and the results of the experiments, in which experiment—Experiment 1 or Experiment 2— was Toluene most likely the unknown organic compound passed through the IR spectrometer?

F. Experiment 1, because Figure 1 shows a high absorbance for the C=C functional group.
G. Experiment 2, because Figure 2 shows a high absorbance for the C=C functional group.
H. Experiment 1, because Figure 1 shows a high absorbance for the C-F functional group.
J. Experiment 2, because Figure 2 shows a high absorbance for the C-F functional group.

The Internet and Changing Reading Habits

The Internet has transformed personal reading habits. The availability of a limitless stream of online text has been linked to the declining ability of both children and adults to read long texts, interpret complex styles and vocabulary, and evaluate texts critically. This transformation has affected the industries of publishing and journalism, which are encouraging writers to develop more accessible and colloquial styles in order to write shorter, less complex pieces of writing. Is this change a positive one? What is gained or lost by the shift in reading habits?

Read and carefully consider these perspectives. Each suggests a particular way of thinking about rhetoric and educational traditions.

Perspective 1	Perspective 2	Perspective 3
The explosion of simplistic and sensationalistic writing on the Internet has greatly damaged the reading skills of many people, children especially. Their exposure to it should therefore be limited.	The massive shift in writing styles brought on by the internet is the latest in a long series of such changes. Readers and writers have adapted to such shifts before and should be encouraged to do so again.	It is unknown if this change in writing styles will benefit or harm readers and writers, since it is a recent phenomenon. Perhaps the shift is a result of changes in people's preferences and not vice-

Essay Task

Write a unified, coherent essay in which you evaluate multiple perspectives on the Internet and changing reading habits. In your essay, be sure to:

- analyze and evaluate the perspectives given
- state and develop your own perspective on the issue
- explain the relationship between your perspective and those given

Your perspective may be in full agreement with any of the others, in partial agreement, or wholly different. Whatever the case, support your ideas with logical reasoning and detailed, persuasive examples.

ACT5 - A0317

Practice Test

ENGLISH TEST
45 Minutes—75 Questions

DIRECTIONS: In the five passages that follow, certain words and phrases are underlined and numbered. In the right-hand column, you will find alternatives for the underlined part. In most cases, you are to choose the one that best expresses the idea, makes the statement appropriate for standard written English, or is worded most consistently with the style and tone of the passage as a whole. If you think the original version is best, choose "NO CHANGE." In some cases, you will find in the right-hand column a question about the underlined part. You are to choose the best answer to the question.

You will also find questions about a section of the passage, or about the passage as a whole. These questions do not refer to an underlined portion of the passage, but rather are identified by a number or numbers in a box.

For each question, choose the alternative you consider best and fill in the corresponding oval on your answer document. Read each passage through once before you begin to answer the questions that accompany it. For many of the questions, you must read several sentences beyond the question to determine the answer. Be sure that you have read far enough ahead each time you choose an alternative.

PASSAGE I

An Unexpected Artist: Julia Margaret Cameron

At the dawn of photography, many were unclear about what the mediums exact use might be. Immediate reactions
$\overline{}$
1

leaned toward the scientific, or commercial, but could
$\overline{}$
2
photography be elevated to a fine art? One answer to that question

murmured from an unexpected but confident source: Julia
$\overline{}$
3
Margaret Cameron.

Julia Margaret Cameron in living her first forty-eight
$\overline{}$
4
years of life as a free-spirited housewife. She married

1. **A.** NO CHANGE
   B. mediums exact using
   C. medium's exact use
   D. medium's exact using

2. **F.** NO CHANGE
   G. scientific, or commercial but
   H. scientific or commercial but
   J. scientific or commercial, but

3. Which of the following choices best reflects Cameron's confident nature later mentioned in the sentence?
   A. NO CHANGE
   B. bellowed
   C. resonated
   D. confided

4. **F.** NO CHANGE
   G. living
   H. having lived
   J. lived

a <u>bearded wizard</u> of an attorney, and the two had five
      5

children of their own. Even with so many mouths to feed,

Cameron also raised <u>five children of family members</u> as
                                           6

well as a young girl she found begging in the streets.

Outside of the home, Cameron rubbed elbows with

<u>the time's leading artists and scientists,</u> including Lord Alfred
                          7

Tennyson—the Poet Laureate of Great Britain and Ireland.

She was a true character in the celebrity culture of Victorian

England long before she called herself an artist.

But <u>fates having it</u> that Cameron's daughter and
                      8

son-in-law would present her with a camera as a gift.

Inscribed on that camera were the words, "It may amuse you,

Mother, to try to photograph during your solitude at

Freshwater." <u>And amuse her it did!</u> Within the eleven years of
                            9

Cameron's photographic endeavors, the artist took nearly 900

photographs. Her first attempt at using the contraption

resulted in a somewhat blurred focus. <u>It wasn't her intention,</u>
                                                        10

this soft focus became a staple in Cameron's photography.

[4]

She photographed friends and family members, never

accepting payment for portrait sittings. Her best known photos

portrayed <u>biblical and literary, scenes</u> as well as portraits of
                              11

her celebrity friends.

Perhaps most interesting, however, were the traces left

on Julia Margaret Cameron's negatives and prints

<u>by the artist herself.</u> Many of her photographs
              12

5. Given that all of the following are true, which option physically describes Cameron's husband?
   - A. NO CHANGE
   - B. kindly soul
   - C. courageous chap
   - D. sweet being

6.
   - F. NO CHANGE
   - G. five children of family members were raised by Cameron
   - H. family members had Cameron raise five children
   - J. raised by Cameron were five children of family members

7.
   - A. NO CHANGE
   - B. time's leading artists, and scientists
   - C. times leading artists, and scientists
   - D. times leading artists and scientists

8.
   - F. NO CHANGE
   - G. fate would have it
   - H. fates would have them
   - J. fates having them

9. If the writer were to delete the underlined portion, the paragraph would primarily lose:
   - A. an example of the camera's importance.
   - B. a description of why Cameron took to photography.
   - C. a useful transition from the quotation.
   - D. an humorous anecdote.

10.
    - F. NO CHANGE
    - G. The blurriness was unwanted,
    - H. She didn't mean to,
    - J. Though originally a mistake,

11.
    - A. NO CHANGE
    - B. biblical and literary scenes:
    - C. biblical and literary scenes,
    - D. biblical, and literary scenes;

12.
    - F. NO CHANGE
    - G. by: the artist herself.
    - H. by the artist, herself.
    - J. by: the artist, herself.

being featured with accidental fingerprints, the shadow of a
13

stray hair, or even a phantom hand holding a drape back to set
14

the scene. Similar mistakes can be found in a variety of art
15
that has been created since this time.
15

13. **A.** NO CHANGE
    B. feature
    C. will feature
    D. have featured

14. **F.** NO CHANGE
    G. by setting
    H. is setting
    J. to be setting

15. Which of the following best concludes both the paragraph and the essay?

    A. NO CHANGE
    B. These seeming mistakes left physical traces of the artist, who is now heralded as one of the most influential artists of her time.
    C. Other artists should think about creating similar personal touches in their own art.
    D. The confines of Victorian England made it difficult to see beauty in mistakes.

PASSAGE II

Crowdfunding for Change

[1]

A new form of investment has emerged, and with
16
it, comes a new term to describe that process. [A]
16
"Crowdfunding" refers to the practice of raising small amounts

of money from a large number of individuals, via the internet.

While that may seem like an obvious innovation to some,
17
crowdfunding has the potential to completely turn our current

socioeconomic system upside down.

[2]

The old model of investing looks something like this:
18
any person with a concept for a new product must prove

16. **F.** NO CHANGE
    G. emerged and with it,
    H. emerged, and with it comes
    J. emerged and with it comes

17. **A.** NO CHANGE
    B. commemoration
    C. condemnation
    D. introspection

18. **F.** NO CHANGE
    G. something like:
    H. something like this,
    J. something like;

it's potentially to a bank or venture capitalist, who may then
₁₉
invest large sums of money into the idea. [B] First,

entrepreneurs with innovative ideas would likely have to

spend large sums of their own cash to prove just how great

their product is. Even so, most people creating new products
₂₀

hail from affluent backgrounds. Consequently, banks are most
₂₁
interested in seeing a return on their investments. That

could exclude products that help create a better

world and instead reward less socially conscious but cheaper
₂₂
versions of these ideas. ⬚23

[3]

Now, any person can invest small sums of money into

whatever cause they deem worthy. That process empowers

entrepreneurs and small-time investors alike. Entrepreneurs no

longer need to appease the banks, allowing it to spend less
₂₄
money, while having more control over how their product is

presented to the public. [C] The public, then, becomes the

deciding vote of which ideas make it to production, and

which do not. From the comfort of their own home,
₂₅
individuals can give small amounts of money to products with

which they feel a personal connection. An elementary school

teacher or housewife can now add the title of "investor" or

"entrepreneur" to their business card more easy than ever.
₂₆

19. **A.** NO CHANGE
B. it's potential
C. its potentially
D. its potential

20. **F.** NO CHANGE
G. Thusly,
H. However,
J. Therefore,

21. **A.** NO CHANGE
B. Continuously,
C. Secondly,
D. For example,

22. Which of the following alternatives to the underlined portion would be LEAST acceptable?

F. world, they instead reward
G. world: Banks instead reward
H. world; rewarded instead are
J. world, and banks could instead reward

23. At this point, the writer is considering deleting the preceding sentence. Should the writer make this deletion?

A. Yes, because it strays too far from the focus of the paragraph.
B. Yes, because it contradicts information provided earlier in the passage.
C. No, because it clarifies a point made earlier in the paragraph.
D. No, because it defines an entrepreneurial term.

24. **F.** NO CHANGE
G. them
H. whoever
J. us

25. **A.** NO CHANGE
B. which does
C. who do
D. who does

26. **F.** NO CHANGE
G. easy then
H. easily than
J. easily then

GO ON TO THE NEXT PAGE.

[4]

Crowdfunding has also championed a new humanitarian form of doing business. [D] People across the globe are giving more money than ever to causes striving to better the world around us. Whether that be <u>investing in environmentally</u> <u>27</u> <u>sustainable products, helping to pay for someone's expensive</u> <u>27</u> <u>surgery, or funding a musician's dream of creating an album,</u> <u>27</u> people are taking to the internet to show the world what matters to them. [28]

27. Which of the following choices most specifically demonstrates the kinds of humanitarian causes using crowdfunding?

A. NO CHANGE
B. finding a positive cause or trying to help an individual,
C. donating money, buying a myriad of humanitarian products, or looking for causes,
D. funding or investing in a nice project,

28. Which of the following, if added here, would best conclude the essay?

F. Surely there must be even more new ways to incorporate the internet into finance.
G. Many experts in the world of finance have weighed in on these matters.
H. Specifically, young people will benefit from crowdfunding.
J. With so much change in so little time, crowdfunding is surely a global phenomenon to watch out for.

Questions 29 and 30 ask about the preceding passage as a whole.

29. Upon reviewing the passage and realizing that a transition has been left out, the author composes the following sentence:

The confines created by the old model are limiting for many reasons.

The most logical placement for this sentence would be:

A. Point A in Paragraph 1.
B. Point B in Paragraph 2.
C. Point C in Paragraph 3.
D. Point D in Paragraph 4.

30. Suppose the writer had chosen to write a brief essay describing a typical day for modern day entrepreneurs. Would this essay successfully fulfill the writer's goal?

F. Yes, because the essay alludes to a daily schedule.
G. Yes, because the breadth of the essay includes a wide array of entrepreneurs within a single day.
H. No, because the essay focuses on a specific development rather than daily happenings.
J. No, because the essay does not refer to a specific entrepreneur by name.

GO ON TO THE NEXT PAGE.

PASSAGE III

Funghi Fanatics

Darting through the forest, the sniffs of Leila the golden
retriever peruse each and every tree trunk of the lush Oregon
$\overline{31}$
forest. Her owners follow closely behind, clocking how she
reacts to each spot. Rather than carelessly playing, this dog
loves recreational time: to sniff out and unearth truffles.
$\overline{32}$

Hunting for truffles—pricey, aromatic mushrooms
$\overline{33}$
used for cooking—with animal assistance dates all the way
$\overline{33}$
back to the Roman Empire. Oddly enough, hogs are the
animals most widely associated with hunting for these

diamonds of the rough. The first documented case of utilizing
$\overline{34}$
a "truffle hog" dates back to the fifteenth century, and they
have been the ultimate choice in truffle detectors ever since.
Most truffles lay underground, attached to the roots of trees.
Hogs search out these mushrooms, in the wild, and can smell
$\overline{35}$
them up to three feet under the earth. Scientists believe that
these fungi produce a smell similar to one involved in the
hormones of male hogs, making them prime candidates for
hunting truffles.

31. **A.** NO CHANGE
    B. Leila the golden retriever carefully sniffs
    C. Leila's golden retriever sniffs search
    D. a keen sense of smell from Leila the golden re-
    triever sniffs

32. Which of the following most clearly contrasts the first
    half of the sentence?
    F. NO CHANGE
    G. must do something else:
    H. cannot believe her luck:
    J. is on a mission:

33. Which of the following is LEAST acceptable?
    A. truffles (pricey, aromatic mushrooms used for
    cooking,)
    B. truffles, which are pricey, aromatic mushrooms
    used for cooking,
    C. truffles (pricey, aromatic mushrooms used for
    cooking)
    D. truffles—those pricey, aromatic mushrooms
    used for cooking—

34. **F.** NO CHANGE
    G. diamonds in
    H. diamond's of
    J. diamonds' in

35. **A.** NO CHANGE
    B. mushrooms in the wild, and can smell
    C. mushrooms, in the wild and can smell
    D. mushrooms in the wild and can smell

[1] Today, hunting for truffles in the Oregon forests become a business in their own right, and dogs are the perfect
36   37
creatures for the job. [2] Perhaps more important, is the

secretly covert nature of truffle hunting; people preferring to
        38   39
search for the fungi in private, allowing them to keep secret

the best spots to look. [3] Though dogs do not naturally seek

out truffles in the wild, they are easily trained to do so and

have many benefits that pigs lack. [4] Dogs, who are much
                                              40
smaller than your average truffle hog, which can weigh

two-hundred pounds, so they are easier to care for. [5]

Trainers often have a difficult time with hogs trying to eat their

findings, while dogs are rewarded with treats of their own. [6]

A dog in the forest is quite a banal sight, but you'd be hard

pressed to inconspicuously follow a hog around those woods

without raising suspicions. ⏐42⏐
        41

36. F. NO CHANGE
    G. have been becoming
    H. has become
    J. are becoming

37. A. NO CHANGE
    B. its
    C. ones
    D. one's

38. F. NO CHANGE
    G. secretively covert
    H. covert, private
    J. covert

39. A. NO CHANGE
    B. having preferred
    C. with preferences
    D. prefer

40. F. NO CHANGE
    G. Dogs are
    H. Dogs, being
    J. Dogs, which are

41. A. NO CHANGE
    B. without suspicions being raised.
    C. sans raising suspicions.
    D. DELETE the underlined portion, ending the sentence with a period.

42. For the sake of the logic and coherence of this paragraph, Sentence 2 should be placed:
    F. where it is now.
    G. before sentence 1.
    H. after sentence 4.
    J. before sentence 6.

GO ON TO THE NEXT PAGE.

<u>Who are the main players in mushroom economics?</u>
43

Market prices for truffles are astounding. <u>Though Oregon</u>
44
white truffles can sell for close to $560 per pound, while ultra

rare white Alba truffles can go for a whopping $2000 per

pound. With such potential for profit, it's no wonder truffle

hounds are more popular than ever!

43. Which of the following questions best helps to introduce this paragraph?

   A. NO CHANGE
   B. For how long will these fungi be so popular?
   C. Why all the fuss?
   D. Where are the main spots for finding truffles?

44. **F.** NO CHANGE
    G. When
    H. Knowing that
    J. DELETE the underlined portion

Question 45 asks about the preceding passage as a whole.

---

45. Suppose the writer had written this as part of a collection of essays spotlighting animals that help people. Would this essay fit with the collection's theme?

   A. Yes, because the essay highlights a single animal that aids humans in completing a task.
   B. Yes, because the essay highlights more than one animal that aids humans in completing a task.
   C. No, because the essay fails to mention what people do after finding truffles.
   D. No, because the essay focuses too heavily on the human component of this task.

PASSAGE IV

A Collegiate Family of Singers

[1]

I will never forget the first time I heard the

<u>crisp chords and syncopated percussion</u> of an a cappella
46
group. At the age of six, I accompanied my family to a

county fair where we were to watch my eldest cousin perform

with her college singing group. I squirmed in my seat as we

waited for the performance to begin, wishing <u>with every</u>
47
<u>cent of my innermost being</u> that we had instead opted to visit
47
the petting zoo. But as soon as those six harmonic voices

46. Which of the following most specifically describes the qualities of the music that the narrator admires?

   F. NO CHANGE
   G. substantial and obvious accomplishment
   H. various melodic qualities
   J. constant musicality

47. **A.** NO CHANGE
    B. with every scent of my innermost being
    C. with all my might
    D. with all my mite

echoed through the crowd, I was hooked. <u>Where were the</u>
<u>instruments? Perhaps there was a backup track?</u> Bopping
my head to the beat, I became too distracted to care.

[2]

It would be three hours before my mother explained to
me that "a cappella" meant creating music <u>using solely and</u>
<u>only the power of the human voice without any accompaniment,</u>
and it would be twelve years before I, myself, could
participate in an a cappella group.[A] A cappella has a deep
collegiate history, beginning with the founding of the Yale
Whiffenpoofs in 1909, so I had waited in <u>eagerly anticipation</u>
for the opportunity to participate in a group of my own when I
attended college. [B]

[3]

The weeks that followed proved even more difficult than
<u>the audition: in which senior members of the group drilled us</u>
bumbling freshmen on eight-part harmonies for what seemed
like an infinite number of songs. [C] Every time I considered
giving up, another member would reach out to offer a helping
hand. <u>One such time,</u> the day before my first show, I had
completely bungled my entrance to our finale song. [D] I
trudged out of the our rehearsal with an <u>embarrassed defeated</u>

look on my face. No less than half an hour <u>later a knock</u>
<u>at my door revealed</u> my "big sibling" of the group with a

warm cup of coffee in hand. ☐55 With her guidance, I was
able to ace my entrance the next day and finish my first show
with pride.

48. If the writer were to delete the two underlined questions, the paragraph would primarily lose:
F. a humorous anecdote.
G. an example of the audience's reactions to the performance.
H. a transition into the main focus of the essay.
J. a concession that the author did not fully understand the music she heard.

49. A. NO CHANGE
B. using solely and only the power of the human voice,
C. using only human voices without any accompaniment,
D. using only human voices,

50. F. NO CHANGE
G. eager anticipation
H. eagerly anticipated
J. eager, anticipated

51. A. NO CHANGE
B. audition; senior members of the group drilling
C. audition, senior members of the group drilled
D. audition; senior members of the group drilled

52. F. NO CHANGE
G. On the occasion,
H. Today,
J. Often,

53. A. NO CHANGE
B. embarrassingly defeated
C. embarrassed defeatingly
D. embarrassed, defeatingly

54. F. NO CHANGE
G. later, a knock at my door revealed
H. later, a knock at my door revealed,
J. later a knock at my door revealed,

55. The use of quotation marks around the phrase in the preceding sentence is most likely intended to:
A. add humor to an otherwise serious tone.
B. voice the author's negative feelings towards the individual.
C. directly quote the individual.
D. identify that the title given is not a literal one.

GO ON TO THE NEXT PAGE.

[4]

The members of my a cappella group grew to become

family. Together, we toured the country, competing in national

events, and <u>even recorded an album!</u> Singing in an a cappella
                   56

group is <u>more difficult but beautiful,</u> but I wouldn't trade the
         57

time with my group for anything in the world. [58]

56. F. NO CHANGE
    G. an album was recorded!
    H. even recording an album was fun!
    J. and record an album on which we sang!

57. A. NO CHANGE
    B. more difficult and beautiful,
    C. as difficult as they are beautiful,
    D. as difficult as it is beautiful,

58. At this point, the writer is considering adding the following true statement:

    > Today, a cappella has gained notoriety in many forms of mainstream media including film and television!

    Should the writer make this addition?

    F. Yes, because it justifies the author's love for a cappella.
    G. Yes, because it makes clear a point made earlier in the passage.
    H. No, because it does not help to conclude the passage.
    J. No, because it does not mention whether or not the author has participated in those programs.

Questions 59 and 60 ask about the preceding passage as a whole.

59. The writer plans to add the following sentence to the essay:

    > After a grueling week of auditions, I landed the role of second soprano in a group of twelve coed singers.

    This sentence would most logically be placed at Point:

    A. A in paragraph 2.
    B. B in paragraph 2.
    C. C in paragraph 3.
    D. D in paragraph 3.

60. Suppose the writer's goal had been to write a persuasive essay advocating that more people should join a cappella groups. Would this essay accomplish that goal?

    F. Yes, because it creates a clear link to her thesis in every paragraph.
    G. Yes, because it makes clear the personal and financial benefits of a cappella.
    H. No, because its pedantic tone is too harsh to be persuasive.
    J. No, because it focuses more heavily on personal anecdotes than persuasion.

PASSAGE V

To Sport or Not To Sport: Olympic Review

Since the first modern games in 1896, the Olympic Games have brought together nations from around the globe. Unnoticed by many, however, <u>is</u> the ever changing landscape
61

of the games. New sports are <u>constantly in review and the</u>
62

decision to add a new game to the Olympic <u>rotation</u> is never
63
taken lightly.

A sport's road to the Olympic Games begins with paperwork—and lots of it. Members of the sport's international federation must submit a proposal nearly one-hundred pages in length, to the ninety member International Olympic Committee <u>(IOC)</u>. Contained in this
64
proposal is a plethora of information, including the sport's olympic history,

global participation rates, gender equity, <u>popularity and</u>
<u>potentially financing.</u>
65
Further lobbying for a sport's entry happens at five continental general assemblies where representatives of various sports meet annually to discuss the merits of <u>it's</u>
66
sport and lobby for Olympic inclusion at lavish events.

61. A. NO CHANGE
B. are
C. have been
D. were

62. F. NO CHANGE
G. constantly in review, and
H. constantly, in review, and
J. constantly in review and,

63. A. NO CHANGE
B. rotating
C. rotated
D. rotator

64. The write is considering deleting the underlined portion, correcting any necessary punctuation. Should they make this edit?

F. Yes, because it introduces an acronym that is not employed again within the passage.
G. Yes, because it detracts from the passage's formal tone.
H. No, because it explains who makes up the International Olympic Committee.
J. No, because it introduces an acronym used later in the passage.

65. A. NO CHANGE
B. popularity, and what they calculate for potentials in financing it.
C. popularity, and the potential it has in financing.
D. popularity, and financial potential.

66. F. NO CHANGE
G. its
H. their
J. they're

The <u>final decision</u>, however, is left in the hands of the IOC,
<u>67</u>
and some decisions may be a matter of personal bias between

committee members. In fact, recent committee decisions have

been largely influenced by a push for youth interest as the IOC

<u>cannot fathom any other option.</u>
<u>68</u>

And finally making it into the Olympic Games <u>being</u>
<u>69</u>
just the beginning of the battle. Many sports must compromise

on exact events and judging methods. <u>For example, the newly</u>
<u>70</u>
<u>admitted event of, climbing</u> is fated to award only two gold
<u>70</u>
medals — one to a male climber and another to a female

climber — <u>based, on a cumulative score, from three events:</u>
<u>71</u>

sport climbing, bouldering, and speed climbing. <u>Typically,</u>
<u>72</u>
professional climbers tend to specialize in only one of these

events. Requiring athletes to participate in all three may leave

some of the <u>worlds' best climbers</u> out of the running, and
<u>73</u>
could possibly endanger others who are stepping outside their

preferred event.

67. **A.** NO CHANGE
B. The ultimate, final decision,
C. The ultimately final decision,
D. In the end, the ultimately final decision,

68. Which of the following most specifically describes the reasoning behind the aforementioned "push?"
F. NO CHANGE
G. fears losing spectators under the age of forty.
H. needs an audience to watch the Games.
J. uses specific marketing tactics.

69. **A.** NO CHANGE
B. was
C. is
D. will be

70. **F.** NO CHANGE
G. For example the newly, admitted, event of climbing
H. For example, the newly admitted event of climbing
J. For example, the newly admitted, event of climbing

71. **A.** NO CHANGE
B. based on a cumulative score from three events:
C. based on a cumulative score from three events;
D. based, on a cumulative score from three events; those include

72. Which of the following alternatives to the underlined portion is LEAST acceptable?
F. Accordingly,
G. Usually,
H. Normally
J. Customarily,

73. **A.** NO CHANGE
B. worlds best climbers'
C. worlds best climber's
D. world's best climbers

Regrettably, a new sport like climbing can be voted out of the Games by a simple majority of the IOC once the season has ended. <u>Furthermore,</u> sports organizations
74
continue to campaign for Olympic entry. So why bother?

<u>Being a part of the Olympic Games means</u> widening your
75
audience, gaining respect, and most importantly, competing for a piece of global history.

74. **F.** NO CHANGE
    G. Still,
    H. Finally,
    J. Seemingly,

75. **A.** NO CHANGE
    B. Being a part, of the Olympic Games, means
    C. Part of the Olympic Games means
    D. Part of the Olympic Games, means

END OF TEST 1.
STOP! DO NOT TURN THE PAGE UNTIL TOLD TO DO SO.

THERE ARE NO TESTING MATERIALS ON THIS PAGE.

MATHEMATICS TEST
60 Minutes — 60 Questions

DIRECTIONS: Solve each problem, choose the correct answer, and then fill in the corresponding oval on your answer document.

Do not linger over problems that take too much time. Solve as many as you can; then return to the others in the time you have left for this test.

You are permitted to use a calculator on this test. You may use your calculator for any problems you choose,

but some of the problems may be best done without using a calculator.

Note: Unless otherwise stated, all of the following should be assumed:
1. Figures are NOT necessarily drawn to scale.
2. Geometric figures lie in a plane.
3. The word *line* indicates a straight line.
4. The word *average* indicates arithmetic mean.

---

1. What value of x makes the equation $\dfrac{4(3x+6)}{5} = 11$ true?

   A. $2\dfrac{7}{12}$

   B. $4\dfrac{1}{2}$

   C. $\dfrac{1}{6}$

   D. $\dfrac{14}{15}$

   E. $10\dfrac{1}{3}$

2. What is the minimum number of students that must be in a class so that the class can be divided evenly into groups of 4, 5, or 6 students?

   F. 20
   G. 24
   H. 30
   J. 60
   K. 120

3. A store sells a jacket for $120. For the upcoming holidays the store is having a sale for 20% off all items. If sales tax is 8%, what is the purchase price, to the nearest cent, of the jacket for the upcoming holidays?

   A. $16.32
   B. $88.89
   C. $96.00
   D. $103.68
   E. $108.00

4. As shown in the figure below, a flagpole, $\overline{AB}$, that is 12 feet tall casts a shadow, $\overline{AE}$, that is 30 feet long. The shadow, $\overline{DE}$, of a vertical post 5 feet in height, $\overline{CD}$, ends at the same point as the shadow of the flagpole. How far is the post from the base of the flagpole along the ground?

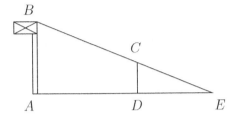

F. 12.5 feet

G. 15 feet

H. 17.5 feet

J. 18 feet

K. 20 feet

5. Erica's grade in history class is based on the average of 6 tests. To make the honor roll, Erica's test average must be at least an 85. She has scored 72, 91, 83, 86, and 82 on the first 5 tests, respectively. What is the minimum score she must receive on her last test in order to make the honor roll?

A. 83

B. 87

C. 91

D. 93

E. 96

6. A bag contains 6 red, 5 green, 11 yellow, and 8 blue marbles. If a marble is selected at random from the bag, what is the probability that the marble selected is NOT green?

F. $\dfrac{1}{6}$

G. $\dfrac{1}{5}$

H. $\dfrac{1}{4}$

J. $\dfrac{3}{4}$

K. $\dfrac{5}{6}$

7. A 17 foot ladder is laid against a wall so that the base of the ladder rests 8 feet from the wall. To the nearest foot, how high up on the wall does the ladder reach?

    A. 12 feet
    B. 13 feet
    C. 15 feet
    D. 17 feet
    E. 18 feet

8. Maria used 210 feet of wooden boards to make the border of the 15 foot wide rectangular bocce court she installed in her back yard. To the nearest square foot, what is the area of the bocce court?

    F. 2700 ft^2
    G. 2070 ft^2
    H. 1463 ft^2
    J. 1350 ft^2
    K. 1050 ft^2

9. In triangle ABC where C is the right angle, what is the cosine of $\angle B$?

    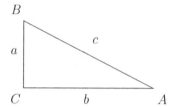

    A. $\dfrac{a}{c}$

    B. $\dfrac{c}{a}$

    C. $\dfrac{c}{b}$

    D. $\dfrac{b}{c}$

    E. $\dfrac{a}{b}$

10. If $f(x) = 3x^2 + 7x - 12$, what is $f(-5)$?

    F. -122
    G. -52
    H. -28
    J. 28
    K. 98

11. Which of the following equations represents a line perpendicular to the line $5x - 3y = 12$?

   A. $y = \dfrac{5}{3}x + 3$

   B. $y = -\dfrac{5}{3}x - 3$

   C. $y = \dfrac{3}{5}x + 4$

   D. $y = -\dfrac{3}{5}x - 4$

   E. $y = -\dfrac{4}{3}x + 5$

12. Which of the following expressions is equivalent to $(5x^2y^5z)(8x^7y^5z)$?

   F. $13x^9y^{10}z$

   G. $13x^{14}y^{25}z$

   H. $40x^9y^{10}z$

   J. $40x^9y^{10}z^2$

   K. $40x^{14}y^{25}z^2$

13. Which of the following expressions is equivalent to:

$$(-4x^2 - 7x + 4) - (7x^2 - 7x + 11)$$

   A. $3x^2 - 14x + 15$

   B. $11x^2 + 15$

   C. $-3x^2 + 7$

   D. $-11x^2 - 14x - 7$

   E. $-11x^2 - 7$

14. Timmy has a collection of 640 baseball cards. He plans to give most of them to his nephew, but wants to keep a few for himself. Every year he plans on giving half his cards to his nephew until he can no longer divide his collection evenly. Assuming Timmy acquires no new cards, for how many years will he be able to give his nephew baseball cards?

   F. 2

   G. 5

   H. 6

   J. 7

   K. 8

15. If $f(x) = x^2 + 3$ and $g(x) = 4x - 5$, which of the following represents $f(g(x))$?

   A. $4x^2 - 2$

   B. $16x^2 - 22$

   C. $4x^2 + 12x - 5$

   D. $16x^2 - 40x + 28$

   E. $16x^2 - 40x - 22$

GO ON TO THE NEXT PAGE.

16. Kenny has planted a garden in the shape of a right triangle. The shortest side of the garden is half the length of the longest side. If the sum of the shortest and longest sides is 75 feet, what is the length, to the nearest foot, of the remaining side?

   F. 35 feet

   G. 43 feet

   H. 56 feet

   J. 70 feet

   K. 87 feet

17. A small school has a class of 24 freshmen, 31 sophomores, 27 juniors, and 25 seniors. If the student council consists of one sophomore, one junior, and one senior, how many different councils are possible?

   A. 83

   B. 107

   C. 1,992

   D. 20,925

   E. 502,200

18. Line segment AB has a midpoint at $(4, -3)$. If point A is located at $(-2, 5)$, what are the coordinates of point B?

   F. $(-8, -15)$

   G. $(-8, 13)$

   H. $(1, 1)$

   J. $(10, 1)$

   K. $(10, -11)$

19. The first matrix below represents the number of patrons who purchased the Quick (q), Standard (s), and Deluxe (d) washes at each of the north and south locations at Jay's Sprays Car Washes last week. The second matrix represents the cost of each type of wash. Based on the matrix data below, how much total revenue did Jay's Sprays make?

$$\begin{array}{ccc} q & s & d \end{array}$$
$$\begin{bmatrix} 140 & 80 & 35 \\ 70 & 115 & 180 \end{bmatrix} \begin{bmatrix} \$8 \\ \$13 \\ \$20 \end{bmatrix}$$

   A. \$2,795

   B. \$2,860

   C. \$5,655

   D. \$8,455

   E. \$8,515

GO ON TO THE NEXT PAGE.

20. A ramp is placed at the top of a shipping container, that is 8.5 feet tall, as shown in the figure below. If the angle formed by the ramp and the ground has a sine of $1/4$, how long is the ramp?

    F.   13 feet

    G. 25 feet

    H. 28 feet

    J.   34 feet

    K. 38 feet

21. In his grading policy, Mr. Garrison drops the highest and lowest scores of 8 given tests. Wendy calculated the mean and median of her 8 tests scores before the application of the grading policy. Which of the following statements *must* be true of Wendy's calculations after Mr. Garrison applies his grading policy?

    A. The mean will be higher

    B. The median will be higher

    C. The mean will be lower

    D. The median will be lower

    E. The median will remain the same

22. The number of diagonals of a polygon with n sides can be calculated using the formula $\dfrac{n(n-3)}{2}$. If a polygon has 35 diagonals, how many sides does that polygon have?

    F. 665

    G. 560

    H. 13

    J.   10

    K. 7

23. If the system of equations shown below has an infinite number of solutions, what is the value of r?

$$8x - 6y = 36$$
$$20x - 15y = 9r$$

    A. 5

    B. 9

    C. 10

    D. 18

    E. 20

24. A pool containing 210 gallons of water is filling at a rate of 20 gallons per minute. A second pool containing 850 gallons of water is draining at a rate of 1 gallon per second. In how many minutes will the two pools contain the same amount of water?

    F.   4
    G.   6
    H.   8
    J.   12
    K.   30

25. Which of these represents the equation of the function $f(x) = x^2$, shifted 2 units up and 7 units to the right?

    A. $f(x) = (x + 7)^2 + 2$
    B. $f(x) = (x - 7)^2 - 2$
    C. $f(x) = (x - 7)^2 + 2$
    D. $f(x) = (x + 2)^2 + 7$
    E. $f(x) = (x - 2)^2 - 7$

26. Points A, B, C, and D lie on a line in that order. If $AD = 28$, $AC = 17$, and $BD = 14$, what is the length of BC?

    F.   3
    G.   5
    H.   21
    J.   31
    K.   59

27. $2 \begin{bmatrix} 4 & 7 \\ 3 & 2 \end{bmatrix} + 3 \begin{bmatrix} 5 & 1 \\ 8 & -3 \end{bmatrix} = ?$

    A. $\begin{bmatrix} 14 & 13 \\ 16 & 4 \end{bmatrix}$

    B. $\begin{bmatrix} 48 & 36 \\ 55 & 0 \end{bmatrix}$

    C. $\begin{bmatrix} 23 & 17 \\ 30 & -5 \end{bmatrix}$

    D. $\begin{bmatrix} 20 & 7 \\ 24 & -6 \end{bmatrix}$

    E. $\begin{bmatrix} 9 & 8 \\ 11 & -1 \end{bmatrix}$

GO ON TO THE NEXT PAGE.

Use the following information to answer questions 28-30.

Stan's first child is applying to colleges, and Stan is trying to calculate how much he can afford to pay for college tuition each year based on his annual salary of $130,000. His partial budget can be found in the table below. Stan's federal income tax rate is 28%, his state income tax rate is 6%, and his other taxes combine for an additional 7% of his annual income.

Expense Category	Budget Amount
Housing / Transportation	$31,000
Food / Clothing	$13,500
Healthcare	$7,900
Entertainment	$10,000
Taxes	?
College	?
Total	$130,000

28. What is the total amount that Stan will have to pay in annual taxes?

    F. $14,300
    G. $36,400
    H. $41,000
    J. $53,300
    K. $67,600

29. Stan's son matriculates to a college which costs $19,500 per year. By how much would Stan need to decrease his Entertainment spending in order to pay the tuition?

    A. $5,200
    B. $4,800
    C. $2,700
    D. $1,100
    E. $1,350

30. If Stan receives a $20,000 raise he will have to pay a total of $61,500 in taxes. Assuming Stan allocates the same amount of money for his expenses, what percent of his income can he devote to college tuition?

    F. 11.0%
    G. 13.3%
    H. 17.4%
    J. 26.1%
    K. 41.0%

31. In the figure below $\overline{AEB}$ is parallel to $\overline{FCDG}$. $\angle ECD = 3x - 9$, $\angle CED = 4x$, and $\angle DEB = 3x + 9$. What is the value of x?

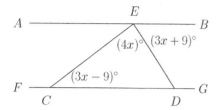

A. $9\frac{1}{2}$

B. $10\frac{1}{2}$

C. 18

D. $25\frac{5}{7}$

E. 36

32. In the parallelogram below, Points A, B, C, and D are located at $(3, -2), (-3, -2), (0, 3)$ and $(6, 3)$ respectively. To the nearest tenth of a square unit, what is the area of the parallelogram?

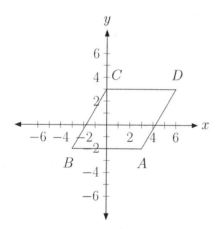

F. 15

G. 23.7

H. 27.6

J. 30

K. 35

33. What is the maximum area of a circle that is contained entirely within a rectangle whose dimensions are 8 by 14?

A. 8π

B. 14π

C. 16π

D. 49π

E. 64π

34. In the figure below, rectangle $ABCD$ is inscribed in circle E. If $\overline{AB} = 15$ cm and $\overline{BC} = 8$ cm, what is the area of the shaded region to the nearest square centimeter?

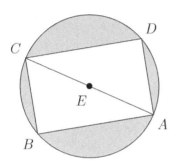

F. 107

G. 120

H. 227

J. 310

K. 788

35. A cylindrical jug 18 inches in diameter contains 25 gallons of water. To the nearest tenth of an inch, what is the height of the water in the jug?

(Note: There are 231 in^3 in 1 gallon.)

A. 5.7

B. 7.2

C. 17.8

D. 22.7

E. 102.1

36. For a school project, Leopold tracked the number of hours he spent working on each of six subjects over the course of a week. His results are displayed in the table below.

Subject	Hours
English	8
Science	3
History	6
Math	11
French	5
Economics	7

He wants to draw a circle graph from his data. What should be the central angle for the Math sector of his circle graph?

F. 72°

G. 84°

H. 99°

J. 120°

K. 137°

37. If $\sin^2 \theta = 0.36$ and $90° < \theta < 180°$, what is the value of $\cos \theta$?

A. −0.8

B. −0.64

C. −0.6

D. 0.64

E. 0.8

38. Colorado license plates consist of three digits (0-9) followed by three letters. If repetition of digits is allowed but repetition of letters is not, and none of the digits are zero, how many unique license plates are possible?

F. 7,862,400

G. 11,232,000

H. 11,372,400

J. 12,812,904

K. 15,600,000

39. Which of the following equations represents a horizontal asymptote for the function $f(x) = \dfrac{12x^2 + a}{4x^2 + b}$ where a and b are integers and $a \neq b$?

  A. $x = 3$

  B. $y = 3$

  C. $y = \dfrac{3a}{b}$

  D. $y = 3x$

  E. $y = -\dfrac{a}{b}$

40. If x is a negative, odd integer, what must be true about y so that the expression $x^3 y^6$ results in a positive, even integer?

  F. y is even and positive

  G. y is even and negative

  H. y is odd and positive

  J. y is odd and negative

  K. y is imaginary

41. Which of the following values of d would result in the product $\left(\dfrac{1}{2 + \sqrt{5}}\right)\left(\dfrac{d}{d}\right)$ having a rational denominator?

  A. $4 - \sqrt{20}$

  B. $2 + \sqrt{5}$

  C. $4 + \sqrt{20}$

  D. $-2 - \sqrt{5}$

  E. $2 + \sqrt{-5}$

42. On January 1st, Bradley placed $50 in a shoe box and slid it under his bed. His plan was to stow away $5 *more* than he did the previous month on the last day of every month for a year. If he met but did not exceed his goal, how much money did he have in his shoe box on January 1st of the next year?

  F. $1,040

  G. $ 990

  H. $ 930

  J. $ 710

  K. $ 440

43. Two dice, each with 6 sides numbered 1-6, are rolled simultaneously. What is the probability that the product of the numbers shown is greater than 21?

  A. $1/6$

  B. $1/8$

  C. $1/9$

  D. $1/12$

  E. $1/36$

44. In car safety crash tests, the force of the car hitting a wall, F, can be modeled by the equation shown below.

$$F = \frac{(\text{mass})(\text{distance})}{\text{time}^2}$$

If two identical cars are tested along the same length of track, how many times more force will the car that reaches the wall in 10 seconds exert compared to the car that reaches the wall in 15 seconds?

F. 2.25 times more force

G. 2.50 times more force

H. 3.00 times more force

J. 4.50 times more force

K. 6.00 times more force

45. A point travels along vector $8\mathbf{i} + 4\mathbf{j}$ and then travels along vector $11\mathbf{j}$. If the distance d between the initial and terminal point of a vector $a\mathbf{i} + b\mathbf{j}$ can be determined by the formula $d = \sqrt{a^2 + b^2}$, how far will the point end up from its starting position to the nearest tenth of a unit?

A. 8.9

B. 17.0

C. 19.4

D. 19.9

E. 23.0

46. If $\log_a(x) = q$ and $\log_a(y) = r$, which expression is equivalent to $\log_a \dfrac{x}{y^3}$?

F. $3q + r$

G. $3(q - r)$

H. $3(r - q)$

J. $q - 3r$

K. $\dfrac{q}{r^3}$

47. A chemistry student designed an experiment to measure the effect of two salts, NaCl and KCl on water temperature. The student prepared two separate beakers of 100 mL of salt-water solutions, one containing 15% NaCl, and one containing 15% KCl, and recorded the initial temperature for each beaker. Using identical heat sources, the student then heated each beaker for an hour, recording the temperature of each beaker every 10 minutes. At the end of the experiment, how many temperature readings will the student have?

A. 6

B. 7

C. 10

D. 12

E. 14

Use the following information to answer questions 48-51.

The figure below shows the overhead view of a Monster Truck tire. The tire itself is 50 inches in diameter and 10 inches wide, while the rims are 34 inches in diameter. The tire is filled with foam to prevent deflation, with an access point labeled A. Point B represents the front of the tire.

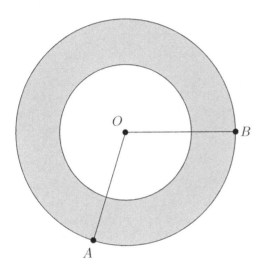

The angular position of the access point relative to the front of the tire is the reflex angle of $\angle AOB$, or θ. (A reflex angle is an angle, ϕ, where $180° \leq \phi \leq 360°$).

48. To the nearest inch, what is the circumference of the *rim* of the tire?

 F. 53

 G. 107

 H. 143

 J. 157

 K. 908

49. If $\dfrac{3\pi}{2} < \theta < 2\pi$ and $\sin\theta = -\dfrac{7}{25}$, what is $\tan\theta$?

 A. $-24/7$

 B. $-24/25$

 C. $-7/24$

 D. $7/24$

 E. $24/7$

50. Which of the following expressions represents the volume, in cubic inches, of foam that can fit in the tire?

F. $25\pi(10) - 17\pi(10)$

G. $25^2\pi(10) - 17^2\pi(10)$

H. $25^2\pi(10) + 17^2\pi(10)$

J. $50\pi(10) + 34\pi(10)$

K. $50^2\pi(10) - 34^2\pi(10)$

51. Which of the following functions, $P(\theta)$, could represent the position of point A, in terms of θ, as the tire rolls along the ground?

A. $P(\theta) = 25\sin\theta + 25$

B. $P(\theta) = 25\cos\theta - 25$

C. $P(\theta) = 25\sin\theta$

D. $P(\theta) = 25\cos\theta$

E. $P(\theta) = 25\tan\theta + 25$

---

52. A cube with side lengths of 10 inches is inscribed in a sphere. What is the radius, in inches, of the sphere?

F. $5\sqrt{2}$

G. $5\sqrt{3}$

H. $10\sqrt{2}$

J. $10\sqrt{3}$

K. 100

53. Consider the following matricies:

$$W = \begin{bmatrix} 11 & 22 \\ 66 & 33 \end{bmatrix} \quad X = \begin{bmatrix} 5 & 10 & 15 \\ -15 & -10 & -5 \end{bmatrix}$$

$$Y = \begin{bmatrix} 2 & -4 \\ -16 & 8 \end{bmatrix} \quad Z = \begin{bmatrix} -3 & 3 \\ 2 & -2 \\ -1 & 1 \end{bmatrix}$$

Which of the following matrix products is undefined?

A. YW

B. ZX

C. XZ

D. WX

E. YZ

54. Consider the map of a region of an ocean shown below. Ship A and Ship B leave port O at the same time, with Ship A traveling 39° South of West, and Ship B traveling 21° South of East. After 5 hours, Ship A had traveled 74 miles and Ship B had traveled 64 miles. At this point, what is the approximate distance, in miles, between the two ships?

Note: for any triangle ABC where a, b, and c are the sides opposite $\angle A$, $\angle B$, and $\angle C$, respectively, the law of cosines states that $c^2 = a^2 + b^2 - 2(a)(b)cos(C)$, and the law of sines states that $\dfrac{sin(A)}{a} = \dfrac{sin(B)}{b} = \dfrac{sin(C)}{c}$.

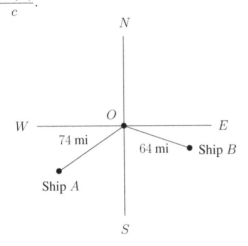

- **F.** 18
- **G.** 54
- **H.** 72
- **J.** 120
- **K.** 138

55. Clyde likes to race Go Carts. He recently purchased a newer version of his Go Cart. In his old cart, a lap around the track took 40 seconds at an average speed of 25 miles per hour. In his new cart, his average speed is 35 miles per hour. How much time will he save on each lap in his new Go Cart?

- **A.** 10 seconds

- **B.** $11\frac{3}{7}$ seconds

- **C.** 20 seconds

- **D.** 25 seconds

- **E.** $28\frac{4}{7}$ seconds

56. In the figure below, circles A, B, and C are tangent. Circle B has an area that is 16 times that of circle A, and circle C has an area that is 9 times that of circle A. If circle A has a radius of r, what is the perimeter of triangle ABC in terms of r?

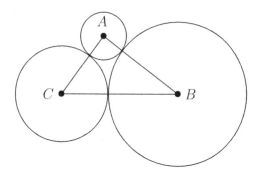

    F. $6r$

    G. $8r$

    H. $9r$

    J. $14r$

    K. $16r$

57. Which of the following data sets has the greatest standard deviation?

    A.   60, 60, 60, 60, 60, 60

    B.   10, 20, 30, 40, 50, 60

    C.   40, 45, 50, 55, 60, 65

    D.   10, 10, 10, 60, 60, 60

    E.   40, 50, 60, 70, 80, 90

58. The table below shows the probability of arbitrarily defined major upsets in a college basketball tournament based on annual historical data.

Number of major upsets	Probability
0	0.156
1	0.250
2	0.375
3	0.219

Based on the data, to the nearest tenth, what is the expected number of major upsets in any given year?

    F.   1.3

    G.   1.4

    H.   1.5

    J.   1.6

    K.   1.7

59. The binomial $(x + 7)$ is a factor of the polynomial $3x^2 + kx - 35$, where k is a constant. Which of the following expressions is the sum of the two solutions of the polynomial?

A. $-7 + \dfrac{5}{3}$

B. $-7 + 5$

C. $-7 + \dfrac{7}{3}$

D. $7 + \dfrac{5}{3}$

E. $5 + \dfrac{7}{3}$

60. In a certain quadrilateral, opposite angles are congruent, but its diagonals are NOT congruent. Which of the following statements regarding this quadrilateral is FALSE?

F. If the diagonals are perpendicular, the quadrilateral is a rhombus

G. Because its diagonals are not congruent, it may be a trapezoid

H. Since opposite angle are congruent, it must be a parallelogram

J. Even though the diagonals will bisect each other, it cannot be a square

K. Without congruent diagonals, it cannot be a rectangle

END OF TEST 2.
STOP! DO NOT TURN THE PAGE UNTIL TOLD TO DO SO.
DO NOT RETURN TO THE PREVIOUS TEST.

READING TEST

35 Minutes — 40 Questions

DIRECTIONS: There are four passages in this test. Each passage is followed by several questions. Choose the best answer to each question and fill in the corresponding oval on your answer document. You may refer to the passages as often as necessary.

Passage I

LITERARY NARRATIVE: This passage is adapted from *11 Kent* by Adelaide Emerson (©2004 by Adelaide Emerson).

The first time I saw Aunt Marguerite in the hallway at school, she pulled me out of the line of students and bent down to give me a big hug. She was smiling broadly and she leaned down with a big crook in her back so that
[5] she could look me straight in the eye. She asked how I was and asked me to come and see her after lunch in her classroom. I was afraid about what she would ask me, but I went. I didn't know how not to go. To my surprise she only asked me about myself and how I liked school, what
[10] I liked to read, who had been my favorite teachers. Since then whenever I see her in the hall she gives me a smile and a sideways glance as if we have a secret.

I don't know why my mother doesn't like Aunt Marguerite, but her disdain is clear and drips from her when-
[15] ever the subject of the other Emerson family comes up. She will slam a pot in the sink if my father reports something as innocuous as the fact that my cousin Patricia is attending secretarial school.

My mother rarely visits my grandmother's house.
[20] When she is with my grandmother, she seems to like her and to have fun talking to her. But she never comes to visit our house and my mother only goes to see her on Christmas and Easter. For many years, we have done these major holidays in shifts—on Christmas my family visits grand-
[25] mother at noon, and Aunt Marguerite's family sees grandmother at four. When my grandmother doles out presents to us, she steps gingerly through the boxes at the foot of their small Christmas tree to make sure she is leaving my cousins' things untouched. At Easter we switch the order.

[30] That night, as I wash the dishes after supper, I am alone in the kitchen with my mother. She is in a good mood. I implore her to tell me the story of the day they moved into this house. It is one of my favorite stories. How my oldest brother was three, my sister had just had
[35] her first birthday, and my mother was going to have my other brother any day. How they rented huge wooden barrels to fill with their clothing and dishes, and how the last one had just been moved into the house when my mother went into labor. How my brother was born that night and

[40] missed being a Leap Year baby by an hour. How the barrels remained unpacked in the house for weeks, giving my brother and sister a hide and seek playground in their house that they were unwilling to give up. My mother is expansive and funny as she tells the story, and I slow down
[45] my rinsing to make the story last longer.

She cycles into a story of the small apartment they lived in before this house and how she had to haul the awkward baby carriage up a flight of stairs in order to leave the house.

[50] "And where did you live before that?" I ask. I know the answer, but it's like I have her in a hypnosis session and want to see how far back I can go. She tells me about living with my grandmother when she was first married to my father. How much she disliked it. How she couldn't
[55] imagine there were people who arrived at the breakfast table fully dressed for the day and never appeared in bare feet in the house. But how much she enjoyed sitting with my grandmother in the long afternoons when she was pregnant with my oldest brother drinking peppermint tea with
[60] dry biscuits as the evening came.

I don't know how to draw her into talking about things that happened further back, which is what I really want to know about now. She looks at me, knowing I want to know, and retreats to the living room to watch television.

[65] Later that week I am told to stop by Classroom 107. Aunt Marguerite is sitting at a low table in the empty classroom, putting papers rhythmically into a series of yellow, brown, and orange folders.

"Hello, Kathleen." She grins at me. Her long nylon
[70] legs are bent at an awkward angle in the small chair. I'm not sure what I'm supposed to do, so I just stand there. As I expected, she fills the silence by describing the one-on-one reading program for seven year olds, telling how sixth grade girls like me can help. "We'll be working dur-
[75] ing lunch," Aunt Marguerite says. "The school has agreed to let us bring in a pizza from Pal Joey's so that we can eat lunch while we work." She smiles. "Will that be acceptable?" She leans over and says quietly in my ear, "I especially asked that you be one of the girls from the sixth
[80] grade."

My instinct is to be suspicious of her, but as she goes to the other side of the table to talk to the other girls, I study her: all I see is kindness. Maybe Aunt Marguerite was different when she was younger, when she first met my
85 mother. Maybe she was selfish and mean like the girls in my own grade. I consider this. When I get home, I decide not to ask my mother any questions about Aunt Marguerite. I decide not to mention her name at all.

1. All of the following are elements of the story the narrator's mother tells in the kitchen EXCEPT:

   A. the narrator's brother missing a leap year birth by an hour.
   B. opening Christmas presents at the narrator's grandmother's house.
   C. the narrator's family packing their belongings in barrels.
   D. the narrator's brother and sister playing hide and seek in their new house.

2. The narrator most nearly portrays her mother as:

   F. maliciously secretive.
   G. expansive and funny.
   H. negligent.
   J. temperamental.

3. The author's tone can best be described as:

   A. conciliatory.
   B. defensive.
   C. curious.
   D. jaded.

4. Which of the following events occurs first chronologically?

   F. The narrator is born.
   G. The narrator sees Aunt Marguerite in the hallway at school.
   H. The narrator's mother lives with the narrator's grandmother.
   J. The narrator's mother lives in a tiny apartment with the narrator's father.

5. The primary purpose of the last paragraph is to:

   A. clarify why the narrator's mother dislikes Aunt Marguerite.
   B. shift the focus of the passage to the narrator's experiences with her classmates.
   C. illustrate that some of the narrator's questions may never be answered.
   D. provide a flashback to when Aunt Marguerite and the narrator's mother first met.

6. What detail in the passage best indicates the narrator's age?

   F. Seven years old
   G. Ten years old
   H. Third grade
   J. Sixth grade

7. Which of the following statements best captures how the narrator's mother feels about Aunt Marguerite?

   A. She dislikes Aunt Marguerite due to a past experience unknown to the narrator.
   B. She hopes to reconcile with Aunt Marguerite at an upcoming family holiday celebration.
   C. She wants the narrator to have a relationship with Aunt Marguerite, despite her own feelings.
   D. She feels slighted because the narrator's grandmother chose Aunt Marguerite over her.

8. In lines 54–60, the narrator's mother describes her relationship with the narrator's grandmother by:

   F. explaining all of the times the grandmother was condescending to her.
   G. giving examples of when she was more and less comfortable at the grandmother's home.
   H. describing the link bewteen the grandmother and Aunt Marguerite.
   J. providing reasons why she was happy to live at the grandmother's home.

9. In the passage, the narrator's interactions with her grandmother take place:

   A. when her mother is not around.
   B. at the same time as Aunt Marguerite's.
   C. in the hallway at school.
   D. on Christmas and Easter.

10. When the narrator first sees Aunt Marguerite at school, she most nearly feels:

    F. happy to finally get to know her aunt.
    G. afraid that her mother will be upset with her.
    H. angry that Aunt Marguerite hugged her in public.
    J. uneasy about what Aunt Marguerite might say to her.

Passage II

SOCIAL SCIENCE: Passage A is adapted from "America's National Parks" by Alice Andrews (©2007 by Alice Andrews). Passage B is adapted from "Stuck in the Woods" by David Schwartz (©2010 by David Schwartz).

Passage A by Alice Andrews

When Woodrow Wilson passed the Organic Act of 1916, he officially launched the National Park Service (NPS) that now protects and manages 450 individual sites across the US. The stated mission for the National Park Project was "to conserve the scenery and the natural and historic objects and the wild life therein and to... leave them unimpaired for the enjoyment of future generations."

Baked into the language of this act was a brewing conflict: a fight between the forces of "conservation" and "enjoyment."

Admittedly, awareness of the contradictions between these two forces was lacking for the first fifty years of NPS management. Allowing for "enjoyment" demanded the paving of roads and the construction of railways, which meant demolishing mountains and displacing animal species. Through the modern lens, we can easily view these projects as blatant violations of conservation, but at the time, the federal government was moving ever forward in full faith of American progress. And to them, progress meant trains and cars in parks.

Although much of this blatantly destructive development has slowed today, a quieter battle carries on between conservation and seemingly innocent recreational activities done in the name of "enjoyment."

Conservationists are quick to point out the damage done by outwardly innocuous activities like hiking, camping, and water sports. For instance, in 2008, the Wildlife Conservation Society published their finding that protected areas in California that allowed quiet recreation activities like hiking (compared to their more restrictive counterparts) saw fivefold declines in populations of bobcats, coyotes and other midsize carnivores. From their point of view, wildlife protection is of the highest importance, and visitor amusement ranks much lower.

But recreationists readily defend and encourage any activity that brings people into nature. What better way to reinvigorate the public's declining interest in the outdoors, than drawing them out into the parks and creating a new generation of stewards to engage with the national treasures?

All of these considerations ultimately bring about questions of ownership. Who do the parks truly belong to—the government, the people, or the wildlife that makes them worth protecting?

Passage B by David Schwartz

Frequently held up as the poster child of mid-19th century thought about man's relation to nature, Henry David Thoreau's quotes find themselves splattered across posters in English classrooms across America. "I went to the woods because I wished to live deliberately." "Simplicity, simplicity, simplicity." Left uninterrogated, quotes like these deliver the sickly sweet punch of an inspirational "quote-of-the-day."

But to what extent should we trust this singer of nature's praises?

In Thoreau's *Walden*, we find the diary of a man running away from the city. A man running from the materialism, industrialism, and group-think of society. A man seeking to experience the individual "self" and the "sublime."

To be fair, at a historical moment obsessed with technological progress and geographical expansion, one can't be blamed for turning inward. In keeping with the Transcendentalist tradition, Thoreau desperately believed in the inherent goodness of people and nature, and, in turn, the capacity of society to corrupt that essential goodness— even if society came with things like trains, medicine, and newspapers.

Clinging to these principles, he set up a social experiment: to live in complete self-reliance, in the isolation of a small cabin on the Walden Pond in Massachusetts. He lived alone, foraging food for himself, and trying as hard as possible to revel in life (only to be found in nature, of course).

He exclaimed: "Think of our life in nature—daily to be shown matter, to come in contact with it—rocks, trees, wind on our cheeks! The solid earth! The actual world! The common sense! Contact! Contact! Who are we? Where are we?"

Admittedly, the experiences Thoreau describes sound somewhat enviable. Who wouldn't want to be prodded into an existentialist fantasia at the sight of a rock?

And yet, many of Thoreau's critics point out that this self-sufficient existence is a farce; how, in fact, can we truly separate ourselves from society in a Thoreauian way? How can he claim to have lived in isolation when his mother occasionally visited to do his laundry?

Surely, taking cues from a man who viewed conversation, community, and tradition as distractions from truth should not be trusted. Why does nature have to exist in the absence of society? Can a sunset be enjoyed if shared?

GO ON TO THE NEXT PAGE.

Questions 11–14 ask about Passage A.

11. As it is used in Passage A, the word *innocuous* (line 26) most nearly means:

    A. hostile.
    B. nontoxic.
    C. harmless.
    D. impulsive.

12. Which of the following details do Conservationists use to illustrate the damage done to the National Parks by recreational activities in Passage A?

    F. "paving of roads and the construction of railways" (line 14)
    G. "demolishing mountains" (line 15)
    H. "trains and cars in parks" (line 20)
    J. "fivefold declines in populations of bobcats, coyotes and other midsize carnivores" (lines 31–32)

13. The main function of the question in lines 42–44 is to:

    A. reveal the author's point of view about land ownership.
    B. prove the merits of the Recreationist beliefs.
    C. explain the Conservationists' views that parks belong to the wildlife that live there.
    D. suggest a continued conflict between the perspectives described.

14. Passage A indicates that people in the early 1900s viewed progress as:

    F. access for vehicles like trains and cars to National Parks.
    G. prioritizing the environment over enjoyment.
    H. restricting park activities to hiking, camping and water sports.
    J. destroying natural features like mountains and animal species.

Questions 15–17 ask about Passage B.

15. The tone of Passage B can best be described as:

    A. critical.
    B. praising.
    C. detached.
    D. sympathetic.

16. The primary purpose of paragraph 6 (lines 74–78) is to:

    F. illustrate the awe-inspiring capacity of nature.
    G. mock Thoreau's ecstatic revelations.
    H. lend the essay credibility by using quotations from Thoreau's writing.
    J. suggest the importance of Thoreau's existential questions.

17. Based on Passage B, Thoreau agreed with the Transcendentalist tradition that:

    A. new technology caused society to become evil.
    B. people and nature could be degraded by forces of society.
    C. nature could not teach as much as other people.
    D. living in parks was the only way to achieve self-realization.

Questions 18–20 ask about both passages.

18. The authors of both passages would most likely agree that:

    F. nature may provide a refuge from the forces of industrialization.
    G. a life lived exclusively in nature is impossible and irresponsible.
    H. it is mankind's responsiblity to protect the American wilderness.
    J. everybody should spend a period of their life alone in nature.

19. The "critics" in Passage B (lines 82–86) would most likely agree with which viewpoint in Passage A?

    A. Recreationists; they both believe that nature and people can coexist.
    B. Recreationists; they both believe that parks are useless in the absence of humans.
    C. Conservationists; they both believe that human activities are harmful to nature.
    D. Conservationists; they both believe that Thoreau's visit to Walden Pond taught people to appreciate nature.

20. Compared to Passage A's discussion of nature and society, Passage B's discussion can best be described as:

    F. more focused on the perspective of one individual and those who oppose his views.
    G. less focused on nature and more on the needs of humans.
    H. disregarding the connection between nature and essential goodness.
    J. comparing modern views with beliefs from previous decades.

Passage III

HUMANITIES: This passage is adapted from *The Works of Sappho* by Maria Demo (©2009 by Maria Demo).

> O dream on your black wings you come when I
> am sleeping.
> Sweet is the god but still I am in agony and far
> from my strength.

5   So reads one of the tantalizing fragments left to posterity by the Greek poet Sappho, a woman from the Mediterranean island of Lesbos who, scholars believe, lived from approximately 630–570 BCE. The mystery of Sappho, in a sense, is contained in these small and frag-
10 mented facts. There are the remnants of poetry, a rough idea of a lifespan, and a legacy of genius that is now more than two thousand five hundred years old.

Who was Sappho? The best place to begin is with her work, which survives today in scattered and cryptic
15 fragments. Though widely known and anthologized in the ancient civilizations of Greece and Rome, the poet's work was mostly lost during the chaos of the barbarian invasions and the medieval period. The oldest extant manuscripts date from the 7th century CE, and an Oxford University
20 metastudy of her work, collating every reference from ancient authors, concludes that out of 10,000 lines of poetry written by Sappho, only 650 survive.

Despite this immeasurable loss, these remaining lines tell us much about the poet and her world. Sappho wrote
25 lyrics, meaning poetry meant to be accompanied by music and delivered in public. The passion of eros—the Greek concept of love between people—is a constant theme, though we do not know if this reflects her entire body of work. Certainly she was preoccupied by the power of hu-
30 man feeling, and how that power it can be likened to a divine force. Her one complete surviving poem, the "Ode to Aphrodite," powerfully conveys this sensibility:

> Iridescent-throned Aphrodite, deathless
> Child of Zeus, wile-weaver, I now implore you,
35 > Don't—I beg you, Lady—with pains and
> torments
> Crush down my spirit,
>
> Skimming down the paths of the sky's bright ether
> On they brought you over the earth's black bosom,
40 > Swiftly—then you stood with a sudden bril-
> liance,
> Goddess, before me.

The feeling of intense vulnerability and the longing for the divine presence are characteristic of Sappho's work,
45 which ancient scholars prized as among the most beauti-fully written Greek poetry in existence. Indeed, Sappho was numbered among the "Nine Lyric Poets" who were looked upon as the greatest artists of language in the an-cient world.

50   Sappho's complete body of work was widely known and influential. Allusions and direct quotations appear in many surviving texts, often ones that are unrelated to po-etry, suggesting that familiarity with Sappho was a basic component of the education of the Greek and Roman aris-
55 tocracies. This was in no small part due to the specific qualities of her work. Sappho's poetry was noted for its direct, clear use of language that was nevertheless capable of inspiring powerful, layered emotions in listeners. Her unaffected vocabulary, coupled with a strong sense of the
60 musical quality of language, remains one of the most strik-ing aspects of her work.

Beyond their artistic quality, the themes of Sappho's poetry also tell us something about the social world in which she was embedded. She was obviously a daughter
65 of privilege on the island of Lesbos (no commoner's poetry has survived), and her lyrics refer to fellow aristocrats and the lives they led at the height of Greek civilization. Her cultural milieu prized leisure and the art it made possible. Art itself was a way for women to display their worth dis-
70 tinct from the competitions of their male counterparts, who pursued distinction through athletic and military prowess. Sappho was immersed in the world of Greek myth, and her lyrics identify friends and companions among the various gods and heroes of the Mediterranean imagination.

75   Her lyrics also contain clues that correlate to various ancient accounts of her life, which blur the line between fact and legend. One account, for example, says that Sap-pho was sent into exile in Sicily for an unknown crime. Certain fragments referencing the loss of family and the
80 bitterness of separation are read as allusions to this sad fate. Another tradition claims that Sappho was a kind of priestess, charged with training young aristocratic ladies in the arts of choral singing, an essential aspect of Greek religious rituals. Various fragments reference the songs
85 sung during animal sacrifices and festivals of the gods, and scholars have studied these lines to determine just what role Sappho played in these rites.

But ultimately, there is no certain way to reconstruct Sappho's life. Ancient sources, already incomplete, dis-
90 agree on the fundamentals, and without the larger context of her complete work we will never uncover what is un-known about this extraordinary poet. Instead we must looks to the fragments, those chance snatches of lyric beauty that have defied the all-consuming voracity of time
95 and have come down to us as the miraculous echoes of an ancient genius.

21. The main purpose of the passage is to:

    A. explain the differences between poetry today and poetry in ancient Greece.
    B. appeal to donors interested in preserving the words of Sappho.
    C. introduce an ancient poet about whose life few details are known.
    D. criticize ancient societies for not saving important literary works.

22. According to the passage, one of the most striking qualities of Sappho's work is its:

    F. music-like use of language.
    G. detailed explanation of her life.
    H. audience of Greek and Roman elites.
    J. discussion of gods and goddesses.

23. In the context of the passage, the excerpt from "Ode to Aphrodite" (lines 33–42) mainly serves to:

    A. show Sappho's need to be the best poet of her time.
    B. provide an example of one of Sappho's many surviving poems.
    C. prove Sappho's desire to become one with the goddess Aphrodite.
    D. illustrate the power of feeling characteristic of Sappho's poetry.

24. The passage suggests that Sappho came from a privileged social class because:

    F. she was one of the nine best lyric poets of her time.
    G. details of her life are well-known.
    H. she pursued poetry and not athletics.
    J. her poetry survived to modern times.

25. The passage indicates that a major theme in Sappho's work is:

    A. the concept of love between people.
    B. the Earth and sky.
    C. her ideas about the future.
    D. festivals of animal sacrifice.

26. As it is used in line 58, *layered* most nearly means:

    F. candid.
    G. complex.
    H. straightforward.
    J. negative.

27. In the passage, all of the following are facts about Sappho EXCEPT:

    A. Only 650 lines of her poetry survive today.
    B. She was born on the island of Lesbos.
    C. She was sent to Sicily in exile.
    D. Her poetry refers to Greek aristocrats.

28. According to the passage, Sappho lived:

    F. in the 20th century.
    G. during an unknown era.
    H. in 630 CE.
    J. more than 2,500 years ago.

29. In the context of the passage, the purpose of the last paragraph is to:

    A. provide facts about Sappho's life as a poet.
    B. demonstrate the secrecy surrounding Sappho's accounts of her life.
    C. explain the need to discover ancient texts with information about Sappho.
    D. reiterate that little is known about Sappho, though readers can still learn from her work.

30. In the passage, Sappho is most nearly described as:

    F. a writer who destroyed her works prior to her death.
    G. an ancient Greek priestess.
    H. an artist who was more popular after her death than while she was alive.
    J. a lyric poet revered by ancient scholars.

Passage IV

NATURAL SCIENCE: This passage is adapted from *Lead and Crime* by Stephanie Feig (©2013 by Stephanie Feig). Lead is a common element that has been used by humans for thousands of years, despite the fact that prolonged exposure is dangerous.

Beginning in the 1960s, a remarkable trend appeared in the United States. Crime rates began a sharp and steady rise. The trend seemed to defy demographic and geographic barriers. In teeming, cosmopolitan New York
5 City, murders, armed robberies, and other violent crimes rose precipitously. But crime rates also exploded in small towns like Raleigh, NC and Flagstaff, AZ. These trends continued for thirty years, peaking in the early 1990s. Then, an equally startling reversal took place, and crime
10 rates began to plummet, and within ten years fell beneath their 1960s-era levels.

Researchers, politicians, and police officials have offered dozens of explanations for this phenomenon but have reached no consensus. The biggest stumbling block is the
15 uniformity of the trend. For example, New York police may credit their sophisticated CompStat system for better channeling resources in the fight against crime, resulting in a murder rate that fell from a high of 2650 in 1990, to 339 in 2015. But many cities without such elaborate police
20 technology, saw equally dramatic drops in crimes like murder over the same period. Regardless of the strategies employed, crime fell across the country at roughly the same rates.

So, what happened? One hypothesis gaining scien-
25 tists' attention suggests that the abrupt spike in crime, and its equally sudden decline, were connected to lead poisoning.

Researchers compare crime waves to epidemics, pointing out that crime waves spread in patterns similar to
30 diseases. If an epidemic spreads via transportation routes, it is caused by a microbe. If it radiates outward, like a fan, it's carried by insects. But if an epidemic is suddenly present everywhere at once, the cause is molecular. The crime spike of the 1960s–1990s followed the latter model
35 and suggests that a widespread factor like lead exposure may be involved.

It has long been known that childhood exposure to lead causes permanent and fundamental damage to the brain. Though lead exposure is always dangerous, chil-
40 dren store more of the element in their bodies following exposure, giving the element more time to create toxic effects. Neurological aspects of lead poisoning are relevant to the 20th century crime epidemic.

In children, lead carried into the bloodstream even-
45 tually reaches the blood-brain barrier, a selectively permeable layer surrounding the brain that regulates which blood-borne substances can get in and which cannot. Lead mimics and displaces enzymes responsible for growing synaptic connections in the cerebral cortex, the part of the
50 brain responsible for learning and impulse control. Usually these enzymes reach the brain and help stimulate the release of neurotransmitters, the chemicals that carry messages to the brain's billions of neurons, a process we experience as thinking and decision-making. When lead is
55 present, it enters the brain instead. The result is a drastic decrease in neurotransmitter production and, as a result, fewer and weaker neuronal connections in the cerebral cortex.

For over a century, researchers have been document-
60 ing the neurological consequences of lead exposure on maturing children. The most common effects are intellectual impairment, diminished impulse control, and a high propensity for risk-taking behavior. These traits correlate with the pathological features of many criminals.

65 Scientists working at Columbia University's Mailman School of Public Health, have found strong circumstantial evidence to back up the hypothesis that widespread lead exposure was related to rising crime rates. According to those scientists, the most important factor was the rise in
70 the use of leaded gasoline beginning in the 1940s. As Americans bought cars in ever-greater numbers, they consumed massive amounts of gasoline treated with lead in order to improve engine efficiency. Lead-laden car exhaust, coupled with the common use of lead paint in low-income
75 apartments and houses, drastically increased levels of lead exposure in children across the country. Children exposed to this in the 40s and 50s entered young adulthood in the 60s and 70s. Young adults are the age range that statistically produces the largest number of criminals.

80 Congress passed environmental legislation in the 1970s that phased out the use of leaded gasoline and required homes with lead paint to be stripped of the toxins. This process took years but led to a nearly 70% drop in ambient lead levels. Children born in the 70s and 80s were
85 thus at a much lower risk of heavy lead exposure, and that generational cohort reached adulthood just as crime rates began their rapid decline.

Studies in this area are only beginning, but the set of facts related to crime and lead exposure offer a compelling
90 explanation for a crime wave whose origins and outcome have so far defied every other proposed explanation.

31. The primary purpose of the passage is to:

   A. prove that lead poisoning caused people to commit crimes in the 1960s.
   B. explain how lead can enter a child's blood stream.
   C. support the U.S. Congress's push for environmental legislation.
   D. provide information about a possible cause of a societal phenomenon.

32. According to the passage, lead in the blood passes through the:

   F. enzymes.
   G. blood-brain barrier.
   H. hippocampus.
   J. skin.

33. As it is used in line 25, *spike* most nearly means:

   A. pierce.
   B. loss.
   C. drop.
   D. increase.

34. In the passage, crime rates in the 1960s rose:

   F. worldwide, affecting most of the planet.
   G. more in small towns, where lead exposure was the most drastic.
   H. in multiple geographic areas with a variety of population sizes.
   J. mostly in large, urban centers throughout the country.

35. According to the passage, New York police attribute the decline in murder rate to:

   A. a new technology.
   B. hiring more detectives.
   C. self-defense training.
   D. movement of criminals from the state.

36. The author most likely included the statistics in paragraph 9 (lines 80–87) in order to:

   F. illustrate a correlation between a decrease in lead levels and crime rates.
   G. prove that lead levels were the clear cause of the crime wave in the 1960s.
   H. praise the political system in the United States.
   J. link lead levels with brain damage in children.

37. All of the following are consequences of lead exposure in children EXCEPT:

   A. criminal behavior.
   B. lowered impulse control.
   C. intellectual impairment.
   D. tendency toward risk-taking.

38. In the passage, the increase in the use of leaded gasoline in the 1940s was due to:

   F. knowledge about its harmful effects on children.
   G. its positive effect on engine efficiency.
   H. its clean-burning properties.
   J. a trend away from use of lead paint.

39. The passage indicates that lead exposure is most dangerous to:

   A. criminals.
   B. children.
   C. police officers.
   D. adults.

40. In lines 28–33, crime waves are most likely compared to diseases in order to:

   F. explain how the crime wave in the 1960s was caused by diseases.
   G. illustrate that insects and microbes can also be exposed to lead.
   H. give examples to illustrate the ways crime waves spread.
   J. show methods to isolate lead exposure to certain geographical areas.

SCIENCE TEST
35 Minutes—40 Questions

DIRECTIONS: There are six passages in this test. Each passage is followed by several questions. After reading a passage, choose the best answer to each question and fill in the corresponding oval on your answer document. You may refer to the passages as often as necessary. You are NOT permitted to use a calculator on this test.

Passage I

A *pedigree chart* is a diagram that displays the phenotypes (appearance of traits) of a particular organism and its ancestors from one generation to the next. Pedigree charts are most commonly used for humans and show dogs.

Study

A group of geneticists mapped a pedigree chart (Figure 1) of a particular family of show dogs for the inheritance of a trait, Trait B. The expression of Trait B in a show dog is determined solely by Gene B. Gene B contains 1 dominant allele, *B*, and 1 recessive allele, *b*.

Each show dog in the pedigree was assigned a number for reference. The geneticists determined the Gene B genotype of all show dogs in the family, three of which are tabulated in Table 1.

Table 1	
Individual	Genotype
1	*bb*
7	*BB*
16	*Bb*

In order to accurately determine the genotype for all members of the family, the geneticists performed a procedure known as a *test cross*. A test cross is used to identify whether an organism expressing the dominant trait is either homozygous or heterozygous for a specific allele. This organism is crossed with another organism that is known to be homozygous recessive for the trait. If the two organisms have at least 1 offspring that expresses the recessive trait, then the original organism is heterozygous. If no offspring expresses the recessive trait, then the original organism is homozygous dominant.

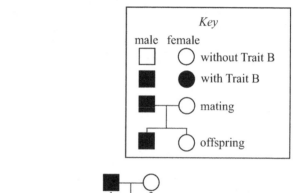

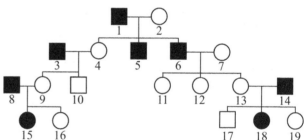

Figure 1

1. What is the relationship of Show Dog 17 to Show Dog 2?

   A. Grandson
   B. Great-Grandmother
   C. Great-Grandson
   D. Great-Granddaughter

2. Based on the pedigree chart, which of the following pairs of show dogs most likely share the most similar genetic code in their genome?

   F. Show Dog 4 and Show Dog 15
   G. Show Dog 5 and Show Dog 6
   H. Show Dog 8 and Show Dog 11
   J. Show Dog 15 and Show Dog 16

3. Suppose Show Dog 16 and a male show dog with genotype *bb* have 8 biological offspring. Based on the results of the study, on average, what percent of the offspring will express Trait B?

- **A.** 0%
- **B.** 25%
- **C.** 50%
- **D.** 100%

4. Which of the following statements *could* be true about the parents of Show Dog 1? For Gene B:

- **F.** the genotype of at least one of the parents was homozygous dominant.
- **G.** the genotype of one parent was homozygous dominant, and the genotype of the other parent was heterozygous.
- **H.** the genotype of one parent was heterozygous, and the genotype of the other parent was homozygous recessive.
- **J.** the genotype of both of the two parents were homozygous dominant.

5. Based on the results of the study, is it likely that Trait B for the given family of show dogs is a sex-linked trait?

- **A.** Yes, because the allele pairs determined in Table 1 for Trait B lie on sex chromosomes.
- **B.** Yes, because the allele pairs determined in Table 1 for Trait B lie on autosomal chromosomes.
- **C.** No, because the allele pairs determined in Table 1 for Trait B lie on sex chromosomes.
- **D.** No, because the allele pairs determined in Table 1 for Trait B lie on autosomal chromosomes.

6. Based on the description of a test cross and the pedigree chart, is the genotype for Show Dog 13 homozygous or heterozygous?

- **F.** Homozygous, because Show Dog 13 produced at least 1 offspring that was homozygous dominant.
- **G.** Homozygous, because Show Dog 13 produced at least 1 offspring that was homozygous recessive.
- **H.** Heterozygous, because Show Dog 13 produced at least 1 offspring that was homozygous dominant.
- **J.** Heterozygous, because Show Dog 13 produced at least 1 offspring that was homozygous recessive.

Passage II

Erosion is a naturally occurring process where the top layer of soil on a plot of land or bedrock wears away due to wind or water. Other factors can promote or limit the rate of erosion, such as the quantity of nearby vegetation or whether trampling of the area by animals has occurred. A team of graduate students conducted three experiments to determine the erosion rate, measured in kilograms per square meter (kg/m^2), of three different types of soil is affected by varying conditions. The three soils differed in their siltstone content. Soil 1 contained 0% siltstone, Soil 2 contained 30% siltstone, and Soil 3 contained 60% siltstone.

Experiment 1

Three 50 square meter plots of soil, with different compositions, were randomly dispersed on top of a greenhouse floor. All doors and windows of the greenhouse were closed. Overhead sprinklers were controlled to simulate rainfall. The floor of the greenhouse was tilted at various angles of elevations (°) and the erosion rate of soil was measured for each type of soil. The results of the experiment are shown in Table 1.

Table 1				
Soil plot	Erosion rate (kg/m^2) at angles of elevations of:			
	0°	10°	20°	30°
1	182	352	462	559
2	219	405	584	671
3	293	449	692	803

Experiment 2

The procedure from Experiment 1 was repeated except nearby vegetation cover was simulated using wire filter screens placed over the plot of soil instead of changing the angle of elevation of the greenhouse floor. The larger the area of the wire filter screens, the greater the percent of the soil area covered by vegetation. The results of the experiment are shown in Table 2.

Table 2				
Soil plot	Erosion rate (kg/m^2) at percent vegetation cover of:			
	0%	30%	60%	90%
1	182	154	132	110
2	219	186	155	132
3	293	265	241	215

Experiment 3

The procedure from Experiment 1 was repeated except animal trampling was simulated using a robotic arm which pressed against the soil that was suspended from the ceiling of the greenhouse, instead of changing the angle of elevation of the greenhouse floor. The robotic arm was controlled from a control room and moved parallel to the floor of the greenhouse. The resulting erosion rate was measured and the percent of the soil floor that was pressed by the robotic arm for the different trials is tabulated in Table 3.

Table 3			
Soil plot	Erosion rate (kg/m^2) of soil plot that was:		
	0% pressed	20% pressed	40% pressed
1	182	221	247
2	219	245	277
3	256	268	303

7. According to the results of Experiments 2 and 3, one can maximize erosion rate by:

   A. increasing vegetation cover and increasing the amount of soil pressed while using Soil Plot 1.
   B. decreasing vegetation cover and increasing the amount of soil pressed while using Soil Plot 1.
   C. increasing vegetation cover and increasing the amount of soil pressed while using Soil Plot 2.
   D. decreasing vegetation cover and increasing the amount of soil pressed while using Soil Plot 2.

8. Which of the following is the most likely reason why the graduate students closed all doors and windows of the greenhouse before conducting Experiment 1?

   F. Remove possible ambient noise from affecting the results of the experiment
   G. Prevent unwanted bacteria from entering the greenhouse
   H. Prevent outside wind from contributing to the soil erosion rate
   J. Shield light from affecting vegetation growth

9. Is the statement "The erosion rate was greatest when the plot of soil contained the highest percentage of silstone" supported by the information given and the results of the experiments?

   A. Yes; the erosion rate was greatest for Soil Plot 1, which contained the highest percentage of siltstone, compared to the two other soil types.
   B. No; the erosion rate was greatest for Soil Plot 1, which contained the highest percentage of siltstone, compared to the two other soil types.
   C. Yes; the erosion rate was greatest for Soil Plot 3, which contained the highest percentage of siltstone, compared to the two other soil types.
   D. No; the erosion rate was greatest for Soil Plot 3, which contained the highest percentage of siltstone, compared to the two other soil types.

10. Which of the following parameters had the same value throughout the trials of Experiment 1, but differed in value throughout the trials in Experiment 2?

    F. Erosion rate (kg/m^2)
    G. Greenhouse floor angle of elevation ($°$)
    H. Percent vegetation cover
    J. Percent of soil floor pressed

11. Suppose that in Experiment 1, soil erosion rate had been calculated in *grams* per square meter instead of kg/m^2. The soil erosion rate for Soil Plot 2 at an angle of elevation of $10°$ would have been:

    A.   0.405 g/m^2.
    B.   40.5 g/m^2.
    C.   4,050 g/m^2.
    D. 405,000 g/m^2.

12. Based on the results of Experiments 1-3, did angles of elevation of the greenhouse floor or percent vegetation have a greater effect on the erosion rate of the soil?

    F. Elevation of the greenhouse floor, because the change in erosion rate per degree was higher than the change of erosion rate per percent vegetation cover.
    G. Elevation of the greenhouse floor, because the change in erosion rate per degree was lower than the change of erosion rate per percent vegetation cover.
    H. Percent vegetation cover, because the change in erosion rate per percent vegetation cover was higher than the change in erosion rate per degree.
    J. Percent vegetation cover, because the change in erosion rate per percent vegetation cover was lower than the change in erosion rate per degree.

13. The graduate students looked to further investigate the effect of animal trampling on erosion rate. The students most likely repeated Experiment:

    A. 2, using no wire filter screens.
    B. 2, with additional trials of varying vegetation percentages.
    C. 3, with a trial that does not use the robotic arm.
    D. 3, with additional trials of varying pressed percentages.

Passage III

In the mid-20th century, astrophysicists demonstrated that predicted Keplerian dynamics did not apply to nearby galaxies. Newtonian gravity and Kepler's laws show that the speed of stars in galaxies should increase sharply as they move away from the center, then gradually drop off. Instead, it was measured that star velocity plateaued and continued to slightly increase at greater distances (see Figure 1).

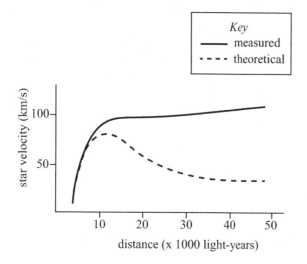

Four 21st century scientists present their theories as to what explains this phenomenon.

Scientist 1

Galactic rotational velocity curves maintain their speed due to undetectable hidden matter. This matter, nicknamed *dark matter*, is called *WIMPs* (Weakly Interactive Massive Particles). WIMPs do not interact, except through gravity. Thus, they are only measurable through gravitational attractions between centers of astral bodies. WIMPs lead to significantly more massive galaxies than the norm and exist in huge clustered spheres around galaxies.

Scientist 2

Scientist 1 is correct with only one exception. The dwarf galaxies around larger galaxies are arrayed in a disc, rather than clustered in spheres. The weak interactions of WIMPs create an initial spherical cluster, but dark matter forces flatten the cluster into a disc. This is due to *partially interactive dark matter* (PIDM). PIDM does not interact with other matter, consistent with the dark matter theory, but it does interact with itself and releases energy. This leads to interactions with different angular momenta, and thus different dark matter structures.

Scientist 3

Dark matter is a theoretical concept with little evidence to solve inconsistencies in the gravitational equations. *Modified Newtonian Dynamics* (MOND) is a theory, however, that explains these inconsistencies. If at great distances gravity is related to distance between bodies in an inverse relationship rather than an inverse square relationship, the observed curves then follow the laws of gravity. The required linearization is found in black-hole thermodynamics, which states that maximal entropy in a region scales with radius squared, not radius cubed, reducing the distance relationship power by 1.

Scientist 4

Scientist 3 is correct with only one exception. MOND, instead, occurs from the existence of gravity as a statistical phenomenon of the *holographic principle* (a three-dimensional system of information coded on a two-dimensional boundary). Our entire universe is a set of information encoded on two dimensions that describes three dimensions, leaving the three-dimensional description only accurate at macroscopic scales.

14. Scientists 1 and 2 agree that dark matter particles cluster due to:

    F. gravitational forces of attraction.
    G. their velocity relative to the central galaxy.
    H. merging with nearby celestial bodies.
    J. similar chemical compositions.

15. Based on Scientist 2's argument, are the reactions within partially interactive dark matter exothermic or endothermic?

    A. Exothermic; According to Scientist 2, partially interactive dark matter reactions release energy.
    B. Exothermic; According to Scientist 2, partially interactive dark matter reactions absorb energy.
    C. Endothermic; According to Scientist 2, partially interactive dark matter reactions release energy.
    D. Endothermic; According to Scientist 2, partially interactive dark matter reactions absorb energy.

16. According to the information provided, at approximately what distance does theoretical star velocity from Newtonian gravity and Kepler's laws begin to deviate from empirical data?

F.   8 light-years
G.   75 light-years
H.   8,000 light-years
J.   10,000 light-years

17. A certain theory of gravity states that at very low accelerations and great distances, the calculated gravity is linearly inverse to the distance of the star from the center of the galaxy. Which of the following scientist(s) would agree with this theory?

A.   Scientist 2 only
B.   Scientists 2 and 3
C.   Scientist 4 only
D.   Scientists 3 and 4

18. Black hole evaporation, or *Hawking radiation*, states that black holes release energy and mass over time due to quantum effects. How does Hawking radiation effect the viewpoints of Scientist 1 and Scientist 3, if at all?

F.   It strengthens Scientist 1's viewpoint only.
G.   It weakens Scientist 3's viewpoint only.
H.   It strengthens both Scientist 1 and Scientist 3's viewpoints.
J.   It has no effect on either scientist's viewpoint.

19. Suppose scientists discovered that dark matter causes the speed of stars to sharply decrease as they move away from the center of their galaxy. This discovery would *weaken* the viewpoints of which scientists?

A.   Scientists 1 and 2
B.   Scientists 1 and 3
C.   Scientists 1, 2, and 3
D.   Scientists 1, 2, 3, and 4

20. Consider the simplified form of *Newton's law of gravity* below between two specified masses:

$$F = k\frac{1}{r^2}$$

where F is the force between masses, k is a constant, and r is the distance between the centers of the masses. Based on Scientist 3's argument, the modified form at great distances for this law would be represented by which of the following?

F. $F = kr^2$

G. $F = kr$

H. $F = k\frac{1}{r}$

J. $F = k\frac{1}{r^3}$

Passage IV

The *Doppler effect* is a phenomenon in which frequency of audio is affected by the relative velocity of a source to the listener. For examples, if a source is approaching the listener, the waves will arrive closer together and the listener will hear a higher frequency. Similarly, when the source is moving away from the listener, the waves will arrive farther apart, resulting in the listener hearing a lower frequency.

A model of the Doppler effect, or *Doppler shift formula*, for a stationary observer is presented below:

$$f_o = \frac{v}{v \pm v_s} f_s$$

where f_o is the frequency heard by the observer, v is the speed of sound (approximately 340 meters per second), v_s is the speed of the source (negative if moving towards the observer and positive if moving away from the observer), and f_s is the frequency of sound emitted by the source.

Study 1

A group of high school students conducted a Doppler shift study. A small speaker emitting a constant frequency of 200 Hz was clamped to the middle of a horizontal moving platform. The platform was adjusted to a different velocity, v_s, for each trial, which is shown in Table 1.

Table 1	
Trial	v_s (m/s)
1	−30
2	−15
3	0
4	15
5	30

One student of the group stood stationary as the observer and recorded the frequency of sound, f_o, using a vibration accelerometer. The results of their study are shown in Figure 1.

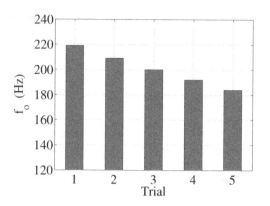

Figure 1

Study 2

The group of high school students repeated the procedure from Trial 1, except the frequency emitted by the speaker was varied for Trials 6-10. The results of the study are shown in Figure 2.

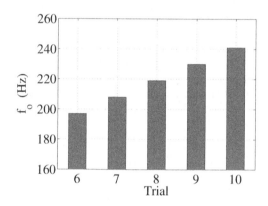

Figure 2

Study 3

The students performed an additional study to verify *Doppler blueshift* (an increase in frequency due to the movement of visible light towards an observer) and *Doppler redshift* (a decrease in frequency due to the movement of visible light away from an observer). The results of their experiment agreed with the known results of Doppler blueshift and Doppler redshift.

21. Based on the results of Study 1, as the velocity of the platform holding the speaker increased, the frequency observed by the students:

    A. increased only.
    B. decreased only.
    C. increased then decreased.
    D. varied, but with no general trend.

22. According to the information provided, which of the following best exemplifies the Doppler effect?

    F. A train sounds it horn while passing through a populated station.
    G. A dog barks at a car while chasing it.
    H. Two kids sing loudly while sprinting side by side.
    J. A guitarist jumps up and down while playing a repetitive note.

23. The high school students unknowingly used the same parameters for a particular trial in Study 2 that was previously recorded in Study 1. Based on the description of Study 2 and the results of Studies 1 and 2, which trial in Study 2 did the students unknowingly repeat?

    A. Trial 6
    B. Trial 8
    C. Trial 9
    D. Trial 10

24. Based on Studies 1 and 2, which of the following parameters had the same value throughout all trials in Study 1, but did not have the same value throughout all trials in Study 2?

    F. The speed of sound
    G. The speed of the speaker
    H. The speed of the stationary student observer
    J. The frequency of sound emitted by the speaker

25. Based on Study 1, which trial served as the standard of comparison?

    A. Trial 1
    B. Trial 2
    C. Trial 3
    D. Trial 5

26. Based on the results of Study 1 and the description of the Doppler shift formula, was the source in Trial 2 moving away or towards the stationary student acting as the observer?

    F. Away from the student, because the resulting frequency was greater than 200 Hz
    G. Away from the student, because the resulting frequency was less than 200 Hz.
    H. Towards the student, because the resulting frequency was greater than 200 Hz
    J. Towards the student, because the resulting frequency was less than 200 Hz

27. Consider the three *wavelengths* of visible light, in nanometers, shown below:

Color	Wavelength (nm)
Red	665
Green	550
Blue	470

Suppose a source emits monochromatic light at 550 nm. Based on the description of Study 3, if the light-emitting source traveled away from a stationary observer, the wavelength of light seen by the observer would be:

    A. greater than 665 nm.
    B. between 665 nm and 550 nm.
    C. between 550 nm and 470 nm.
    D. less than 470 nm.

Passage V

True harmonic distortion (THD) is the accuracy measurement of an *amplifier* (a device used to increase the volume of an audio input signal). When a microphone is sent through an amplifer, a lower THD value will result in a more natural and clean sound. There are various amplifer setups, one of which uses a *vacuum tube valve* (a lightbulb-like glass cylinder). Figure 1 shows an apparatus drawing and a circuit diagram for a vacuum tube valve.

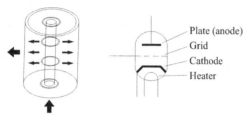

Plate (anode)
Grid
Cathode
Heater

Figure 1

In a vacuum tube valve, electrical current flows into the center cathode from a power supply and drifts across the vacuum to the outer layer, connecting to an output stage. The signal charges a grid, which modifies the flow of electrons from the power supply to imitate the initial signal.

Experiment 1

Two audio engineers ran a recording microphone through three different amplifier setups—a triode, pentode, and solid state transistor—to measure the percent THD of the amplification method. A sound source was recorded from a relative input level of 0 dB (decibels) to 36 dB, with measurements every 3 db. The amplifiers operated at 600 ohms (Ω) with a fixed gain of 40 dB. Figure 2 shows the distortion characteristics of each setup.

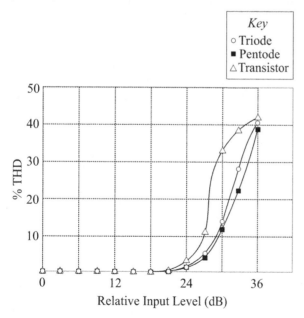

Figure 2

Experiment 2

The audio engineers further investigated the characteristics of each amplifier setup. Harmonic distortion manifests as an increase in second, third, and fourth harmonics. The procedure from Experiment 1 was repeated for the triode. The audio engineers measured the onset of each harmonic. The results of this experiment are shown in Figure 3.

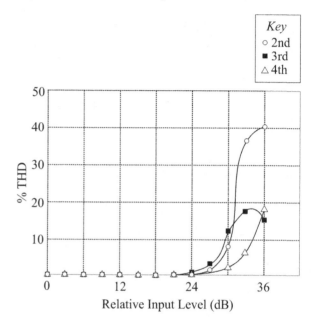

Figure 3

Experiment 3

The procedure from Experiment 2 was repeated using the pentode. The results of this experiment are shown in Figure 4.

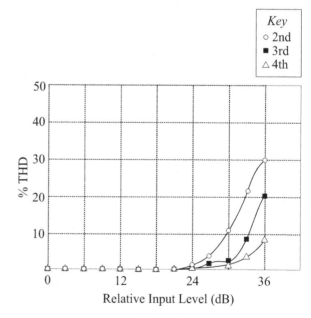

Figure 4

Experiment 4

The procedure from Experiment 2 was repeated using the solid state transistor. The results of this experiment are shown in Figure 5.

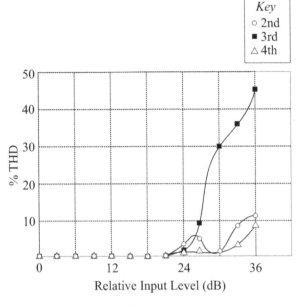

Figure 5

28. Suppose the audio engineers tested the fifth harmonic for the pentode tube preamplifier. Based on the results of the experiment, at a relative input level of 36 dB, the %THD recorded would be:

F. less than 10%.
G. between 10% and 15%.
H. between 15% and 20%.
J. greater than 20%.

29. A triode and pentode both utilize a vacuum tube valve, unlike a solid state transistor amplifier. Which of the following statements is most consistent with the results of Experiments 1-4?

A. At 36 dB, the pentode tested resulted in a higher % THD than the triode.
B. The triode, pentode, and solid state transistor all began showing % THD values above 0 at different relative input levels.
C. The triode tested resulted in the overall highest % THD when compared to the pentode or solid state transistor results.
D. Vacuum tube valves show high % THD levels at the 2nd harmonic, and the solid state transistor at the 3rd harmonic.

30. Vacuum tube valves contain a volume of empty space between the center cathode and the anode. According to the description of Figure 1, the vacuum was most likely designed to:

F. match the ambient temperature of the testing room.
G. increase the temperature of the space between the cathode and anode.
H. prevent the flow of electrons between the cathode and anode.
J. promote the flow of electrons between the cathode and anode.

31. A third audio engineer hypothesized that tube-based preamplifiers and solid state transistor-based amplifiers have noticeable differences in sound. Do the results of the experiments agree with this hypothesis?

A. Yes, because Experiment 1 shows clear differentiation between the triode and pentode data, versus the transistor data.
B. Yes, because Experiments 2-4 show clear differentiation between the triode and pentode data, versus the transistor data.
C. No, because Experiment 1 shows clear differentiation between the triode and pentode data, versus the transistor data.
D. No, because Experiments 2-4 show clear differentiation between the triode and pentode data, versus the transistor data.

32. According to Experiments 2-4, what is the most likely reason why the audio engineers did not record a significant THD percentage until the relative input level was greater than 22 dB?

F. The sound source did not produce recordable sound at input levels less than 22 dB.
G. Significant distortion is first experienced by amplifiers at input levels greater than 22 dB.
H. The 5th and 6th harmonics distort at input levels greater than 22 dB.
J. Electrical current does not run through vacuum tubes at input levels less than 22 dB.

33. *Odd harmonics* produce an edgy metallic tone, while *even harmonics* produce a full choral tone. The 2nd and 3rd harmonics have the greatest effect on the tone of the instrument. Which of the following best describes the difference between triodes and transistors? As relative input level increases:

A. triodes become full, while transitors become harsh.
B. triodes become harsh, while transitors become full.
C. both triodes and transistors become clear.
D. both triodes and transistors become full.

Passage VI

Polymerase Chain Reaction (PCR) is a technique used by molecular biologists to duplicate a single copy of DNA many times over. Each DNA strand consists of four nitrogenous bases: adenine (A) and thymine (T) are base pairs, as are guanine (G) and cyosine (C). *DNA Polymerase* is an enzyme responsible for helping to synthesize complimentary strands of DNA from the original strand. A thermostable DNA Polymerase typically used in PCR is *Taq Polymerase*, which can replicate a 1000 base pair strand of DNA in less than 10 seconds at 72°C. Figure 1 shows the effective reaction rate of PCR utilizing Taq Polymerase at varying temperatures.

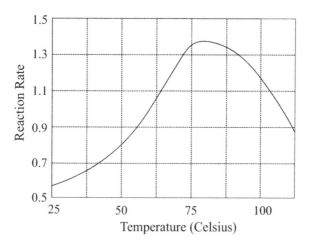

Figure 1

PCR is a four-step process shown below in Figure 2.

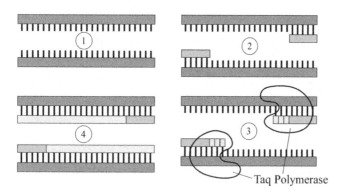

Figure 2

1. The temperature of the reaction chamber is raised to 98°C for 10 minutes, causing each DNA strand to *denature* into two single-stranded DNA molecules.

2. The temperature of the reaction chamber is lowered to 60°C for 30 seconds to allow for *annealing*, where strands of amino acids called *primers* stick to targeted DNA strands.

3. The temperature of the reaction chamber is raised to 72°C for 10 minutes to activate Taq Polymerase and start the *extension* phase, wherein Taq Polymerase duplicates the primed DNA strands.

4. Steps 1-3 are repeated 24 additional times, resulting in large scale DNA replication.

To determine if PCR was successful, agarose gel electrophoresis is performed to separate the PCR products based on size.

Experiment

A team of scientists conducted a standard agarose gel electrophoresis procedure on three PCR products derived from a father, mother, and child. Each PCR product was loaded onto 2% agarose gel. The agarose gel was made using 2 grams of agarose mixed in 100 mL of *TAE buffer* (Tris-acetate-EDTA). A bromophenol blue loading dye was added to assist visualization of the sample migrating through the gel. The gel was seen using ultraviolet light and a photo was taken. The photo is shown in Figure 3.

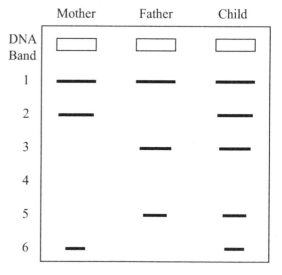

Figure 3

34. Which of the following best explains why raising the temperature of the reaction chamber is essential to begin the first step of the PCR process?

F. Taq Polymerase is an enzyme that denatures at $72°$ C, because that is the optimal efficiency point of the protein.

G. Taq Polymerase is an enzyme that denatures at $98°$ C, because that is the optimal efficiency point of the protein.

H. DNA strands denature at $72°$ C, resulting in accessible single-strands for duplication.

J. DNA strands denature at $98°$ C, resulting in accessible single-strands for duplication.

35. Consider the temperature at which liquid water boils given standard conditions. Based on Figure 1, at this temperature, which of the following is closest to the effective reaction rate of PCR utilizing Taq Polymerase?

A. 1.0
B. 1.1
C. 1.2
D. 1.3

36. With each full completion of the PCR process, Taq Polymerase helps to triple the existing set of DNA strands. Based on the description of the PCR process, which graph best describes the growth of DNA strands when undergoing multiple runs of the PCR process?

F.
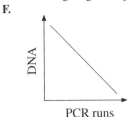

H.
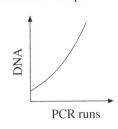

G.
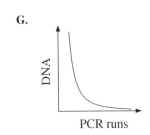

J.
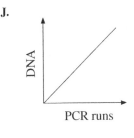

37. Suppose a new polymerase enzyme, Polymerase A, was discovered to perform optimally at $60°$ C. Based on Steps 2 and 3, is Polymerase A a good candidate to complete the current PCR process effectively?

A. Yes, because annealing and extension could occur simultaneously and speed up the process.

B. Yes, because extension would start prematurely and interrupt the annealing process.

C. No, because annealing and extension could occur simultaneously and speed up the process.

D. No, because extension would start prematurely and interrupt the annealing process.

38. Based on the description of the experiment, how would the team of scientists make a 15% agarose gel solution?

F. 2 grams of agarose mixed with 15 mL of TAE
G. 15 grams of agarose mixed with 85 mL of TAE
H. 15 grams of agarose mixed with 100 mL of TAE
J. 85 grams of agarose mixed with 100 mL of TAE

39. Taq Polymerase has a *half-life* (the amount of time elapsed for half of an original sample to decay) of approximately 25 minutes at $98°$ C as it approaches the temperature of full denaturation. If an intern scientist mistakenly sets Step 1 to 30 minutes, approximately what percent of the starting Taq Polymerase would remain to complete the PCR process?

A. 98%
B. 56%
C. 50%
D. 44%

40. Consider the following DNA sequence shown below:

A—G—T—G—T—A—C—C—C—C

Which of the following represents the complimentary DNA strand?

F. T—C—A—C—A—T—G—G—G—G
G. T—C—A—C—A—U—C—C—G—G
H. U—G—T—G—T—A—C—C—C—C
J. U—C—A—C—A—U—G—G—G—G

Communication and Relationships

Modern communication technology presents a paradox. On the one hand, email and cell phones and social media allow us to stay in constant contact with friends and family, even across great distances. On the other hand, this form of mediated communication distracts us from the reality of life all around us. Face-to-face relationships are the traditional norm for human beings, and indeed helped drive the evolution of human social intelligence. But we are less and less inclined to pursue relationships in real life, and instead spend our time socializing through technological means. How should we think about this transformation in human interaction? Have we gained more or lost more through this change?

Read and carefully consider these perspectives. Each suggests a particular way of thinking about communication and relationships.

Perspective 1	Perspective 2	Perspective 3
Social media and related technologies have revolutionized communications. This new means of interacting might seem jarring, but it is the beginning of a new and fuller means of being human.	Modern technology undermines the ancient modes of social interaction that were crucial to human evolution. Without face-to-face relationships we will lose a sense of what it means to be human.	The recent revolution in communication technology is too new, and too unprecedented, to be predictable. We cannot yet know if humans will live better or worse social lives through this technology.

Essay Task

Write a unified, coherent essay in which you evaluate multiple perspectives on communication and relationships. In your essay, be sure to:

- analyze and evaluate the perspectives given
- state and develop your own perspective on the issue
- explain the relationship between your perspective and those given

Your perspective may be in full agreement with any of the others, in partial agreement, or wholly different. Whatever the case, support your ideas with logical reasoning and detailed, persuasive examples.

ACT6 - A0118

Practice Test

ENGLISH TEST
45 Minutes—75 Questions

DIRECTIONS: In the five passages that follow, certain words and phrases are underlined and numbered. In the right-hand column, you will find alternatives for the underlined part. In most cases, you are to choose the one that best expresses the idea, makes the statement appropriate for standard written English, or is worded most consistently with the style and tone of the passage as a whole. If you think the original version is best, choose "NO CHANGE." In some cases, you will find in the right-hand column a question about the underlined part. You are to choose the best answer to the question.

You will also find questions about a section of the passage, or about the passage as a whole. These questions do not refer to an underlined portion of the passage, but rather are identified by a number or numbers in a box.

For each question, choose the alternative you consider best and fill in the corresponding oval on your answer document. Read each passage through once before you begin to answer the questions that accompany it. For many of the questions, you must read several sentences beyond the question to determine the answer. Be sure that you have read far enough ahead each time you choose an alternative.

PASSAGE I

Roots of Responsibility

Childhood lessons in responsibility can take many forms, made up of various activities. Some care for a pet, keep a paper route, or try to finish their homework on time. Unfortunately, my childhood had some very particular restraints on such activities. Allergies kept me from the loving licks of a dog or cat, my city didn't have a local newspaper, and I needed to learn responsibility. When I asked for a pet snake, knowing full well that my mother was terrified of the

species, my parents opting for a practical responsibility rooted in an ancient cultural tradition: a bonsai tree.

These masterful miniature trees come in various shapes, and sizes, but each and every one is contained in a pot.

1. **A.** NO CHANGE
   B. forms with various activities.
   C. forms of various activities.
   D. forms.

2. Which choice most clearly addresses an option mentioned previously in the passage?
   F. NO CHANGE
   G. I attended a school that didn't assign homework.
   H. many other activities bored me.
   J. my high school years were quickly approaching.

3. **A.** NO CHANGE
   B. opted
   C. who opted
   D. when opting

4. **F.** NO CHANGE
   G. shapes, and sizes but
   H. shapes and sizes but,
   J. shapes and sizes, but

In fact, the term "bonsai" can be traced back to a

Japanese translation of the Chinese "penzai," meaning

"planted in a container." [5] Each Bonsai tree is unique,

twisting and turning to resemble clouds of smoke in a
<u>   </u>
6

breeze. [A] <u>Their clean streamlined</u> curvatures seem almost
7
too perfect, alluding to the balance of man and nature. Unlike

many plants, bonsai trees are not used for human consumption,

but instead serve as an act of patient cultivation and shaping.

Its meditative growing process was first recorded in Japanese

art of the sixth-century, and <u>remains</u> a popular practice even
8
today. [B]

So how did a tree teach me responsibility? Bonsai trees

don't grow into those <u>snakelike, serpentine</u> shapes on their
9
own. Every day before school, I tended to my bonsai tree.

<u>However,</u> I carefully wrapped wire around its supple
10
branches, pushing its growth to mimic a winding river.

Then, <u>tending to its needs and helping it grow,</u> I spent hours
11
creating the exact look I desired, down to the individual

leaf. [C]

5. The writer is considering deleting the preceding sentence. Should the sentence be kept or deleted?
   A. Kept, because it adds a fact pertaining to the previous sentence.
   B. Kept, because it offers a plausible motivation for the narrator's hobby.
   C. Deleted, because the narrator is unconcerned with the heritage of bonsai trees.
   D. Deleted, because it detracts from the narrator's childhood narrative.

6. F. NO CHANGE
   G. twisting and turning, they
   H. it twists and turns to
   J. they twist and turn to

7. A. NO CHANGE
   B. There clean streamlined
   C. Their clean, streamlined
   D. There clean, streamlined

8. F. NO CHANGE
   G. they remain
   H. it remained
   J. it remains

9. A. NO CHANGE
   B. serpentine, coiled
   C. twisting serpentine
   D. serpentine

10. F. NO CHANGE
    G. Haphazardly,
    H. Conversely,
    J. OMIT the underlined portion

11. Given that all of the choices are accurate, which one provides the most precise description of the narrator's bonsai responsibilities?
    A. NO CHANGE
    B. continuously trimming and pruning and potting and repotting,
    C. creating the perfect tree conditions,
    D. fulfilling each responsibility listed in the guide book,

Throughout my childhood, my bonsai tree sat in my

room amongst my toys and drawings. [D] Twenty years later,
12

that same tree sits in the living room of my own home.

Although maintaining the tree, requires an immense
13

amount of care, I will happily maintain the responsibility of
13

this plant that will live with me long into my old age.

12. Which of the following alternatives to the underlined portion would NOT be acceptable?

   F.   with
   G. surrounded by
   H. among
   J.   compiled with

13. A. NO CHANGE
   B. tree requires an immense amount, of care
   C. tree requires an immense amount of care,
   D. tree requires an immense about of care

> Questions 14 and 15 ask about the preceding passage as a whole.

14. Upon reviewing the essay and finding that some information has been left out, the writer composes the following sentence incorporating that information:

> Every tree variety requires a different watering schedule, so I had to be careful to stick to my bonsai calendar.

If the writer were to add this sentence to the essay, it would most logically be placed at:

   F. Point A in Paragraph 2.
   G. Point B in Paragraph 2.
   H. Point C in Paragraph 3.
   J. Point D in Paragraph 4.

15. Suppose the writer's primary purpose had been to describe the historical evolution of bonsai tree care. Would this essay accomplish that purpose?

   A. Yes, because it sets up contrasting bonsai tree practices with specific examples of each.
   B. Yes, because it creates a clear timeline of said evolution.
   C. No, because it does not attribute bonsai tree care to specific historical figures.
   D. No, because it focuses primarily on the narrator's personal relationship with bonsai trees.

PASSAGE II

Queen Bessie: Aviation Royalty

Beyond Amelia Earhart, the women of aviation largely remain nameless. Within this class, consequently, exist numerous trailblazers. One such trailblazer—the first ever African-American and Native American woman to hold a pilots license—was named Bessie Coleman.

[1] Born in 1892, the childhood of Bessie Coleman was spent in Texas with her parents and twelve siblings. [2] Tenacious, Bessie continued her education in Oklahoma for one year of university upon graduating high school. [3] With such a large household, every family member expected to help as best as they could. [4] When finances forced her to drop out, Bessie packed to join her brother in Chicago. [5] In Bessie's case, that meant walking four miles daily to her one-room school house while maintaining a work schedule during the cotton harvest season. 21

It was in the Windy City where Coleman, then working as a manicurist, found her interest piqued upon hearing tales of World War I aviation missions. She buckled down, devouring every book and article she could find on the subject. With unwavering spirit, Coleman could not be stopped.

---

16. **F.** NO CHANGE
G. consequently, exists
H. however, exist
J. however, exists

17. **A.** NO CHANGE
B. pilot's license–was
C. pilot's license, was
D. pilots license, was

18. **F.** NO CHANGE
G. Bessie Coleman spent her childhood
H. Bessie Coleman's early years were spent
J. the early years of Bessie Coleman were spent

19. **A.** NO CHANGE
B. Callous,
C. Fanciful,
D. Irresolute,

20. **F.** NO CHANGE
G. was expecting
H. was expected
J. expecting

21. Which of the the following sequences of sentences makes this paragraph most logical?

A. NO CHANGE
B. 1, 3, 5, 2, 4
C. 5, 4, 1, 3, 2
D. 1, 5, 2, 3, 4

22. **F.** NO CHANGE
G. Coleman then working as a manicurist,
H. Coleman, then working as a manicurist
J. Coleman then working as a manicurist

23. Given that all of the choices are true, which one most effectively concludes this paragraph and provides a transition to the following paragraph?

A. NO CHANGE
B. With unwavering spirit, Coleman let her intentions be known: she was to become a pilot.
C. Coleman read every single publication on the subject she could find.
D. Coleman would have to leave her job as a manicurist.

However, doing so had an intense level of difficulty. At
the time, aviation schools across the United States denied

access to people of African-American descent and to women.

Being both, Coleman had no chance of entry. Rather than quit,

she taught herself French while saving every penny she earned.

Not long after, Coleman attended flight school in France.

Bessie Coleman officially became the first

civilian-licensed, African-American pilot in the world.

Commercial flights yet weren't a staple of American society,
so she—like

most aviators of her time—made a living as a stunt flier. 26

She toured the nation, performing death-defying feats in her

plane for large crowds. Her figure eights, loops, and daring

drops earned her the nickname "Queen Bess." Throughout her

career, Coleman championed civil rights by refusing to

perform for segregated audiences, and passing on stereotyped

film roles. Her fanbase reached far and wide, crossing barriers

of both race and gender. 27

Unfortunately, Coleman's life was cut short due

to a plane malfunction during an everyday flight with

a normal mission. Bessie Coleman was only thirty-four

24. F. NO CHANGE
  G. was truly the opposite of very easy.
  H. proved quite difficult.
  J. happened in a desperately difficult manner.

25. A. NO CHANGE
  B. weren't yet a staple to
  C. were not yet a staple of
  D. were not yet a staple to

26. If the writer were to delete the word "yet" from the preceding sentence, the sentence would primarily lose a word that:

  F. helps describe Coleman's motivation for becoming a pilot.
  G. emphasizes the fleeting nature of this technological advancement.
  H. implies commercial flights did eventually become normalized in America.
  J. an unnecessary word that has no use within the sentence.

27. At this point, the writer is considering adding the following true statement:

  > Willa Brown, the first African-American woman to earn her pilot's license in the United States, even cited Bessie Coleman as a source of inspiration!

  Should the writer make this addition here?

  A. Yes, because it adds an important detail that supports a previous claim.
  B. Yes, because it reveals the extent of Coleman's influence.
  C. No, because it shifts the essay's focus from Coleman to her influencers.
  D. No, because it distracts from the essay's main focus.

28. F. NO CHANGE
  G. an ordinary, typical flight.
  H. an ordinary flight, customary of her normal skillset.
  J. a routine flight.

GO ON TO THE NEXT PAGE.

years old at the time of her death, not affording her the time to

<u>understand</u> her dream of opening an aviation school for all
29
genders and races. Even so, Queen Bessie's legacy lives on.

<u>A member of</u> the National Aviation Hall of Fame, Bessie
30
Coleman remains a righteous role model: unwilling to accept

limitations, gravitational or societal.

29. **A.** NO CHANGE
    B. find
    C. compose
    D. realize

30. Which choice best emphasizes the continuous nature of Coleman's legacy?

    F. NO CHANGE
    G. Inducted into
    H. Portrayed in
    J. Immortalized in

PASSAGE III

The Renaissance of Paint Itself

Leonardo da Vinci's Mona Lisa, perhaps the world's

most famous <u>painting is an</u> exemplar of the European
31
Renaissance. Facing her audience with an enigmatic smile, the

subject of this work reflects the advent of humanism during

this period that reigned supreme. Following the extreme

religious piety of the medieval period, the Renaissance

celebrated the human form, just as this painting does. While

changes in artistic style and subject matter are highlighted in

descriptions of the Renaissance, often overlooked <u>are</u> the
32
changes in the actual paint that fostered these innovations.

<u>Paint is a super important aspect of the art world.</u>
33

31. **A.** NO CHANGE
    B. painting, an
    C. painting, is an
    D. painting. An

32. **F.** NO CHANGE
    G. is
    H. was
    J. have been

33. **A.** NO CHANGE
    B. The Renaissance was a time of many changes.
    C. The actual paint used to create a work of art is important!
    D. DELETE the underlined portion.

[1] Conversely, this paint consisted of an egg yolk

"binder," or basic mixing agent, that was combined with

pigments and various liquids, <u>then</u> painted directly onto a
34

34. **F.** NO CHANGE
    G. undeniably
    H. for example
    J. however

wooden panel. [2] Tempera paint <u>requiring</u> artists to work
<u>35</u>
quickly before its binder had completely dried, creating a

myriad of artistic limitations. [3] At the dawn of the

Renaissance, tempera paint reigned supreme. [4] The act of

painting with this medium was similar to today's drawing —

<u>a precise, flat, and linear endeavor during which</u> colors could
<u>36</u>

not be mixed or blended together. [5] <u>On the other hand,</u>
<u>37</u>
combining colors took the form of cross-hatching, which

describes drawing thin lines of paint to create the illusion of a

mixed palette. [6] Tempera paintings exhibited high skill

levels but did not perfectly align with the Renaissance's focus

on humanism. |38|

    Not until the sixteenth century, nearly two centuries into

the Renaissance, did oil paint begin to <u>integrate</u>
<u>39</u>

European artists. |40| Oil paint, which replaced

<u>temperas</u> egg-yolk binder with oil, is said to have originated in
<u>41</u>
the Middle East between the fifth and ninth centuries, only

making its way westward during the Middle Ages.

35. A. NO CHANGE
    B. required
    C. that required
    D. has required

36. Which choice most specifically illustrates the physical nature of the comparison within this sentence?
    F. NO CHANGE
    G. unlike paintings because the
    H. vast similarities including that the
    J. various artistic similarities to the medium of drawing included that the

37. A. NO CHANGE
    B. Furthermore,
    C. Instead,
    D. To define,

38. For the sake of logic and cohesion, Sentence 3 should be placed:
    F. where it is now.
    G. before Sentence 1.
    H. after sentence 4.
    J. after sentence 5.

39. A. NO CHANGE
    B. impel
    C. bewitch
    D. derive

40. At this point, the writer is considering adding the following true statements:

    Paint consists of three main components: pigment, solvent, and binder.

Should the writer make this addition here?
    F. Yes, because it provides details about the significance of using oil.
    G. Yes, because it contains information necessary to understanding what follows.
    H. No, because it contradicts the time's need for an innovative medium.
    J. No, because it detracts from the main topic of the paragraph.

41. A. NO CHANGE
    B. tempera's
    C. temperas and its
    D. tempera's and its

Oil paint was not confined by the same limitations as tempera: its liquid quality allowed for longer brush strokes.
42

Pigments could be mixed directly on canvases, and painters
43
could even remove layers of paint before the oil had dried. Together, these qualities made oil paint capable of depicting abstract atmospheres in ways that were unimaginable before its popularization.

    Now, returning to da Vinci's masterful portrait, the Mona Lisa seems not only a product of artistic innovation but also of technical innovation. In fact, da Vinci, himself,
44
pioneered a technique, "sfumato," that would have otherwise been impossible without oil paint. Dark background colors
45
melt together to form a smoky haze, drawing audiences
45
into a mysterious yet familiar state.
45
    So yes, encourage museum patrons to celebrate the Renaissance—lest they forget the artistic advancement that a bit of oil can foster.

42. F. NO CHANGE
    G. one's
    H. their
    J. some of which had

43. A. NO CHANGE
    B. Pigments, which could
    C. Pigments that could
    D. Pigments are to

44. F. NO CHANGE
    G. In fact, da Vinci himself
    H. In fact, da Vinci, himself,
    J. In fact, da Vinci himself,

45. The writer is considering deleting the underlined sentence. Should the sentence be kept or deleted?

    A. Kept, because it gives an example supporting a claim.
    B. Kept, because it helps to define a previously mentioned term.
    C. Deleted, because it detracts from the main focus of the passage.
    D. Deleted, because it does not properly contextualize the information.

PASSAGE IV

Dung Beetle Navigation Study

    As the pungent smell of fresh animal feces have permeated the South African air,
46

and a race begins. Dung beetles flock to the site of the odor
47
and roll a single piece of dung into a ball weighing up to fifty times their own weight. Work too slowly and a cunning beetle might steal their newly formed treasure.

46. F. NO CHANGE
    G. having permeated
    H. permeate
    J. permeates

47. A. NO CHANGE
    B. beginning a race.
    C. a race begins.
    D. which a race begins.

Each dung beetle makes a speedy exit by pushing their dung

ball in a straight line away from its original site. During the
           48

day, dung beetles use polarized light surrounding the sun to

guide this straight-line path. For nocturnal dung beetles,

though, navigation is quite a different matter.

At University of Lund in Sweden, biologist Eric
                                      49
Warrant was determined to solve the mystery of nocturnal
49

dung beetle navigation. The initial phase of his work came in

the form of luring wild beetles with buckets of dung, then

observing their behaviors. Warrant and his team noted that the

beetles still traveled in a straight line when the moon wasn't

within the vicinity. That meant moon beams weren't the
          50

only beetles guiding light. Perhaps stars were the cause?
     51

Warrant tested this new theory, he placed beetles on enclosed
                         52

tables with varying conditions; beetles that could see the
                      53
Milky Way kept their travels in a straight line while all others

roamed aimlessly. These findings were corroborated with one

final test: a dung beetle field trip to the planetarium. The

beetles could orient itself even in a superficial environment,
                     54

as long as they saw the replicated Milky Way ⎣55⎦ .

[4]

These findings marked dung beetles as the first known

species to use the Milky Way for navigational purposes.

48. **F.** NO CHANGE
G. ball, in a straight line away
H. ball, in a straight line, away
J. ball in a straight line away,

49. **A.** NO CHANGE
B. Sweden, biologist, Eric Warrant
C. Sweden, biologist, Eric Warrant,
D. Sweden, biologist Eric Warrant,

50. **F.** NO CHANGE
G. visible.
H. present after the sun had gone down.
J. apparent in the nighttime sky.

51. **A.** NO CHANGE
B. only beetle's
C. beetles'
D. beetles

52. **F.** NO CHANGE
G. theory he placed
H. theory by placing
J. theory. By placing

53. Which of the following alternatives to the underlined portion is LEAST acceptable?

A. conditions. Beetles
B. condition: beetles
C. conditions, beetles
D. condition: Beetles

54. **F.** NO CHANGE
G. oneself
H. themselves
J. them

55. At this point, the writer is considering adding the following information:

even though it was an imitation.

Given that the information is accurate, should the writer make this addition here?

A. Yes, because it clarifies the false nature of the Milky Way in the experiment.
B. Yes, because it specifies the limitation of this experiment.
C. No, because it fails to relate the information to the experiment's findings.
D. No, because it contains redundant information.

GO ON TO THE NEXT PAGE.

The gradient light patterns created by the Milky Way <u>allows</u>
₅₆ dung beetles to travel straight-line paths at any angle from this luminous galaxy. Saving their precious dung balls from the clutches of other <u>insects is an</u> imperative process to the dung
₅₇ beetle, as this ball will later become food for its offspring.

Of course, as is the case with many scientific <u>discoveries. This</u> new knowledge opens up yet another
₅₈ set of questions. How might artificial lights like city street lamps affect this process? Do other species have similar navigational tools? ☐₅₉

56. F. NO CHANGE
G. allow
H. has allowed
J. will allow

57. A. NO CHANGE
B. insects, an
C. insects, being an
D. insects—an

58. F. NO CHANGE
G. discoveries—this
H. discoveries this
J. discoveries, this

59. At this point, the writer is considering adding the following information:

> Regardless of which unanswered question leads to the next dung beetle discovery, we now know that humans aren't the only ones looking at the stars.

Given that the information is accurate, should the writer make this addition here?

A. Yes, because it succinctly concludes the paragraph.
B. Yes, because it makes clear an otherwise mysterious aspect of the passage.
C. No, because it adds superfluous information.
D. No, because it does not conclude the passage better than the previous sentence.

Questions 60 asks about the preceding passage as a whole.

---

60. Suppose the writer's primary purpose had been to describe the process used to solve a specific scientific mystery. Would this essay accomplish that purpose?

F. Yes, because it validates the experiment with expert opinions.
G. Yes, because it provides an overview of the experiment as well as its results.
H. No, because it does not describe the experiment's findings.
J. No, because the writer interjects too many personal opinions.

PASSAGE V

Realistic Visions within Romantic Comedies

During America's Great Depression, the untimely trip of
61
the stock market worked to completely overhaul national

social structures. [A] With such substantial changes occurring

in such a condensed period of time, social anxieties became
62
a nearly inevitable byproduct of this process and left many
62
without the proper tools to fully understand the ever changing

world. Oddly enough, romantic comedy films attempted to

help bridge that gap.

[63] During the Great Depression, social unease

stemmed largely from mass unemployment and economic

troubles that plagued the nation. Distinctions between "rich"
64
and "poor" were difficult to escape in everyday life, spurring

new artistic vices that distracted from these hardships.

Romantic comedies engaged with the social issues of the

day by undermining the economic hardships with tales of

quick social mobility adventures that bridged the gap between
65
rich and poor. Films often maintained a sense of

pride having also respect in depicting the less
66
fortunate to avoid offending moviegoers.

61. **A.** NO CHANGE
    B. sudden crash
    C. catastrophic outburst
    D. faulty drop

62. **F.** NO CHANGE
    G. became, a nearly inevitable byproduct,
    H. became, a nearly inevitable, byproduct
    J. became a nearly, inevitable byproduct

63. At this point, the writer is considering adding the following true statement:

    The Great Depression occurred during the "screwball" age of the film genre.

    Should the writer make this addition here?

    A. Yes, because it contains necessary details for understanding the passage.
    B. Yes, because it contextualizes the sentence that follows.
    C. No, because it is tonally different from the rest of the passage.
    D. No, because it distracts from the main topic of the paragraph.

64. Which of the following alternatives to the underlined portion is LEAST acceptable?

    F. troubles, they plagued the nation.
    G. troubles plaguing the nation.
    H. troubles, both of which plagued the nation.
    J. troubles.

65. Which choice is clearest and suggests the cunning, devious nature of the acts?

    A. NO CHANGE
    B. convoys
    C. cohorts
    D. schemes

66. **F.** NO CHANGE
    G. and was intending
    H. so they maintained a sense of
    J. and

[B] The films follow those struggling men falling for rich heiresses who might help advance its social status in the blink
67
of an eye.

However, narratives like those not only created small
68

moments of nonmembership from America's economic
69

hardships, but also left audience members believing that
70
they too might one day suddenly be thrust into the lap of luxury. [C]

[1] Articles like "Poor Prospector Finds 726-Carat Diamond" followed the same narrative of downtrodden individuals instantly finding financial success. [2] In doing so, newspapers strayed from the real issues of social discomfort caused by large-scale poverty. [3] Instead, they hinted

alternatively with the promise of quickly returning the nation
71

to what this nation had been. [4] In fact, other mediums,
72
including newspapers, used similar narratives of social

mobility. 73

67. **A.** NO CHANGE
B. one's
C. their
D. his

68. **F.** NO CHANGE
G. To provide an example, narratives
H. Secondly, narratives
J. Narratives

69. **A.** NO CHANGE
B. purposeful avoidance
C. escapism
D. quickly running away

70. **F.** NO CHANGE
G. leaving
H. having left
J. leaves

71. **A.** NO CHANGE
B. for
C. within
D. at

72. **F.** NO CHANGE
G. the poverty-stricken nation
H. this downtrodden nation
J. it

73. For the sake of logic and cohesion, Sentence 4 should be placed:

A. where it is now.
B. before Sentence 1.
C. before Sentence 2.
D. before sentence 3.

Analyzing the film and media outlets of any time period can bring to light the anxieties of a given moment in history. Catastrophic events, like those in the Great Depression, do not happen only within the realm of the real. As was the case with romantic comedy films during the Great Depression, the thoughts and fears of a <u>nations people</u> bleed into its artistic tapestry. [D]

74

74. **F.** NO CHANGE
     G. nation's people
     H. nations people's
     J. nation's people's

Question 75 asks about the preceding passage as a whole.

---

75. Upon reviewing the essay and finding that some information has been left out, the writer composes the following true sentence:

> Films like *Bringing Up Baby, It Happened One Night,* and *Holiday*, for example, all followed hardworking men down on their luck.

If the writer were to add this sentence to the essay, it would most logically be placed at:

A. Point A in Paragraph 1.
B. Point B in Paragraph 3.
C. Point C in Paragraph 4.
D. Point D in Paragraph 6.

END OF TEST 1.
STOP! DO NOT TURN THE PAGE UNTIL TOLD TO DO SO.

THERE ARE NO TESTING MATERIALS ON THIS PAGE.

MATHEMATICS TEST
60 Minutes — 60 Questions

DIRECTIONS: Solve each problem, choose the correct answer, and then fill in the corresponding oval on your answer document.

Do not linger over problems that take too much time. Solve as many as you can; then return to the others in the time you have left for this test.

You are permitted to use a calculator on this test. You may use your calculator for any problems you choose,

but some of the problems may be best done without using a calculator.

Note: Unless otherwise stated, all of the following should be assumed:
1. Figures are NOT necessarily drawn to scale.
2. Geometric figures lie in a plane.
3. The word *line* indicates a straight line.
4. The word *average* indicates arithmetic mean.

---

1. What is the average depth, in feet, of a swimming pool that contains 3,000 cubic feet of water and has a rectangular surface with an area of 600 square feet?

   A. 1,800,000 ft
   B. 2,400 ft
   C. 122.5 ft
   D. 5 ft
   E. 0.2 ft

2. Joelle has scored a 73, 89, 77, 83, and 78 on five 100 point tests this semester. In order to make the honor roll, Joelle must have a test average of 85. If all tests are equally weighted, what score must Joelle get on her sixth and final test (also out of 100 points) in order to make the honor roll this semester?

   F. 80
   G. 81
   H. 85
   J. 100
   K. Joelle cannot score high enough

3. The volume of a rectangular pyramid is one-third the volume of a rectangular prism with the same length (l), width (w), and height (h). If a certain rectangular prism has dimensions $l = 6$, $w = 4$, and $h = 11$, what is the volume of a rectangular pyramid with the same dimensions?

   A. $9\frac{7}{9}$
   B. 24
   C. 88
   D. 264
   E. 792

4. The expression $(4z - 3)(2z + 5)$ is equivalent to:

    F. $8z^2 - 2$
    G. $8z^2 - 15$
    H. $8z^2 + 5z + 15$
    J. $8z^2 + 14z - 15$
    K. $8z^2 + 26z - 15$

5. Gerrit's school cafeteria offers 6 types of beverage, 5 types of sandwich, 3 types of fruit, and 2 types of cookie. Gerrit's lunch always consists of 1 beverage, 1 sandwich, 1 piece of fruit, and 1 cookie. If Gerrit wants to have a different lunch combination each school day, how many school days will pass before Gerrit has to repeat a lunch combination?

    A. 5
    B. 6
    C. 16
    D. 36
    E. 180

6. On a school trip, Mr. Casson brought 1 movie from each of his five favorite genres to show on the bus. Each of his 28 students wrote down their preferred genre on a piece of paper. These preferences are shown in the table below:

Genre	# of Students
Action	7
Comedy	8
Drama	5
Sci-Fi	2
Animated	6

    Mr. Casson will draw one piece at random that will determine what movie they watch. Assuming a fair and random selection, what is the probability that Mr. Casson will select a comedy?

    F. $\dfrac{1}{14}$

    G. $\dfrac{5}{28}$

    H. $\dfrac{3}{14}$

    J. $\dfrac{1}{4}$

    K. $\dfrac{2}{7}$

7. What is the value of $|-12| - |7 - 23|$?
   A. -28
   B. -4
   C. 4
   D. 28
   E. 42

8. Erik's moped gets 75 miles per gallon of gas. Keara's sedan gets 28 miles per gallon. They are both driving from Charlotte to the Grand Canyon, which is approximately 2,100 miles. If gas costs an average of $3 per gallon, how much *more* money will Keara have to pay for gas than Erik on a one-way trip?
   F. $28
   G. $75
   H. $84
   J. $141
   K. $225

9. When Erin flew to visit her grandmother, her grandmother gave her a $1/2$ gallon jug of homemade apple cider. However, travel restrictions require a maximum of 3.4 ounces of liquids in any one container on a flight. How many 3.4 ounce containers would Erin need in order to legally transport the full half gallon of apple cider on her flight home?

   (Note: 1 gallon = 128 fluid ounces)

   A. 18
   B. 19
   C. 37
   D. 38
   E. 74

10. Which of the following equations is equivalent to $8x - 2y - 14 = 0$?
    F. $y = -4x + 7$
    G. $y = \ \ \ 4x - 7$
    H. $y = -4x - 7$
    J. $y = \ \ \ 4x + 14$
    K. $y = -4x - 14$

11. What is the smallest integer greater than $\sqrt{14}$?
    A. 3
    B. 3.8
    C. 4
    D. 7
    E. 15

Use the following information to answer questions
12-14

Two car rental companies, Carl's Cars and Ray's Rides, offer discounted car rentals for customers whose cars are getting fixed at Aldo's Auto Repair. For each company, there is a linear relationship between the price of a rental and the number of days that the car will be rented for. The table below lists the price of a rental for select days for each company.

Days	Carl's Cars	Ray's Rides
5	$150	$200
10	$200	$230
15	$250	$260
20	$300	$290
25	$350	$320

12. At Carl's Cars, what is the average cost per day of a 25 day rental?

   F. $30
   G. $20
   H. $16.67
   J. $15
   K. $14

13. Which of the following equations gives the relationship between the price (p) and number of days (d) of a rental at Ray's Rides?

   A. $p = 40d$
   B. $p = 10d + 100$
   C. $p = 6d + 170$
   D. $p = 30d + 200$
   E. $p = 5d + 50$

14. Aldo recommends Carl's Cars to his short term repair customers and Ray's Rides to his long term repair customers based upon his estimate of the number of days a repair will take. How many days must the repair estimate be before Aldo recommends Ray's Rides over Carl's Cars?

   F. 16
   G. 17
   H. 18
   J. 19
   K. 20

15. If $\cos^2(\theta) = \dfrac{7}{17}$, what is $\sin^2(\theta)$?

   A. $\dfrac{7}{10}$

   B. $\dfrac{10}{7}$

   C. $\dfrac{10}{17}$

   D. $\dfrac{17}{10}$

   E. $\dfrac{17}{7}$

16. If 60% of a given number is 15, what is 15% of the given number?

   F.   2.25
   G.   3.75
   H.   9
   J.   100
   K.   166 2/3

17. Erica, Kaitlyn, Hayley, and Suzanne are sharing a 2,400 ft^2 fitness studio, where rent is $5,760 per month. They decide to split the rent proportionally based upon the amount of square footage that each of them needs for their classes. Suzanne uses 500 ft^2, Kaitlyn uses 800 ft^2, Hayley uses 400 ft^2, and Erica uses the rest. How much of the rent does Erica need to pay each month?

   A. $ 700
   B. $ 960
   C. $1,200
   D. $1,440
   E. $1,680

18. If $f(x) = 3x + 9$ and $g(x) = x^2 + 11$, what is the value of $g(f(-5))$?

   F.   −216
   G.   −33
   H.   −25
   J.   47
   K.   117

19. James rides a sports bike with a front wheel diameter of 18 inches along a straight track 200 yards in length. To the nearest full spin, how many rotations does the front wheel make when James travels from one end of the track to the other?

    (Note: 12 inches = 1 foot; 3 feet = 1 yard)

    A. 33
    B. 127
    C. 133
    D. 400
    E. 1,257

20. A jacket originally priced at $75 is on sale for 25% off. Ignoring sales tax, if Jenny has a coupon for an additional 15% off the sale price, how much will her jacket cost?

    F. $ 2.81
    G. $30
    H. $35
    J. $45
    K. $47.81

21. Cube A has a volume of 8 cm^3. If the side lengths of Cube B are triple the side lengths of Cube A, what is the volume of Cube B?

    A. 36
    B. 152
    C. 216
    D. 512
    E. 13,824

22. An isosceles trapezoid has a bottom base that is twice the length of its top base, a top base that measures 15 inches, and a perimeter of 67 inches. If it can be determined, what are the lengths, in inches, of the other 3 sides?

    F. 11, 11, 30
    G. 22.5, 22.5, 7.5
    H. 18.5, 18.5, 30
    J. 26, 26, 15
    K. Cannot be determined from this information

23. In the figure below, $\triangle ABC \sim \triangle DEF$. If $\overline{AB} = 5$ cm, $\overline{BC} = 3$ cm, $\overline{AC} = 7$ cm, and $\overline{DE} = 12.5$ cm, what is the perimeter, in centimeters, of $\triangle DEF$?

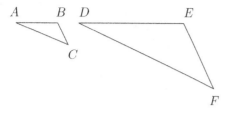

- **A.** 2.5 cm
- **B.** 17.5 cm
- **C.** 24.5 cm
- **D.** 37.5 cm
- **E.** 62.5 cm

24. The numbers below represent the number of points the Marauders scored in each of their 10 regular season football games. What is their median score?

48, 21, 43, 23, 22, 14, 21, 47, 28, 41

- **F.** 25.5
- **G.** 28
- **H.** 34.2
- **J.** 34.5
- **K.** 41

25. Which of the following expressions is equivalent to $\dfrac{3}{5 - \sqrt{7}}$?

- **A.** $\dfrac{5 + \sqrt{7}}{6}$
- **B.** $\dfrac{25 + 5\sqrt{7}}{18}$
- **C.** $\dfrac{15 + 3\sqrt{7}}{32}$
- **D.** $\dfrac{5 - \sqrt{7}}{35}$
- **E.** $\dfrac{8 + \sqrt{7}}{-2}$

26. When measured counter-clockwise, major $\angle XYZ$ measures 225°, as shown in the figure below. What is the equivalent radian measure of major $\angle XYZ$?

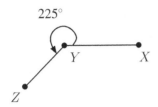

225°

F. $\dfrac{\pi}{4}$

G. $\dfrac{3\pi}{4}$

H. $\dfrac{3\pi}{2}$

J. $\dfrac{5\pi}{4}$

K. $\dfrac{5\pi}{2}$

27. Conor runs at a constant speed of 15 miles per hour, while Jack runs at a constant speed of 12 miles per hour. The two of them are running on the same straight line path, starting from the same point. If Conor gives Jack a 5 minute head start, after how much time will Conor catch up to Jack?

A. 20 mins

B. 40 mins

C. 60 mins

D. 75 mins

E. 90 mins

28. An Irish soda bread recipe calls for $1\frac{1}{3}$ cups of flour, $1\frac{1}{2}$ tablespoons of sugar, 1 egg, $1/3$ cups of butter and $1/2$ a teaspoon of baking soda. If McGregor has 10 cups of flour, 12 tablespoons of sugar, 20 eggs, 4 cups of butter, and 5 teaspoons of baking soda, how many full loaves of Irish soda bread can McGregor make?

F. 7

G. 8

H. 10

J. 12

K. 20

29. In circle O below, chord $\overline{AB}$ intersects diameter $\overline{CD}$ at point E and $\angle ABC$ measures $50°$. Which of the following pieces of information CANNOT be proven true?

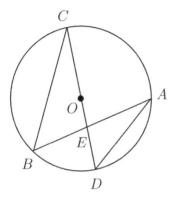

A. $\angle CDA$ measures $50°$
B. $\angle CEB \cong \angle AED$
C. $\overline{CO}$ is a radius of circle O
D. $\angle A \cong \angle C$
E. $\overline{CB} \parallel \overline{AD}$

30. The expression $\dfrac{(3x^3)^3}{9x^2}$ is equivalent to which of the following?

F. $3x^7$

G. $3x^4$

H. $2187x^7$

J. $\dfrac{x^7}{3}$

K. $\dfrac{x^4}{3}$

31. If $\triangle ABC$ is an equilateral triangle, what is the value of y?

A. 4
B. 7
C. 10
D. 19
E. 57

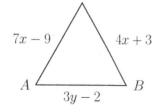

Use the figure below to answer questions 32-35

In the figure below, the vertices of $\triangle MAX$ have (x, y) coordinates of $(-7, 1)$, $(0, 7)$, and $(4, 1)$, respectively.

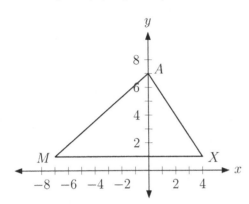

32. In coordinate units, what is the area of $\triangle MAX$?

    F. 27

    G. 30

    H. 33

    J. 42

    K. 66

33. What are the coordinates of the centroid (the average coordinate point of the 3 vertices of a triangle) of $\triangle MAX$?

    A. $(-1\frac{1}{2}, 1\frac{2}{3})$

    B. $(-1, 3)$

    C. $(-\frac{1}{2}, 3\frac{1}{2})$

    D. $(-1\frac{1}{2}, 1)$

    E. $(0, 4)$

34. What is the value of $\tan X$?

    F. $\frac{3}{2}$

    G. $\frac{2}{3}$

    H. $\frac{6}{7}$

    J. $\frac{7}{6}$

    K. $\frac{11}{2}$

35. To the nearest tenth, what is the length of $\overline{MA}$?

    A. 6

    B. 7.2

    C. 9.2

    D. 10.1

    E. 11

36. Bob is at the top of a tree 5 meters in height. Annie is standing 12 meters from the tree, as shown in the figure below. To the nearest degree, what is the angle of depression (θ) from Bob to Annie?

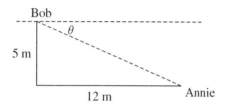

F. 13°

G. 23°

H. 25°

J. 39°

K. 67°

37. If x is an integer, which of the following could NOT be the value of y when $y = i^{3x}$? (Note: $i = \sqrt{-1}$)

A. -1

B. $-i$

C. 0

D. i

E. 1

38. Which of the following is the solution set for the equation $|x|^2 - |4x| - 5 = 0$

F. $\{-5, 0, 5\}$

G. $\{-5, 5\}$

H. $\{-1, 5\}$

J. $\{-5, 1\}$

K. $\{-5, -1, 1, 5\}$

39. For what value of q would the lines represented by the system of equations below be *perpendicular*?

$$9x - 5y = 18$$
$$15x + qy = 30$$

A. -27

B. $-8\frac{1}{3}$

C. -3

D. 3

E. 27

GO ON TO THE NEXT PAGE.

40. Since complex numbers (in the form $a + bi$) are imaginary, their absolute value (or modulus) is the distance a point is from the origin on the complex plane, where the horizontal axis is the *real axis*, and the vertical axis is called the *imaginary axis*, and is given by the Pythagorean formula $\sqrt{a^2 + b^2}$. Which of the following complex numbers has the greatest absolute value?

   F. $6 - 8i$

   G. $2 + 7i$

   H. $5 + 5i$

   J. $-7 - 6i$

   K. $-9 + i$

41. As shown in the figure below, a can with an 4 inch radius and a height of 10 inches is filled with pineapple chunks. The pineapple chunks take up 425 in³ of space. If the rest of the can is to be filled with preservative syrup, what is the maximum integer amount of syrup, in cubic inches, that can fit in the can?

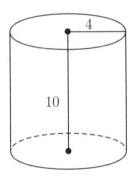

   A.   77 in³

   B.   78 in³

   C.   160 in³

   D.   265 in³

   E.   831 in³

42. If $\dfrac{3x - y}{x + y} = \dfrac{2}{5}$, then $\dfrac{x}{y} = ?$

   F. $\dfrac{3}{17}$

   G. $\dfrac{1}{8}$

   H. $\dfrac{7}{10}$

   J. $\dfrac{13}{5}$

   K. $\dfrac{7}{13}$

43. In Alaska, license plates consist of three letters followed by three digits, with a possible 26 letters and 10 digits. If repetition of letters and digits is NOT allowed, which expression gives the number of distinct license plates that are possible?

A. $(26^3 \cdot 10^3)$

B. $(26!)^3(10!)^3$

C. $(3+3)^{26+10}$

D. $(_{26}C_3)(_{10}C_3)$

E. $(_{26}P_3)(_{10}P_3)$

44. In the standard (x, y) coordinate plane, line m contains the points $(-5, 2)$ and $(-2, -3)$, while line n contains the points $(0, 11)$ and $(0, 5)$. At what point does line m intersect line n?

F. $(-\frac{7}{15}, 11)$

G. $(-\frac{55}{3}, 5)$

H. $(-\frac{19}{5}, 0)$

J. $(\frac{11}{5}, \frac{5}{3})$

K. $(0, -\frac{19}{3})$

45. Ward drove his delivery truck from Albertson to Bortown, made a delivery, and then drove from Bortown to Charcity. He logged the mileage from Bortown to Charcity, but forgot to log his miles from Albertson to Bortown. Given the information below, which of the following expressions represents the straight line distance he traveled from Albertson to Bortown?

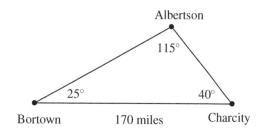

A. $\dfrac{170 \sin(40°)}{\sin(115°)}$

B. $\dfrac{170 \sin(25°)}{\sin(115°)}$

C. $\dfrac{170 \sin(115°)}{\sin(40°)}$

D. $\dfrac{170 \sin(115°)}{\sin(25°)}$

E. $\dfrac{170 \sin(40°)}{\sin(25°)}$

46. Which of the following lists the factors of $(8x^3 + 125)$?

    F. $(2x - 5)(4x^2 + 10x + 25)$

    G. $(2x + 5)(4x^2 - 10x + 25)$

    H. $(2x + 5)(4x^2 + 10x + 25)$

    J. $(2x + 5i)(2x - 5i)(2x + 5)$

    K. $(2x + 5)^3$

47. On the first day of a four-day long fundraiser, Bridget sold paintings for $25 each and made a profit of $750. The next day she raised the price to $26 dollars each, and made a profit of $728. On the third day she raised the price to $27 and made a profit of $702. She found that for every dollar she increased the price, she sold two fewer paintings. If that is the case, at what price should she sell her paintings on the last day in order to maximize the amount of profit she will make?

    A. $30

    B. $25

    C. $24

    D. $22

    E. $20

48. Which of the following are the *asymptotes* of the function $f(x) = \dfrac{3x - 15}{x^2 - 2x - 15}$?

    F. $y = 0, x = -3$

    G. $y = 0, x = -3, x = 5$

    H. $y = 0, x = 5$

    J. $y = 3, x = -3$

    K. $y = 3, x = \pm 3, x = 5$

49. The set of which values of x satisfy the parameters:

    i. x is a natural number

    ii. $x^2 \le 25$

    iii. $-|x| > 1$

    A. $\emptyset$

    B. $\{1, 2, 3, 4, 5\}$

    C. $\{2, 3, 4, 5\}$

    D. $\{1, 2, 3, 4\}$

    E. $\{2, 3, 4\}$

50. The definition of which of the items below is the set of points equidistant from a point (called the *focus*), and a line (called the *directrix*)?

    F. A circle

    G. A parabola

    H. A hyperbola

    J. An ellipsis

    K. A plane

Use the graph below to answer questions 51-53

In the figure below, $f(x) = x^4 - 3x^3 + 3x$ and $g(x) = -x$

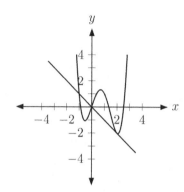

51. What real values, if any, satisfy the inequality
$f(x) < g(x)$
A. No real values
B. $-1 < x < 0$
C. $0 < x < 1$
D. $0 < x < 2$
E. $x < -1 \bigcup x > 2$

52. If $h(x) = f(x) - g(x)$, which of the following is $h(x)$?
F. $h(x) = x(x+1)$
G. $h(x) = (x+1)(x-2)^2$
H. $h(x) = (x-1)(x+2)^2$
J. $h(x) = x(x+1)(x-2)^2$
K. $h(x) = x(x-1)(x+2)^2$

53. The graph below represents which of the following functions?

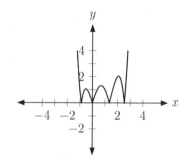

A. $-f(x)$
B. $f(-x)$
C. $|f(x)|$
D. $-|f(x)|$
E. $f(x)^2$

54. Private High School encourages each athlete to take up to three AP classes a year. The table below shows the probability of the number of AP classes a given athlete takes. If there are 15 students on the basketball team, about how many total AP courses can the basketball team expect to take in any given year?

AP Courses	Probability
0	0.15
1	0.45
2	0.35
3	0.05

F. 45

G. 30

H. 24

J. 19

K. 15

55. What value of x would make the determinant of the matrix $\begin{bmatrix} 8 & 6 \\ -12 & x \end{bmatrix}$ equal to 0?

A. -16

B. -9

C. -4

D. 0

E. 9

56. Which of the following represents the domain of the function $f(x) = \ln(x^2 - 9x + 14)$?

F. $\{x | x < 2 \cup x > 7\}$

G. $\{x | 2 < x < 7\}$

H. $\{x | x > e\}$

J. $\emptyset$

K. $\mathbb{R}$

57. What is the period of the function $f(x) = \cot(3x)$?

A. $\dfrac{\pi}{3}$

B. $\dfrac{2\pi}{3}$

C. $\dfrac{3\pi}{2}$

D. π

E. 3π

58. If the equation $ax^2 + bx + c = 0$ has no *real* solutions for *x*, what must be true about the relationship between the constants *a*, *b*, & *c*?

   F. $b^2 < 4ac$

   G. $|b| < 4ac$

   H. $b^2 = 4ac$

   J. $|b| > 4ac$

   K. $b^2 > 4ac$

59. In the figure below, the dark-shaded ring region and the light-shaded circle region each have areas equal to 36 square inches. To the nearest tenth of an inch, what is the width of the dark-shaded region?

   A. 1.4 in

   B. 2.4 in

   C. 2.8 in

   D. 3.4 in

   E. 4.8 in

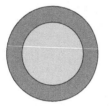

60. At Dai's daycare center, parents are often late to pick up their kids. Dai decided to track how many parents were late to pick up their child on any given evening over a period of a year. The first 5 rows of her results are shown on the table below:

Late Parents	Probability
0	0.255
1	0.221
2	0.192
3	0.159
4	0.113

Based on her findings, what is the probability that there will be *more* than one late parent on any given night?

   F. 0.225

   G. 0.464

   H. 0.476

   J. 0.524

   K. 0.745

END OF TEST 2.
STOP! DO NOT TURN THE PAGE UNTIL TOLD TO DO SO.
DO NOT RETURN TO THE PREVIOUS TEST.

THERE ARE NO TESTING MATERIALS ON THIS PAGE.

READING TEST

35 Minutes — 40 Questions

DIRECTIONS: There are four passages in this test. Each passage is followed by several questions. Choose the best answer to each question and fill in the corresponding oval on your answer document. You may refer to the passages as often as necessary.

Passage I

LITERARY NARRATIVE: This passage is adapted from *A Life Apart* by Adena Robinson (©2014 by Adena Robinson).

Even with his back to the window and the blinds down, Don could feel the thunderstorm gathering—mostly in his right ankle but also, to a lesser degree, in his wrists. He'd gotten more used to it over the last ten years, but it
5 was still an uneasy, unnatural feeling. He glanced at the clock. 4:30. Another half hour and Cody would be pulling into the driveway, along with his fiancée. He smiled. It was nice that his son had finally decided to get serious, and from what he could tell she was a good match for him—
10 though given his own history he couldn't really consider himself much of an expert on romance, let alone matrimony. Still, before Janet left and the arthritis and cynicism had set in, he'd had a decent idea of love and the happiness it could bring, even if it was never what you saw in the
15 movies or read about in novels.

He thought back to one summer in particular, when they'd been staying in a little place in Cape Cod—or was it Martha's Vineyard?—with a screened-in porch and a little gurgling marble fountain you could hear from the bedroom
20 whenever the cicadas quieted down for a bit. There were tiger lilies too, and a huge honeysuckle vine out back. He could remember showing her how to pinch off the green ends of the blossoms and suck out the nectar. But he could also remember how they'd had so many petty arguments:
25 cook vs. eat out, see a play vs. visit the marina. Most of it seemed pretty empty to him now, but it hadn't at the time. It had left him feeling unsettled, and he sensed it had been the same for her.

His mind jumped forward to walking around their
30 house what seemed like a lifetime later, and a lifetime before now, looking at the packed-up boxes, half of the paintings gone from the walls, half the family photos, half of everything. So much stuff that they'd gathered together, made together, over twenty years, and it didn't
35 seem strange at all that it fit into a handful of boxes. What seemed strange was how separable it all was, as if the objects themselves had developed some kind of amnesia and had forgotten why they existed in the first place. When the time came for him to move his own things out, he'd taken
40 nearly everything, though he didn't see much meaning in

it then. Now, looking at a family Christmas photo on the fridge from over two decades ago, he understood.

He stood to straighten up a bit more, though he knew the house didn't really need it. Cody and Marina weren't
45 the kind to put much stock in appearances, and a few crumbs on the tablecloth or a grease spot on the counter would probably go unnoticed, but it gave him something to do while he waited, and helped him to ignore the dull, deep throbbing that had been steadily building for the last
50 hour or so. He paced around the kitchen, swiping at invisible stains with a sponge.

Then it came. Lightning flashed through the glass back door, and torrents broke loose on the patio and hammered the roof. He started to worry a bit about Cody driv-
55 ing, but caught himself and let it go—he was a good driver, and it was only about 90 minutes from the airport. Besides, Cody had always been, if anything, overly cautious, and he'd made the trip a few times now. He decided to worry about dinner instead.

60 Putting on some heavy mitts, he pulled open the oven door and peered in. The parmesan had just started to brown, and though he liked the pasta on the top a bit on the crispy side, he didn't want to risk burning it. So, he slid the sturdy pan out of its place on the oven rack. Once
65 it was cooling on a couple of coasters on the counter, he turned his attention to the asparagus. His grandmother had taught him how to prepare it when he was only eight or nine, and he'd never forgotten. Picking up the stalks one at a time, he held each one at the middle and end and bent
70 it until it snapped.

He was nearly finished when he saw the thin, yellow glow of headlights through the downpour. Quickly washing off his hands and toweling them dry, he walked over to the front door, opened it, and flicked on the outside light.
75 Then he put both hands in his back pockets and stood there, looking out into the storm, straining to see a familiar face.

GO ON TO THE NEXT PAGE.

1. The point of view of the passage can best be described as:

   A. first person; multiple characters tell their sides of a story.
   B. first person; the main character relates his thoughts and feelings.
   C. third person; a narrator tells the story of multiple characters.
   D. third person; a narrator tells the story from the main character's perspective.

2. Which of the following events mentioned in the passage occurs first chronologically?

   F. Don's wife leaves him.
   G. Don puts pasta into the oven.
   H. A thunderstorm begins to roll in.
   J. Cody and his fiancée arrive at Don's house.

3. The narrator mentions the Christmas photo on Don's fridge in order to:

   A. demonstrate how difficult it was for Don and Janet to divide their possessions.
   B. give an example of an item Don was happy he had kept.
   C. identify a reason that Don wishes Marina were not coming to his house.
   D. provide insight into a painful memory for Don.

4. As it is used in line 26, *empty* most nearly means:

   F. nostalgic.
   G. distasteful.
   H. bare.
   J. meaningless.

5. The narrator indicates that Don had learned some of his cooking skills from:

   A. a cookbook.
   B. his grandmother.
   C. his ex-wife Janet.
   D. his son Cody.

6. In the last paragraph, Don is most likely straining to see a familiar face because:

   F. it is late and completely dark out.
   G. it is difficult to see through the heavy rain.
   H. he has forgotten what his son looks like after many years apart.
   J. he does not see well at his age.

7. Based on the passage, the "uneasy, unnatural feeling" the narrator mentions in line 5 most nearly refers to:

   A. a sensation in the character's joints.
   B. feelings of anticipation before a loved one's arrival.
   C. lightning striking the house.
   D. regret over a failed marriage.

8. It can most reasonably be inferred from the fourth paragraph (lines 43–51) that Don was straightening up because:

   F. it distracts him from his unease.
   G. he needs to clean the grease spot from the counter.
   H. he fears that Cody and Marina will be disappointed by his house.
   J. the lightning makes him feel anxious.

9. The main idea of the fifth paragraph (lines 52–59) is that:

   A. Don channels his worry about Cody driving in the storm into preparing dinner.
   B. Don is concerned about getting along with Marina.
   C. Cody is taking his time to avoid arriving at Don's house.
   D. Cody's fiancée dislikes driving in rainy weather.

10. The author most likely mentions a summer in Cape Cod in order to:

   F. demonstrate how a character's perspective has changed over time.
   G. shift the passage's focus to Cody's childhood.
   H. describe the setting of the passage.
   J. give details about Janet's early life.

Passage II

SOCIAL SCIENCE: This passage is adapted from *Revolutionary Waves* by David Xiao (©2016 by David Xiao).

In February 1848, revolutionary crowds took to the streets of Paris and forced King Louis-Philippe from power. In itself, this was not a remarkable event: the French had a long history of revolt. What was remarkable
5 was what followed in cities throughout Europe. Within days of Louis-Philippe's flight and the foundation of a new French republic, thrones in Germany, Italy, Austria-Hungary, Romania, and Poland were shaken by popular rebellions. Ordinary people toppled centuries-old monar-
10 chies and demanded elections, constitutions, and civil rights.

A wave of revolution swept Europe, disregarding political, religious, and social boundaries. Rulers in vastly different countries were simultaneously challenged by cit-
15 izens championing radical ideas that had been suppressed for decades, including nationalism, liberalism, and socialism. The speed and vigor of the revolts overturned Europe's political order in a matter of weeks. But the new republics and constitutions created during the extraordinary
20 summer of 1848, were all stamped out by the end of the year. Kings returned to their thrones and re-established their power by imprisoning, exiling, or killing the revolutionary leaders who had challenged them. The ideas that briefly inspired dreams of a new society were once
25 again suppressed. Like a plague, the revolutionary wave advanced by leaps and bounds, then quickly burnt itself out.

The concept of "bounded rationality" has been used to explain the wave's speed. Bounded rationality attempts
30 to take into account the tension between emotional impulses and reasoned decision-making within the human mind. Many social scientists work under the assumption that human beings are utility-maximizing agents; that is, our actions are determined by a rational assessment of our
35 own self-interest. We do what we think will be beneficial to ourselves, and we avoid doing what we think will be harmful. But this assumption makes it hard to understand the often irrational actions of humans, as individuals and as groups. Bounded rationality accounts for this by point-
40 ing out that, in order to act in our own self-interest, we have to understand every possible factor relevant to our self-interest. This perfect understanding is impossible; no one can ever know all of the possible consequences of their action or the external factors that could impact their deci-
45 sions. Instead, people make the most rational decisions possible in an imperfectly understood context. The result is very often action that appears irrational, despite being carried out by rational actors.

In 1848, communication between the cities of Europe
50 was rudimentary. There were very few railroads and no telegraphs. The fastest mode of transportation was sea travel, and ships were still powered by sails rather than steam. Consider the situation of potential revolutionaries in Prussia. When news of the revolution in France first
55 arrived in the capital city of Berlin, rebels made two assumptions. First, the fact that the French king had been overthrown meant that it was possible for the Prussian king to meet the same fate. Second, conditions in Berlin were similar enough to those in Paris to warrant an attempt
60 to achieve the same result. The French example meant that it was rational, in principle, to envision a scenario in which the Prussian king could also be driven from power. But that piece of sound inductive reasoning was bounded by the fact that Berlin rebels did not understand the spe-
65 cific context of the Paris rebellion. A thousand subtle differences that could not be communicated over distances meant that observers in Berlin had a flawed understanding of the factors that led to revolutionary success in Paris. Instead, the rebellion in Berlin was launched on the assump-
70 tion that if one king was vulnerable, all kings were vulnerable. The immediate success of the revolution in Berlin obscured this fatal mistake, which became clear as the king and his allies regrouped and steadily undermined the haphazard revolutionary efforts to build a new government.

75 Indeed, the weaknesses of the new governments—not just in Berlin, but all over Europe—can in part be explained by the structural weakness of non-governmental political institutions in general. In 1848, there were no political parties, trade unions, or public associations com-
80 parable to the ones that exist today. The only durable forms of political organization were the monarchies and their governments. The absence of political organization, not only helps explain the sudden, impulsive uprisings, but also the failure of the rebels to build a lasting replacement
85 for the regimes they temporarily stunned. Without the leadership provided by party and union leaders or the organization necessary for rebels to stand up to disciplined, professional armies, the revolts could only last until the forces of the old order could rally and reassert themselves.

11. Which of the following questions is directly answered by the passage?

   A. When did governments become democracies in the majority of European countries?
   B. By what means did monarchs restore their power?
   C. How many continents experienced revolutions in the 1800's?
   D. What were the main differences between revolutions in different countries in Europe?

12. As it is used in line 20, *stamped out* most nearly means:

   F. suppressed.
   G. encouraged.
   H. advanced.
   J. communicated.

13. According to the passage, many social scientists believe that humans:

    A. are naturally drawn to revolutions.
    B. act rationally and in their own self-interest.
    C. choose to make irrational decisions to confuse others.
    D. should not be governed by oppressive monarchies.

14. The main idea of the second paragraph (lines 12–27) is that in Europe in the 1800's:

    F. revolutions were not sustained over time.
    G. it was impossible for democracy to exist.
    H. radical ideas like liberalism and socialism were accepted by the ruling class.
    J. rebellions were dangerous for citizens who got involved.

15. The main idea of the fourth paragraph (lines 49–74) is that:

    A. sea voyage was the preferred mode of travel in the 1800's.
    B. Prussian revolutionaries ignored lessons from their French counterparts.
    C. the success of the French revolution was the downfall of the Prussian revolution.
    D. slow communications bounded revolutionaries from understanding the full context of other revolutions.

16. According to the passage, the center of the revolution in Prussia was located in:

    F. Germany.
    G. Austria-Hungary.
    H. Berlin.
    J. Paris.

17. The author most likely lists the countries in lines 7–8 in order to:

    A. illustrate France's significance in Europe in 1848.
    B. emphasize the number of popular rebellions.
    C. compare rebellions in Europe to those in other regions of the world.
    D. create a visual of the order in which the rebellions occurred.

18. It can most reasonably be inferred from the passage that bounded rationality results in:

    F. monarchs re-establishing power after halting a political revolution.
    G. citizens making choices in the best interest of other people.
    H. the dissolution of political parties and public associations.
    J. choices that seem rational to the decision-maker but irrational to others.

19. As it is used in line 82, *absence* most nearly refers to:

    A. the lack of political parties and trade unions at the time.
    B. the desire of traditional monarchs to step down from power.
    C. citizens' irrational thinking during rebellions.
    D. monarchies toppled during European rebellions.

20. It can most reasonably be concluded from the passage that:

    F. the Prussian revolution was the most successful of all revolts.
    G. a lack of leadership and organization caused revolts to be unsuccessful.
    H. elections became commonplace as a result of the European revolts.
    J. rebels preferred to stay out of positions of power.

Passage III

HUMANITIES: Passage A is adapted from "Why Hide?" by Robert Thomas (©2010 by Robert Thomas). Passage B is adapted from "Another Name" by Yvette Maltono (©1999 by Yvette Maltono).

Note: A pseudonym, or pen name, is the fictitious name used by an author in place of his or her own name to sign his or her work.

Passage A by Robert Thomas

Now you must understand that I am not entirely against the practice of adopting a pseudonym. In not-so-distant times, it was something of a necessity for members of the gentler sex, for whom to be discovered would have
5　meant not only abundant social criticism (so limited were the roles of women in society) but, paradoxically perhaps, a lack of criticism altogether. That is to say, if the publishers were aware that these authors were women, they most likely would have refused to publish them. Thus, by
10　choosing an alternate name, just as Mary Anne Evans (better known to us as George Eliot), and all three Brönte sisters (Charlotte, Emily, and Anne, known respectively as "Currer, Ellis, and Acton Bell") did, to name just a few, these brave souls provided us with such masterpieces as
15　"Middlemarch," "Silas Marner," "The Mill on the Floss," "Wuthering Heights," "Jane Eyre," "Agnes Grey," and others that would never have seen the light of day otherwise.

In modern times, however, when gender is no longer considered the best, or even a relevant, factor in judging
20　the literary output of an author, choosing to write under a pseudonym cannot be attributed to a search for freedom of expression. Agatha Christie, who is the best-selling author of all time (excepting only the Bible and Shakespeare) and who, by the way, did not seem to find it necessary to
25　use a pen name, is well-acknowledged as the best mystery writer of all time—not only among female writers, mind you, but all writers of that genre. No, in modern times, a pseudonym must be viewed, if we are to be honest, as a form of pretension. It is a way of the author making him
30　or herself appear to be fancier, more mysterious, high, and unapproachable, than they really are, or, alternatively, to escape from criticism of the work itself.

Consider, for example, writers such as Gore Vidal (whose given name is Edgar Box) or Victoria Lucas
35　(known to us as Sylvia Plath), whose original names are just as melodious and attractive as their false ones, eliminating the consideration that they changed names just to sell more copies of their works. No, these people wanted to add some sense of secrecy or mystery to their lives and
40　works by writing under another name, as if to say that real writing, and real authors, cannot exist in this world. But despite the high-quality output of these writers, the truth is just the opposite: the best writing comes from the real world and is separated from it only through the thinnest of
45　literary devices. Otherwise, it would fail to move us or to deserve our reading it in the first place.

Passage B by Yvette Maltono

I can clearly recall writing my first poem at the age of eleven. It wasn't much in retrospect (it focused mainly on butterflies and flowers, and the rhymes were forced
50　to say the least), but at the time I was quite proud of it, and I couldn't wait to show it to my father when he returned from another hectic day at the office. You should understand, before I describe that encounter, that my father was a very encouraging parent. He had always shown
55　me unconditional love and support, but even more so since my mother had passed away, two years prior. So when I showed him this, my very first poem, it was only natural that I expected if not joy, then at least some sort of positive feedback. What I got instead, as he sat down, unfolded it,
60　and started to read, was a stern warning: "Chickpea (that was his nickname for me), this is a beautiful thing to have done, and I want you to be proud of yourself. But I also want you to know that your time and energy would be better spent elsewhere. You know your cousin Antonio, the
65　writer? I cannot tell you how often he has had to return home to live with his parents or even to borrow money from friends. The life of a writer is noble but very, very difficult."

I surprised myself by not crying, nor indeed by even
70　showing how disappointed I felt. I simply nodded quietly and accepted the hug he offered. I was a child who liked to make plans, and I was as stubborn as any adult. Even as my father was issuing his warning, I had decided that I would—no, that I must—find a way to write poetry any-
75　way.

So when I was in my early thirties, having spent four long years writing, revising, tearing up (and, on one occasion, burning) poems, and a friend offered to publish them, there was no doubt in my mind that I would say yes.
80　However, I was still dependent on my father for some of my rent money, and he was just as stubborn as I was. I was also aware that in my community back home, it was looked upon very poorly for an unwed woman to write—writing was considered a hobby for a wife, not a serious
85　endeavor, and certainly not a way to make money (for that would have been seen as a dangerous threat to a husband's or potential husband's sense of self-worth). In addition, I knew that many people, despite all the evidence of the centuries, thought that the writing of a Latina had to be limited
90　to certain themes, themes which I personally did not connect with. So it was that I chose for myself the name of Thomas Alliston, and I proceeded to enjoy the communication with a wider audience, without harming my father's feelings or prospects for future marriage and avoiding the
95　preconceptions of my would-be critics.

Questions 21–23 ask about Passage A.

---

21. For the author of Passage A, the best writing comes from:

   A. the nonfiction genre.
   B. the real world.
   C. women more often than men.
   D. writers who use pseudonyms.

22. As it is used in line 29, *pretension* most nearly means:

   F. resentment.
   G. friendliness.
   H. conceit.
   J. criticism.

23. Which of the following statements regarding female writers in the past is best supported by Passage A?

   A. They should have avoided using pseudonyms because Agatha Christie did not use one.
   B. Women did not often choose to become literary critics.
   C. Critics were appropriately harsh because the women lacked the necessary education to become writers.
   D. They were likely to receive societal criticism for their work but not attention from publishers.

Questions 24–27 ask about Passage B.

---

24. In line 64 of Passage B, the narrator's father most likely mentions cousin Antonio in order to:

   F. support his argument with an example.
   G. illustrate the reasons why he disdains writers.
   H. encourage the narrator to write under a pen name.
   J. inspire the narrator to follow her dreams.

25. The "wider audience" in line 93 of Passage B most nearly refers to readers the narrator can reach due to:

   A. support from her father and his relatives.
   B. her mother's past success as a writer.
   C. being less limited to Latina themes only.
   D. sales from male readers who prefer books written by male writers.

26. In Passage B, which of the following actions best captures the narrator's reaction to her father's warning?

   F. She is caught off guard by his opinion but not surprised.
   G. She cries because she was proud of her work.
   H. She stubbornly tells her father that she will become a writer.
   J. She hides her disappointment and hugs her father.

27. It can most reasonably be inferred from Passage B that the narrator chooses to writer under a pen name due to:

   A. her desire to marry someone from outside of her culture.
   B. average book sales, which are higher for male versus female writers.
   C. cultural pressure from her family and community.
   D. pressure from her friends to hide her identity.

Questions 28–30 ask about both passages.

---

28. Which of the following elements is most clearly similar in the two passages?

   F. The shift from first person to third person point of view
   G. The inclusion of pen names used by one or more authors
   H. The use of dialogue between two characters
   J. The time period in which each passage is set

29. The passages most strongly indicate that both authors agree that women writers:

   A. create work of inferior quality as compared to male writers' work.
   B. are constrained by family situations.
   C. should not use gender as a reason to use a pen name.
   D. have been subject to social criticism at some point in time.

30. Which of the following statements best describes how the author of Passage B would feel about the author of Passage A's opinion about writing under a pen name in modern times?

   F. Sympathetic; she regrets her own choice to use a pen name.
   G. Supportive; she would agree that women should never use a pen name.
   H. Disapproving; she had a positive outcome from using a pen name herself.
   J. Frustrated; she believes that all women should use pen names.

Passage IV

NATURAL SCIENCE: This passage is adapted from the article *Wildfires and Chaparral Biomes* by Henriette Cavendish (©2017 by Henriette Cavendish).

In October 2017, 150,000 acres of the state of California were burning. An area the size of Chicago had been reduced to charred carbon and ash. Entire towns were evacuated as thousands of firefighters struggled to merely slow
5 down the spread of the inferno.

For all the horror of the fires—the lives lost, the neighborhoods gutted, the choking ash spread over dozens of miles, and the terrible speed at which the flames spread—there was nothing unnatural about the disaster. In fact, con-
10 ditions were ripe. Years of a once-a-millennium drought desiccated the countryside, providing an abundance of fuel.

One common condition in the area contributed to the speed of the flames. Each October, California is sub-
15 jected to weeks of intense winds, called the Santa Ana winds in the south and, perhaps more appropriately, the Diablo winds in the north. Beyond the peaks of the Sierra Nevada mountains in the deserts of the Great Basin, hot, dry masses of air condense throughout the summer. The
20 pressure builds up until in the early fall, low pressure fronts along the Pacific coast draw the air through the gaps in the Sierra Nevada like water spilling through a dam. The winds accelerate through canyons and across plains, pushing moist air out to sea and scouring California's lowlands
25 with hot air gusting up to seventy miles an hour. Wind speeds can reach levels comparable to a level one hurricane, only in this case the wind is exceptionally dry.

Dry vegetation whipped by intense winds is the ideal starting point for wildfires, which routinely plague the
30 state. A small spark can be carried miles by wind gusts, setting fires as it goes. Especially intense fires in recent years, crowned by the fires that destroyed the vineyards of Napa and Sonoma, have been blamed on climatic shifts. But while it is true that the dynamics of climate change are
35 causing longer droughts and more intense winds, wildfires have long been a fact of life in this part of the world. Indeed, California's ecology has evolved in adaptation to the regular infernos.

California's fire-vulnerable regions are all within
40 what scientists call a chaparral biome. Though a biome contains multiple habitats and a diverse population of flora and fauna, all of the life within a biome shares common adaptations to a particular climate cycle. For example, both tropical rainforests and subarctic taiga forests contain
45 a wide variety of plants and animals, but the populations in each biome are adapted to very different climate conditions.

The chaparral biome is characterized by a Mediter-

ranean climate of hot, dry summers and mild, wet win-
50 ters. California's chaparral averages between 10 and 17 inches of rain per year, almost all of which falls between November and March. This period of comparatively heavy rainfall must sustain life for the longer stretch of the year during which there is almost no precipitation. Accord-
55 ingly, much of the chaparral is dominated by scrubland and woodland, expanses of tough shrubs and trees adapted to long periods of minimal rainfall. Manzanita shrubs and scrub oak trees, two of the most common species in the biome, have evolved to store water in the winter and very
60 slowly absorb its supply during the progressively drier summer months. These adaptations cope with water shortages as well as provide a defense against fire. But, drought tolerance is not enough: these plants also thrive because of their unique seeds.

65 In milder, wetter climates, plant seeds are dispersed as soon as they mature, leading to rapid expansion for as long as a plant is fertile. Serotineous plants, however, have evolved the capability of retaining mature seeds, which are only released in response to some environmental cue. In
70 the chaparral, the most common environmental cue is wildfire. These plants hoard their seeds until fire scorches the surrounding landscape, clearing tangled underbrush and promoting nutrient renewal in the soil. The seeds are released into the post-fire environment, where they take ad-
75 vantage of soil cleared of competitors and packed full of nutrients. In California, since the most intense fires occur just before the rainy season, burned land is richly fortified by winter rains just as seeds are establishing themselves.

Of course, this evolutionary pattern is not shared by
80 human beings, whose habitats are less well-suited to the chaparral. Low-density settlement in the chaparral biome leaves homes and other structures vulnerable to autumn fires, requiring extensive investments in firefighting capabilities. The human presence raises the chances of out-of-
85 season fires—downed power lines, construction, and accidents can provoke more wildfires than would naturally occur, burning stretches of land too often to allow new plant life to develop the tough bark and leaves that protect them from flames and give them time to mature. In
90 these cases, even species adapted to fire can be worn down by too-frequent blazes.

The result of this collision between humans and nature can be seen in the 2017 fires. Vineyards and estates built in the oak-strewn woodlands are especially vulnera-
95 ble to fire and hard to defend, while residential subdivisions built on the edge of chaparral scrublands can be devoured by wind-whipped flames in a matter of hours. Like the long-established life of the biome has done, humans must take into account the inescapable fact that fire is inte-
100 gral to the chaparral.

31. Which of the following best expresses the main idea of the passage?

    A. Studying plant adaptations can help prevent wildfires.
    B. California's chaparral biome is suited to wildfires.
    C. Chaparral biomes have a rainy Mediterranean climate.
    D. Humans must avoid living in California due to wildfires.

32. According to the passage, which of the following statements best describes the role of climate change in the California wildfires?

    F. Climate change will soon force people to move away from California.
    G. Climate change worsens conditions but does not cause the fires.
    H. The long drought caused by climate change is the sole reason for the wildfire.
    J. Climate change played no role in the destructive fires.

33. As it is used in lines 62–63, *drought tolerance* most nearly refers to:

    A. unique seeds that can survive high temperatures.
    B. human adaptation to years with little to no rainfall.
    C. heavy rainfall that takes place unexpectedly in drier months.
    D. chaparral plants' ability to store water in the winter.

34. The passage directly compares the air pressure building up in the mountains to:

    F. choking ash from wildfires.
    G. wind speeds of a level one hurricane.
    H. water spilling through a dam.
    J. a once-a-millennium drought.

35. The last paragraph most strongly suggests that the author's attitude toward human presence in the chaparral is one of:

    A. skepticism of people's ability to coexist with the natural world.
    B. respect for people's determination to live in fire-prone areas.
    C. alarm that people have not yet evacuated their homes.
    D. optimism for new technologies that can fight wildfires.

36. Which of the following questions is most directly answered in the passage?

    F. What kinds of animals thrive in chaparral biomes?
    G. How many homes were destroyed in California?
    H. Where are chaparral biomes outside of the United States?
    J. How many inches of rain, on average, fall per year in California's chaparral?

37. It can reasonably be inferred from the seventh paragraph (lines 65–78) that compared to plant seeds in milder climates, seeds in chaparral biomes:

    A. release seeds during the rainy season.
    B. hold on to already mature seeds.
    C. insulate themselves from high heat.
    D. are protected in pods rather than exposed.

38. The author refers to the size of Chicago primarily in order to:

    F. indicate the danger of wildfires in the Midwest.
    G. compare the measurement in acres with city blocks.
    H. synthesize an argument about chaparral biomes.
    J. emphasize the magnitude of wildfires in California.

39. According to the passage, the most intense fires in California occur:

    A. near the Sierra Nevada mountains.
    B. before the rainy season.
    C. in October.
    D. in areas with high populations of people.

40. It can reasonably be inferred from the passage that human presence influences the chaparral by:

    F. decreasing natural fires with improved firefighting capabilities.
    G. causing animal species to migrate to areas outside of the biome.
    H. creating conditions that cause wildfires outside of the natural season.
    J. building types of homes particularly prone to fire damage.

SCIENCE TEST
35 Minutes—40 Questions

DIRECTIONS: There are six passages in this test. Each passage is followed by several questions. After reading a passage, choose the best answer to each question and fill in the corresponding oval on your answer document. You may refer to the passages as often as necessary. You are NOT permitted to use a calculator on this test.

Passage I

Physics students conducted a study to analyze the effects of various parameters of a sphere rolling from different points on a halfpipe. The apparatus they used throughout the study is shown in Figure 1. The students marked 5 different points on the halfpipe: Point A (9.2 cm), Point B (4.1 cm), Point C (1.3 cm), Point D (3.0 cm), and Point E (6.2 cm).

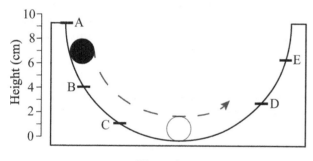

Figure 1

Experiment 1

Students constructed a wooden mini halfpipe and placed a steel orb at three different starting heights, Points A, B, and C. The orb was released from rest (starting velocity of 0 cm/s) at these points for different trials and allowed to roll to the opposite side of the halfpipe. The final height reached on the opposite side of the halfpipe, in centimeters, of the orb was recorded, as well as the speed of the orb while passing Point C (see Table 1).

Table 1			
Trial	Release point	Final height (cm)	Speed at C (cm/s)
1	A	8.5	13.5
2	B	3.5	11.0
3	C	0.8	0

Experiment 2

Experiment 1 was repeated, except two additional surface materials were tested: felt and sandpaper. The felt and sandpaper were glued to the wooden surface for their respective trials. The orb was also placed at Point A for each trial. The results are shown in Table 2.

Table 2			
Trial	Surface material	Final height (cm)	Speed at C (cm/s)
4	Wood	8.5	13.5
5	Felt	7.4	11.2
6	Sandpaper	8.9	14.0

Experiment 3

Experiment 1 was repeated, except the orb was made of three different types of material: steel, marble, and glass. Each orb was produced to be otherwise identical with the other orbs. The orb was also placed at Point A for each trial. The results are shown in Table 3.

Table 3			
Trial	Orb material	Final height (cm)	Speed at C (cm/s)
7	Steel	8.5	13.5
8	Marble	8.2	13.1
9	Glass	8.1	13.0

1. Based on the results of Experiment 1, as the initial height of the orb decreases, the final height measured on the opposite side of the halfpipe:

   A. increases only.
   B. decreases only.
   C. remains constant.
   D. varies, but with no general trend.

2. Based on the results of Experiments 2 and 3, which combination of parameters would result in the lowest final height reached on the opposite side of the halfpipe?

Surface	Orb
F. Wood	Steel
G. Wood	Marble
H. Felt	Steel
J. Felt	Marble

3. Which of the following is the most likely reason why the experimenters glue the material down every time they re-attached a new material?

   A. The glue acts as a lubricant to help the sphere roll down the halfpipe.
   B. The glue is an independent variable designed to generate another set of results.
   C. The glue prevents the new material from sliding due to friction from the sphere.
   D. The glue is an unnecessary step but a part of the experimental design.

4. Based on the descriptions of Experiments 1 and 2, which initial height was the orb placed at in Trial 5?

   F. 4.1 cm
   G. 6.2 cm
   H. 7.4 cm
   J. 9.2 cm

5. For a spherical object to maintain maximum kinetic energy, a high-friction surface is superior to a low-friction surface. A low-friction surface causes slippage, which can absorb some of the kinetic energy as the ball attempts to roll at severe angles. Which pair of trials illustrate this concept?

   A. Trials 5 and 6, because sandpaper, which has more friction than felt, resulted in a higher speed at Point C.
   B. Trials 5 and 6, because felt, which has more friction than sandpaper, resulted in a higher speed at Point C.
   C. Trials 7 and 9, because sandpaper, which has more friction than felt, resulted in a higher speed at Point C.
   D. Trials 7 and 9, because felt which has more friction than sandpaper, resulted in a higher speed at Point C.

6. According to Figure 1 and Table 1, if a ball is released from Point C, if it can be determined, what will the final height of the ball be on the right side of the halfpipe?

   F. Less than the height of Point D
   G. Between the heights of Point D and Point E
   H. Greater than the height of Point E
   J. Cannot be determined from the given information

7. Assume the physics students conducted a trial where a steel orb was released from Point A on a wooden surface. Based on the information provided, at what point on the halfpipe would the orb have the most *kinetic energy*?

   A. Point B
   B. Point C
   C. Point D
   D. Point E

Passage II

The *internal combustion engine* functions via alternating pairs of pistons compressing combustible fuel to the point of explosion, which drives that piston down and the opposing piston up, reversing the process. There are many variations of executing the design of an engine that appears in a vehicle. A *diesel engine*, named for Rudolf Diesel, differentiates itself from the now-standard gasoline engine, by not requiring an electric starter system. The engine starts itself through mechanical compression of air until the temperature of the air is sufficiently raised to ignite diesel fuel. As such, diesel fuel has a different chemical design than gasoline, and those differences allow for many design and results variations between diesel and gasoline engines.

A group of engineers gathered data on a current diesel engine to analyze for design improvements. The output of an engine's strength is measured through *torque* (rotational force) and *power* (speed of delivery of force). *Fuel consumption* measures how many gallons of fuel per mile are being consumed. The pistons of an engine fluctuate at a certain rpm (revolutions per minute) which interfaces with the moving driveshaft at different gearings selected by the transmission (see Figure 1).

Additional internal measurements of the piston chambers are useful for examining the efficiency and power of diesel engines. A piston moves up and down within a combustion chamber, compressing air and fuel to ignition and then rotating the driveshaft as it is driven downward. The *compression ratio* represents the ratio of the largest volume of a combustion chamber (piston in bottom position) to the smallest volume (piston in top position).

Maximum temperature and pressure values inside of the combustion chamber are correlated to a changing compression ratio (see Figure 2).

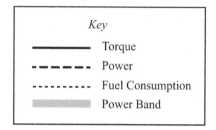

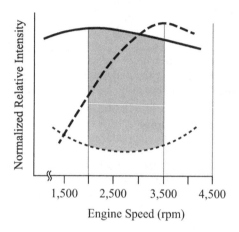

Figure 1

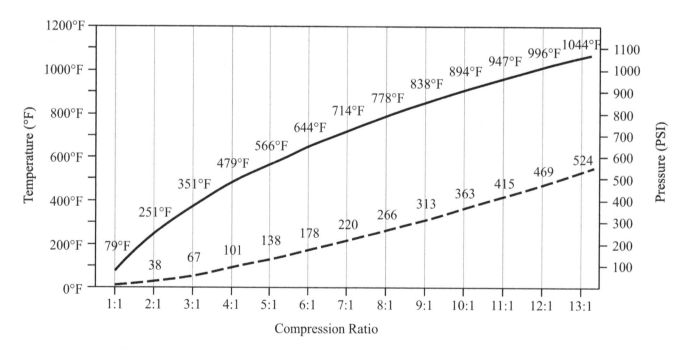

Figure 2

8. Based on Figure 1, at which of the following engine speeds does torque equal power?

    F. 2,000 rpm
    G. 2,500 rpm
    H. 2,900 rpm
    J. 3,500 rpm

9. Based on Figure 2, when the pressure of the diesel engine is 300 PSI, the temperature is approximately:

    A. 650°F.
    B. 710°F.
    C. 800°F.
    D. 840°F.

10. According to the information provided, which of the following units represents how fuel consumption is measured ?

    F. $N\,s^{-1}$
    G. $N{\cdot}s$
    H. $gal\,mi^{-1}$
    J. $gal{\cdot}mi$

11. Which of the following best describes the relationship between power and torque in diesel engines?

    A. Power and torque are directly related
    B. Power and torque are inversely related
    C. Power is independent of a change in torque
    D. None of the above accurately describes the relationship between power and torque

12. Based on the data and other information provided, if a driver pushes a diesel vehicle to a rpm value beyond its power band, which of the following results does NOT occur?

    F. Fuel consumption rises
    G. Power decreases
    H. Torque decreases
    J. Temperature decreases

13. Consider the following data of the top and bottom piston position of a diesel engine at a certain point in time:

Piston position	Volume (L)
top	2
bottom	10

Based on Figure 2 and other information provided, which of the following represents the pressure, in PSI, of the diesel engine at that point in time?

    A. 67 PSI
    B. 101 PSI
    C. 138 PSI
    D. 178 PSI

Passage III

Gibbs free energy is a concept that defines the amount of free energy available in a set system. Whether G is positive, negative, or zero determines if spontaneous reactions will occur within the given system. At constant volume the change in Gibbs free energy can be defined as:

$$\Delta G = \Delta H - T\Delta S$$

where T is measured in Kelvins, and G, H, and S are measured in joules. Entropy, S, is a measure of disorder within a system. It changes with state changes and excitement due to temperature shifts. The energy (or enthalpy), H, of a system is the kinetic and potential energy contained within a system and can be modified by work done on the system. A positive ΔG is telling of a non-spontaneous reactions, while a negative ΔG yields a spontaneous reaction. When ΔG is zero the system is at equilibrium.

Figure 1 illustrates different possible positions within the changing energy, H, and entropy, S, of a system.

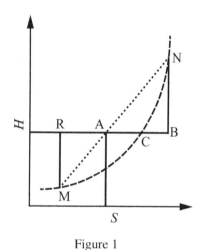

Figure 1

Line $\overline{MAN}$ represents the equilibrium line. $\overline{MR}$ maintains a constant entropy while only increasing energy. $\overline{RAB}$ holds energy constant while increasing entropy.

The changes of energy and entropy result in different possible Gibbs free energy values, which are detailed in Figure 2.

	$\Delta H < 0$	$\Delta H > 0$
$\Delta S > 0$	Spontaneous at all T ($\Delta G < 0$)	Spontaneous at high T (when TΔS is large)
$\Delta S < 0$	Spontaneous at low T (when TΔS is small)	Non-spontaneous at all T ($\Delta G > 0$)

Figure 2

14. Based on Figure 2, if ΔH is positive and ΔS is negative will a reaction occur spontaneously?

    F. Yes, because ΔG will be negative
    G. Yes, because ΔG will be positive
    H. No, because ΔG will be negative
    J. No, because ΔG will be positive

15. Based on Figure 2, when a process is *exothermic* ($\Delta H < 0$) and the entropy of the system increases, ΔG is:

    A. positive at only high temperatures.
    B. positive at all temperatures.
    C. negative at only high temperatures.
    D. negative at all temperatures.

16. Based on Figure 1 and other information provided, which of the following best describes the change that occurs along the path from Point M to Point A?

    F. The change in both enthalpy and entropy is negative
    G. The change in both enthalpy and entropy is positive
    H. The change in enthalpy is positive, whereas the change in entropy is negative
    J. The change in Gibbs free energy, enthalpy, and entropy is zero

17. Consider the following equation that defines temperature:

$$T = \frac{\Delta H}{\Delta S}$$

where T is temperature, H is enthalpy, and S is entropy. Based on the equation in the passage, if it can be determined, the above equation is a result of which of the following? The reaction in the system:

A. occurs spontaneously.
B. does NOT occur spontaneously.
C. is at equilibrium
D. cannot be determined from the given information.

18. Based on Figures 1 and 2, which of the following paths in Figure 1 is best described as "spontaneous at low T (when TΔS is small)"?

F. Point R to Point M
G. Point R to Point A
H. Point M to Point C
J. Point N to Point C

19. Consider a system at 298 K. Suppose when the temperature of this system increases, the ΔG also increases. Based on the equation in the passage, which of the following is true?

A. $\Delta S > 0$ and $\Delta H = 0$
B. $\Delta S < 0$ and $\Delta H < 0$
C. $\Delta S = 0$ and $\Delta H > 0$
D. $\Delta S = 0$ and $\Delta H < 0$

GO ON TO THE NEXT PAGE.

Passage IV

Muscle contractions occur when tension-gathering sites within muscle fibers are activated. The muscle does not need to change in length in order to contract; an isometric exercise uses a muscle contraction to maintain a weight at a fixed joint angle. If a contraction leads to a shortening of the muscle, it is called a *concentric* (shortening) contraction. If the muscle lengthens, it is an *eccentric* (lengthening) contraction. Depending on the initial position of the muscle and the movement of the contraction, a muscle can exert various degrees of *tension* (force – measured in N) and *power* (mechanical output – measured in J/s).

Experiment 1

The bicep muscles of the 15 female athletes were measured during concentric and eccentric activity during 15 trials, where each trial utilized a different athlete. For each trial, the athletes tested 50 different weighted values. Each athlete held the weight isometrically at $90°$, then completed the trial by concentrically contracting the weight as fast as possible. The force or tension, T, of the muscle fiber was measured and normalized relative to the initial tension, T_0, as the speed of application, v, was increased. The speed of application was normalized against the maximum speed of unweighted contraction, v_0. The mechanical power output was then calculated from those results. The average results of all 15 athletes are displayed in Figure 1.

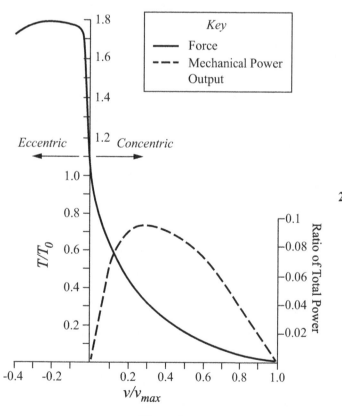

Figure 1

Experiment 2

A small electrical stimulus was applied to different muscles in the body of the 15 female athletes and the tension of the muscle over time was measured. The tension was normalized relative to the maximum tension recorded. The muscles examined included the *extraocular muscle* (controls eyelid retraction), the two muscles that make up the calf muscles – the *gastrocnemius* (large upper muscle), and the *soleus* (the flat lower muscle). The average results of all 15 athletes are displayed in Figure 2.

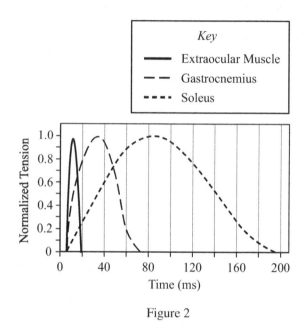

Figure 2

20. According to Figure 1, at what percentage of maximum concentric velocity does peak mechanical power output occur?

    F. 0%
    G. 25%
    H. 50%
    J. 75%

21. According to Figure 2, compared to the Soleus, the Gastrocnemius reaches maximum tension:

A. in less than half the amount of time.
B. between half the amount of time and the same amount of time.
C. with the same amount of time.
D. with twice the amount of time.

22. Based on Figure 2, if the total time of the Soleus contraction was measured in seconds instead of milliseconds, the result would be:

F. 0.002 s.
G. 0.02 s.
H. 0.2 s.
J. 2 s.

23. The procedure of Experiment 1 differed from that of Experiment 2 in which of the following ways?
The procedure of Experiment 1:

A. tested only a single muscle type, whereas Experiment 2 tested multiple muscle types.
B. tested multiple muscle types, whereas Experiment 2 tested only a single muscle type.
C. utilized only a single athlete, whereas Experiment 2 utilized many athletes.
D. utilized many athletes, whereas Experiment 2 utilized a single athlete.

24. Based on Figure 1 and other information provided, which of the following values for v/v_{max} is possible when a bicep muscle lengthens?

F. −0.3
G. 0.0
H. 0.3
J. 0.5

25. Suppose an athlete's maximum velocity of bicep contraction is 8 m/s. Based on this information and the results of Experiment 1, at what speed will the athlete exhibit a maximum mechanical power output?

A. 1 m/s
B. 2 m/s
C. 4 m/s
D. 8 m/s

26. Suppose an athlete can hold a 20 N force completely still. Based on the results of Experiment 1, which of the following is closest to the quantity of force the athlete can move at half the maximum velocity?

F. 40 N
G. 20 N
H. 10 N
J. 4 N

Passage V

Electrons and protons are elementary-charged particles that experience a negligible force from gravity, due to their small mass. Instead, electrons and protons largely experience *electric force* (measured in N). Electric force is experienced either from another point source (other charged particles) or within an *electric field* (a region of uniform electric force). An electric field uses a flat surface of conductive material that has either had electrons added, or stripped away, to create a uniform force along the length and breadth of the surface. *Point source charges* have strength relative to the inverse square of the distance from the point, while *uniform plates* have strength relative to the linear inverse of the distance.

Apparatus

To examine the effects of an electric field on the flight path of electrons, a group of scientists designed an apparatus consisting of a tube-shaped charged plate and an emitter. A single electron or clusters of electrons are emitted into an electric field with two negative plates, one above and one below the electron path, at varying starting velocities. The electron is launched at a starting angle, θ, towards the top plate. The path of the electron is represent by the solid sinusoidal black line (see Figure 1).

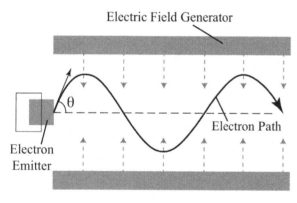

Figure 1

Experiment 1

The apparatus was utilized to emit a single electron at three different launch angles: 20°, 30°, and 40°. The electron was launched at a speed of 2.0 km/ms. As the horizontal position of each electron increased in the electric field generator, the vertical position was measured in picometers. The result is shown in Figure 2.

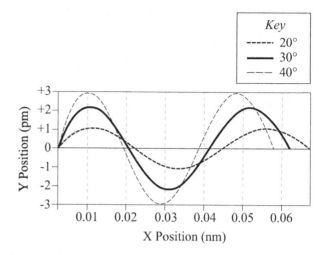

Figure 2

Experiment 2

The apparatus was utilized to emit a single electron at three different launch speeds: 1.8 km/ms, 2.0 km/ms, and 2.2 km/ms. The electron was launched at an angle of 30°. As the horizontal position of each electron increased in the electric field generator, the vertical position was measured in picometers. The result is shown in Figure 3.

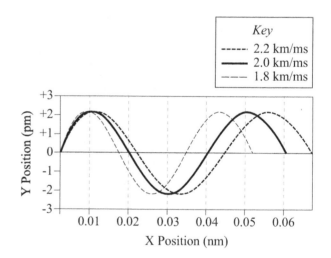

Figure 3

Experiment 3

The apparatus was utilized to emit different quantities of electrons through the electric field generator: one, two, and three electrons. As the horizontal position of the electron(s) increased in the electric field generator, the vertical position was measured in picometers. The results are shown in Figure 4.

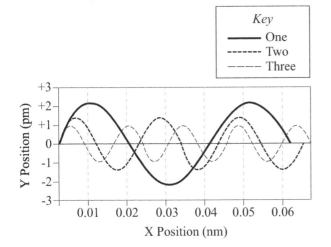

Figure 4

27. According to Experiment 2, as velocity increases, the maximum Y position:

   A. increases only.
   B. decreases only.
   C. decreases, then increases.
   D. remains constant.

28. According to the results of Experiments 1 and 3, which combination of launch angle and electron quantity would result in the least *magnitude* (absolute value) for Y position?

	Angle	Quantity
F.	40°	3
G.	40°	1
H.	20°	3
J.	20°	1

29. Suppose a particle was launched at 35° with a speed of 2.5 km/ms. According to the results of Experiments 1 and 2, how far from the center will the particle travel?

   A. Less than 1.0 pm
   B. Between 1.0 pm and 2.0 pm
   C. Between 2.0 pm and 3.0 pm
   D. Greater than 3.0 pm

30. Which of the following statements can best be deduced from the results of Experiment 3?

   F. Groups of electrons are heavier than a single electron, and thus have more inertia, causing them to change direction more slowly.
   G. Groups of electrons are affected more strongly by the electric field than a single electron, causing them to change direction more swiftly and reach a lower amplitude.
   H. A single electron is lighter than a group of electrons, and thus have less inertia, causing them to change direction more swiftly.
   J. A single electron is affected just as strongly by the electric field as a group of electrons, causing all particle groups to move the same.

31. According to Experiment 3, when two electrons are launched together, the period of their sinusoidal path is:

   A. less than 0.02 nm.
   B. between 0.02 nm and 0.03 nm.
   C. between 0.03 nm and 0.04 nm.
   D. greater than 0.04 nm.

32. Suppose the emitter fired clusters of protons instead of electrons. Based on the passage, which of the following is most likely to occur? The emitted protons would:

   F. repel the negative charge of the plate, yielding similar results.
   G. attract the negative charge of the plate, yielding similar results.
   H. repel the negative charge of the plate, resulting in all of the protons to stick to the plate immediately after launch.
   J. attract the negative charge of the plate, resulting in all of the protons to stick to the plate immediately after launch.

33. Based on the passage, if an electron is located twice as close to a negatively charged plate as another electron, the ratio of forces experienced by both electrons will be closest to which of the following?

   A. 1:1
   B. 1:2
   C. 1:4
   D. 1:8

Passage VI

The *Global Positioning System*, or GPS, is a location tracking technology that is used by many modern applications and devices. The technology allows the device to obtain geolocation and time information anywhere on or near the Earth. Four students debate the process behind GPS tracking.

Student 1

The Global Positioning System functions by triangulating distance from cell service towers. A phone of an individual continually checks the distance to each nearby tower. With three discrete distances to three distinct towers, the specific location of the phone can be pinpointed with accuracy. A mathematical process of *trilateration* occurs: distance to a single tower gives us a circle of possible locations; distance to two towers narrows that down to the intersection of two circles, or two points of possible location; the third tower distance then selects our existing location from those two points. As such, the distance an individual is from the cell service towers is needed, not the angle of elevation or directional information.

Student 2

Student 1 is correct, except instead of cell service towers, the distance is measured to nearby satellites. An array of thirty plus satellites in *geosynchronous orbit* (orbiting at a speed matched to Earth's rotation in order to stay fixed over a single coordinate on Earth's surface) can be referenced for trilateration. Satellites are more reliable than cell service towers, which can be obstructed by mountains and obstructed sight lines. Because satellites require more sophisticated data than cell service towers, distance from the satellite, angle of elevation, and directional information are all required.

Student 3

The Global Positioning System functions by using the internal accelerometer of the phone of an individual to track movement in a two-dimensional plane and reference those movements to a saved map. A detailed map is constructed by engineers with reference points of locations and roads within each GPS application, allowing location to have some *jitter* (unregulated variation in electrical signals). Saved locations in the device allow the device to reset from jitter by snapping to those locations when nearby and stopped. Due to the fact that the two-dimensional plane is utilized, distance traveled and directional information are required, but not the angle of elevation to any object above.

Student 4

The Global Positioning System is based on motion-tracking software paired with the open network of cameras distributed through every major metropolitan area and nation. The network of traffic cameras, security cameras, and other video-recording devices attached to the internet are utilized to visually track the movements of each individual. GPS applications request location data from this central system, which include the distance from the open network of cameras and angle of elevation, but not any directional information.

34. Earth rotates at a speed of 460 m/s. Based on Student 2's explanation, if a satellite is locked into geosynchronous orbit, the speed at which the satellite moves would be:

    F. 115 m/s.
    G. 230 m/s.
    H. 360 m/s.
    J. 460 m/s.

35. Based on the description of trileration by Student 1, which of the following equations are most likely used?

    A. $r^2 = (x - h)^2 + (y - k)^2$
       $c^2 = a^2 + b^2$

    B. $r^2 = (x - h)^2 + (y - k)^2$
       $A = \frac{1}{2}bh$

    C. $C = \pi D$
       $A = \frac{1}{2}bh$

    D. $C = \pi D$
       $c^2 = a^2 + b^2$

36. Suppose GPS can be used on devices that lack an accelerometer. This statement would support the viewpoint(s) of which of the following student(s)?

    F. Student 1 only
    G. Students 1 and 3
    H. Students 1, 2, and 4
    J. Students 2, 3, and 4

37. A scientist claims that each Global Positioning System data point can only utilize one parameter. Is this claim more strongly supported by Student 1 or Student 2?

A. Student 1, because according to Student 1, only the distance from a cell service tower is needed for GPS.
B. Student 2, because according to Student 2, only the distance from a cell service tower is needed for GPS.
C. Student 1, because according to Student 1, only the distance from nearby satellites is needed for GPS.
D. Student 2, because according to Student 2, only the distance from nearby satellites is needed for GPS.

38. Suppose a scientist claimed to use the Global Positioning System tracking technology to aid with navigation in remote locations, such as deserts, oceans, forests, and mountains. The viewpoints of which students would be *weakened* by this claim?

F. Students 1 and 2
G. Students 1 and 3
H. Students 1 and 4
J. Students 2 and 4

39. Suppose it was noted that GPS was designed to work internally on a device and not require any signal connection. Based on this note, which of the following students would then be correct?

A. Student 1
B. Student 2
C. Student 3
D. Student 4

40. Consider a singular point of GPS data that includes the following: (50 m, North, 35°). Which of the following students would agree that GPS data would look like the singular point described above?

F. Student 1
G. Student 2
H. Student 3
J. Student 4

Too Sweet?

Some cities have taken steps to heavily tax or ban the sale of sugary foods and drinks, arguing that these products contribute to a variety of illnesses. Proponents argue that these regulations would both increase the general health of the population and save money in healthcare costs. Critics say that city governments should not attempt to guide the choices of their citizens by making certain foods and drinks either more expensive or impossible to legally purchase. Does the government have a right to discourage the purchase of certain products in order to promote better health?

Read and carefully consider these perspectives. Each suggests a particular way of thinking about regulating unhealthy products.

Perspective 1	Perspective 2	Perspective 3
City governments have an obligation to promote the health of their citizens. Products found to pose a health risk should therefore be taxed or banned.	People should not be penalized for buying foods or drinks high in sugar. Encouraging individual responsibility and healthier habits would be preferable to taxing or banning these products.	Governments already ban the use of many dangerous items, e.g., narcotics. Banning sugary foods and drinks is a logical extension of an existing power.

Essay Task

Write a unified, coherent essay in which you evaluate multiple perspectives on regulating foods and drinks that are high in sugar. In your essay, be sure to:

- analyze and evaluate the perspectives given
- state and develop your own perspective on the issue
- explain the relationship between your perspective and those given

Your perspective may be in full agreement with any of the others, in partial agreement, or wholly different. Whatever the case, support your ideas with logical reasoning and detailed, persuasive examples.

ACT7 - A0119

Practice Test

ENGLISH TEST

45 Minutes—75 Questions

DIRECTIONS: In the five passages that follow, certain words and phrases are underlined and numbered. In the right-hand column, you will find alternatives for the underlined part. In most cases, you are to choose the one that best expresses the idea, makes the statement appropriate for standard written English, or is worded most consistently with the style and tone of the passage as a whole. If you think the original version is best, choose "NO CHANGE." In some cases, you will find in the right-hand column a question about the underlined part. You are to choose the best answer to the question.

You will also find questions about a section of the passage, or about the passage as a whole. These questions do not refer to an underlined portion of the passage, but rather are identified by a number or numbers in a box.

For each question, choose the alternative you consider best and fill in the corresponding oval on your answer document. Read each passage through once before you begin to answer the questions that accompany it. For many of the questions, you must read several sentences beyond the question to determine the answer. Be sure that you have read far enough ahead each time you choose an alternative.

PASSAGE I

Ants and Bees: A Family Tree

Far below the flights of majestically buzzing bees, creepy-crawly ants rule the subterranean pockets and floor of the forest. These powerhouses of the insect world have long been of scientific interest, with over 12,000 species in existence, the ability to lift twenty times their own weight, and a complete lack of ears and lungs, ants are far more interesting than their stature might suggest. Surprisingly, though, the ant may also be the genetic key to the evolution of bees. The ant and bee—both members of the Hymenoptera clade—have recently been discovered to be genetic cousins.

The research that unearthed this genomic family tree was made possible by technological innovations: technologies that could compare only a few genes across species of various

1. **A.** NO CHANGE
   B. interest, with over 12,000 species,
   C. interest; with over 12,000 species
   D. interest with over 12,000 species

2. **F.** NO CHANGE
   G. bee both members of the Hymenoptera clade—
   H. bee, both members of the Hymenoptera clade—
   J. bee—both members of the Hymenoptera clade

---

kinds, just ten years ago, now have the power to compare

thousands. ☐3 Researchers sought out evolutionarily

conserved genomes <u>who</u> had remained similar or identical
4

between wasps, bees, and ants. <u>Contrastingly,</u> by aligning
5
those genes across species, researchers could determine

evolutionary relationships between these seemingly unrelated

<u>insects. Comparing</u> core regions of larger variability. The
6

results <u>ended</u> a scientific debate that had spanned decades: the
7
closest living relative of the ant was indeed the bee.

Suspicion of relation between the two species, before

this confirmation, stemmed from behavioral similarities. Ants

and bees both <u>build structurally constructed nests and are</u>
8
central–

place foragers. <u>The act of bringing back foraged food to a</u>
9
<u>given locale</u> is sometimes an
9

3. The writer is considering deleting the following clause from the preceding sentence (adjusting the punctuation as needed):

    of various kinds

Given that the information is accurate, should the writer make this deletion?

- **A.** Yes, because the information is irrelevant to the scope and focus of the paragraph.
- **B.** Yes, because the information is already implied within the sentence.
- **C.** No, because the information clarifies how the technology was used within this study.
- **D.** No, because the information clarifies the technology as applicable to bees and ants.

4. **F.** NO CHANGE
   G. that
   H. they
   J. of which

5. **A.** NO CHANGE
   B. Then,
   C. Besides,
   D. Similarly,

6. **F.** NO CHANGE
   G. insects and comparing
   H. insects by comparing
   J. insects; by comparing

7. **A.** NO CHANGE
   B. conquered
   C. forecasted
   D. convoluted

8. **F.** NO CHANGE
   G. build constructed nests and are
   H. build formatted nests, being
   J. build nests and are

9. Given that all of the choices are accurate, which one most effectively clarifies a term in the previous sentence?

- **A.** NO CHANGE
- **B.** Defining behavior, such as was previously mentioned,
- **C.** Although such behavior is not unique to these species, it
- **D.** Throughout the globe, this behavior is

aspect <u>to</u> both species' social behaviors. All ants and ten
        10
percent of the bee population display some form of advanced

sociality, which includes behaviors like group decision

making, reproductive divisions of labor, and cooperative care

of juveniles. Scientists posit from their <u>flowering</u> genomic
                                                11
findings, that these characteristics—working in tandem—just

may have made ants the dominant terrestrial habitat insects

and bees the most important pollinators of plants.

These behavioral similarities can now <u>surmise</u> from
                                              12
ecological examination to the realm of evolutionary biology as

scientists <u>forcefully</u> map the genomic origins of such
           13
behaviors. In other words, the new phylogeny creates a

framework in which scientists can map the evolution of

nesting, feeding, and social behaviors. While the

consequences of such work may go unnoticed in everyday

<u>life. The</u> findings have already created tangible differences in
    14
the scientific community: a fossil, once classified as the oldest

evidence of ant life only to be later reclassified as a

spheciform wasp, can now rightfully take its place

<u>into the root underneath</u> the ant-apoid family tree.
        15

10. **F.** NO CHANGE
    G. for
    H. of
    J. since

11. The best placement for the underlined portion would be:

    A. where it is now.
    B. after the word *these*.
    C. after the word *habitat*.
    D. before the word *plants*.

12. **F.** NO CHANGE
    G. consecrate
    H. transition
    J. formulate

13. The writer wants to emphasize that scientists have created a genetic tree with less errors than previous trees. Which choice best accomplishes that goal?

    A. NO CHANGE
    B. more accurately
    C. less fortifyingly
    D. more diversely

14. **F.** NO CHANGE
    G. life, and the
    H. life and the
    J. life, the

15. **A.** NO CHANGE
    B. at the root underneath
    C. at the root of
    D. into the root of

PASSAGE II

The Relic of the S.S. Palo Alto

Off the coast of California's Monterey Bay Seacliff sits a

decrepit 420 foot concrete tanker with colorful history.

Although passersby today would assume the S.S. Palo Alto to

serve no <u>purpose in its current state,</u> the giant ship works as
         16

16. **F.** NO CHANGE
    G. purpose (in its current state)
    H. purpose, in its current state,
    J. purpose, in it's current state

an artificial reef and hub of marine life. |17| In fact, this concrete colossus was originally fabricated as a WWI vessel.

Engineers of WWI looked to concrete as steel—the era's material of choice for ship construction—that had become
                                                              18

less and less available to the masses for usage. The United
                      19
States ordered twenty-four ships of ferroconcrete—a cheaper, more abundant resource of concrete reinforced with steel. To this day, therefore, the utility of military ferroconcrete ships
            20
remains unknown, as the ships were completed only after WWI had already ended. The ferroconcrete Palo Alto, therefore, would never see battle and required immediate repurposing.

    The remarketing of the Palo Alto followed its purchase by a private company that aimed to refashion the vessel into one of entertainment. Their ample remodeling of the
                              21

420 foot tanker included a fifty-four foot heated pool, a full
22
casino, and a dance floor. The elegant tanker was built into the

pier, where it served as a tourism hub for only two years.
23
Unfortunately, the Great Depression snuffed out much of the entertainment industry, and with it the Palo Alto's business.

17. Which of the following true statements, if added here, would provide the best transition between the current state of the Palo Alto and the reason for its construction?

    A. While the Palo Alto has had various purposes throughout its near century of life, the ship has always been a tourist attraction of sorts.
    B. Playing an integral role in the Monterey Bay marine ecology is about as far from the Palo Alto's intended purpose as could be.
    C. Ownership of the Palo Alto has bounced between private companies and the state, adding layers to its historical significance.
    D. As one of twenty-four of its kind, a ship constructed of this material is a rare sighting.

18. F. NO CHANGE
    G. which had become
    H. having become
    J. became

19. A. NO CHANGE
    B. useably available in mass.
    C. readily available.
    D. optionable.

20. F. NO CHANGE
    G. for example,
    H. of course,
    J. DELETE the underlined portion.

21. Which choice most clearly emphasizes the lavish nature of the ship's remodeling?

    A. NO CHANGE
    B. opulent
    C. abundant
    D. copious

22. F. NO CHANGE
    G. this ferroconcrete tanker
    H. the now-broken military ship
    J. the ship

23. A. NO CHANGE
    B. pier, there
    C. pier; where
    D. pier,

[1] The state of California purchased the ship after it had fallen to ill will, making use of it as a public fishing pier. [2] Even so, California didn't see the spill as cause to remove the Palo Alto, so it still sits today right in its normal spot.

[3] The concrete mass was reborn, and reclaimed as a place of leisure—soirees traded for fishing lure. [4] With the passage of time came further decay, beginning a cycle of restoration attempts. [5] The largest attempt occurred when a crack in the vessel's fuel tank caused an oil leak. [6] Though the spill was contained, its effects were far from negligible: the surrounding wildlife suffered while California footed a $1.7 million bill to clean up five-hundred gallons of gunk. [28]

Now, algae coats the hull of the Palo Alto. While the ship is closed to the public, different generations remember the ship at its various stages—some remember it as a dance hall, others as a spot to fish, and still others are a mysterious relic of its own fascinating past.

24. **F.** NO CHANGE
    G. into disrepair,
    H. in pieces,
    J. unwittingly broken,

25. **A.** NO CHANGE
    B. at the Seacliff.
    C. where it goes.
    D. right there.

26. **F.** NO CHANGE
    G. reborn and reclaimed
    H. reborn, and reclaimed,
    J. reborn and reclaimed,

27. Which of the following alternatives to the underlined portion would NOT be acceptable?

    A. negligible; unfortunately, the
    B. negligible as the
    C. negligible, the
    D. negligible. The

28. For the sake of logic and coherence of this paragraph, Sentence 2 should be placed:

    F. where it is now.
    G. after sentence 3.
    H. after sentence 4.
    J. after sentence 6.

29. **A.** NO CHANGE
    B. generations both young and old
    C. various age groups both young and old
    D. various age groups at different stages of their lives

30. **F.** NO CHANGE
    G. to be
    H. being
    J. as just

Synesthesia

When first gazing upon one of Melissa McCracken's

pieces, viewers are often shocked to learn that the

<u>various paintings for sale</u> are depictions of what McCracken
    ₃₁

sees when she listens to music. This <u>aptitude, having sensory</u>
                ₃₂

<u>perceptions involuntarily unified—is called</u>
    ₃₂

<u>synesthesia. People</u> with synesthesia can have their senses
    ₃₃

intertwined in different manners, though the most common

variety involves seeing colors and patterns based on music.

For decades, the <u>numeral</u> of synesthesia within the
           ₃₄

scientific community had been one of a neurological disorder.

Early scientific research suggested that crossed wires in the

brain were to blame for the confusion of senses. The auditory

cortex, responsible for the processing of sound, is located

<u>so wicked close</u> to the occipital lobe that processes colors and
    ₃₅

shape. An excess of neurological connections might, therefore,

trigger multiple senses. However, current research suggests

that the senses of infant primates are a hyperconnected blend

for the first few weeks of infancy, so all individuals may be

synesthetes at birth. What, then, could be responsible for

adults tasting music or seeing colors associated with certain

numbers?

31. Which choice most clearly describes the visual and material aesthetics of McCracken's work?
    A. NO CHANGE
    B. art gallery's pieces
    C. the different paintings, each unique in specific ways,
    D. complex abstractions of colorful oil paints

32. **F.** NO CHANGE
    G. aptitude—having sensory perceptions involuntarily unified—
    H. aptitude—having sensory perceptions involuntarily unified,
    J. aptitude, having sensory perceptions involuntarily unified

33. **A.** NO CHANGE
    B. synesthesia and those people
    C. synesthesia and people
    D. synesthesia, people

34. **F.** NO CHANGE
    G. figure
    H. classification
    J. fortification

35. **A.** NO CHANGE
    B. within problematically close quarters of the area next
    C. in close proximity
    D. like totally next

One study at the University of London Oxford, in suggesting that adult development of synesthesia is a learned skill. Brain scans of synesthetes provided no evidence of structural neurological differences, leading researchers to believe that connections between various senses are learned. This theory seems to have been at least partially falsified by a study at the University of Amsterdam, which successfully

trained participants to associate colors with letters. Even so, scientists are still endeavoring to answer two particular questions: How do children learn sound-color synesthesia, and why do some children retain the ability to do so while others do not?

While there is still research to be done regarding synesthesia, often mentioned facts of its rarity dissipate as more and more individuals come forward as synesthetes.

Synesthetes who see patterns of color while listening to music are more likely to dedicate their lives to creative pursuits. In the future, as scientists define the mechanisms for maintaining synesthesia into adulthood, which can someday include exercises to increase the chance of retaining the neurological condition. 42 Such lessons would enhance the students' experience of music, creating a more full sensory

36. F. NO CHANGE
G. Oxford suggests
H. Oxford. It suggests
J. Oxford, that suggesting

37. A. NO CHANGE
B. frowned upon
C. corroborated
D. confiscated

38. F. NO CHANGE
G. In the first place,
H. For example,
J. Besides,

39. Given that all the choices are accurate, which one most clearly suggests that the perceived rarity of synesthesia is changing?
A. NO CHANGE
B. formulated investigations
C. previously held assumptions
D. manifestations

40. F. NO CHANGE
G. Synesthetes who, see patterns of color,
H. Synesthetes who see patterns, of color
J. Synesthetes, who see patterns of color

41. A. NO CHANGE
B. arts education could
C. that will
D. DELETE the underlined portion.

42. At this point, the writer is considering dividing the paragraph into two. Should the writer begin or not begin a new paragraph here, and why?
F. Begin a new paragraph, because it would separate the ideas about future education from the essay's conclusion.
G. Begin a new paragraph, because the essay shifts from focusing on education of synesthesia to those who have already been educated about it.
H. DO NOT begin a new paragraph, because doing so would establish a link between teaching methods and talent levels.
J. DO NOT begin a new paragraph, because doing so would interrupt the discussion of teaching synesthesia in the future.

GO ON TO THE NEXT PAGE.

experience. As for synesthetes like Billy Joel, Lady Gaga, and
                                    _____
                                        43
Mary J. Blige who have synesthesia, each experiences a

unique color association: while some see a minor chord as a
            _____
                44
green streak, others as a blue wave, the visual component of

their music can't help but influence their compositions.

43. A. NO CHANGE
    B. those with the intertwined mechanisms of sense
       processing
    C. grown synesthete individuals with the gift
    D. popular artists

44. F. NO CHANGE
    G. association: and
    H. association,
    J. association

Question 45 asks about the preceding passage as a whole.

45. Suppose the writer's primary purpose had been to suggest ways in which synesthesia could be introduced into music education. Would this essay accomplish that purpose?

    A. Yes, because it considers classroom integration of synesthesia throughout history.
    B. Yes, because it includes a list of artists who have already introduced synesthesia into education.
    C. No, because it focuses generally on understandings of synesthesia rather than offering tangible examples of classroom integration.
    D. No, because the main suggestions address how to conduct further research rather than classroom integration.

PASSAGE IV

The Ansel Adams Wilderness

Complete with towering peeks and glacial lakes, the
               _____
                    46

Ansel Adams Wilderness is a lesser known patch of land
                            _____
                                47
cradled between Yosemite National Park and Mammoth Lakes.

While some naturally protected lands are named for explorers

or native tribes, this particular stretch bears the name of
                                                        __
                                                        48

46. F. NO CHANGE
    G. towering peaks
    H. tower peeks
    J. tower peaks

47. A. NO CHANGE
    B. less of known
    C. least of known
    D. least knowing

48. F. NO CHANGE
    G. with
    H. for
    J. upon

GO ON TO THE NEXT PAGE.

America's most beloved photographer and environmentalist
                                                        49
held in high regard.
      49

San Francisco native, Ansel Adams, lived a quiet,
                  50
reserved childhood. A shy boy with undiagnosed learning

disabilities, he took to solitary activities like playing the piano

and he traversed the outdoor terrain. During annual family
    51

trips to the Yosemite Sierra, which was where Adams
                                  52
expanded his artistic endeavors by taking photographs on a

camera his parents had given him. His intentions had always

been to pursue a career in music, but when employment as the

official photographer of the Sierra Club proved lucrative, he

changed course and was established as the official artist of

Sierra Nevada.

Adams quickly rose the artistic ranks while honing his

craft and technical abilities. He often worked eighteen hours

daily until fatigue-induced illness allowed him to take time off
                                    53
to recover. While much of that time was spent with his art, a

large portion was dedicated to commercial photography gigs

that enabled Adams to pay his rent. Even after his first ever

one-man museum show in 1932, the artist could not survive on

art photography alone. Still, Adams pushed himself to author
    54
ten volumes of technical photography manuals that are, to this

day, regarded as the most influential books on the subject.

Now, Adams' photography is notable. Each black and
                              55
white photo transcends realistic documentation of the

wilderness into an ethereal, idealized wilderness—a

49. A. NO CHANGE
B. cherished environmentalist.
C. highly cherished environmentalist.
D. environmentalist.

50. F. NO CHANGE
G. native, Ansel Adams
H. native Ansel Adams,
J. native Ansel Adams

51. A. NO CHANGE
B. being an outdoorsman.
C. outdoor-minded motivations.
D. exploring the outdoors.

52. F. NO CHANGE
G. it was at here that
H. where
J. DELETE the underlined portion.

53. Which choice most effectively emphasizes Adams' resistance to stop working?
A. NO CHANGE
B. coddled
C. forced
D. authorized

54. F. NO CHANGE
G. the art photos that had earned him a museum show
H. the photos he considered artistically fulfilling
J. it

55. Given that all of the statements are true, which one provides the most effective transition from the preceding paragraph into this paragraph?
A. NO CHANGE
B. Adams' fierce work ethic and prolific nature made his work a defining cannon of nineteenth century American landscape photography.
C. Many of the artist's photos were used to promote environmentalist causes.
D. Adams took countless photos of the land that would become the Ansel Adams Wilderness.

wilderness free of <u>human trace,</u> amplified to its ultimate
                              56
manifestation. Adams' photography purifies the psychological

experience of natural beauty to unimaginable heights.

    Lesser known than his artwork, <u>consequently,</u> was
                                                    57
Adams' relentless advocacy for all forms of environmentalism.

While his photographs did function as unintentional advocacy

in <u>it's</u> beautiful portrayals of nature, Adams himself attended
   58
countless environmentalist meetings, and wrote thousands of

letters to newspapers and politicians, in support of his

conservation philosophies. The causes he championed ran the

entire range of environmentalism, including wishes to

maintain the lands of Yosemite near his namesake patch of

wilderness. While fighting to save the American wilderness,

Ansel Adams <u>became famous without acquiring riches.</u> [60]
                                    59

56. **F.** NO CHANGE
    G. people having touched the land,
    H. legitimate humanity,
    J. humanitarian diatribe,

57. **A.** NO CHANGE
    B. all in all,
    C. however,
    D. for example,

58. **F.** NO CHANGE
    G. its
    H. they're
    J. their

59. Which choice most effectively concludes the sentence and the essay?

    A. NO CHANGE
    B. is often studied in art history courses.
    C. created art that became symbolic of wild America.
    D. was unlike any artist of his day and is highly regarded.

> Question 60 asks about the preceding passage as a whole.

60. Suppose the writer's primary purpose had been to describe the current lack of funding for American photographic arts. Would this essay accomplish that purpose?

    F. Yes, because the writer indicates that funding for all artists is substantially lacking.
    G. Yes, because the writer hints that Adams' lack of funding is symptomatic of a larger financial issue.
    H. No, because the writer focuses on Adams' general artistic and environmental history.
    J. No, because the writer admits that other artists had no such issues with financing.

PASSAGE V

Interactive Art or Selfie Backdrop?

In 2015, the Renwick Gallery at the Smithsonian Museum opened "Wonder," an exhibit showcasing immersive and interactive pieces by nine contemporary artists. One work featured sixty miles of thread forming a prismatic rainbow; another adorned towering walls with dead insects. Prompted by social media, visitors flocked at record rates to the exhibit
61
for a chance to snap a photo in front of the massive installations. In fact, the exhibit attracted more visitors during

its six-week continuity than did the museum for the entire
62
year. Though the popularity confounded the exhibit's curators, there had been no mistake: The success of similarly immersive works, like Yayoi Kasuma's "Infinity Mirrored Room", proved that museum visitors now craved becoming the star of these pieces—and that they wanted to post the experiences on their social media accounts.

Queue the conceptualization in a never-before-seen
63
business: the pop-up museum. Only a year after the "Wonder" exhibit became a viral hit, the Museum of Ice Cream opened in New York City. Meanwhile this museum wasn't explicitly
64
made for social media photos, its appealing aesthetics give hint that the subject wasn't completely ignored. Museum guests walk through colorful sprinkles, swing on a yellow
65
banana dangling from the ceiling, or walk among illuminated

---

61. Which of the following alternatives to the underlined portion would NOT be acceptable?
- **A.** Because visitors had been prompted by social media, they
- **B.** Social media, which had prompted visitors,
- **C.** Visitors, prompted by social media,
- **D.** Social media prompted visitors; they

62. **F.** NO CHANGE
- **G.** conservancy
- **H.** duration
- **J.** perpetuation

63. **A.** NO CHANGE
- **B.** from
- **C.** of
- **D.** as

64. **F.** NO CHANGE
- **G.** However
- **H.** Furthermore
- **J.** While

65. The writer wants to emphasize the depth and configuration of the sprinkles. Which choice best accomplishes that goal?
- **A.** NO CHANGE
- **B.** crunch the underfoot,
- **C.** sparkle photographically among
- **D.** wade in a pool of

fluffy clouds. The entire exhibit being drenched in whimsical
66
pink and lit to photograph well.

The Museum of Ice Cream was a great success, boasting
67

over 200,000 followers on social media and selling out of their
68
pricey $38 tickets for a six-month stint in San Francisco in

less than ninety minutes. New pop-up museums formed

quickly in its likeness, they mirrored this new balance of
69

artistry and commercialization. Pop-up museum curator
70
Kat Dennison admits to knowingly formatting the interactive
70

layout to cater to social media participants. Many pop-up
71
museums even have commercial sponsors. Such blatant

participation in commercialization is not typical of what is

usually classified as a "museum," giving these experiences
72
a unique classification.
72

Though first inspired by the installation art of formal

museums, the pop-up museum experience offers something

less formal than did its predecessors. Rather than seeing the
73

66. F. NO CHANGE
G. exhibit, which is
H. exhibit is
J. exhibit

67. A. NO CHANGE
B. Cream, in becoming
C. Cream that was
D. Cream, becoming

68. F. NO CHANGE
G. one's
H. that
J. its

69. A. NO CHANGE
B. such museums mirrored
C. mirroring
D. they attempted to mirror

70. F. NO CHANGE
G. curator—Kat Dennison—
H. curator, Kat Dennison,
J. curator Kat Dennison,

71. A. NO CHANGE
B. participants who will visit the pop-up museum.
C. personas who post such museums on their accounts.
D. fanatics who enjoy pop-up museums like hers.

72. Given that all the choices are accurate, which one best supports the idea that some individuals do not support mixing art and commercialization?
F. NO CHANGE
G. allowing for participants to freely photograph themselves in the exhibits.
H. creating a safe space of child-like play.
J. leaving many hesitant to classify such pop-up museums as true *museums*.

73. A. NO CHANGE
B. then did it's
C. then did its'
D. than did it's

art, the goal becomes being seen within the

art—by the audience— that is social media. [75]
————————
74

74. F. NO CHANGE
    G. art by the audience
    H. art, by the audience,
    J. art by the audience,

Question 75 asks about the preceding passage as a whole.

75. Suppose the writer's primary purpose had been to offer an overview of a cultural phenomenon. Would this essay accomplish that purpose?

    A. Yes, because it describes the effect of social media on culture beyond the pop-up museum.
    B. Yes, because it briefly traces the development, popularity, and cultural effects of pop-up museums.
    C. No, because it explains what pop-up museums are but suggests they won't last very long.
    D. No, because it focuses only on the Museum of Ice Cream.

END OF TEST 1.
STOP! DO NOT TURN THE PAGE UNTIL TOLD TO DO SO.

THERE ARE NO TESTING MATERIALS ON THIS PAGE.

MATHEMATICS TEST
60 Minutes — 60 Questions

DIRECTIONS: Solve each problem, choose the correct answer, and then fill in the corresponding oval on your answer document.

Do not linger over problems that take too much time. Solve as many as you can; then return to the others in the time you have left for this test.

You are permitted to use a calculator on this test. You may use your calculator for any problems you choose,

but some of the problems may be best done without using a calculator.

Note: Unless otherwise stated, all of the following should be assumed:
1. Figures are NOT necessarily drawn to scale.
2. Geometric figures lie in a plane.
3. The word *line* indicates a straight line.
4. The word *average* indicates arithmetic mean.

---

1. Last week, Sally babysat for her niece for 12 hours at a rate of $15.00 per hour, and she spent 7 hours life guarding at a rate of $8.50 per hour. What was the average amount of money she made per hour last week?

   A. $6.60
   B. $10.90
   C. $11.75
   D. $12.60
   E. $14.50

2. In the figure below, $g(x)$ is a translation of $f(x)$ such that $g(x) = f(x + a) + b$, where a represents a horizontal shift of $f(x)$ and b represents a vertical shift of $f(x)$. Which of the following *must* be true?

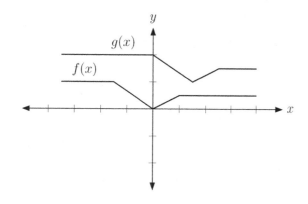

   F. $a = 0$
   G. $a > 0$
   H. $b < 0$
   J. $b = 0$
   K. $b > 0$

3. Larry lives 75 miles from his office. In the morning, his commute to his office took him 3 hours due to traffic. In the afternoon, his trip home from the office took him only 1.5 hours. To the nearest whole number, what was his average speed on his round-trip from his home to his office and back in miles per hour?

   A. 17 mph
   B. 25 mph
   C. 33 mph
   D. 42 mph
   E. 50 mph

4. For shipments from New Jersey to Hawaii, a postal carrier charges $8.00 to ship a package of up to 5 pounds, and then $1.50 for each additional pound the package weighs. If Derek paid $24.50 to ship a package, approximately how much did the package weigh?

   F. 3 lbs
   G. 4.5 lbs
   H. 7.5 lbs
   J. 11 lbs
   K. 16 lbs

5. The ages of the 21 children in a pre-school class are shown in the table below. What is the median age of the children in the class?

Age	Frequency
Two	3
Three	8
Four	6
Five	3
Six	1

   A. Two
   B. Three
   C. Four
   D. Five
   E. Six

6. Which of the following is the equation of a line perpendicular to the line whose equation is $3x + 4y = 5$?

   F. $-4x + 3y = 5$
   G. $4y + 3x = 5$
   H. $4x + 3y = 5$
   J. $4y - 3x = 5$
   K. $6x + 8y = 10$

Use the following information to answer questions 7-9.

The Ward and Wolf families went out for burgers and fries. The quantity of burgers and orders of fries each family ordered and the initial cost (before tax and coupons) are shown in the table below:

Family	Burgers	Fries	Total
Ward	5	3	$32.00
Wolf	4	6	$31.00

7. Which of the following augmented matrices represents the table above as a system of equations

A. $\begin{bmatrix} -5 & -3 & | & -32 \\ 4 & 6 & | & 31 \end{bmatrix}$

B. $\begin{bmatrix} 5 & -4 & | & 31 \\ 3 & -6 & | & 32 \end{bmatrix}$

C. $\begin{bmatrix} 5 & 4 & | & 0 \\ 3 & 6 & | & 63 \end{bmatrix}$

D. $\begin{bmatrix} 5 & 3 & | & 32 \\ -4 & -6 & | & -31 \end{bmatrix}$

E. $\begin{bmatrix} 5 & 3 & | & 32 \\ 4 & 6 & | & 31 \end{bmatrix}$

8. What is the cost of a single burger?
   F. $1.50
   G. $4.50
   H. $5.00
   J. $5.50
   K. $7.00

9. If p represents the initial cost of the Ward family's meal, which of the following expressions represents the total cost of their meal if they had a coupon for 20% off and were charged 7% sales tax?
   A. $(1.07)(0.80)p$
   B. $(0.93)(1.20)p$
   C. $(1.27)p$
   D. $(1.13)p$
   E. $(0.93)p$

10. In the figure below, points D, E, and F are the midpoints of the sides of triangle ABC. If the perimeter of triangle ABC is 34 units, what is the perimeter of triangle DEF?

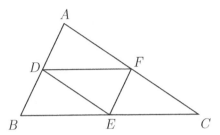

   F. $8\frac{1}{2}$
   G. $11\frac{1}{3}$
   H. 17
   J. $25\frac{1}{2}$
   K. 68

11. A school polled 300 parents as to whether they think that a high school should ban football. 87 parents voted "Yes", 168 parents voted "No", and the remaining parents voted "No Opinion." What is the probability that a randomly selected parent voted "No Opinion?"

   A. 0.15
   B. 0.27
   C. 0.29
   D. 0.45
   E. 0.56

12. In the figure below, $\angle AED$ measures $110°$ and $\overline{ED} \cong \overline{CD}$. What is the measure of $\angle JDH$?

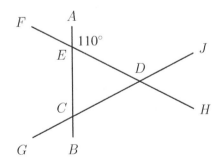

   F. $35°$
   G. $40°$
   H. $55°$
   J. $70°$
   K. $140°$

GO ON TO THE NEXT PAGE.

13. What is the difference between the largest root and the smallest root of the function $f(x) = x^2 - 11x - 60$?

  A. 0
  B. 11
  C. 15
  D. 19
  E. 60

14. The volume of a cone with radius r and height h is $\frac{1}{3}\pi r^2 h$. Which of the following expressions represents the volume of a cone with a *diameter* of 12?

  F. $9\pi h$
  G. $12\pi h$
  H. $16\pi h$
  J. $36\pi h$
  K. $48\pi h$

15. Peyton's teacher assigned her a project where she must construct as many triangles as she can, where one side is 4 inches long, another side is 6 inches long, and a third side with an integer length. How many different triangles can Peyton construct?

  A. 0
  B. 5
  C. 7
  D. 9
  E. An infinite number of triangles

16. Consider the following true statement: "If it is raining, then I'm carrying an umbrella." Which of the following statements MUST also be true?

  F. If I'm NOT carrying an umbrella, then it is NOT raining
  G. If I'm carrying an umbrella, then it is raining
  H. If it is NOT raining, then I am NOT carrying an umbrella
  J. I am carrying an umbrella IF AND ONLY IF it is raining
  K. It is raining IF AND ONLY IF I am carrying an umbrella

17. Point C lies on line segment $\overline{AB}$ in the coordinate plane. The distance between points A and C is half the distance between points B and C. If point A has coordinates $(2, 9)$ and point C has coordinates $(5, 7)$, what are the coordinates of point B?

  A. $(8, 5)$
  B. $(6\frac{1}{2}, 6)$
  C. $(-1, 11)$
  D. $(-4, 13)$
  E. $(11, 3)$

GO ON TO THE NEXT PAGE.

18. The table below shows the sums of all 36 possible outcomes from rolling two standard six-sided dice, with the top row representing the number shown on the first die and the first column representing the number shown on the second die.

	One	Two	Three	Four	Five	Six
One	2	3	4	5	6	7
Two	3	4	5	6	7	8
Three	4	5	6	7	8	9
Four	5	6	7	8	9	10
Five	6	7	8	9	10	11
Six	7	8	9	10	11	12

What are the odds of rolling a sum that is a prime number AND is either even OR double digits on a single roll of the two dice?

- **F.** 1:2
- **G.** 1:7
- **H.** 1:8
- **J.** 1:11
- **K.** 1:12

19. When water freezes to ice, it expands to take up approximately 9% more volume than when it is in its liquid state. A container that is 5 inches wide and 8 inches long is filled with water to a height of 10 inches and placed in a freezer. If the length and width remain constant, to what height will the ice reach once the water freezes?

- **A.** 10.30 in
- **B.** 10.90 in
- **C.** 11.72 in
- **D.** 12.95 in
- **E.** 13.60 in

20. The figure below represents the template for the print of a digital photograph, where the shaded region represents the photograph itself and the non-shaded region represents the border of the photo so that it can be framed once printed. If the area of the entire figure is 1 and each of the grid lines is a square, what is the area of the photograph?

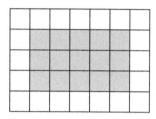

F. 3/5

G. 3/7

H. 5/7

J. 8/11

K. 10/17

21. Rectangle $ABCD$ is shown below. What is the value of y?

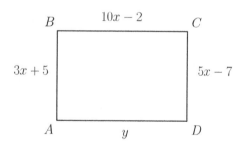

A. 6

B. 23

C. 35

D. 58

E. 60

22. Tripper has 5 plates (shown below) that he wants to display on his mantle. In how many different ways can he arrange these plates?

   F. 5
   G. 15
   H. 25
   J. 120
   K. 3,125

23. 180% of 15 is equivalent to which of the following?
   A. 25% of 108
   B. 15% of 108
   C. 30% of 88
   D. 80% of 35
   E. 33% of 81

24. If $f(x, y) = \dfrac{3x^2 - 5y}{3y^2 - 5x}$, what is $f(10, 4)$?

   F. -140
   G. $-1/140$
   H. 1
   J. $1/140$
   K. 140

25. Rhombus $ABCD$ (shown below) has a perimeter of 60 cm and the length of diagonal $\overline{AC}$ is 24 cm. What is the length of diagonal $\overline{BD}$?

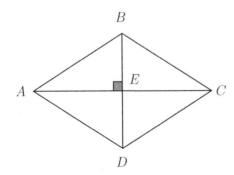

   A. 5 cm
   B. 9 cm
   C. 12 cm
   D. 13 cm
   E. 18 cm

26. If Joe can paint a house in 4 hours, and Sam can paint the same house in 6 hours, how long would it take for them to paint it together?

    F. 1 hour and 30 minutes
    G. 2 hours and 24 minutes
    H. 2 hours and 30 minutes
    J. 2 hours and 40 minutes
    K. 5 hours

27. To the nearest square inch, what is the area of the largest circle that can fit entirely inside a square whose side lengths are 12 inches?

    A. 36 in^2
    B. 113 in^2
    C. 226 in^2
    D. 144 in^2
    E. 452 in^2

28. The chance that the Giants win a football game is 40%. The probability that the Jets win a *different* football game is 25%. What is the probability that the Giants and Jets both LOSE their respective games?

    F. 10%
    G. 35%
    H. 45%
    J. 65%
    K. 90%

29. The point (7,2) lies on a circle whose center is (3,5). Which of the following is another point that lies on the same circle?

    A. $(6, 9)$
    B. $(10, -1)$
    C. $(5, 3\frac{1}{2})$
    D. $(7, 5)$
    E. $(3, 2)$

30. A basketball is dropped from a height of 10 feet. Each time it bounces, it reaches a maximum height that is $3/5$ its previous height. To the nearest *inch*, what is the maximum height that the ball will achieve *after* its third bounce?

    F. 1 foot 4 inches
    G. 2 feet 2 inches
    H. 2 feet 6 inches
    J. 3 feet 7 inches
    K. 8 feet 2 inches

GO ON TO THE NEXT PAGE.

Use the following information to answer questions
31-33

Woodland's Rock Quarry contains 2.8×10^9 tons of rock, which is hauled away by dump trucks that each have the capacity to carry 500 tons of rock in a single load. In one section of the quarry, the dump trucks carry their payload along a 200 yard incline from the base of the quarry to the top, as shown in the figure below. The incline (θ) steepens as rock is removed.

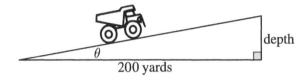

The quarry owns 75 dump trucks, each of which is capable of hauling 5 full loads out of the quarry each day. The quarry operates for 250 days each year.

31. If the maximum incline (θ) that the dump trucks can handle is $10°$, what is the maximum depth, to the nearest yard, that this section of the quarry can reach?

  A. 3 yards
  B. 20 yards
  C. 30 yards
  D. 35 yards
  E. 203 yards

32. Each load of rock it hauls away costs the quarry $4,500 for man-hours, $3,750 for vehicle expenses, $6,850 in machinery, and $2,400 for other miscellaneous expenses. How much revenue will the quarry need to make on each ton of rock in order for the amount of money they make in profit to equal the cost of mining the rock?

  F. $2
  G. $35
  H. $70
  J. $105
  K. $140

33. Operating at the given capacities, approximately how many years would it take to completely empty the quarry of rock?

  A. 20 years
  B. 40 years
  C. 60 years
  D. 80 years
  E. 100 years

34. Angle θ has its vertex at the origin, an initial side that is the positive ray of the x-axis, and a terminal side that bisects the second quadrant. Which of the following statements regarding θ is true?

    F. The sine of θ is positive and the cosine of θ is negative

    G. The sine of θ is negative and the cosine of θ is positive

    H. Both the sine and cosine of θ are both positive

    J. Both the sine and cosine of θ are both negative

    K. The cosine of θ is 0 and the tangent of θ is undefined

35. Kelly's scores on 7 biology tests this semester were as follows: 85, 89, 83, 91, 66, 93, and 87. If her teacher drops her highest and lowest test scores, what will happen to the current mean (x) and median (y) of her scores?

    A. x will increase and y will stay the same

    B. x will stay the same and y will increase

    C. Both x and y will stay the same

    D. Both x and y will increase

    E. Both x and y will decrease

36. Which of the following expressions is equivalent to $(x+5)^{-2}$?

    F. $-2x - 10$

    G. $\dfrac{1}{x^2} + \dfrac{1}{25}$

    H. $-x^2 - 10x - 25$

    J. $\dfrac{1}{2x + 10}$

    K. $\dfrac{1}{x^2 + 10x + 25}$

37. Consider three real numbers x, y, and z, such that $xy \neq 0$ and $yz = 0$. What *must* be true about $\dfrac{x}{z}$? The expression $\dfrac{x}{z}$ is:

    A. equal to 0.

    B. a real number NOT equal to 0.

    C. an imaginary number.

    D. undefined.

    E. unable to be determined by the given information.

38. Vector $\mathbf{w} = \langle 8, 3 \rangle$ and is the sum of vectors $\mathbf{u}$ and $\mathbf{v}$. If $\mathbf{u} = \langle p, -2 \rangle$ and $\mathbf{v} = \langle 12, s \rangle$, what are p and s?

   F. $p = -20$, $s = -1$

   G. $p = 5$, $s = -4$

   H. $p = 1.5$, $s = -1.5$

   J. $p = -4$, $s = 5$

   K. $p = 4$, $s = -5$

39. The formula for the annual depreciation of an item is given by $C = I(1-r)^t$, where C is the current value, I is the initial value, r is the rate of depreciation, and t is the time in years. Which of the following expressions is equal to r in terms of C, I, and t?

   A. $1 + \sqrt[t]{\dfrac{C}{I}}$

   B. $\sqrt[t]{\dfrac{C}{I}} - 1$

   C. $1 - \dfrac{\sqrt[t]{C}}{I}$

   D. $\dfrac{\sqrt[t]{C}}{I} - 1$

   E. $1 - \sqrt[t]{\dfrac{C}{I}}$

40. Given $f(x) = x^2 - 2x + 1$ and $g(x) = x - 5$, what is $f(g(x))$?

   F. $x^2 - 2x - 4$

   G. $x^2 - 12x + 26$

   H. $(x - 6)^2$

   J. $x^2 - 12x - 4$

   K. $x^2 - 2x + 11$

41. In creating a new flat screen television, Sandspoke Electronics increased the length of the base of their current model by 10%, but the total area of the television decreased by 12%. By how much must the height of the television have decreased?

   A. 2%

   B. 10%

   C. 18%

   D. 20%

   E. 22%

42. The prime factorization of which of the following numbers (all of which have exactly four single-digit prime factors) contains four *unique* factors?

   F. 84

   G. 210

   H. 294

   J. 315

   K. 525

43. The graph of which of the following functions passes through the 4 points shown below?

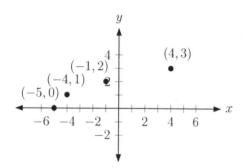

   A. $f(x) = x^2 - 5$

   B. $f(x) = -\frac{1}{2}x + 2$

   C. $f(x) = \log_2(x + 5)$

   D. $f(x) = (x + 5)^{\frac{1}{3}}$

   E. $f(x) = \sqrt{x + 5}$

GO ON TO THE NEXT PAGE.

44. In circle O below, $\triangle ABC$ is inscribed in Circle O, $\overline{AB} = 6$ cm, $\overline{BC} = 8$ cm, and $\overline{AC}$ is a diameter of the circle. What is the area of Circle O?

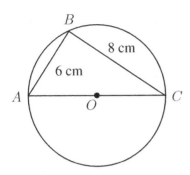

   F. 16π

   G. 25π

   H. 36π

   J. 49π

   K. 100π

45. For which of the following inequalities does the solution set contain *multiple* integers?

   A. $x - 7 < x - 11$

   B. $-1 < x < 1$

   C. $-|x + 5| > 0$

   D. $|x - 3|^{-1} < 0$

   E. $\dfrac{|x|}{x} < 0$

Use the following information to answer questions
46-49

Trapezoid $WXYZ$, shown below, is made up of four right triangles, with diagonals $\overline{WY}$ and $\overline{XZ}$ perpendicular at K. $\overline{WX} \cong \overline{KY}$ and $\triangle KXW \sim \triangle KYZ$. a, b, and c represent the lengths of line segments.

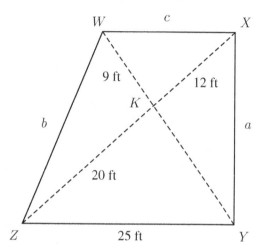

46. If it can be determined, which of the following correctly relates the values of a, b, and c?

F. $a < b < c$

G. $c < b < a$

H. $a < c < b$

J. $c < a < b$

K. Cannot be determined from the given information

47. To the nearest degree, what is the measure of $\angle KZY$?

A. $24°$

B. $37°$

C. $39°$

D. $53°$

E. $61°$

48. Point Y will be moved along $\overline{WY}$ towards point K, until trapezoid $WXYZ$ becomes Kite $WXYZ$ (making $\triangle KWX \cong \triangle KYX$). When this happens, by what percent will the length of $\overline{XY}$ be *decreased*?

F. 22%

G. 25%

H. 28%

J. 33%

K. 40%

49. What is the area of trapezoid $WXYZ$?
- **A.** 180 ft^2
- **B.** 204 ft^2
- **C.** 384 ft^2
- **D.** 440 ft^2
- **E.** 484 ft^2

---

50. The graph of $f(x) = \dfrac{x^2 - 2x - 15}{x^2 - 8x + 15}$ is shown in the figure below, with a vertical asymptote at $x = 3$ and a hole at $x = 5$. Which of the following functions is an equivalent function, except that it is continuous (plugs in the hole) at $x = 5$?

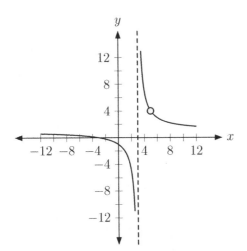

- **F.** $f(x) = \dfrac{x - 3}{x + 3}$

- **G.** $f(x) = \dfrac{x - 5}{x - 3}$

- **H.** $f(x) = \dfrac{x + 3}{x - 5}$

- **J.** $f(x) = \dfrac{x + 5}{x - 5}$

- **K.** $f(x) = \dfrac{x + 3}{x - 3}$

51. For all positive values of x, which of the following is equivalent to $\dfrac{\frac{5}{x+3}}{1 + \frac{2}{x+3}}$?

A. $\dfrac{5}{x+5}$

B. $\dfrac{1}{x} + 1$

C. $\dfrac{8}{(x+3)^2}$

D. $\dfrac{2}{x+3}$

E. $\dfrac{5}{3}$

52. The table below shows the number of diagonals that can be drawn in certain polygons:

Polygon	Diagonals
Triangle	0
Quadrilateral	2
Pentagon	5
Hexagon	9

How many diagonals can be drawn in a decagon?

F. 10

G. 16

H. 19

J. 28

K. 35

53. In the New York Metro area, if the ratio of Islanders fans to Devils fans is 5:8, and the ratio of Devils fans to Rangers fans is 5:16, what is the ratio of Islanders fans to Rangers fans?

A. 1:2

B. 3:11

C. 5:24

D. 2:25

E. 25:128

54. In the figure below, the equation of the outer circle is $x^2+y^2 = a^2$ and the equation of the inner circle is $x^2+y^2 = b^2$. The ellipse (dashed) is internally tangent to the outer circle, externally tangent to the inner circle, and has an area of πab. What is the area of the ellipse?

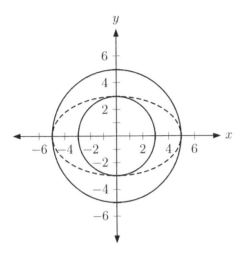

 F. 4π

 G. 9π

 H. 15π

 J. 25π

 K. 225π

55. Given that $\sin^2(x) + \cos^2(x) = 1$, which of the following is also equal to 1 for all values of x? Note:

$$\sec(x) = \frac{1}{\cos(x)}, \csc(x) = \frac{1}{\sin(x)}, \cot(x) = \frac{1}{\tan(x)}$$

 A. $\cot^2(x) - \csc^2(x)$

 B. $\tan^2(x) - \sec^2(x)$

 C. $\sec^2(x) - \tan^2(x)$

 D. $\csc^2(x) + \cot^2(x)$

 E. $\sec^2(x) + \tan^2(x)$

56. The function $f(x) = 5^{\frac{x}{x^2-7x+10}}$ is defined for all real values of x *except*:

 F. 0 only

 G. 0 and -5

 H. 2 and 5

 J. 7 and -10

 K. x is defined for all real numbers

57. In the figure below of $\triangle ABC$, Point A is located at $(1, 3)$, Point B is located at $(1, 8)$, and Point C is located at $(5, 5)$. Which of the following is an equation of a line that would cut $\triangle ABC$ into two smaller triangles of equal area?

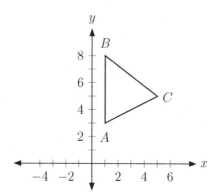

A. $y = -2x + 10$
B. $y = \frac{1}{2}x + 5$
C. $y = x + 4$
D. $y = 5$
E. $x = 3$

58. Consider all rectangles with longest side x and perimeter $P \geq 10$, where the measures of both the length and width are whole number values. In terms of x, what is the range of the ratio of the perimeter of the rectangle to the area, A, of the rectangle?

F. $\dfrac{x}{4} \leq \dfrac{P}{A} \leq x + \dfrac{1}{2}$

G. $4x \leq \dfrac{P}{A} \leq x^2$

H. $\dfrac{1}{4} \leq \dfrac{P}{A} \leq \dfrac{2}{x+2}$

J. $4 \leq \dfrac{P}{A} \leq x + 2$

K. $\dfrac{4}{x} \leq \dfrac{P}{A} \leq 2 + \dfrac{2}{x}$

59. The graphs of hyperbolas $x^2 - y^2 = 9$ and $y^2 - x^2 = 9$ and their asymptotes $y = \pm x$ are shown in the figure below. For any hyperbola in the form $\dfrac{x^2}{a^2} - \dfrac{y^2}{b^2} = 1$ or $\dfrac{y^2}{a^2} - \dfrac{x^2}{b^2} = 1$, the distance ($c$) from the vertex (where the asymptotes intersect) to the foci is $a^2 + b^2 = c^2$. What would be the area of a circle that is centered at the intersection of the asymptotes and passes through the four foci?

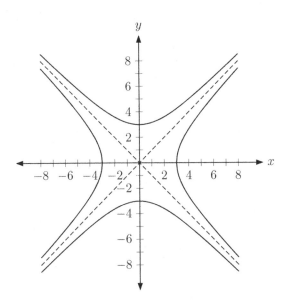

A. $2\pi\sqrt{3}$
B. 9π
C. 18π
D. 36π
E. 81π

60. A committee of 6 randomly selected members will be formed from a group of 10 people, half of whom are Democrats and half of whom are Republicans (5 of each). To the nearest hundredth, what is the probability that the committee will consist of *exactly* 3 Democrats and 3 Republicans?

F. 0.20
G. 0.25
H. 0.27
J. 0.48
K. 0.50

READING TEST

35 Minutes — 40 Questions

DIRECTIONS: There are four passages in this test. Each passage is followed by several questions. Choose the best answer to each question and fill in the corresponding oval on your answer document. You may refer to the passages as often as necessary.

Passage I

LITERARY NARRATIVE: This passage is adapted from the novel *Someone Else's Name* by Valerie Prant (©2015 by Valerie Prant).

Only with the grasslands dwindling to a thin yellow line in the fingerprint-smeared rearview mirror, did Jane pause to think about what had happened at the diner and to wonder if she'd been in the wrong. She still felt unsure, un-
5 settled to the point where her thoughts and the new scenery of squalid houses and high evergreens seemed inseparable. A boy playing outside of a yellow clapboard house—was that a rabbit's foot or a mouse he was holding?—flashed by, his eyes raised briefly to her level before he went back
10 to whatever invented adventure he was on.

And what about her? How many unsettling encounters was she meant to face in order to find out whether she had the right to feel uncomfortable, if others' perceptions of and reactions to her were perfectly reasonable, or, as she
15 often felt, completely unwarranted? The waiter obviously hadn't meant to offend her, at least she didn't think so now, but it was impossible to tell how much of her anger came from his ignorance or his tone. But it had been totally neutral, hadn't it? She asked herself for the third or fourth
20 time, annoyed that her anger had so clouded her impressions at the time, that she was now unable to say for certain. After all, she looked and acted the part—her hands were covered with dirt, the sunburn on her face and shoulders had only recently begun to resemble a tan, two of her front
25 teeth were gone, and she spoke with a twang that was pure Appalachia. So, it really was likely an honest mistake.

Maybe it's because growing up, she had come so close to being like the Sutton clan who lived up the mountain, keeping to themselves more than was healthy, getting
30 up to nothing good and apparently existing well beyond the reach or the desire of the local law. When the waiter asked if she was one of them, it really stung. She didn't flatter herself into thinking she was any better than they were—she, like them, had committed more than her fair
35 share of questionable actions to survive—but if only to some small degree, if only in her mind, she hadn't become quite like them. Yes, she'd broken the law as well, but it was different...somehow, in some way she was certain was there, even if she was completely unable, even after
40 all these years, to say what it was.

She knew now it had been a mistake to drive back this way. Even within the realm of the practical, it didn't really make sense: it took her a full day's drive off her path to the Pacific, where friends and some sense of comfort were
45 still waiting for her. And it didn't really make much sense emotionally either. There was nobody, nothing waiting for her in her hometown, not even the vague notion of some force with which she might still share some connection. Nevertheless, crossing the state line, she'd felt that distinct
50 pull in the pit of her stomach, the gravitational tug that only nostalgia can bring.

So she'd come back. She'd passed the tumbledown mill where her father had worked and contracted the cancer that had killed him, and she'd passed the empty, grass-
55 covered lot where her family's trailer home had once been (she couldn't remember if it was, in the end, an uncle or a distant cousin who'd come to sell what little could be sold and drive it off to the junkyard; she hadn't bothered to keep in touch and neither had they). The school hadn't
60 changed, although the groups of kids outside cutting class looked younger than she remembered. Even the diner still stood, the place where she had worked as a dishwasher for three consecutive high school summers while her friends were out getting into whatever teenage trouble they could
65 find.

She smiled bitterly at her own foolishness. What had she expected—a warm greeting from the manager who simple math dictated must have passed away a long time ago? Some sense of self-worth that she had been so lack-
70 ing in of late? She didn't know then and, she realized, she probably wouldn't ever really know. Whatever lay behind the impulse had been as instinctual as any basic human reaction. So what if she'd told the waiter he should keep his mouth shut? She felt bad, all these miles later, but a part
75 of her still held on to the humor of it: she, a forty-two year old, washed-up woman telling off some kid who couldn't have been more than 14, who probably, from the look of him, already kept his mouth shut most of the time. She laughed a little, and savored it. She knew that part of her,
80 at least, was one of the things that had, somehow, kept her going.

1. The author most likely includes the parenthetical statement in lines 56–59 in order to:

   A. contrast Jane's family relationships with those of the Sutton clan.
   B. explain the disdain that Jane felt for her uncles and cousins.
   C. indicate the distance that Jane feels from her past.
   D. provide evidence of property values in the region.

2. Which of the following events referred to in the passage occurred first chronologically?

   F. Jane passed through her hometown on her drive to the Pacific.
   G. Jane worked as a dishwasher at the diner.
   H. Jane lashed out at the waiter in the diner.
   J. A boy played outside of a clapboard house.

3. Based on the passage, when the waiter asks if Jane is part of the Sutton clan, she feels:

   A. elated; she is happy for someone to acknowledge her identity.
   B. hurt; she considers herself to be different from the Sutton clan.
   C. defensive; she has not broken the law like people in the Sutton clan.
   D. appreciative; she feels connected to the people she used to live near.

4. The main idea of the fourth paragraph (lines 41–51) is that:

   F. Jane's sentimental feelings drew her to her hometown.
   G. no one remembered Jane in her hometown.
   H. adding a full day to a drive is impractical.
   J. Jane's strong ties to the community drew her to her hometown.

5. The tone of the passage can best be described as:

   A. reflective and self-critical.
   B. angry and combative.
   C. thoughtful and condescending.
   D. reverent and proud.

6. The passage indicates that when Jane's father was alive, he worked:

   F. with the Sutton clan.
   G. as a dishwasher.
   H. at the mill.
   J. as a teacher at the school.

7. The interaction between Jane and the waiter that is described in the passage most strongly suggests that Jane feels:

   A. frustrated that the waiter is unable to see past her physical appearance.
   B. content to fit in with people in her hometown.
   C. slighted that the waiter would talk to her in an arrogant way.
   D. uncomfortable with the way other people view her.

8. The author refers to Jane's age in the last paragraph mainly to:

   F. imply that emotional maturity is based solely on age.
   G. emphasize the irrationality of Jane's reaction to the waiter.
   H. suggest that Jane has not visited her hometown in many years.
   J. prove that Jane should face consequences for her behavior toward the waiter.

9. As it is used in line 67, the word *warm* most nearly means:

   A. friendly.
   B. heated.
   C. irritated.
   D. wanton.

10. According to the passage, the scenery Jane passes while driving includes:

    F. views of the Pacific ocean.
    G. mountainous terrain.
    H. houses and trees.
    J. animals like rabbits and mice.

Passage II

SOCIAL SCIENCE: This passage is adapted from *Romanesque Architecture* by Pranay Akhudh (©2018 by Pranay Akhudh).

Sometime in the 8th century, an anonymous English poet marveled at the ruins of the town of Bath. He had never seen anything like it. Five hundred years earlier, Bath had been a renowned resort town, patronized by the
5 wealthy elite of Roman Britain who endowed it with temples, markets, townhouses, and theaters. Now it was forlorn, a slumping and rain-scoured ruin abandoned since time, out of mind. But this empty city was built of marble and concrete, timber and iron, and on a scale absolutely
10 unlike anything else in the rough-and-tumble England of the Early Middle Ages.

Roman-style architecture as seen in Bath reflected the ideals of Roman civilization. Consider the triumphal arch, built to commemorate foreign conquests and the prowess
15 of successful emperors. Arches were sophisticated constructions, intricate towers of marble or concrete up to one hundred feet tall and covered in elaborate, finely-carved sculptures that told the tale of the conqueror who commissioned it. Building a triumphal arch required a highly de-
20 veloped body of knowledge that could draw upon a large, reliable pool of labor and materials to execute an intricate project. In the ancient world, cities were the only sites that drew together all the necessary factors for this monumental architecture. Without the city's inherent facility
25 in concentrating population and talent, many of the refinements identified with civilized life fell apart. As citizens fled, trade declined, and life became more precarious, the ancient art of building vanished.

The Early Middle Ages in Europe were once called
30 the Dark Ages, because they were so poorly documented. That is, from the perspective of modern scholars and researchers, very little of the evidence that is necessary to cast light on an era in time survived. We know a great deal about the ancient world and the world of the High
35 Middle Ages, in part, because so much of their architecture survived, even if it went through periods of decline or ruin. But hardly anything of enduring quality was built in Europe between the 6th and 10th centuries. The few surviving attempts at large-scale architecture from the darkest
40 decades of the Middle Ages underscore just how much had been lost. Whereas Roman monuments emphasized sculptures and elaborate symbolism, these buildings were covered in repetitive abstract patterns and designs, with no attempt to represent the human form or convey obvious sym-
45 bolic meaning. But, there are some common features— notably rounded arches and thick load-bearing walls—that anticipate the development of Romanesque architecture.

Scholars debate exactly when Romanesque emerged as a distinct mode of architecture. Though its roots are in
50 the Roman ruins that remained as examples to later artists, it wasn't until the 11th century that its recognizable forms

and standards appeared all over Europe, from the Mediterranean to the North Sea. Though its most striking examples are cathedrals and palaces, there are buildings of vir-
55 tually every sort done in the Romanesque style.

And what led to this revival of large-scale architecture? The pioneering architects of the style were plainly influenced by the example of the Roman past—the name says it all. But this influence was drawn from a specific
60 episode of that past. Architects did not look to the classical style of Roman art, which was associated with the pre-Christian pagan order and its suppressed universe of gods and heroes. Instead they looked to the so-called "Constantinian style," named for the emperor who made Christian-
65 ity the faith of the empire and broke with the traditions of the earlier Roman Empire. The rounded arches and cupolas, the arcades and columns, were directly inspired by this late imperial architecture that, in the Middle Ages, signified the power of both the emperor and God.

70 Romanesque architecture was not daunted by the monumental, in no small part because projects were often commissioned by the spiritual and political rulers of European societies. By the 11th century, invasions had ceased, plagues had abated, and populations slowly began to re-
75 bound. New lands were brought into cultivation, and the shells of ancient cities were reinhabited and began to grow into new urban centers called communes. Once again, the talent and resources needed to build on a grand scale were available.

80 Romanesque architecture typically expresses confidence, with finely wrought and soaring forms signaling energy and optimism. This reflected the mood of societies in which life was, slowly but surely, becoming richer and more secure. Those cities that could concentrate the sur-
85 plus needed to encourage abundance, became sites of a renewed cultural complexity that borrowed from the past, while building a world that reflected new values and visions. Romanesque architecture in time evolved in two directions, one stream trending toward the somber Gothic
90 of the High Middle Ages while another trended toward the Classical Revival of the Renaissance. Romanesque marked the point at which one civilization transformed into another.

11. Which of the following events referred to in the passage happened first chronologically?

  A. Romanesque architecture split into Gothic and Classical Revival.
  B. Emperor Constantine made Christianity the faith of the Roman Empire.
  C. An English poet visited the ruins of Bath.
  D. People began to move to urban centers called communes.

12. As it is used in line 23, the word *drew* most nearly means:

    F. gathered.
    G. illustrated.
    H. forced.
    J. created.

13. It can most reasonably be inferred from the passage that the English poet marveled at the ruins of Bath because:

    A. Romanesque architecture had never before existed in Britain.
    B. most of the buildings had been renovated by citizens.
    C. they were not able to visit the temples they planned to.
    D. the town had undergone a drastic change over time.

14. The author most likely includes the description of 11th-century Europe in the sixth paragraph (lines 70–79) in order to:

    F. explain the reasons why architecture once again became popular in urban areas.
    G. prove that people living in rural areas caused the downfall of architecture in the Dark Ages.
    H. list the locations in Europe where Romanesque architecture was most popular.
    J. indicate the types of buildings favored by spiritual leaders.

15. According to the passage, the most striking examples of Romanesque architecture are:

    A. entire cities.
    B. triumphal arches.
    C. cathedrals and palaces.
    D. townhouses and theaters.

16. One function in the passage of including information about the Dark Ages is to create a contrast between the:

    F. amount of documentation from that era and the information known about eras before and after.
    G. decline of architecture in ancient times and its rebirth in the Dark Ages.
    H. population distribution of urban centers and areas of the countryside.
    J. religious and secular styles of architecture.

17. The main idea of the fourth paragraph (lines 48–55) is that Romanesque architecture:

    A. became popular well after the 11th century.
    B. is not recognized by all architecture scholars.
    C. appears in vast areas and building types.
    D. is a style only popular for palaces in Europe.

18. The passage indicates that the triumphal arch was built in order to:

    F. replace the sculptures that were once popular.
    G. help unskilled laborers learn the trade of architecture.
    H. provide a place to use the surplus of marble.
    J. celebrate successful emperors and foreign conquests.

19. Which of the following best captures the passage's characterization of the role of cities in architecture?

    A. The decline of cities fueled the development of Romanesque architecture.
    B. Cities were responsible for the popularity of the somber Gothic architectural style.
    C. Cities attracted the resources and people necessary to build major architecture.
    D. Rome was the birthplace of all major architecture that followed.

20. As it is used in lines 83–84, the phrase "richer and more secure" refers to the fact that:

    F. people became more energetic and optimistic in modern times.
    G. citizens began to prefer more serious and somber forms of architecture.
    H. societies were developing new visions for the future.
    J. invasions and plagues had become less prevalent.

Passage III

HUMANITIES: Passage A is adapted from *Journey through the Sun* by Elissa Bathwaite (©1842 by Elissa Bathwaite). Passage B is adapted from "Foreigners to Ourselves" by Edward Thomas (©1974 by Cambridge Critical Review).

Passage A by Elissa Bathwaite

"And why should I do anything of the kind?" Victor replied, his tone of voice and tilt of head at an angle Thomas felt if not quite contemptuous, still far from the casual warmth he'd come to expect of his traveling com-
5 panion.

"Well, putting aside the obvious desires of the locals to have us participate in the local customs, there's our general health to consider. While I have yet to develop a full history of the fashions native to this part of the world, I
10 can nevertheless, confidently state, that they never have, and never will, include proper breeches. Not only have I acquired on my person this morning alone enough sand to fill at least two hourglasses, but I'm sweating so much I might as well be in a Turkish sauna." Sensing that he'd
15 gone perhaps a bit to far, he hastily added, "surely you wouldn't wish to add to our list of discomforts those that illness are sure to burden us with?"

Victor appeared either not to have heard him or to consider that this outburst didn't warrant a response. Looking
20 lazily around the tent for a few moments, he once again turned his attention to the thawbs, turbans, and other articles that had been left for them, giving them a suspicious poke with his cane, as if they might at any moment rise up to offer him bodily or mystical harm. Giving the room an-
25 other slow once-over, he at last managed a somewhat civil, "It is especially unpleasant today. I'll grant you that."

In the awkward silence that ensued, Thomas repeatedly tried, and failed, to recollect not only why he had agreed to take part in this diplomatic expedition, but why
30 he'd agreed to do so with Victor, whom he'd known since their time together at Eton. He'd certainly never harbored more than a distant interest for Victor, let alone the kind of camaraderie one normally took for granted between people who agreed, whether for the greater love of country or the
35 more personal love of leisure, to advance together into the unknown that lay outside their Island, which, while powerful in scope, was, at least relatively, quite diminutive in scale.

Passage B by Edward Thomas

The Elissa Bathwaite of literary legend—the woman
40 who dared, when so few of her sex would have thought to, much less managed, to visit those glittering provinces of the East and to simultaneously turn upon not only them but also upon her fellow countrymen her deeply perceptive gaze—is alive and quite well in the minds of most of our

45 men and women of letters. One need hardly look further than the 100th Anniversary celebration invitations (with which the salvers of the well-to-do in this town have been loaded nearly past the point of the butler's ability to carry) to see that Ms. Bathwaite is enjoying a renaissance far
50 greater than was the appreciation of her works in her own time.

But why such a celebration of her in particular? Avid fans of her work are quick to point out that Bathwaite's perceptions, if not proven correct then certainly not overruled
55 by latter observations, were unique; no one else before or since has managed to capture so truly and vividly our national, twofold obsession with ourselves and those who are "other." It is indeed through her works alone that we can find and come to terms with the driving forces of those
60 of us, past and present, who have had cause, be it business or leisure, to travel into the unknown. But a writer must—must she not?—be judged by more than the power of her observations. Just as there are countless mathematicians and scientists who have made invaluable discoveries
65 and have passed them on to future generations, yet whose names lie lost beneath the sands of time, surely there is many a writer of keen observation whose anniversaries and names are equally unknown to us.

A good writer must possess more than liquid syntax,
70 deep observation, musical language, and the power to tug at the heart's strings, and more, indeed than their sum; a great writer must, beyond these, possess a voice distinctly his or her own. To what degree voice and observation are separable is something for our good professors to hash out
75 in their thundering lectures. I will submit merely that there is a distinction to be made, and an important one. For if we look closely at nearly any given page of, say, "The Eastern Star" or "Journey through the Sun," the observations do indeed stand out a great deal more than the fashion in which
80 they are transmitted: no doubt Bathwaite displayed original ideas, but the same claim cannot be supported for her writing, which seems, at least to me, strikingly unremarkable. The syntax is flabby, the diction flat, the dialogue as dry as the deserts in which her characters so often find
85 themselves. Whether such a writer is deserving of these upcoming celebrations is, however, something I must ultimately leave to her readers.

Questions 21–23 ask about Passage A.

21. The author most likely includes the description of thawbs and turbans (lines 19–24) in order to:

A. portray the clothing popular among the locals.
B. indicate a character's discomfort in an unfamiliar environment.
C. compare the practicality of Western and Eastern fashion.
D. explain the reason for animosity between Thomas and Victor.

22. In Passage A, all of the following are true of Victor and Thomas EXCEPT that they:

F. agreed to join a diplomatic expedition.
G. both come from the same country.
H. both enjoy the excitement of visiting a new place.
J. met when they were students at Eton.

23. As it is described in Passage A, the relationship between Victor and Thomas can best be described as:

A. tense.
B. amicable.
C. relaxed.
D. violent.

Questions 24–27 ask about Passage B.

24. In Passage B, the main idea of the last paragraph is that:

F. popular writing should be able to influence the reader's emotions.
G. Elissa Bathwaite's writing style is not as strong as her ideas and observations.
H. the characters in Elissa Bathwaite's writing spend most of their time in a desert.
J. most readers continue to find "Journey through the Sun" entertaining.

25. As it is used in line 79, the word *fashion* most nearly means:

A. idea.
B. writing style.
C. configuration.
D. trend.

26. According to Passage B, Elissa Bathwaite's fans appreciate her writing because she:

F. uses striking syntax and diction.
G. writes about her countrymen in a positive light.
H. makes perceptive observations.
J. has made mathematical and scientific discoveries.

27. The author of Passage B most likely references the 100th Anniversary celebration in order to:

A. illustrate the present-day popularity of Elissa Bathwaite's writing.
B. compare the success of books written earlier and later in Elissa Bathwaite's career.
C. provide examples of Elissa Bathwaite's most popular books.
D. describe Elissa Bathwaite's reaction to fame.

Questions 28–30 ask about both passages.

28. The author of Passage B would most likely characterize the dialogue in the second paragraph of Passage A (lines 6–17) as:

F. "unique" (line 55).
G. "invaluable discoveries" (line 64).
H. "musical language" (line 70).
J. "strikingly unremarkable" (lines 82–83).

29. Both passages support the idea that Elissa Bathwaite:

A. used intricate diction to describe characters.
B. was one of the most visionary writers of an era.
C. wrote about scenes of travel to the East.
D. was a popular writer during her lifetime.

30. Which of the following statements best captures a difference in the purposes of the passages?

F. Passage A provides a description of Bathwaite's most well-known characters, while Passage B provides a summary of Bathwaite's early life.
G. Passage A provides an example of Bathwaite's writing, while Passage B provides a critique of the author's style.
H. Passage A provides an excerpt of a novel written by Bathwaite, while Passage B provides a synopsis of that novel.
J. Passage A provides a response to modern-day critics, while Passage B provides support for Bathwaite's success.

Passage IV

NATURAL SCIENCE: This passage is adapted from *Ants and Humans: Social Creatures* by Sara Worth (©2017 by Sara Worth).

Comparing a human to an ant is likely to draw some skeptical responses. However, the comparison is not as far-fetched as it appears. Obviously, human beings don't hatch from eggs, they don't communicate through pheromones, and they don't build massive underground nests. But a number of behaviors common to both humans and ants suggest surprising social similarities.

Ant societies are centered around a queen, the literal mother of the colony. The queen ant is the only members of the colony that reproduces, tended by specialized worker ants so that she is healthy enough to lay eggs continuously. Her larval children—called brood ants, or the brood—grow up to take on any number of specialized roles in the colony, such as hunting, burrowing, tending the young, and guarding the colony from intruders. Studies suggest that ants take on particular roles to which they are best suited. This suggests that ants have an unusual ability to learn from experience and adapt their behavior. Indeed, they are the only non-mammal species to demonstrate social learning by teaching.

Scientists experimenting with *Ooceraea biroi*, the South American clonal raider ant, found that worker ants slot themselves into particular social roles based on their past experience. Ants that show a particular skill at a task tend to stick with that work, while those that handle a task poorly shuffle through a number of jobs in the colony until they find one that suits them. Behavior like this has led some scientists to describe ant societies as a kind of "superorganism." The smallest ant colonies consists of a few dozen worker ants and a queen living on a tree branch, while the largest cover hundreds of square miles and include millions of ants and dozens of queens living together in communal cooperation. Each can be thought of as a single organism made up of many parts, coordinated and directed toward the colony's survival and reproduction by a collective intelligence.

There is no single source of this intelligence. The "queen" is not really in charge of anything, she merely serves a single, if crucially important, specialized role in breeding. Nor are the ants that scout for food or excavate new additions to the colony. The ants' activity is collectively self-directed. A recent study showed that when ants dig a new tunnel in underground colonies, only about twenty percent of the ants are working at any given time, while the others appear idle. In fact, the twenty percent of ants at work in the tunnels are constantly switched out among the other eighty percent, ensuring that all contribute to the common project.

This collective activity, though common in social animals, bears a striking resemblance to some human social practices, even though ants and humans are remote from each other in the evolutionary tree of life.

Ants are generally omnivorous, feeding on all manner of plants and animals. Usually ants scavenge for food, taking advantage of whatever they can find. But some species—like the Central American *Acromyrmex*, or Leaf Cutter ant—feed themselves through a form of agriculture. Leaf Cutter colonies subsist on the *Leucocoprinus* fungus, a kind of mushroom. Instead of hunting for them in the wild, parties of Leaf Cutter harvest tree and flower leaves and bring them back to the colony, where the ants chew the leaves into a paste. This paste serves as the fertilizer for *Leucocoprinus*, which is raised and harvested within the colony in much the same way human farmers sow, nurture, and harvest our own food.

Some ants have independently evolved their own versions of the worst vices of human behavior. *Formica sanguinea*, found all over the Northern Hemisphere, supply their colonies' labor needs by slave raiding. Specialized worker ants raid neighboring nests to carry off as much of the brood as possible. The brood are raised in captivity and put to work on behalf of their captors, who display a noticeably less intense pace of activity relative to their slaves. Some species, like *Polyergus*, the Amazon ant, have become so inured to living off of the labor of stolen neighbors that they have lost the capacity to feed themselves, relying entirely on the work of their slaves to keep themselves alive.

And just as humans have spread all over the surface of the earth in a chain of linked societies, so have ant colonies. While scientists have long known of "megacolonies" that cover hundreds of miles, recent work has uncovered the existence of a linked society of *Linepithema humile*, or Argentine ants, on four different continents. These ants, when placed together, will not fight each other, even though they are derived from Europe, the Americas, and Asia. These same ants, when confronted with members of a different colony adjacent to their own, immediately become aggressive. The Argentine ants recognize each other as kin despite the vast distance between them, suggesting that ants have achieved a developmental milestone thought to be unique to humans: the establishment of a global society.

31. The main purpose of the passage is to use the examples of ant species to show that:

A. ants and humans have some similar social behaviors.
B. ants perform specialized roles within their colonies.
C. ants have learned negative behaviors like slavery from humans.
D. some adaptations benefit ants more than other adaptations.

32. As it is used in line 36, the word *collective* most nearly refers to:

F. the ability of ants to find food sources.
G. collaboration of scientists to gather data about ants.
H. cooperation of groups of ants.
J. the birth of multiple ants from the same queen.

33. It can most reasonably be inferred from the passage that ants are different from humans because they:

A. have developed the ability to harvest food.
B. work together in communal groups.
C. eat an omnivorous diet.
D. communicate through pheromones.

34. The passage author most likely includes the information in the fifth paragraph (lines 49–52) in order to:

F. provide an example of an ant species that exhibits social behavior.
G. transition to examples of ant behavior that is similar to human behavior.
H. highlight the close evolutionary relationship between humans and ants.
J. dispute a claim that humans and ants have genetic similarities.

35. According to the passage, brood ants can take on any of the following roles in the ant colony EXCEPT:

A. hunting.
B. reproducing.
C. guarding.
D. burrowing.

36. The main idea of the sixth paragraph (lines 53–65) is that Leaf Cutter ants:

F. use similar feeding methods to human agriculture.
G. prefer to eat tree and flower leaves over fungus.
H. are the only omnivorous species of ant.
J. hunt for *Leucocoprinus* fungus in the wild.

37. The passage indicates that the Amazon ant's use of stolen labor has resulted in:

A. raids on neighboring nests.
B. the spread of the species across multiple continents.
C. collective intelligence among the worker ants.
D. the species relying completely on that labor for food.

38. Which of the following best summarizes the author's claims about the relationships between groups of Argentine ants?

F. Despite being members of the same species, Argentine ants from different continents will not recognize each other.
G. Argentine ants recognize members of their species, even when they are from other parts of the world.
H. Argentine ants have communicated across the world to form a global society including only their members.
J. Argentine ants are one of the most aggressive species of ant.

39. As it is used in line 23, the word *slot* most nearly means:

A. force.
B. endure.
C. study.
D. place.

40. In the passage, a common reaction to the comparison of ants and humans can best be described as:

F. antagonistic.
G. convinced.
H. doubting.
J. trusting.

SCIENCE TEST
35 Minutes—40 Questions

DIRECTIONS: There are six passages in this test. Each passage is followed by several questions. After reading a passage, choose the best answer to each question and fill in the corresponding oval on your answer document. You may refer to the passages as often as necessary. You are NOT permitted to use a calculator on this test.

Passage I

Noise-canceling headphones are a consumer and professional device that use technology to reduce or remove ambient noise and sound. Four students each propose a hypothesis describing how the noise-canceling technology functions within the headphones.

Student 1

The noise-canceling functionality within these headphones is achieved via passive insulation. A careful combination of cork, foam, and fiberglass coated in plastic, creates a system that uses *reflection* (sound waves bouncing off the hard plastic exterior), *refraction* (waves changing angle when they enter a new medium), and *absorption* (waves reducing in amplitude as they change media) to eliminate outside noise. The key element here is 705 fiberglass, a material which exhibits an even absorption characteristic across all frequencies. The 705 fiberglass has a *noise reduction coefficient* (NRC) rating of 0.95, which indicates it absorbs 95% of incoming sound.

Student 2

While passive insulation can create a reduction in ambient sound, the only technology that can create the drastic level of noise reduction is *active noise control* (ANC). ANC requires powered built-in speakers on the headphone that face outwards, creating high-frequency impulses that meet incoming sound waves and diffuse them, like a force field around the headset. This works best on frequencies above 400 Hz.

Student 3

Student 2 is correct that ANC is required and passive insulation is not enough. However, the way ANC works is by using powered speakers to create a loud drone. The human ear acclimates to levels of noise quickly, which is why it is hard to hear your friend talking to you when at a concert. As such, the ear acclimates to this loud drone tone and quickly ignores it, and the net effect is a perceived reduction of all other outside sounds while the drone overpowers them. This works best on frequencies below 5 kHz.

Student 4

Active noise control works by using four powered microphones on the headphones to detect incoming sound. The headphones then create the same signal as the one coming in, but with the wave inverted, or upside-down. When a wave combines with an inverted wave, they experience destructive interference and cancel each other out. We experience this as noise cancellation. It works effectively across the entire range, depending on the microphones used on the headset.

1. Which of the students believes noise-canceling headphones can function without battery power?

   A. Student 1
   B. Student 2
   C. Student 3
   D. Student 4

2. Neuroscience research has determined that the human ear acclimates to sound over a period of minutes, not seconds. This research weakens the viewpoint(s) of which student(s)?

   F. Student 3 only
   G. Student 4 only
   H. Students 1 and 3 only
   J. Students 2, 3, and 4 only

3. Noise-canceling headphones are used by airplane mechanics working on engines and around active airplanes. These large machines often create loud, resonant sounds around 200 Hz. Which headphone designs would work best in this application?

   A. Students 1 and 4 only
   B. Students 2 and 4 only
   C. Students 1, 3, and 4 only
   D. Students 2, 3, and 4 only

GO ON TO THE NEXT PAGE.

4. Which process is visualized in the following diagram?

- **F.** Reflection, as described by Student 1
- **G.** Absorption, as described by Student 1
- **H.** ANC, as described by Student 3
- **J.** ANC, as described by Student 4

5. Which headphone designs project additional sound inward towards the ears?

- **A.** Student 2 only
- **B.** Student 4 only
- **C.** Students 3 and 4 only
- **D.** Students 2, 3 and 4 only

6. A pair of headphones was analyzed, and no fiberglass or cork was found in the design. Which student's argument is weakened by this discovery?

- **F.** Student 1
- **G.** Student 2
- **H.** Student 3
- **J.** Student 4

7. According to the passage, if a given material does NOT absorb 80% of the sound that hits it, the given material is best described by which of the following ratings?

- **A.** ANC of 0.2
- **B.** NRC of 0.2
- **C.** ANC of 0.8
- **D.** NRC of 0.8

Passage II

Chromosomes undergoing *meiosis* (a specialized form of cell division that occurs in all reproducing eukaryotes), sometimes encounter errors due to DNA polymerase slippage. Changes to chromosomal content are classified in four ways: *Insertion*, where a piece of one chromosome is taken from that chromosome and inserted into another chromosome; *fusion*, where two previously separate chromosomes are linked into a single piece; *inversion*, where a piece of one chromosome flips orientation while otherwise remaining in place; and *translocation* where pieces of different chromosomes swap places.

Translocation has a specific notation for compact descriptions of chromosomal exchanges, called the International System for Human Cytogenetic Nomenclature (ISCN). In this notation, t(A;B)(p1;q2) indicates that section p1 from chromosome A has exchanged places with section q2 from chromosome B. A "p" refers to the short arm of a chromosome, while "q" refers to the long arm. Numbers indicate subsections of the corresponding segments.

Figure 1 displays, from left to right for each of 4 different chromosomes, a human, chimpanzee, gorilla, and orangutan, respectively.

Table 1 displays translocation notations that correspond to specific conditions.

Table 1	
Gene Translocation	Associated Condition
t(8;14)(q24;q32)	Burkitt's Lymphoma
t(2;3)(q13;p25)	Follicular Thyroid Cancer
t(12,21)(p12;qq2)	A.L.L.
t(1;11)(q21;q21)	Schizophrenia
t(11;22)(q24;q12)	Ewing's Sarcoma
t(1;12)(q21;p13)	Leukemia

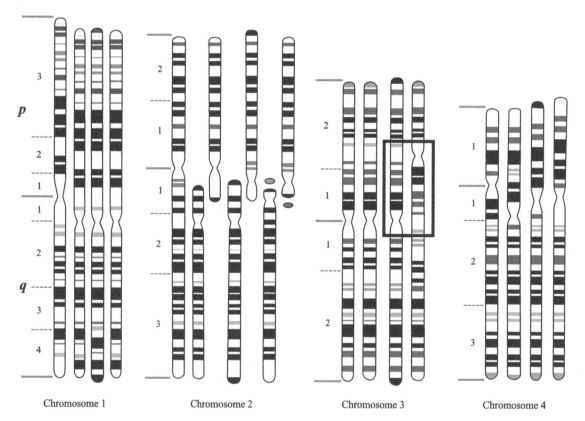

Chromosome 1   Chromosome 2   Chromosome 3   Chromosome 4

Figure 1

8. According to Figure 1, which of the following meiosis errors explains the highlighted chromosome variation on Chromosome 3 comparing gorilla DNA and orangutan DNA?

   F. Inversion
   G. Translocation
   H. Fusion
   J. Insertion

9. According to Figure 1, which set of chromosomes displays the process of fusion when comparing chimpanzees to humans?

   A. Chromosome 1
   B. Chromosome 2
   C. Chromosome 3
   D. Chromosome 4

10. Which process is illustrated by this procedural diagram?

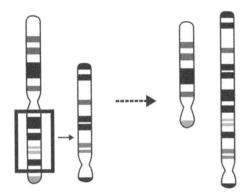

   F. Inversion
   G. Translocation
   H. Fusion
   J. Insertion

11. Based on Table 1 and the passage, the translocation of segment q21 between genes 1 and 11 would correspond with which of the following conditions?

   A. Lymphoma
   B. Leukemia
   C. Infertility
   D. Schizophrenia

12. In Figure 1, which of the following genetic mutations occurs to go from gorilla Chromosome 1 to orangutan Chromosome 1?

   F. Inversion of p2
   G. Inversion of q2
   H. Inversion of q4
   J. None of the above

13. Based on Figure 1, which of the following sections of Chromosome 4 are unique for each species?

   A. p1 and q1
   B. q2 and q3
   C. q3 only
   D. p1, q1, and q2

Passage III

Genetic theory predicts that height of children will be based off the genetic coding of their parents. In 1997, a group of seven statisticians undertook a study to examine the statistical patterns of hereditary height.

Study

An oral survey of 325 adults between the age of 25 and 35 was conducted. Each participant provided age and height, and the height of each of their parents. All the data was collected and a basic statistical analysis was performed.

From the data, a mean height of 68.25" was calculated for both the surveyed young adults and the average of their parents' height. A measure of deviation, or how far a measurement strays from the mean, was found for each height value. Deviation was calculated using the following formula:

$$\text{Deviation} = (\text{measured height}) - (\text{mean height})$$

Table 1 displays the height of adult children (in deviations) versus the average height of their parents (in deviations). The data is graphed as a frequency table, where each numerical value represents the number of height occurrences within that deviation zone. The highlighted diagonal indicates individuals whose height deviation is the same as their parental average height deviation. The bolded axes indicate central mean values.

Table 1

Adult Children Height (in +/- from 68.25")

Parent Height (in +/- from 68.25")

Parent Height	−4	−3	−2	−1	0	+1	+2	+3	+4
+3					1	2	2	2	1
+2			2	4	5	5	4	3	1
+1	1	2	3	5	8	9	9	8	5
0	2	3	6	10	12	12	2	10	6
−1	3	7	11	13	14	13	10	7	3
−2	3	6	8	11	11	8	6	3	1
−3	2	3	4	6	4	3	2		

14. According to Table 1, if an individual matures to a height of 70", what is the most likely average height of the individual's parents?

    F. 67"
    G. 68"
    H. 69"
    J. 70"

15. According to the data, which average parent height was most common?

    A. 67"
    B. 68"
    C. 69"
    D. 70"

16. Based on the data in Table 1, as average parent height increases, the expected adult children height:

    F. increases only.
    G. decreases only.
    H. increases, then decreases.
    J. decreases, then increases.

17. One scientist claims that the normal distribution predicts that children should end up at the same height deviation as their parents more often than not. Do the data in Table 1 support the claim from the scientist?

    A. Yes, because the height deviation in inches for adults matched the most frequent height deviation in inches of their adult children more than 3 times.
    B. Yes, because the height deviation in inches for adults matched the most frequent height deviation in inches of their adult children less than 3 times.
    C. No, because the height deviation in inches for adults matched the most frequent height deviation in inches of their adult children more than 3 times.
    D. No, because the height deviation in inches for adults matched the most frequent height deviation in inches of their adult children less than 3 times.

18. A statistical anomaly is defined as an observation that breaks the trend otherwise observed strongly in the data. Which of the following data points is an example of a statistical anomaly in the data in Table 1?

Height Deviation (in)

	Parent	Adult children
F.	0 to +1	+1 to +2
G.	0 to −1	0 to −1
H.	−1 to −2	−4 to −5
J.	+2 to +3	0 to +1

19. Which of the following statistical facts could have created error in the data analysis?

    A. 99% of children stop growing after age 23
    B. Males, on average, are 5 inches taller than females
    C. There were more parents with a height of 67.5 inches than any other height surveyed
    D. Age and height data were provided by the participants, not measured by the statisticians

20. The statisticians looked to further investigate the relationship between height of adult children versus average height of their parents. Which of the following actions would NOT aid in additional investigations?

    F. Conducting the same survey with adults between ages 36 to 46
    G. Conducting the same survey with children ages 5 to 15
    H. Conducting the same survey with female adults between ages 25 and 35
    J. Conducting the same survey in a different geographical location

Passage IV

As part of a college physics curriculum, a group of students calculated atomic volume and then performed a laboratory experiment to attempt to verify their results.

Theoretical

The students gathered information of the number of protons (based on atomic number) and the configuration of electrons in all the elements of the periodic table. A sample of their results is displayed in Table 1. Electron configuration is ordered by an integer value indicating the layer (innermost to outermost) that the electrons are on. The letters s, p, d, and f indicate an electron orbit. An electron configuration of $1s^2 2s^2 2p^6 3s^1$ has two electrons in layer 1 (in s orbits), eight electrons in layer 2 (two in s orbits, six in p orbits) and one electron in layer 3.

Table 1			
Element	Element Symbol	# of Protons	Electron Configuration
Lithium	Li	3	$1s^2 2s^1$
Beryllium	Be	4	$1s^2 2s^2$
Boron	B	5	$1s^2 2s^2 2p^1$
Carbon	C	6	$1s^2 2s^2 2p^2$
Oxygen	O	7	$1s^2 2s^2 2p^3$
Nitrogen	N	8	$1s^2 2s^2 2p^4$
Fluorine	F	9	$1s^2 2s^2 2p^5$

As atoms add electrons to outer layers and protons to the nucleus, the innermost layer of electrons remains constant with two electrons. As a result, as atomic number increases, the positive charge of the growing nucleus draws in the electron shells, reducing the overall atomic volume. This trend continues until the atom grows large enough to add another layer, increasing its size significantly. Students performed computer assisted measurements to display these measurements in Figure 1.

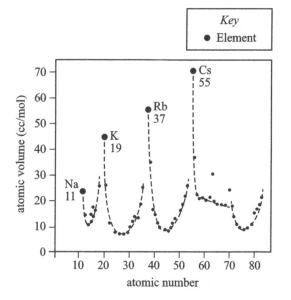

Figure 1

Experiment

To verify their results, the students took a small cubic block of element Ag. They measured the mass and volume. From the data, they calculated the density (ρ) of the block. The students multiplied the density with the molar mass (M) of Ag and Avogadro's number (N_A) to convert density from grams to atoms. Next, they calculated the relationship between the atomic radius of spherical crystal structures as they fit into a cubic shape. The final result converts measurements of mass and volume into atomic radius using the following equation:

$$r = \sqrt[3]{\frac{0.555M}{\pi \rho N_A}}$$

428

GO ON TO THE NEXT PAGE.

21. According to Figure 1, from Cesium (atomic number 55) to Ytterbium (atomic number 70), as atomic number increases, atomic volume:

A. increases only.
B. decreases only.
C. decreases, then increases.
D. increases, then decreases.

22. Based on the information in the passage and Table 1, how many electrons are in the second layer of Nitrogen (N)?

F. 1
G. 2
H. 4
J. 6

23. Based on the passage, which of the following possible electron configurations for sodium (Na) could be used to explain the difference in atomic volume between flourine and sodium observed in Figure 1 and Table 1?

A. $2s^22s^22p^62s^1$
B. $1s^22s^22p^63s^1$
C. $1s^21s^22p^62s^1$
D. $1p^22p^22s^61p^1$

24. According to information provided, if one element has 8 times the density of another, but their molar mass is approximately the same, the radius of the denser element compared to the radius of the less dense element would be:

F. one-fourth the size.
G. one-half the size.
H. twice the size.
J. four times the size.

25. Which one of these forces describes the force that reduces atomic volume as the atomic number increases?

A. Gravitational
B. Normal
C. Electrical
D. Air Resistance

26. In the experiment, which pair of measurement tools are required to complete the procedure and calculation?

F. Scale and measuring tape
G. Pipette and test tube
H. Microscope and clamp
J. Voltmeter and ammeter

27. As displayed in the figure below, different bond types create different atomic structures.

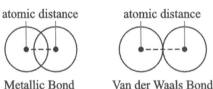

Metallic Bond   Van der Waals Bond

Assuming the students used a material with metallic bonding in their experiment, their atomic volume measurements from their results would be:

A. inaccurate and smaller than the accepted value, while the Van der Waals would give an accurate result.
B. inaccurate and larger than the accepted value, while the Van der Waals would give an accurate result.
C. accurate, while the Van der Waals would give an overestimate.
D. accurate, while the Van der Waals would give an underestimate.

Passage V

Four students undertook a study to examine the effects of various methods of water filtration on the metal and bacterial content of the filtered water.

Experiment

In each of Trials 1-4, Steps 1-4 were repeated 5 times and averaged into the results displayed in Figure 2:

1. Sixty mL of contaminated water were measured for heavy metals and minerals.

2. A filter was prepared by placing two coffee filters in a cone, then adding 4 inches of the filtering material, as shown in Figure 1.

3. Contaminated water was poured through the filter over the course of 1 minute, working its way through to a clean beaker below.

4. The resulting water in the beaker was tested for metals and minerals by the same procedure as in Step 1. Changes were recorded.

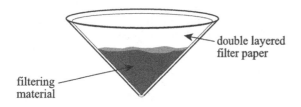

Figure 1

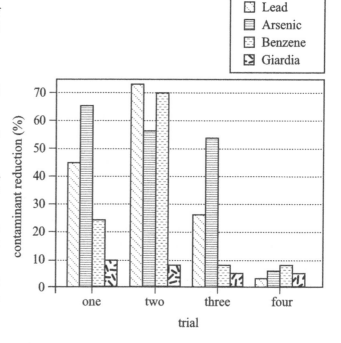

Figure 2

Table 1 displays the filtration materials used per trial in the experimental process.

Table 1	
Trial	Filtration material
1	Ceramic
2	Activated carbon
3	Sand and gravel
4	None (coffee filter only)

28. When filter materials are combined within the same 4-inch filter, their results are averaged as compared to a single-material filter. If a 4-inch filter is created from ceramic and activated carbon, what would be the expected value of percent reduction of benzene?

    F. Less than 8%
    G. Between 8% and 25%
    H. Between 25% and 70%
    J. Greater than 70%

29. Which measured contaminant was least affected by the filtration systems?

    A. Lead
    B. Arsenic
    C. Benzene
    D. Giardia

30. Suppose the initial contaminated water measured 22 ppm (parts per million) of lead. On average, how much lead would remain after ceramic filtration as described in the procedure?

    F. 0.45 ppm
    G. 10 ppm
    H. 12 ppm
    J. 45 ppm

31. If an activated charcoal filter was used for a 2 minute period, which of the following results, if it can be determined, would describe the arsenic levels in the filtered water?

    A. Less than 44%
    B. Between 44% and 56%
    C. Greater than 56%
    D. Cannot be determined from the given information

32. Based on the results of the experiment, approximately how much benzene reduction does sand and gravel offer without a coffee filter?

    F. 0%
    G. 8%
    H. 92%
    J. 100%

33. Suppose the students completed a second experiment which placed the filtration processes in sequential order. Which order would result in the greatest reduction in lead content?

    A. (1) Sand and gravel, (2) Activated carbon, (3) Ceramic
    B. (1) Sand and gravel, (2) Ceramic, (3) Activated carbon
    C. (1) Activated carbon, (2) Ceramic, (3) Sand and gravel
    D. (1) Activated carbon, (2) Sand and gravel, (3) Ceramic

34. A contaminated sample with 10 ppb (parts per billion) of arsenic is processed three times in a row by a ceramic filter. After the third process, the remaining arsenic would be:

    F. approximately 0.3 ppb, because the ceramic filter removes around one-third of the arsenic in the sample each time it is processed.
    G. approximately 0.3 ppb, because the ceramic filter removes around two-thirds of the arsenic in the sample each time it is processed.
    H. approximately 3 ppb, because the ceramic filter removes around one-third of the arsenic in the sample each time it is processed.
    J. approximately 3 ppb, because the ceramic filter removes around two-thirds of the arsenic in the sample each time it is processed.

GO ON TO THE NEXT PAGE.

Passage VI

California's centralized farm system provides efficient farming techniques for growing produce, but suffers losses due to inefficiencies in the truck transport industry. Trucks without refrigeration or roofs lose significant amounts of fresh produce due to improper climate control, excessive sun exposure, and pollution.

Fourteen environmental scientists studied truck routes from central valley farms to a processing plant in Bakersfield, and then from the processing plant to four destinations. Produce loss was measured along the way by stopping trucks every 15 minutes and examining moisture and coloration of produce with the same accept/reject methods used by the Bakersfield processing plant. The results were plotted in Figure 1, with key checkpoints organized in Table 1.

Table 1		
Checkpoint	Description	Produce lost* (lbs)
A	I-5 mile 40	0
B	I-5 mile 80	11
C	I-5 mile 120	27
D	Bakersfield processing plant	88
E	San Luis Obispo	14
F	Ventura	6
G	Barstow	22
H	Los Angeles†	0

* produce lost since last checkpoint

† utilizes better truck technology

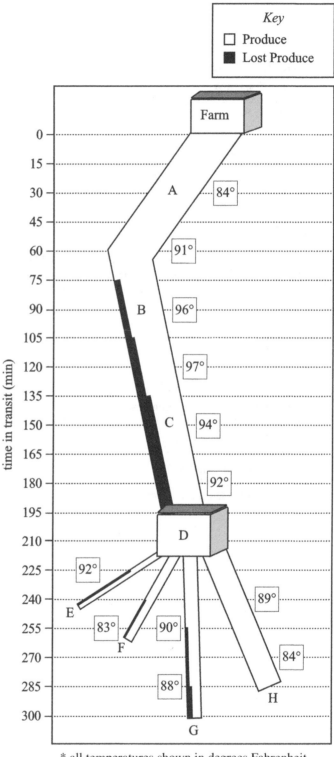

* all temperatures shown in degrees Fahrenheit

Figure 1

35. Based on the figure, starting from the farm, on which route does the produce spend the most time in the vehicle?

A. Barstow
B. Los Angeles
C. Ventura
D. San Luis Obispo

36. According to Table 1, between mile 40 and mile 80, how much produce was lost?

F. 11 pounds
G. 16 pounds
H. 27 pounds
J. 38 pounds

37. Based on Figure 1 and Table 1, which graph accurately depicts temperature and produce lost versus time on the Farm to Bakersfield route?
(Note: temperature is represented by the dashed line.)

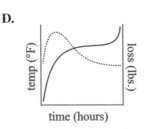

38. A new refrigerated-bay truck design could reduce losses due to high temperatures by 50%. On which segment of the trip would these trucks have the greatest effect?

F. Farm to Bakersfield
G. Bakersfield to Barstow
H. Bakersfield to Ventura
J. Bakersfield to Los Angeles

39. According to Figure 1 and Table 1, if 210 pounds of produce leaves the Bakersfield processing plant for Ventura, how much arrives safely?

A. 6 pounds
B. 78 pounds
C. 82 pounds
D. 204 pounds

40. Which of the following theories could explain why the Bakersfield to Los Angeles route has 0 lbs of produce loss? The route from Bakersfield to Los Angeles:

F. is a shorter travel time than the other routes.
G. leaves the earliest, reducing produce losses due to produce aging.
H. utilizes refrigerated trucks, which protects produce from high temperatures
J. utilizes open-top trucks, reducing produce losses due to increased sun exposure.

High School Trade Courses

Many high schools are experimenting with classes designed to prepare students for work in trades or artisanal professions on the grounds that not everyone wants to or is able to succeed in a purely academic environment. Proponents say that this system better reflects not only the interests of many students but also the needs of the economy and workforce. However, critics say that such courses categorize students at too young an age and narrows educational options for them. Is it appropriate for high schools to offer trade classes?

Read and carefully consider these perspectives. Each suggests a particular way of thinking about tracking high school students.

Perspective 1	Perspective 2	Perspective 3
Rather than be forced to complete a course of education that does not address their interests, students should be able to focus on job-training courses that will allow them to find good work upon graduation.	Forcing students to forgo a standard education may prevent them from acquiring the skills to change careers at some point in their lives or from discovering a new interest or passion.	Education is already too focused on teaching students skills that will be useful in the job market. Education should instead be about cultivating a sense of self and acquiring well-rounded knowledge of several areas of study.

Essay Task

Write a unified, coherent essay in which you evaluate multiple perspectives on trade and career classes for high school students. In your essay, be sure to:

- analyze and evaluate the perspectives given
- state and develop your own perspective on the issue
- explain the relationship between your perspective and those given

Your perspective may be in full agreement with any of the others, in partial agreement, or wholly different. Whatever the case, support your ideas with logical reasoning and detailed, persuasive examples.

Answer Key and Curves

ACT0 - A0318 - Answer Key

#	Grammar	Math	Reading	Science	#	Grammar con't	Math con't
1	A	E	D	A	41	A	A
2	H	G	G	F	42	F	J
3	D	D	A	D	43	D	A
4	H	K	F	J	44	H	H
5	D	D	D	C	45	D	A
6	F	H	G	J	46	J	G
7	B	A	C	B	47	D	B
8	H	F	H	H	48	J	H
9	C	B	C	D	49	C	A
10	F	J	J	J	50	G	K
11	D	C	A	C	51	A	E
12	H	G	J	H	52	H	F
13	D	E	A	C	53	A	C
14	G	G	H	F	54	J	J
15	C	C	A	D	55	C	B
16	G	G	J	G	56	J	F
17	A	E	B	B	57	B	D
18	J	G	G	H	58	H	H
19	D	B	A	D	59	B	D
20	G	J	F	G	60	H	K
21	A	B	A	D	61	A	
22	J	H	F	J	62	G	
23	B	C	A	B	63	A	
24	H	F	J	J	64	F	
25	A	D	B	A	65	B	
26	F	G	G	F	66	H	
27	D	D	B	B	67	D	
28	H	H	H	F	68	J	
29	D	A	B	C	69	D	
30	J	F	F	G	70	G	
31	C	B	D	C	71	B	
32	J	H	G	H	72	G	
33	A	A	C	A	73	C	
34	H	H	H	F	74	J	
35	C	D	B	C	75	D	
36	J	K	H	J			
37	B	A	B	B			
38	G	K	G	F			
39	D	E	A	A			
40	J	K	J	H			

ACT0 - A0318 - Curve

Grammar score		Math score		Reading score		Science score		
Raw	Scaled	Raw	Scaled	Raw	Scaled	Raw	Scaled	
75	36	60	36	40	36	40	36	
74	36	59	36	39	36	39	34	
73	35	58	35	38	35	38	33	
72	35	57	35	37	35	37	32	
71	35	56	34	36	34	36	31	
70	34	55	34	35	33	35	30	
69	34	54	33	34	32	34	29	
68	33	53	33	33	31	33	28	
67	33	52	32	32	31	32	27	
66	33	51	32	31	30	31	26	
65	32	50	31	30	29	30	25	
64	32	49	31	29	28	29	24	
63	31	48	30	28	27	28	24	
62	31	47	29	27	26	27	23	
61	30	46	28	26	25	26	23	
60	30	45	28	25	24	25	22	
59	29	44	28	24	23	24	22	
58	29	43	27	23	23	23	21	
57	28	42	27	22	22	22	21	
56	28	41	27	21	22	21	20	
55	27	40	26	20	21	20	20	
54	27	39	26	19	20	19	19	
53	26	38	25	18	19	18	19	
52	25	37	25	17	18	17	18	
51	25	36	25	16	17	16	18	
50	24	35	24	15	16	15	17	
49	24	34	24	14	15	14	16	
48	23	33	23	13	14	13	16	
47	23	32	23	12	13	12	15	
46	22	31	22	11	13	11	15	
45	22	30	21	10	12	10	14	
44	21	29	20	9	12	9	13	
43	21	28	20	8	11	8	12	
42	20	27	19	7	10	7	11	
41	20	26	19	6	9	6	10	
40	19	25	18	5	8	5	9	
39	19	24	17	4	7	4	8	
38	18	23	17	3	5	3	7	
37	18	22	17	2	4	2	5	
36	17	21	17	1	2	1	3	
35	17	20	16	0	1	0	1	
34	16	19	16					
33	16	18	16					
32	16	17	16					
31	15	16	15					
30	15	15	15					
29	15	14	15					
28	14	13	14					
27	14	12	14					

ACT1 - A0116 - Answer Key

#	Grammar	Math	Reading	Science	#	Grammar con't	Math con't
1	B	B	D	D	41	D	A
2	H	J	H	G	42	J	K
3	A	D	B	A	43	C	D
4	H	J	H	G	44	H	J
5	C	D	B	C	45	D	E
6	F	H	J	G	46	F	H
7	A	B	C	D	47	A	C
8	J	H	G	J	48	H	F
9	B	D	A	A	49	A	E
10	F	G	F	F	50	J	F
11	D	D	A	A	51	C	E
12	H	F	H	H	52	G	J
13	A	C	A	D	53	D	C
14	F	K	G	J	54	H	F
15	C	A	D	B	55	A	C
16	H	F	H	H	56	J	F
17	B	C	D	B	57	B	A
18	H	J	G	F	58	F	H
19	B	E	C	C	59	A	B
20	H	H	G	J	60	G	J
21	D	C	A	C	61	C	
22	J	J	J	J	62	F	
23	A	B	D	D	63	B	
24	J	J	G	J	64	H	
25	B	C	A	D	65	C	
26	F	J	H	G	66	F	
27	D	B	D	C	67	B	
28	H	G	H	J	68	G	
29	A	C	A	B	69	C	
30	F	G	G	G	70	J	
31	C	E	A	C	71	B	
32	H	H	H	F	72	G	
33	B	C	B	A	73	B	
34	F	H	J	H	74	G	
35	D	E	D	B	75	B	
36	G	H	F	G			
37	D	C	A	D			
38	H	G	H	G			
39	C	E	C	A			
40	G	H	G	G			

ACT1 - A0116 - Curve

Grammar score		Math score		Reading score		Science score	
Raw	Scaled	Raw	Scaled	Raw	Scaled	Raw	Scaled
75	36	60	36	40	36	40	36
74	36	59	36	39	36	39	34
73	35	58	35	38	35	38	33
72	35	57	35	37	35	37	32
71	35	56	34	36	34	36	31
70	34	55	34	35	33	35	30
69	34	54	33	34	32	34	29
68	33	53	33	33	31	33	28
67	33	52	32	32	31	32	27
66	33	51	32	31	30	31	26
65	32	50	31	30	29	30	25
64	32	49	31	29	28	29	24
63	31	48	30	28	27	28	24
62	31	47	29	27	26	27	23
61	30	46	28	26	25	26	23
60	30	45	28	25	24	25	22
59	29	44	28	24	23	24	22
58	29	43	27	23	23	23	21
57	28	42	27	22	22	22	21
56	28	41	27	21	22	21	20
55	27	40	26	20	21	20	20
54	27	39	26	19	20	19	19
53	26	38	25	18	19	18	19
52	25	37	25	17	18	17	18
51	25	36	25	16	17	16	18
50	24	35	24	15	16	15	17
49	24	34	24	14	15	14	16
48	23	33	23	13	14	13	16
47	23	32	23	12	13	12	15
46	22	31	22	11	13	11	15
45	22	30	21	10	12	10	14
44	21	29	20	9	12	9	13
43	21	28	20	8	11	8	12
42	20	27	19	7	10	7	11
41	20	26	19	6	9	6	10
40	19	25	18	5	8	5	9
39	19	24	17	4	7	4	8
38	18	23	17	3	5	3	7
37	18	22	17	2	4	2	5
36	17	21	17	1	2	1	3
35	17	20	16	0	1	0	1
34	16	19	16				
33	16	18	16				
32	16	17	16				
31	15	16	15				
30	15	15	15				
29	15	14	15				
28	14	13	14				
27	14	12	14				

ACT2 - A0316 - Answer Key

#	Grammar	Math	Reading	Science	#	Grammar con't	Math con't
1	C	C	B	D	41	C	D
2	J	F	J	G	42	G	J
3	B	A	A	C	43	B	A
4	J	K	G	H	44	J	G
5	C	C	A	C	45	C	D
6	H	K	J	G	46	J	J
7	B	C	C	B	47	B	C
8	J	F	H	G	48	H	K
9	D	C	A	A	49	A	A
10	G	H	J	H	50	J	H
11	C	E	A	D	51	C	C
12	F	G	H	J	52	F	H
13	C	B	A	C	53	A	B
14	F	H	F	G	54	G	G
15	D	C	A	C	55	A	D
16	F	J	F	F	56	F	F
17	C	E	D	C	57	B	C
18	F	F	J	F	58	F	G
19	D	D	B	B	59	D	E
20	G	H	H	G	60	J	F
21	C	C	C	B	61	A	
22	G	H	G	H	62	G	
23	D	B	D	D	63	A	
24	H	F	G	H	64	J	
25	A	C	B	C	65	A	
26	J	F	G	J	66	H	
27	D	D	C	B	67	D	
28	G	H	J	G	68	H	
29	A	A	B	C	69	D	
30	F	F	G	J	70	G	
31	C	C	A	C	71	C	
32	G	J	H	G	72	F	
33	D	E	B	D	73	C	
34	J	G	J	F	74	G	
35	D	A	D	D	75	A	
36	G	F	F	H			
37	A	D	A	B			
38	H	F	H	H			
39	B	A	B	A			
40	J	F	G	F			

ACT2 - A0316 - Curve

Grammar score		Math score		Reading score		Science score	
Raw	Scaled	Raw	Scaled	Raw	Scaled	Raw	Scaled
75	36	60	36	40	36	40	36
74	36	59	36	39	34	39	35
73	35	58	35	38	33	38	34
72	35	57	35	37	32	37	33
71	34	56	34	36	31	36	33
70	34	55	33	35	30	35	32
69	33	54	33	34	29	34	31
68	33	53	32	33	28	33	30
67	32	52	31	32	27	32	30
66	32	51	30	31	26	31	29
65	31	50	30	30	26	30	28
64	31	49	29	29	25	29	27
63	30	48	29	28	25	28	25
62	30	47	28	27	24	27	25
61	29	46	27	26	24	26	24
60	29	45	27	25	23	25	23
59	28	44	26	24	23	24	23
58	27	43	26	23	22	23	22
57	26	42	26	22	22	22	22
56	25	41	25	21	21	21	21
55	24	40	25	20	21	20	21
54	24	39	25	19	20	19	20
53	24	38	24	18	19	18	20
52	23	37	24	17	18	17	19
51	23	36	24	16	17	16	18
50	23	35	23	15	16	15	17
49	22	34	23	14	15	14	16
48	22	33	22	13	14	13	16
47	22	32	22	12	13	12	15
46	21	31	21	11	13	11	15
45	21	30	21	10	12	10	14
44	21	29	21	9	12	9	13
43	20	28	20	8	11	8	12
42	20	27	20	7	10	7	11
41	20	26	19	6	9	6	10
40	19	25	18	5	8	5	9
39	19	24	17	4	7	4	8
38	18	23	17	3	5	3	7
37	18	22	17	2	4	2	5
36	17	21	17	1	2	1	3
35	17	20	16	0	1	0	1
34	16	19	16				
33	16	18	16				
32	16	17	16				
31	15	16	15				
30	15	15	15				
29	15	14	15				
28	14	13	14				
27	14	12	14				

ACT3 - A0516 - Answer Key

#	Grammar	Math	Reading	Science	#	Grammar con't	Math con't
1	A	B	B	B	41	B	B
2	H	G	G	F	42	H	F
3	A	B	A	C	43	A	D
4	H	J	H	J	44	H	F
5	D	B	A	C	45	A	E
6	H	H	F	G	46	F	K
7	C	D	D	C	47	D	C
8	G	G	H	H	48	G	J
9	D	E	C	D	49	C	C
10	G	F	H	H	50	H	H
11	C	C	D	C	51	D	C
12	H	J	F	G	52	J	H
13	C	C	A	B	53	D	A
14	J	H	F	F	54	H	K
15	D	C	B	B	55	D	C
16	G	H	F	J	56	H	H
17	B	C	C	B	57	B	D
18	G	K	G	H	58	J	F
19	A	C	B	A	59	D	B
20	J	J	H	J	60	G	H
21	B	B	C	D	61	C	
22	J	G	G	J	62	G	
23	B	A	B	D	63	B	
24	F	F	J	J	64	F	
25	C	D	B	A	65	B	
26	J	F	J	J	66	F	
27	C	A	A	B	67	B	
28	G	J	G	J	68	F	
29	D	B	C	A	69	A	
30	F	J	H	J	70	H	
31	C	B	D	D	71	D	
32	G	F	F	H	72	G	
33	D	D	A	C	73	B	
34	F	F	G	H	74	H	
35	D	B	D	D	75	C	
36	G	G	G	G			
37	C	A	C	B			
38	F	G	H	G			
39	C	E	B	B			
40	J	F	F	J			

ACT3 - A0516 - Curve

Grammar score		Math score		Reading score		Science score	
Raw	Scaled	Raw	Scaled	Raw	Scaled	Raw	Scaled
75	36	60	36	40	36	40	36
74	36	59	36	39	36	39	35
73	35	58	35	38	35	38	34
72	35	57	35	37	35	37	33
71	34	56	34	36	34	36	32
70	34	55	34	35	33	35	31
69	33	54	33	34	32	34	30
68	33	53	33	33	31	33	29
67	33	52	32	32	31	32	28
66	32	51	31	31	30	31	27
65	32	50	30	30	29	30	26
64	31	49	30	29	28	29	25
63	31	48	29	28	27	28	24
62	30	47	29	27	26	27	23
61	30	46	28	26	25	26	23
60	29	45	28	25	24	25	22
59	29	44	28	24	23	24	22
58	28	43	27	23	23	23	21
57	28	42	27	22	22	22	21
56	27	41	27	21	22	21	20
55	26	40	26	20	21	20	20
54	26	39	26	19	20	19	19
53	25	38	25	18	19	18	19
52	25	37	25	17	18	17	18
51	24	36	24	16	17	16	18
50	24	35	24	15	16	15	17
49	23	34	23	14	15	14	16
48	22	33	22	13	14	13	16
47	22	32	22	12	13	12	15
46	21	31	21	11	13	11	15
45	21	30	20	10	12	10	14
44	21	29	20	9	12	9	13
43	20	28	19	8	11	8	12
42	20	27	19	7	10	7	11
41	20	26	18	6	9	6	10
40	19	25	18	5	8	5	9
39	19	24	17	4	7	4	8
38	18	23	17	3	5	3	7
37	18	22	17	2	4	2	5
36	17	21	17	1	2	1	3
35	17	20	16	0	1	0	1
34	16	19	16				
33	16	18	16				
32	16	17	16				
31	15	16	15				
30	15	15	15				
29	15	14	15				
28	14	13	14				
27	14	12	14				

ACT4 - A0117 - Answer Key

#	Grammar	Math	Reading	Science	#	Grammar con't	Math con't
1	D	B	D	D	41	B	E
2	J	J	H	G	42	F	F
3	B	D	A	A	43	B	C
4	G	K	J	J	44	J	H
5	D	A	A	C	45	D	D
6	F	K	G	J	46	H	F
7	C	B	A	A	47	B	C
8	H	J	G	J	48	H	G
9	B	C	D	B	49	B	E
10	F	G	G	G	50	J	G
11	D	D	D	D	51	C	D
12	G	H	F	G	52	F	H
13	C	D	B	D	53	A	C
14	J	J	H	J	54	G	F
15	B	B	C	C	55	B	C
16	J	K	F	F	56	H	J
17	D	C	B	A	57	D	A
18	F	J	F	G	58	F	K
19	B	A	A	D	59	A	D
20	J	H	H	J	60	J	H
21	B	E	B	B	61	B	
22	G	G	F	H	62	J	
23	D	B	D	B	63	C	
24	G	H	G	F	64	G	
25	D	B	C	B	65	D	
26	J	H	F	J	66	G	
27	C	E	D	A	67	C	
28	F	F	F	G	68	H	
29	D	C	C	D	69	A	
30	G	K	H	F	70	H	
31	D	A	D	B	71	B	
32	G	J	H	F	72	H	
33	C	B	D	A	73	A	
34	J	K	F	H	74	J	
35	B	E	B	B	75	C	
36	H	H	F	G			
37	A	B	D	C			
38	J	G	H	H			
39	A	C	A	D			
40	H	F	H	F			

ACT4 - A0117 - Curve

Grammar score		Math score		Reading score		Science score	
Raw	Scaled	Raw	Scaled	Raw	Scaled	Raw	Scaled
75	36	60	36	40	36	40	36
74	36	59	36	39	36	39	36
73	35	58	36	38	35	38	35
72	35	57	35	37	35	37	35
71	35	56	35	36	34	36	34
70	34	55	34	35	33	35	33
69	34	54	34	34	32	34	33
68	33	53	33	33	31	33	32
67	33	52	33	32	31	32	31
66	33	51	32	31	30	31	30
65	32	50	32	30	29	30	29
64	32	49	31	29	28	29	28
63	31	48	31	28	27	28	27
62	31	47	30	27	26	27	26
61	30	46	29	26	25	26	25
60	30	45	29	25	24	25	25
59	29	44	28	24	23	24	24
58	29	43	28	23	23	23	24
57	28	42	27	22	22	22	23
56	28	41	27	21	22	21	22
55	27	40	26	20	21	20	21
54	27	39	26	19	20	19	20
53	26	38	25	18	19	18	19
52	25	37	25	17	18	17	19
51	25	36	25	16	17	16	18
50	24	35	24	15	16	15	18
49	24	34	24	14	15	14	17
48	23	33	24	13	14	13	16
47	23	32	23	12	13	12	16
46	22	31	23	11	13	11	15
45	22	30	22	10	12	10	14
44	21	29	22	9	12	9	13
43	21	28	21	8	11	8	12
42	20	27	21	7	10	7	11
41	20	26	20	6	9	6	10
40	19	25	20	5	8	5	9
39	19	24	19	4	7	4	8
38	18	23	19	3	5	3	7
37	18	22	18	2	4	2	5
36	17	21	17	1	2	1	3
35	17	20	16	0	1	0	1
34	16	19	16				
33	16	18	16				
32	16	17	16				
31	15	16	15				
30	15	15	15				
29	15	14	15				
28	14	13	14				
27	14	12	14				

ACT5 - A0317 - Answer Key

#	Grammar	Math	Reading	Science	#	Grammar con't	Math con't
1	C	A	B	C	41	D	A
2	J	J	J	G	42	J	F
3	B	D	C	C	43	C	A
4	J	H	H	H	44	J	F
5	A	E	C	D	45	B	B
6	F	K	J	J	46	F	J
7	A	C	A	D	47	C	E
8	G	J	G	H	48	J	G
9	C	A	D	C	49	D	C
10	J	J	J	H	50	G	G
11	C	D	C	D	51	D	A
12	F	J	J	F	52	F	G
13	B	E	D	D	53	B	E
14	F	J	F	F	54	G	J
15	B	D	A	A	55	D	B
16	H	G	H	H	56	F	K
17	A	D	B	D	57	D	D
18	F	K	F	J	58	H	K
19	D	E	A	D	59	B	A
20	J	J	F	H	60	J	G
21	C	E	C	B	61	A	
22	F	J	F	F	62	G	
23	C	C	D	B	63	A	
24	G	H	J	J	64	J	
25	A	C	A	C	65	D	
26	H	F	G	H	66	H	
27	A	C	C	B	67	A	
28	J	J	J	F	68	G	
29	B	A	D	D	69	C	
30	H	H	J	J	70	H	
31	B	C	D	A	71	B	
32	J	J	G	G	72	F	
33	A	C	D	A	73	D	
34	G	F	H	J	74	G	
35	D	D	A	C	75	A	
36	H	H	F	H			
37	B	A	A	D			
38	J	H	G	H			
39	D	B	B	D			
40	G	K	H	F			

ACT5 - A0317 - Curve

Grammar score		Math score		Reading score		Science score	
Raw	Scaled	Raw	Scaled	Raw	Scaled	Raw	Scaled
75	36	60	36	40	36	40	36
74	36	59	36	39	36	39	36
73	35	58	36	38	35	38	35
72	35	57	35	37	35	37	35
71	35	56	35	36	34	36	34
70	34	55	34	35	33	35	33
69	34	54	34	34	32	34	32
68	33	53	33	33	31	33	31
67	33	52	33	32	31	32	30
66	33	51	32	31	30	31	29
65	32	50	32	30	29	30	28
64	32	49	31	29	28	29	27
63	31	48	30	28	27	28	27
62	31	47	30	27	26	27	26
61	30	46	29	26	25	26	25
60	30	45	29	25	24	25	25
59	29	44	28	24	23	24	24
58	29	43	28	23	23	23	24
57	28	42	27	22	22	22	23
56	28	41	27	21	22	21	23
55	27	40	26	20	21	20	22
54	27	39	26	19	20	19	21
53	26	38	25	18	19	18	20
52	25	37	25	17	18	17	20
51	25	36	25	16	17	16	19
50	24	35	24	15	16	15	18
49	24	34	24	14	15	14	17
48	23	33	24	13	14	13	16
47	23	32	23	12	13	12	15
46	22	31	23	11	13	11	15
45	22	30	23	10	12	10	14
44	21	29	22	9	12	9	13
43	21	28	22	8	11	8	12
42	20	27	21	7	10	7	11
41	20	26	21	6	9	6	10
40	19	25	20	5	8	5	9
39	19	24	20	4	7	4	8
38	18	23	19	3	5	3	7
37	18	22	19	2	4	2	5
36	17	21	18	1	2	1	3
35	17	20	18	0	1	0	1
34	16	19	17				
33	16	18	16				
32	16	17	16				
31	15	16	15				
30	15	15	15				
29	15	14	15				
28	14	13	14				
27	14	12	14				

ACT6 - A0118 - Answer Key

#	Grammar	Math	Reading	Science	#	Grammar con't	Math con't
1	D	D	D	B	41	B	A
2	G	K	F	J	42	F	K
3	B	C	B	C	43	A	E
4	J	J	J	J	44	G	K
5	A	E	B	A	45	B	A
6	F	K	G	F	46	J	G
7	C	B	A	B	47	C	E
8	J	J	F	H	48	F	F
9	D	B	A	C	49	A	A
10	J	G	F	H	50	G	G
11	B	C	B	C	51	C	B
12	J	K	F	J	52	H	J
13	C	C	B	C	53	C	C
14	H	H	F	J	54	H	J
15	D	C	D	D	55	D	B
16	H	G	H	G	56	G	F
17	B	E	B	C	57	A	A
18	G	J	J	J	58	J	F
19	A	B	A	B	59	A	A
20	H	K	G	G	60	G	J
21	B	C	B	A	61	B	
22	F	F	H	H	62	F	
23	B	D	D	A	63	D	
24	H	F	F	F	64	F	
25	C	A	C	B	65	D	
26	H	J	J	J	66	J	
27	D	A	C	D	67	C	
28	J	F	G	H	68	J	
29	D	E	D	C	69	C	
30	J	F	H	G	70	F	
31	C	B	B	B	71	D	
32	F	H	G	J	72	J	
33	D	B	D	B	73	B	
34	F	F	H	J	74	G	
35	B	C	A	A	75	B	
36	F	G	J	H			
37	C	C	B	A			
38	G	G	J	H			
39	C	E	B	C			
40	J	F	H	G			

ACT6 - A0118 - Curve

Grammar score		Math score		Reading score		Science score	
Raw	Scaled	Raw	Scaled	Raw	Scaled	Raw	Scaled
75	36	60	36	40	36	40	36
74	36	59	36	39	36	39	36
73	35	58	36	38	35	38	35
72	35	57	35	37	35	37	35
71	35	56	35	36	34	36	34
70	34	55	34	35	33	35	33
69	34	54	34	34	32	34	32
68	33	53	33	33	31	33	31
67	33	52	33	32	31	32	30
66	33	51	32	31	30	31	29
65	32	50	32	30	29	30	28
64	32	49	31	29	28	29	27
63	31	48	30	28	27	28	27
62	31	47	30	27	26	27	26
61	30	46	29	26	25	26	25
60	30	45	29	25	24	25	25
59	29	44	28	24	23	24	24
58	29	43	28	23	23	23	24
57	28	42	27	22	22	22	23
56	28	41	27	21	22	21	23
55	27	40	26	20	21	20	22
54	27	39	26	19	20	19	21
53	26	38	25	18	19	18	20
52	25	37	25	17	18	17	20
51	25	36	25	16	17	16	19
50	24	35	24	15	16	15	18
49	24	34	24	14	15	14	17
48	23	33	24	13	14	13	16
47	23	32	23	12	13	12	15
46	22	31	23	11	13	11	15
45	22	30	23	10	12	10	14
44	21	29	22	9	12	9	13
43	21	28	22	8	11	8	12
42	20	27	21	7	10	7	11
41	20	26	21	6	9	6	10
40	19	25	20	5	8	5	9
39	19	24	20	4	7	4	8
38	18	23	19	3	5	3	7
37	18	22	19	2	4	2	5
36	17	21	18	1	2	1	3
35	17	20	18	0	1	0	1
34	16	19	17				
33	16	18	16				
32	16	17	16				
31	15	16	15				
30	15	15	15				
29	15	14	15				
28	14	13	14				
27	14	12	14				

ACT7 - A0119 - Answer Key

#	Grammar	Math	Reading	Science	#	Grammar con't	Math con't
1	C	D	C	A	41	B	D
2	F	K	G	F	42	J	G
3	B	C	B	C	43	D	E
4	G	K	F	G	44	F	G
5	B	B	A	C	45	C	E
6	H	F	H	F	46	G	J
7	A	E	D	B	47	A	B
8	J	J	G	F	48	F	F
9	A	A	A	B	49	D	C
10	H	H	H	J	50	J	K
11	D	A	B	D	51	D	A
12	H	G	F	J	52	J	K
13	B	D	D	D	53	C	E
14	J	G	F	G	54	F	H
15	C	C	C	B	55	B	C
16	F	F	F	F	56	F	H
17	B	E	C	A	57	C	A
18	J	K	J	F	58	J	K
19	C	B	C	D	59	C	C
20	J	G	J	G	60	H	J
21	B	D	B	B	61	B	
22	J	J	H	J	62	H	
23	A	A	A	B	63	C	
24	G	F	G	G	64	J	
25	B	E	B	C	65	D	
26	G	G	H	F	66	H	
27	C	B	A	A	67	A	
28	J	H	J	H	68	J	
29	A	A	C	D	69	C	
30	J	G	G	G	70	F	
31	D	D	A	D	71	A	
32	G	G	H	F	72	J	
33	A	C	D	C	73	A	
34	H	F	G	J	74	G	
35	C	A	B	A	75	B	
36	G	K	F	F			
37	C	D	D	A			
38	F	J	G	F			
39	C	E	D	D			
40	F	H	H	H			

ACT7 - A0119 - Curve

Grammar score		Math score		Reading score		Science score	
Raw	Scaled	Raw	Scaled	Raw	Scaled	Raw	Scaled
75	36	60	36	40	36	40	36
74	36	59	36	39	36	39	36
73	35	58	36	38	35	38	35
72	35	57	35	37	35	37	35
71	35	56	35	36	34	36	34
70	34	55	34	35	33	35	33
69	34	54	34	34	32	34	32
68	33	53	33	33	31	33	31
67	33	52	33	32	31	32	30
66	33	51	32	31	30	31	29
65	32	50	32	30	29	30	28
64	32	49	31	29	28	29	27
63	31	48	30	28	27	28	27
62	31	47	30	27	26	27	26
61	30	46	29	26	25	26	25
60	30	45	29	25	24	25	25
59	29	44	28	24	23	24	24
58	29	43	28	23	23	23	24
57	28	42	27	22	22	22	23
56	28	41	27	21	22	21	23
55	27	40	26	20	21	20	22
54	27	39	26	19	20	19	21
53	26	38	25	18	19	18	20
52	25	37	25	17	18	17	20
51	25	36	25	16	17	16	19
50	24	35	24	15	16	15	18
49	24	34	24	14	15	14	17
48	23	33	24	13	14	13	16
47	23	32	23	12	13	12	15
46	22	31	23	11	13	11	15
45	22	30	23	10	12	10	14
44	21	29	22	9	12	9	13
43	21	28	22	8	11	8	12
42	20	27	21	7	10	7	11
41	20	26	21	6	9	6	10
40	19	25	20	5	8	5	9
39	19	24	20	4	7	4	8
38	18	23	19	3	5	3	7
37	18	22	19	2	4	2	5
36	17	21	18	1	2	1	3
35	17	20	18	0	1	0	1
34	16	19	17				
33	16	18	16				
32	16	17	16				
31	15	16	15				
30	15	15	15				
29	15	14	15				
28	14	13	14				
27	14	12	14				

ABOUT PRIVATE PREP

Private Prep is an education services company that offers individually customized lessons in all K-12 academic subjects, standardized test prep, and college admissions consulting. We believe personal attention is fundamental to academic achievement and lies at the forefront of every student-tutor relationship. Designing curriculum for each student's unique learning style, we focus not only on improving grades and increasing test scores but also on building confidence and developing valuable skills—like work ethic, growth mindset, and anxiety management—that will last a lifetime.

One of the most significant points of differentiation between us and other educational services companies is our team approach. Our directors work in tandem with tutors and support staff to provide comprehensive, collaborative support to families.

We also focus on giving back to the communities in which we work. Through the Private Prep Scholarship Program, we place high-achieving students from low-income or underserved backgrounds with individual tutors, who work with them to navigate the test prep and college application process and ultimately gain admission to best-fit colleges.

At Private Prep, we deliver a superior academic experience—in the U.S., abroad, and online—that is supported by diverse and excellent resources in recruitment, curriculum design, professional training, and custom software development.

Made in the USA
Monee, IL
17 February 2020